Fasten Your Seat Belts

BOOKS BY LAWRENCE J. QUIRK

Robert Francis Kennedy

The Films of Joan Crawford

The Films of Paul Newman

The Films of Fredric March
Foreword, Photoplay Magazine
Anthology

The Films of William Holden

The Great Romantic Films

The Films of Robert Taylor

The Films of Ronald Colman

The Films of Warren Beatty

The Films of Myrna Loy

The Films of Gloria Swanson

Claudette Colbert:
An Illustrated Biography

Bette Davis: Her Films and Career
(Update from 1965)

Lauren Bacall:
Her Films and Career

Jane Wyman:
The Actress and the Woman

The Complete Films of
William Powell

Margaret Sullavan:
Child of Fate

Norma:
The Story of Norma Shearer

The Complete Films of
Ingrid Bergman

Some Lovely Image (A Novel)

Fasten Your Seat Belts:
The Passionate Life of Bette Davis

Lawrence J. Quirk

Fasten Your Seat Belts

THE PASSIONATE LIFE OF
BETTE DAVIS

WILLIAM MORROW AND COMPANY, INC.
New York

Library of Congress Cataloging-in-Publication Data

Quirk, Lawrence J.
  Fasten your seat belts: the passionate life of Bette Davis / Lawrence J.
Quirk.
    p.   cm.
  ISBN 0-688-08427-3
  1. Davis, Bette, 1908–1989. 2. Motion picture actors and
actresses—United States—Biography.   I. Title.
PN2287.D32Q57   1990
791.43'028'092—dc 20
[B]   89-29771
                                                                              CIP

Printed in the United States of America

First Edition

1   2   3   4   5   6   7   8   9   10

BOOK DESIGN BY KATHRYN PARISE

For Daniel A. Strone,
Agent and Friend

Acknowledgments

FASTEN YOUR SEAT BELTS: The Passionate Life of Bette Davis, is based on the research of forty-three years, and my interviews over that period with those living and dead, those named throughout this book, and others who requested not to be named, all of whom generously shared their memories of Bette Davis with me, as well as their thoughts and opinions regarding her life and career. Since the beginning of my career, Bette Davis has led the list of film stars on whom I assiduously collected all sorts of material, with a view to one day writing her biography.

My deep appreciation to Doug McClelland for the interviews he contributed, as well as clippings and other memorabilia. To Douglas Whitney, who lent me many fascinating photographs of Bette Davis. To William Schoell, for his helpful suggestions and advice and for sharing his revisionist theories on certain Bette Davis films, as well as a younger generation's attitude toward her. Also to Mike Ritzer and Arthur Tower for research and many other forms of help, and to Albert B. Manski and Donald Collins, Jr., for various memorabilia.

My gratitude also to: John Cocchi, Don Koll, the James R. Quirk

Memorial Film Symposium and Research Center, New York; Mary Corliss and the Museum of Modern Art Department of Film's photo archives; the staff of the Margaret Herrick Library of the Academy of Motion Picture Arts and Sciences, Hollywood; the British Film Institute, London; Dorothy Swerdlove, Rod Bladel, and their associates at the Billy Rose Theater and Film Collection, New York Public Library at Lincoln Center; Ernest D. Burns of Cinemabilia, New York; Mark Ricci and The Memory Shop, New York; Jerry Ohlinger's Movie Material Store, New York; and Photofest.

Also thanks to: Lou Valentino; Terry Geesken of the Museum of Modern Art Film Library; John W. M. Phillips, London; Ken Sephton, London; Eduardo Moreno, Ben Carbonetto, Manuel Cordova, Barry Paris, John Gallagher, the late DeWitt Bodeen, and Henry Hart, editor of *Films in Review* from 1950 to 1971, who published my pioneering life story of Bette Davis in *Films in Review*'s December 1955 issue.

Also my appreciation to James E. Runyan, John A. Guzman, Robert Heide, John Gilman, Mike Snell, Jim McGowan, Frank Rowley of the Biograph Cinema, New York; Howard Otway of Theatre 80, New York; and Barbara Barondess MacLean, actress, designer, writer, and a contemporary of Bette Davis.

And with sincere thanks to Daniel Strone, my agent and friend, to whom this book is dedicated; to my editor, Douglas Stumpf; and to Jared B. Stamm. And to the memory of Michael Lavelle Scuffle III (1962–1989), my young writer friend who loved Bette Davis movies and saw many of them with me.

Contents

Introduction

I N JANUARY 1988, Bette Davis was a guest on *The Tonight Show*. She
came out looking like a skeletal marionette, limping on legs that were
toothpick-thin and wearing a white hat shaped like an inverted kettle,
straight on top of her head, and a blue knit dress with horizontal white
stripes. Her makeup did not hide the pallor of her skin, nor her ancient,
wrinkled neck.

She wobbled over and sat down, waving her arms, cigarette in hand,
looking for all the world like a carefully caparisoned death's-head—until
she spoke. Then the blue eyes sparkled as of yore, and the famous
voice, projected from a stroke-twisted mouth, came down on the
consonants and pushed hard on the vowels with its fabled authority.
Everyone realized that the legendary Bette Davis was on hand and accounted for.

In spite of her frail appearance, her well-publicized health problems,
the career that seemed all but over, she was still the Warner Brothers
queen of four decades before.

She was still feisty: She had found Faye Dunaway unprofessional to
work with, and said so. She told a fellow guest, a young comedian who

had done a lame imitation of her, that he could "skip it." She was still stubborn: Her smoking must be okay, she claimed, if she had lived as long as she had. She could be as vulgar as ever: She laughed at Johnny Carson's statement that champagne made him fart, and even topped his ace with a story about Disraeli and Queen Victoria.

She could still kid herself: A photographer had told her he preferred her legs to her face. She played schoolmistress with her audience, putting them down when they laughed at her saying how she had loved working with Lillian Gish in *The Whales of August*.

Then it was time to go, and Bette Davis wobbled out into the night, to the waiting car, leaving in the minds of her audience a kaleidoscope of her eighty-plus films, her two Oscars and ten Oscar nominations, the studio battles, the four husbands and myriad lovers, the retarded daughter and the treacherous other daughter, and the solid-citizen lawyer son far away in Boston with his wife and children—the one she kept in touch with—somewhat.

They had—at least the Bette Davis devotees among them had—read about the waiting Forest Lawn tomb and the mother and sister who had preceded her there. They could chant by rote her oft-repeated statement, "I did it the hard way," and such famous lines from her films as, "What a dump!" "Fasten your seat belts—it's going to be a bumpy night!" "I'd love to kiss ya but I just washed ma hair" (reportedly her favorite), "With all my heart, I still love the man I killed!" and above all, "Jerry, don't let's ask for the moon; we have the stars!"

The true fans of Bette Davis glued to TV sets around the nation that night knew that her career had always been her life. That career had always been the constant, the safety valve, the refuge. It would not divorce her, turn on her, parasitize her, play games with her. She would declare her passionate love, wreak murder and vengeance, exorcise epic hurts and jealousies and rages forever—courtesy of revival house screens, television reruns, and a million videocassette recordings.

They had called her witch incarnate, force of nature. They had spoken of her demon within, of the lightning nature that could not seem to find any ordinary outlet. Within two years of that January 1988 TV appearance, the frail body would finally fail her—but the spirit within, fierce, persistent, undying, would endure forever. Bette Davis, actress, will always be a force to reckon with.

1

Spawned in Witch Country

BETTE DAVIS was born Ruth Elizabeth Davis in the mill city of Lowell, Massachusetts, on April 5, 1908. There was, later, considerable hoopla to the effect that she had debuted, with histrionic suitability, in a welter of lightning and thunder, but in actuality it was a day of mild wind and a little rain. Though the city in the main was an industrial community where textile workers were constantly on strike and ugly worker-police battles took place regularly on the streets, Davis was from one of the "old families." She was born in her maternal grandmother's house on upper-class Chester Street. Her father, Harlow Morrell Davis, was a young Bates College graduate who would go on to Harvard Law School and become a prosperous patent lawyer and government consultant. He was descended from the Welch James Davis, who had come to New England in 1634 and had helped found the community of Haverhill. Her mother, the former Ruth Favor, was a descendant of seventeenth-century English and Huguenot pioneers. The Huguenot Favors had blended their blood so thoroughly with the old Brahmins as to qualify as bluebloods through and through. There was even a Salem witch in the ancestry.

Her father was a cold, unemotional, detached man; her mother, whom she was always to call "Ruthie," a woman who lived in her emotions. They were a strange, ill-suited pair. They separated when "Betty" (as she was then known—Betty with a *y*) was seven and her younger sister Barbara—called Bobby—was six. Three years afterward, in 1918, came a full-fledged divorce which horrified all their staid, straitlaced relatives in an era when divorce was almost a synonym for depravity.

Later she remembered that during the first seven years of her life, she "could not recall one moment of affection between my parents." While treated kindly by her mother's relations, and while not lacking for any of the necessities, Davis was strongly affected by this unloving marriage. She said, "I was fed on impermanence and insecurity. Men made vows they did not keep. They left women in the lurch, as my father left my mother. Nothing lasted—not love, not even life itself. One lived from day to day. One made do, cherishing the moment. The past was beyond retrieving. The future was a challenge, a danger."

At the beginning—the very beginning—she got off to a bad start with her father. He had married her mother on July 1, 1907, and she arrived nine months later, almost to the day. Her father had not planned to have a child so soon. His studies, his strict budget, did not provide for it. He tried to force the idea of an abortion on her mother, which horrified Ruth's brother, an Episcopal clergyman. Harlow Morrell Davis was an agnostic, a pragmatist. He dealt with facts. The rest was romantic fluff. Dissuaded from his intention to terminate Betty's life before it had even begun, he punished her for it later with unloving coldness and indifference. This was an attitude that Davis was to maintain toward both his daughters all his life.

Unwanted—and later deserted—by the first man in her life, Betty—later re-spelled Bette because a friend of her mother's had read Balzac's *Cousin Bette* and felt the *e* at the end sounded more glamorous and actress-y—developed a distrust of men that stayed with her all her life. "Childhood shows the adult," as a famed apothegm has it. As a result of the psychic wounds that Harlow Morrell Davis inflicted on his two daughters, Bette grew to think of men as rivals to be bested and Bobby regarded them as frightening threats. Many years later, after her fourth and last divorce, Bette Davis said, "I always knew I would end up an old woman alone on a hill."

Ruthie, her mother, was a loving flibbertigibbet of a woman, childlike and feminine during the years of her marriage to Davis. She seemed to her relatives and friends to be all sugar water, devoted to her babies, scrupulous about her maternal duties. But looks can deceive. Her husband's desertion and the divorce in 1918 brought the real woman to the fore. From then on she thought of herself and her two little ones as the Three Musketeers, Three Against the World, iron-willed survivors, come what might.

Bette's attitude toward younger sister Bobby was always ambivalent. Basking in her mother's adoration, in her sure knowledge that Ruthie thought her the talent to be nurtured, the white hope, she sensed that Bobby felt neglected, almost unwanted. In truth, Bobby always felt inferior to Bette in looks, brains, and creative talent. Lacking her mother's and sister's strong ego and will to survive, Bobby failed in all her pursuits, personal and professional. In time her feelings of inferiority progressed to mental illness that waxed and waned like a recurrent fever.

Harlow Morrell Davis left Ruthie with an alimony that provided only bare subsistence, in spite of the fact he was making excellent money as a major patent lawyer. After a few ill-advised and fruitless attempts to get more money from her frugal ex-spouse, Ruthie showed the true mettle of her hardy Huguenot and Yankee ancestors and went to work as a housekeeper and a dormitory mother in various colleges. This woman who loved art and music, who was a photographer, a painter, and a fine public speaker, was without false pride. She took any job that came to hand and that suited her immediate needs, and she taught Bette that a person was not to be judged by the job she held but by who she showed herself to be—*that* was where true dignity lay. Later, when she was attending an academy, Bette would wait on tables to earn her keep.

By necessity, Ruthie and her two daughters went where the work was. Sometimes it was New York City. Sometimes it was Boston or Newton, Massachusetts, or Maine. Bette Davis later estimated that they had lived in some seventy-five apartments, furnished rooms, or houses in the period between 1918 and 1926.

During those years, from the time she was ten until she was sixteen, Bette Davis learned that life was a battle. You had to fight for everything. Fight for self-respect. Fight for survival itself, because the male was more dangerous than the most ferocious tiger or the fiercest bird. Women had to look out for themselves, Ruthie taught Bette. She herself had been willing to be Harlow Morrell Davis's homemaker, helpmeet, loyal and loving little wife through life, but he had pulled the rug out from under her. All right, if that was how men were, she would be tough and self-sufficient.

Some thirty years later, teenage Barbara Davis Sherry heard the echoes of that long-ago refrain from the world-famous film star who was *her* mother: Men were unreliable, love tarried but a while. After the initial sexual thrill and romance were gone, men went wandering, looking for something or someone new, fresh, and exciting. Men craved novelty and lacked constancy. They were cold, tyrannical, brutal. Women must always be on their guard.

After matriculating in the public schools of Lowell and Winchester, a neighboring Massachusetts town, the Davis girls were sent to Crestalban, a rural academy in the Berkshires where outdoor life and wholesome pursuits were encouraged. By working as a governess for various wealthy families, Ruthie made sure that her girls were dressed nicely, but they were painfully aware that other children had prosperous fathers and loving, intact families with the snug joys and securities all that implied. Bobby reacted by shrinking into her own world. Bette responded by competing for prizes and acting in school plays. She was determined to be the best, the biggest, the brightest. She lived for the day when Ruthie wouldn't have to work so hard, when she would be the provider.

It was at Crestalban that Davis, playing Santa Claus, got too near a Christmas tree and sustained severe facial burns that blistered painfully. The outer layer of her skin had to be removed, and she was in pain for months while her mother kept her face constantly oiled. Thanks to good care, the skin healed, but with the outer layer missing, it was sensitive to sun, harsh makeup, and other irritants. Although her eyesight was not affected, her blue eyes became prominent because she bulged them outward compensatively as if to assure herself they were still functioning.

During the years between 1922 and 1926, Bette's high school years, the Davises moved frequently. While working in a photographic studio in New York, Ruthie took the girls to live in a one-room apartment on the Upper West Side. Later they moved to East Orange, New Jersey, where they lived in a bleak little flat that Davis always remembered for its claustrophobic, drab ambience. Then it was back to Newton, Massachusetts, where the girls went to the local high school. After a few more stopovers, Bette and Bobby wound up at Cushing Academy in Ashburnham, Massachusetts, where Bette spent her junior and senior years.

Davis was sixteen and Henry Fonda a gangling nineteen when they met in 1924. On a double date with a friend of his and her sister, Davis got a crush on Hank, which was not reciprocated. He later said he forgot all about her once she was out of sight. She seems to have carried a torch for some months, writing him letters he did not trouble to answer. They were not to meet again for thirteen years, and then under entirely different circumstances.

During her geographical and scholastic peregrinations, Bette attracted a number of beaux, most of whom she kept at a friendly distance. Ruthie, who harbored firm puritanical attitudes toward the opposite sex, drummed into the girls that the loss of virginity before marriage was the worst thing that could happen to a woman. Boys and men, she declared, were passionate, driven creatures, slaves of their genital urges; they sought only to pleasure themselves, leaving the consequences—venereal disease, pregnancy, the loss of reputation and self-respect—to their hapless female encounters of the moment. Ruthie told the girls that a woman's virginity was her integrity, her suit of armor, her defense against the rampaging, predatory male. Retain it and men would accord respect from a dutiful distance; surrender it and they would treat her as a plaything to be discarded. Total love, total surrender were only to be found in marriage—and even that called for a wary, considered approach.

The girls reacted to this advice according to their differing natures: To unstable, fragile Bobby it meant fear and distrust of the male, and to self-confident, strong Bette it spelled aggression, challenge, and role-playing.

The first man to get through Bette Davis's defenses emotionally, but certainly not sexually (she remained a virgin until she finally married him at twenty-four), was the shy, gangling Harmon Oscar "Ham" Nelson, who was a year ahead of her at Cushing Academy. Big, gawky, awkward, with liquid brown eyes and a large nose, his vulnerable essence appealed to Bette, brought out an element of the maternal and protective in her. Her fundamental attitudes toward men surfaced unmistakably in this, her seventeenth year. Ham was too weak to be a threat; he seemed to be in doubt of his masculinity. Certainly he never made passes, never tried to be alone with her, never pawed her, never maneuvered for kisses. Sometimes she wished he would. When he acted in plays with her, he was cast in character rather than romantic lead roles. He played in the school orchestra, and Davis would watch her shy swain nervously tinkling on his piano or tootling his trumpet. Though he was a talented musician, she regarded him half-protectively, half-contemptuously. This was no dashing Sir Galahad ready to sweep her off her feet, no take-charge male who would aggressively pitch for what he wanted. Although she responded to Ham and liked him, part of her longed to be totally feminine, yielding, dominated by a man she could adore and totally respect.

This dichotomy in Bette Davis's nature—a longing for a dominant man to whom she could surrender herself without reserve and attraction to weak, clinging, passive men—was a conflict she never resolved.

Meanwhile, at Cushing, Davis profited from the instruction of such fine dramatic coaches as Lois Cann, who taught her a special form of expressionism—a vital, disciplined projective technique that she permanently incorporated in her acting. She starred in many school plays at Cushing, including *Seventeen* by Booth Tarkington. Ham had a character role in this with her. When he graduated a year ahead of her in the class of 1925, she missed him. Ham went off to an uncertain career. After matriculating at an agricultural college, he eventually landed at Amherst after doing some band work. He finally graduated at the ripe (for college) age of twenty-five, after which playing in bands became his life. He and Bette continued to keep in touch over the years, meeting when their schedules permitted. Ruthie approved of him: His family was right, his Yankee background was right, and above all, in her view, he was docile and manageable, a kind, affectionate puppy dog. That was the kind of man she wanted for her daughters. It was tacitly understood that however much Bette might wander in the male forests, Ham was the man she would eventually marry.

During the summer between her junior and senior years, Davis went with her mother to Peterboro, New Hampshire, where Ruthie had obtained work as a photographer. She enrolled, at her mother's urging, in a dance school there that also had drama on the curriculum. The school was called Mariarden. While there she fell under the influence of a dance teacher who rather grandly called herself Roshanara, though her origin was plebeian English. Roshanara was a self-made woman who had turned her life into what she called "a thing of beauty and glamor and elegance." It was from Roshanara, Davis said, that she developed the grace of movement that later served her well in acting.

While at Mariarden that summer of 1925, the seventeen-year-old Bette acted and danced in an outdoor production of *A Midsummer Night's Dream*. It was directed by Frank Conroy, a seasoned Broadway and classical actor and later a prominent character actor in talking films. It was here that Conroy first noticed her, and later he was even more impressed by her in another production in which Roshanara cast her, *The Moth*. She danced the title role with such distinctive grace and style that Conroy told her mother, "That girl must continue as an actress. There is something so glowingly individual and distinctive about her that you can't take your eyes away from her. She belongs on the stage, and no-where else."

Davis graduated in the class of 1926 from Cushing Academy, her future unclear despite Conroy's encouraging words. She worked as a secretary and at other odd jobs, feeling that she had been enough of a burden to her mother. Some months later, as a treat, Ruthie took her on a theater outing to Boston. There she saw Henrik Ibsen's touching and powerful *The Wild Duck*, with Blanche Yurka, a noted stage actress with wild eyes and a flashing, driving style, and Peg Entwisle, a sensitive young actress of great promise who in the 1930s despaired over her lack of success in talkies and jumped to her death from one of the mammoth letters of the HOLLYWOOD sign. Seeing the plays, she was to recall, firmed her resolve to become an actress. She could be happy in no other way of life, she told her mother. There were strong, stormy, elemental feelings inside of her that she had to purge, she said, and acting was the only way to do it.

Convinced now that Bette's future lay in acting, and that all other efforts must be subordinated to that end, Ruthie took Davis (Bobby was in school) to New York in the fall of 1927 when Bette was nineteen. The distinguished Eva Le Gallienne, one of the country's most accomplished and celebrated actresses, had founded a group she called the Civic Repertory Theatre, which offered reasonably priced tickets and well-directed, well-acted versions of the classics, all on a shoestring budget. Miss Le Gallienne, philanthropic and dedicated to encouraging young talent, was also a thorough technician and a stern perfectionist who insisted on high standards, even for newcomers. She was not impressed with the young Bette Davis. Asked to read a part beyond her ability at the time, that of an old woman, Bette flubbed and fumbled her way through it with disastrous results. She reminisced years later that if she felt someone did not like her or was down on her from the word go, she froze up. When Miss Le Gallienne pointed out flaws in her trial inter-pretation, Davis irritated the Great Lady by replying that she was a beginner, not a finished technician, and that she had come to Le Gallienne to learn, not to demonstrate.

Mistaking Davis's humility for conceit, Le Gallienne coolly told the aspirant that she would hear from her by letter. A week or so later the frosty judgment came. It was along the lines that Bette Davis did not reflect a sufficiently serious or professional approach to her would-be profession to warrant taking her on.

Asked about this many years later, Eva Le Gallienne shrugged and replied, "So many youngsters came down to Fourteenth Street in those days, hoping and seeking. I simply don't remember her."

Crushed by the rejection, Davis mooned around the house in Newton, Massachusetts, where she and Ruthie and Bobby were then living. Around this time, Bobby elected to go to college in the Midwest. She sensed she was forgotten and that all the chips, as usual, were on Bette. Davis said years later, "I don't blame her for beating a retreat to someplace far away where, for a while anyway, she could feel like her own person."

Then Ruthie had another idea. Again she and Bette took the train to New York, but this time they headed for the Robert Milton—John Murray Anderson School of the Theatre. Just before leaving Boston, they had been disheartened by a letter from Harlow Morrell Davis, who disdained the idea of Bette as an actress. "She doesn't have what it takes for it. She ought to be practical, try for work as a secretary."

Ignoring the paternal vote of nonconfidence, Ruthie marched into the school and told the director, "My girl wants to be an actress. She's very talented. Frank Conroy thinks her potential is unlimited. I haven't got the money to pay your tuition but will you please accept her either on a scholarship or on a deferred-payment arrangement?" Moved by the aggressive yet somehow plaintive and touching request, the director accepted Bette.

That was when Bette Davis's real career began. The instructors at the Milton-Anderson school were the best. She took classes from George Arliss, one of the greats of the British and American stage and screen, who came as a guest instructor and inspired his young charges with his interpretive skills. Later he became an important factor in her life. Martha Graham, also an instructor, taught Davis the principles of full bodily expression on stage. Later, Graham, a disciplined, objective artist who did not bestow praise easily, said of her, "She had control, discipline, electricity. I knew she would turn out to be something out of the ordinary." During her two years there, Bette shone in such roles as Mrs. Fair in *The Famous Mrs. Fair*, played on Broadway by the then-popular star Margalo Gillmore.

Armed with her Milton-Anderson background, she alternated over the next two years between summer stock on the Cape and in companies in Rochester, New York, and elsewhere. Frank Conroy, who had kept in close touch with her, introduced her to George Cukor, who in 1928 was running a repertory group in Rochester. Given a small role in *Broadway* as a gum-chewing, tough chorus girl, she played the lead when the star was indisposed.

After a promise from Cukor that she would be rehired in the fall as a resident ingenue, Davis went to the Cape Playhouse in Dennis, Massachusetts. At first all she was offered was work as an usher. Undaunted, she accepted and awaited her chance. It came when the famous actress and veteran of numerous Broadway shows, Laura Hope Crews, who was directing and playing the lead in a warhorse called *Mr. Pim Passes By*, sent out an SOS for a girl who could assume an English accent. Davis overheard the request from the aisle where she was dusting seats and sorting out the evening's programs and shouted that she could fill the bill. Counting herself lucky that she had practiced accents while at Milton-Anderson, Davis got a commitment for the role—but only on condition that she would sing and play a certain ballad, *I Passed by Your Window*. Unfamiliar with the song, Davis and Ruthie scoured the music stores of the neighboring towns until they found the sheet music. Thanks to musician boyfriend Ham's tutelage in piano and singing at Cushing, Davis performed expertly and won her share of applause. Acting with Laura Hope Crews was another matter. While too shrewd and professional not to recognize her nascent talents, Crews was particularly vexed by some of Bette's mannerisms, especially her tendency to wave her arms around. At one point the Great Lady was *so* vexed that she slapped Davis full in the face. On another occasion she pushed her. The arms stayed at her sides for the rest of the Cape run.

Soon Davis was heading off to Rochester again, her mother, as always, in tow, to fulfill her engagement with the Cukor stock company. It was the fall of 1928, and she found herself up against such solid professionals as Frank McHugh, Louis Calhern, Wallace Ford, and Elizabeth Patterson, all of whom later wound up in Hollywood films.

Also in the company was Miriam Hopkins. Already a seasoned Broadway leading lady at twenty-six, Miriam was autocratic, demanding, temperamental, and a scene-stealer par excellence. Even then she had perfected her standard attention-getting tricks, including fluttering handkerchiefs, picking up books, stroking her throat, anything to distract attention, even from a bit player. Though she had already gone through several husbands, lesbian rumors about her were rife; she fanned them by having in tow a beautiful young girl she called her "protégé," who disappeared with her into her bungalow right after dinner, each and every night. She befuddled Davis by patting her on the fanny and telling her she had a sexy, swanlike neck. One night she invited Davis to join her and the girl in her bungalow; a horrified Ruthie pulled her away on a pretext. "Stay away from her—she's trouble!" she told Bette.

After this, Miriam became short with Bette when they played scenes together. One night Miriam screamed at Cukor, "She's stepping on my lines! The bitch doesn't know her place! *I'm* the star of this show—not that little nobody!" Enraged and humiliated, Davis pulled in her horns through sheer willpower.

Years later George Cukor denied that he fired Davis peremptorily. He told me, "Her talent was apparent. She did buck at direction, yes. She had her own ideas, and though she only did bits and ingenue roles, she didn't hesitate to express them. Her mother, as I recall, pushed her like crazy, was always lurking about. But I did not fire her. She insists I did, says I had a low opinion of her then. But I deny it all!" Whatever the nitty-gritty of the situation, she did leave the stock company rather abruptly. Louis Calhern, the accomplished and seasoned character star, had complained in a play called *Yellow* that Davis looked more like his daughter than his mistress, and she was replaced. Calhern said later that, moreover, she was too standoffish with the resident Lotharios and wouldn't "put out," which made her unpopular.

2

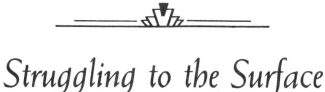

Struggling to the Surface

D AVIS'S BRIEF TENURE at Rochester proved to be the darkness before
the dawn, however. The brilliant James Light asked her to take a
role in *The Earth Between* by Virgil Geddes, produced at Light's Provincetown Playhouse in New York's Greenwich Village. Davis and Ruthie
found a small apartment on West Eighth Street that winter of 1929, and
happily and excitedly joined the famous community of bohemian artists
of all stripes and persuasions, political, sexual, and cultural. There, as
one writer put it, "People can call their souls their own, and see who
cares!"

To be sure, the theater on MacDougal Street was small and poorly
heated and not very clean. But it was redolent with memories of great
actors and great plays, including those of Eugene O'Neill, and young
Geddes, fresh from Nebraska, was as excited over his brain-and-spirit-
child getting produced there as Davis was to be starring in it. Washington Square was nearby, and over on Sixth Avenue and beyond in
Sheridan Square were wonderful little clubs and coffee shops where the
current political and art trends were earnestly debated. Davis and
Ruthie, sometimes accompanied by Geddes or male cast members, en-

joyed the Village atmosphere. Many years later she recalled "that wondrous sense of ecstatic freedom I knew while living there. There was a
sense of the unexpected and the magical. I am sorry for any artist of any
persuasion who has not, for however long or briefly, sampled the life of
Greenwich Village."

There has been some debate as to whether Davis completely understood the plot of *The Earth Between,* or whether her Village-tour companion, the young playwright Geddes, ever cared to enlighten her.
Certainly by age twenty-one, in 1929, Davis, who had cultivated a
wide-ranging sensibility through voracious reading and constant observation, must have been familiar with the phenomenon of incest, at least
in general terms. And incest, however subtly conveyed, was what *The
Earth Between* was all about. Davis must have sensed the play's underlying
currents, for her performance as the fragile, sensitive, delicate-spirited
daughter isolated on a Nebraska farm under the pervading influence of
her father's powerful personality won unreserved kudos from a number
of critics.

Many of her friends and neighbors were on hand to root for her that
evening of March 5, 1929. Armed with a run-of-the-play contract for
thirty-five dollars a week (which sufficed far more handsomely than it
would sixty years later), Davis used all her instincts and emotions to
bring the hapless girl to life. The two-act play was preceded by a brief
Eugene O'Neill piece, *Before Breakfast,* but this was one night when
O'Neill, who had helped make the Provincetown Players famous some
years before, took a back seat. The evening was hers. With Grover
Burgess as the ominous father and William Challee as her younger romantic vis-à-vis, Davis responded with wild delight to the cheers and
bravos of an intelligent and responsive audience.

She was later to say that nothing in her life could ever equal the
deep emotions and the wild elation that night brought her. New York
had accepted her without reservation. Her only sadness was that her
father remained in Massachusetts; instead of attending the performance
he sent a basket of flowers—without a note.

Bobby, Ruthie, and Uncle Paul Favor, a minister, all waited until the
morning papers appeared at the stand at the corner of West Eighth
Street and Sixth Avenue. They brought them home to Davis, who wept
tears of joy as the first reviews were read to her.

Brooks Atkinson in *The New York Times* had written: "Miss Davis . . .
is an entrancing creature who plays in a soft, unassertive style." St. John
Ervine wrote in *The New York World* that she had ably suggested the girl's
disturbed mind. And from the *New York Daily News:* "The performances

are good, especially that of Miss Davis, a wraith of a child with true emotional insight."

The Earth Between played to full houses and garnered flattering press interviews for Davis, who got yet another lift when Blanche Yurka, the famed actress and producer, asked to see her.

Miss Yurka was a formidable theatrical presence on the New York scene in 1929. By no means a beautiful or even handsome woman, she nevertheless took complete command on stage by dint of hypnotic, flashing eyes, a dynamic, compelling chemistry, and a fierce theatrical aura that commanded immediate attention. She had produced and starred in many fine classical and modern, as well as repertory, plays, and at that moment was casting for the role of Hedvig in Ibsen's *The Wild Duck*. She had gone to watch Davis after reading the reviews, and was sure she would be right for the vulnerable, impassioned Hedvig, who reacts to the news that she is an unwanted child, adopted by an indifferent father, by committing suicide.

Miss Yurka wasted no time. When Davis arrived with Ruthie, she told Davis that an audition was unnecessary and offered the role of Hedvig to her. There was one minor trial to be weathered before Hedvig was hers, however. One morning Davis woke up with a bad case of measles. Fortunately *The Earth Between* had run its course, and Miss Yurka, determined that Davis should play in *The Wild Duck*, held up rehearsals for several weeks until she recovered.

Miss Yurka said later that during rehearsals and during the run, Davis had presented problems. "She attacked the role too passionately at first. I wanted her to give it all she had—and that was considerable—but I had to temper and restrain her. I was troubled by her apron-strings ties to her mother, whom I thought a silly, flighty woman who had made her daughter her career and indeed her whole life. She was the archetype of the classic stage mother—only worse. She was always around. She watched every man who came near Bette—even her fellow actors. I think she had the idea that even a man's look could rape and/or impregnate!"

But Miss Yurka, who was also acting in the play, responded to Davis's dedicated intensity by generously handing her whole scenes. "I've had my day—let's see this eager, talented young girl commence to have hers!" she told the press. When the play opened in New York, Davis garnered more fine reviews. "She acts with all her heart and being," one critic commented. "On view here is a sincerity that is as compelling as it is electric."

Miss Yurka took the play on tour. The critics in Philadelphia

were equally good. The *Philadelphian* critic called Davis "strikingly effective . . . [she] thrills us with the poignant grief that comes with the
revelation of the child's great tragedy." Washington was next, with *The
Post* rhapsodizing, "Bette Davis is a young woman who is going to advance far in her stage endeavors. She was . . . profoundly sympathetic
and appealing." By this time Miss Yurka was bringing Davis out to take
curtain calls with her; she treated her like a co-star, to Davis's everlast-
ing gratitude. Years later, Davis was to say of Yurka: "People thought
her formidable, frightening, and cold. I came to know, first-hand, the
warm heart, the appreciation for good work, the fervent dedication to
the acting art that were at the core of this great woman."

The tour of *The Wild Duck* reached Boston—Boston, where she had
nurtured youthful dreams and hopes and had known the depths of despair during times when she feared nothing would ever happen, nothing
would ever begin. Again the accolades were fervent, with the *Boston Post*
declaring, "Our Miss Davis, practically our native daughter with her
birth in Lowell and her former residence in our suburbs, does us proud
in one of Ibsen's finest, most demanding classic roles. Heartbreaking and
compelling is she as she expresses her profound grief and lostness."

Friends poured in from Lowell, Lynn, Winchester, Newton, and
Cushing Academy. Then, at long last, Harlow Morrell Davis appeared
in the audience, and later in her dressing room. As usual unable to
convey what he was feeling (or possibly *not* feeling), he remarked on the
accomplishments of other cast members, the direction, the play itself,
then went on to the weather. Of her performance he said nothing.
Later, at home, he penned her a formal, correct note, the highlight of
which, after perfunctory congratulations, was an injunction to eat properly, for he thought she looked peaked.

During the tour Davis had also cut her teeth on another Ibsen play,
The Lady From the Sea. Yurka felt this would be good contrast for her, as
she played a happy, young, and carefree girl, demonstrating that she
could convey youthful lightheartedness and expectancy as well as tragic
grief. All in all, the Yurka-Ibsen tour vastly expanded Davis's capacities
and convinced her, once and for all, that she had a future in acting.

After the tour ended, Davis went back to the Cape Playhouse for
more seasoning. Her ushering and bit-playing days firmly behind her,
she spent the summer of 1929 honing her talents in a variety of interesting roles. She said of her experiences with summer stock, "It keeps you
on your toes; it teaches you timing, discipline, control."

The director Marion Gering, who was later to do some compelling
early-thirties talkies, saw her in the spring of 1929 in *The Lady From the*

Sea and asked her to try out for the ingenue role in a play by Martin Flavin called *Broken Dishes*, which was to open on November 5, 1929, at Broadway's Ritz Theater. In it, she would act with the comical yet poignant actor Donald Meek, a fussy, bald-headed little man whose uniquely androgynous, put-upon, aura would bring him a considerable measure of fame as a character actor in Hollywood later.

In *Broken Dishes* Meek plays a milquetoast worm who turns on his tyrannical battle-ax of a wife with the aid of his feisty daughter, played by Davis. As Elaine, the intrepid daughter, Davis makes a speech in Act III in which she tells off her mother and her friends in fine, rousing style. The audience cheered her loudly at curtain time, and as Blanche Yurka had, the generous Mr. Meek, though technically the star, called her out for curtain calls with him. Davis remembered that prior to the opening, Meek had lost his life's savings in the disastrous Wall Street crash of October 1929, yet came on and played his role with all his customary squirrelly sharpness that same night. She later called it "one of the most prime examples of the old saw about the show must go on that I was ever to witness. The memory of it was to sustain me in later years when I felt too sick to get out of bed, yet forced myself to drive to work where I knew the cast and crew and director of an expensive production that depended on my presence were waiting."

Of her performance in *Broken Dishes*, the *New York World* reporter declared: "Here is a young woman born for the theatre. The play is slight and even a little worn in its worms-turning plotting, but Miss Davis and Mr. Meek make it seem fresh and new—and yes, even meaningful."

Broken Dishes turned into a big hit. Young women and men wrote Davis fan letters telling her they recognized themselves in her character and in her family troubles. It ran for 178 performances into the spring of 1930, and Davis's name was enlarged in the ads and on the billboards. She was now a well-known Broadway personality, mentioned frequently in the gossip columns. Success was sweet, though she and Ruthie knew she had as yet a long way to go. Occasionally they would take the subway from their East Fifty-third Street apartment down to the Village, to look in at the latest Provincetown production. Davis loved the Village, and for a while contemplated taking a permanent apartment in one of the ancient nineteenth-century houses on Patchin Place. Ruthie and Bobby felt she ought to stay as close as possible to her Broadway theater, however.

It was at this time that a Samuel Goldwyn talent scout saw her in *Broken Dishes* and got her her first screen test. Goldwyn was casting his new Ronald Colman movie, *The Devil to Pay*, and the scout felt she might be right for a role in it. Davis made the long trip to the Astoria studios in Queens more than once because of delays in scheduling and false-alarm photographic experiments, but the test that eventually resulted left the Hollywood Powers-That-Were feeling that Bette Davis had no future in films. "Her features are too irregular. She isn't glamorous or beautiful enough. She is a problem to light and she doesn't have enough 's.a.'" (1929 parlance for sex appeal), Goldwyn's scouts told him. Reportedly he went to see her test himself, and came out barking, "Who in hell did this to me? She's a dog!" Some twelve years later he would find himself shelling out $385,000 to get that same "dog" on loanout for a picture.

Davis for her part reacted indifferently to the screen test results. Her ambition was to be a success on the stage, which she was, and she shared with many of her colleagues a suspicious, indeed disdainful attitude toward the West Coast movie factories. She shrugged it all off without a thought. She was far more excited when her beloved "Madame," Grandmother Favor, the mater familias, came to see her in *Broken Dishes* and with uncharacteristic effusiveness pronounced her granddaughter a signal success and a credit to the long line of Favors and Davises.

After *Broken Dishes* closed on Broadway, Davis went on a tour with it, then returned to the Cape for her third season. Another tour of the popular *Broken Dishes* was projected for the fall, but while she was in Washington, she was asked to replace the actress who played Alabama in *The Solid South*, starring the redoubtable old theater luminary Richard Bennett. He was the father of Joan, Barbara, and the Constance with whom Davis would one day be compared in Hollywood, a once-handsome man now gone to colorful seed via drink and dissipation who was nevertheless still a stage personality to be reckoned with. His outrageous improvisations and insulting, raging asides kept audiences as entertained as his still-excellent acting exhilarated them. Rouben Mamoulian, later the prestigious Hollywood director of Garbo and Dietrich among others, directed, and his battles with old Bennett kept the rehearsals in a constant uproar.

Bennett insisted on approval of everyone with whom he appeared, and when Davis arrived at rehearsal after a tiring trip from Washington, he barked, "You're another of those young kids who think your eyes will do your acting for you, eh?" Davis, tired from being on the train all night, drew herself up in twenty-two-year-old dudgeon and gave Bennett and the onlookers a preview of Mildred and Margo Channing by barking back, "I don't need this! I can always go right back to Washington, Mr. Bennett!"

Taken aback, then amused and intrigued, Bennett told her she was going to be just fine as Alabama. *The Solid South* is a rather chaotic mélange of farce and melodrama, and Bennett hogged the action as a flamboyant old colonel who dominates his plantation and his children and drives everyone to distraction. As his daughter Alabama (a preview of her screen work), Davis was the perfect loving and tender plantation belle. Her light o' love in the play was handsome, sensitive Owen Davis, Jr., with whom she "fell in crush," as she put it to Ruthie, for a while. He was the son of the playwright who later wrote *Jezebel*.

Bennett, ever the cutup, would fall out of character periodically to demand a cigar "if I am to keep concentrating on this damned pap!" One night, when the audience refused to respond to his comic sallies, he went to the footlights and barked, "I suppose I'll have to tell you fools a dirty story to get you to laugh! You have no taste! You're stupid as all get out! If you can't enjoy what you're seeing, then get up and leave!"

Bobby thought Owen Davis, Jr. "a dreamboat" and kept teasing Bette about him. "And think, if you married him you wouldn't even have to change your name!" she giggled, which won her a slap from her sister. Probably the Owen Davis, Jr., encounter would have developed had he not been romantically preoccupied elsewhere, or so her friends felt. He was the latest of a dozen young men she encountered during her theater period. One young man of impeccable aristocratic lineage gave her a rush for a while, then pulled out by writing her a Dear John letter that stated his parents didn't approve of actresses and he couldn't see her anymore. But luckily for her emotional health as of 1930, Davis's mind was primarily on her career ambitions. And Ham was always there, an augury for the future.

Possibly because the public tired of Richard Bennett's unreliable shenanigans, *The Solid South* closed after only thirty-one performances. Again at liberty, Davis was contacted by talent scout David Werner of Universal Pictures. The studio was about to cast a film version of Preston Sturges's *Strictly Dishonorable*, and she seemed right for the lead, he told her. Again she went across the river to Astoria to test. But this time she took more care with her grooming and makeup, and she passed the test—minimally. "They'll fix you up out there to look better," Werner told her, with a minimum of tact, as he presented her with a contract for $300 a week, with three-month options. "You're not the most sexy or glamorous girl I've sent out West, but you've got *intensity*," he said. "I think you'll go a long way in Hollywood."

3

Hollywood

AFTER A THREE-DAY train trip that they recalled as "dusty, messy, and endless," Davis and Ruthie arrived in Hollywood on December 13, 1930. That thirteenth was not a good omen, Bette told her mother, as they alighted from the train. Ruthie rejoined that a fortune teller had said that the name Bette Davis would one day be known all around the world, and maybe—just maybe—movies would make that possible. After all, wasn't movie star Charlie Chaplin known all around the world? "I'm not a comedian, Ruthie," Davis sniffed disdainfully.

The Hollywood of late 1930 was still reeling from the Talkie Revolution of the year before. In 1927, the year Jolson's *The Jazz Singer* debuted, silence was still king. By 1929 the overwhelming majority of pictures talked—or squawked—or squealed—depending on the quality of the sound recording in a given studio. Many a romantic star who had specialized in kinetic face-making accompanied by full orchestra went down the chute when his or her voice turned out to be a Bronx honk or a Southern drawl of the less euphonious kind. Talkies had spelled death to great stars like Norma Talmadge and John Gilbert, though the latter was rumored to have been a victim of a sound-tampering plot on the part of his MGM boss Louis B. Mayer in order to kill his expensive contract. The scene was changing, though. Great silent stars like Mabel Normand and Lon Chaney would die in 1930. Garbo had triumphed in *Anna Christie*; fans were enchanted by her deep, compelling Swedish inflections. An influx of musicals had run their course, and new talkie personalities like Clark Gable were about to burst onto the screen with maximum impact.

The great studios such as MGM, Paramount, and United Artists were importing stage stars by the carload, and Ruth Chatterton, Clive Brook, Kay Francis, and other Broadway luminaries were talking their way into expensive contracts and an ecstatic screen following. Warners had made a breakthrough with crime films.

Universal Pictures was among the second-raters of late 1930, along with RKO and Columbia, though all three would shortly move up to more prestigious status. Universal had made a breakthrough with the splendid *All Quiet on the Western Front*, based on the Erich Maria Remarque novel. The fresh new horror cycle, *Frankenstein* and *Dracula* among them, also enriched Universal's coffers that year and the next. Under old Carl Laemmle, one of the original film pioneers, and his young son, Carl Laemmle, Jr., Universal had big plans for the future, and importing prominent stage players was part of their program.

But Davis was in trouble from the start. The man assigned to meet her went back to the studio claiming no one had gotten off the train who looked even remotely like an actress. Apprised of his blunder, he rushed back in time to escort the bewildered Bette and Ruthie to their hotel. The photograph that the Universal camera aide took that day at the Plaza Hotel tells the story clearly enough: Davis seems shy and tentative, her smile hesitant. Ruthie, drably attired in a nondescript cloche hat and a drab black coat, like Bette, seems more determined in her look but still doubtful.

Carl Laemmle, Jr., whose taste ran to more glamorous, "obvious" examples of feminine appeal, thought Davis drab and unappetizing. He assigned *Strictly Dishonorable* to Sidney Fox—a more blatant sexpot—considered Davis, "since we're stuck with her," for Walter Huston's *A House Divided*, then changed his mind. While waiting outside his office one day, Davis heard him tell an aide, "That Davis dame has about as much appeal as Slim Summerville"—the ultimate ignominy, since Slim was an angular, homely, stupid-looking comedian whose stocks in trade were his befuddled look and awkward, shambling mannerisms. But the ultimate insult came from the *House Divided* director, William Wyler. The wardrobe department forced her to wear an extremely low-cut dress for her test, and Wyler guffawed, "What do you think of these dames who show their chests and think they can get jobs!"

Next she was called in to an office that didn't have a name or department heading on the door, where she was informed in no uncertain terms that the name "Bette Davis" sounded like a servant or a nurse, and that something more glamorous had been concocted for her. "Bettina Dawes" was the inspiration unveiled. Davis, surprising them with a hitherto unseen burst of spirit, informed them that she refused to go through life with a name that sounded like Between the Drawers. Then she imperiously walked out. When her rejoinder—and her attitude— were reported to Junior Laemmle, he decided to let her keep her name. And the glimmer of a suspicion that there might be more to her than her appearance suggested hit him briefly, but shortly disappeared, unfortunately for Davis.

At a loss for the moment to know what to do with Bettina-Determined-to-Stay-Bette, they sent her to the photo gallery to pose in all manner of outfits—swim suits, negligees, street clothes. The photographs left them unimpressed. Davis spent the final weeks of 1930 reading about Richard Bennett's glamorous daughter Constance in *Photoplay*—she had ascended to a $30,000-a-week salary range and was the envy of every actress in Hollywood. Since the only screen actress up to that time that Davis had ever taken seriously was Greta Garbo, whose screen image enchanted her, she went with Ruthie to advance screenings of *Inspiration*, the new Garbo film, and when it went to theaters, followed it there. For hours she studied Garbo's peculiar chemistry, her mannerisms, her facial expressions, the odd, intriguing way the camera had of making love to her.

At the studio, they were keeping her busy on a couch, while some twenty men lay on top of her playing love scenes to test their on-camera "capabilities." They came and they went, "like wooden soldiers" as she later told Ruthie, and only the courtly Gilbert Roland had the taste and tact to whisper to her, just before he imposed his 170 pounds on her bosom, "It will be okay. Really! Everybody out here has to go through this at the beginning."

The dictionary defines the word "lugubrious" as "exaggeratedly or affectedly mournful"—and that is the word *The New York Times* used in March 1931 to describe Bette Davis's performance in her first picture. Davis was heartened somewhat when told she would appear in a film version of Booth Tarkington's *The Flirt*, but then she discovered that she was to play the good sister, Laura, quiet, unassuming, virtuously predictable—and dull as dishwater.

British-born Sidney Fox, from *Strictly Dishonorable*, got to play the girl of the title—which ran through such changes as *What a Flirt* and *Gambling Daughters* before Junior Laemmle settled on *Bad Sister*, reportedly to favor Fox, whom he was grooming for stardom. According to Davis herself, Junior and Sidney had a hot romance going, and this underlay all the favoritism shown her. Fox was to play Marianne, bold, bad, flirtatious, irresistible, and much sought after by the men of a small Indiana town. Charles Winninger was her merchant father and Humphrey Bogart, in films only a year, was the naughty con-man who seduces then abandons Fox. Sadder and wiser, the onetime hey-hey girl marries staid solid-citizen Bert Roach, and drab Laura wins the handsome doctor, Conrad Nagel, who realizes his infatuation for Fox was just that.

It is interesting that Davis's first part should showcase her as an unrequited lover—at least until the upbeat ending—as unrequited love was to become one of her specialties. She languishes mightily over the handsome Nagel, who for sixty-two of the sixty-eight minutes the film runs, wastes his sterling, upright emotions on the sluttish Fox.

Bogart might have been in her first film, and even had some scenes with her, but Davis disliked him from the start, and nothing changed her opinion in later years, even when they did good work together. "How can you act so well with him if, as you say, you dislike Bogie so?" Louella Parsons once asked Davis, who tartly replied, "Because that's what I am—an actress! I'll whip up an acting storm with Lucifer himself if it's worth it to me!"

Bogart was certainly playing a variant of Lucifer in *Bad Sister*. First he gets Fox to forge her dad's signature to an endorsement with which he hopes to raise money to get a factory started; then he absconds with the dough and the daughter—and later abandons her. Some of the Tarkington flavor was retained by Raymond Schrock and Tom Reed, with additional dialogue by Edwin Knopf. The photographer was Karl Freund, famed for his German masterpieces in the silent era, who in 1931 Hollywood found himself mightily flummoxed by the stationary cameras, noisy traffic intrusions, and awkward microphone placements. Freund planted a small mike between Davis's breasts, which forced her to limit her head movements; she spent most of the time talking down directly into her mammaries.

Conrad Nagel, who played her love interest, had had a big career in the silents and helped Louis B. Mayer found the Academy of Motion Picture Arts and Sciences while tutoring Mayer for a more "cultured" accent. Nagel had an excellent voice for talkies, but strangely enough

Mayer neglected him in the early talkie era, and his acting career gradually declined. "It's bad luck to help Louie Mayer—he never forgets to repay favors with unkindness," Hedda Hopper once said of the MGM mogul, and Nagel discovered this was only too true. But Adela Rogers St. Johns opined that Nagel had offended Mayer by telling one person too many how he had worked overtime to "refine L.B.'s accent into something civilized."

In 1960 Conrad Nagel talked to me at length about Davis and her first film.

"She was very shy and very insecure. I think she realized she was not wanted by the powers-that-be, and of course this undermined her confidence. She was, I learned later, completely inexperienced about sex and easily embarrassed. A virgin of twenty-three in distinctly unvirginal Hollywood! That was a phenomenon for nineteen thirty-one!" Nagel laughed.

Asked for his thoughts on why Davis disliked Bogart so much, he recalled that in one scene with him Davis had to diaper a baby; she had expected it would be a girl; when she discovered that she had to handle a boy's genitals, doubtless the first male genitals she had ever seen and at twenty-three yet!—she blushed deep red through the scene, which came off gray on screen, as Davis herself recalled. Nagel hypothesized that Bogart was onto her virginity and had rounded up cast and crew to watch her reaction. He seemed to think it was all a big laugh. Bogart could be vulgar, too. "That dame is too uptight; what she needs is a good screw from a man who knows how to do it," he told Nagel.

"She didn't understand anything about makeup or eyelining or rouging or the right kind of lipstick for the camera, and nobody went out of their way to enlighten her," Nagel continued. "She had to stand by and watch all those prissy makeup men buzzing around court favorite Sidney Fox making her look divine; Marie Antoinette in her beginnings must have felt that way about DuBarry!"

Nagel also recalled that Sidney Fox pulled rank, knowing her clout in the front office, and, in his opinion, enjoyed making Davis look drab and unwanted. "Her hair was an ash-blonde then, and it photographed a mousy brown. She told me later that she and her mother left the San Bernardino preview before it was over, she felt that humiliated, absolutely hated herself on the screen; did for years in fact." Even *Variety's* kind reference to her ("Bette Davis holds much promise in her handling of Laura, sweet, simple, and the very essence of repression") did little to console her. All she could talk about was that the *Times* had called her "lugubrious." Only Karl Freund saw her potential: "She has lovely eyes," he told Junior Laemmle. That comment reportedly saved her at Universal—for a while, anyway.

John M. Stahl, a director regarded as one of the screen's arch sentimentalists, was about to begin a film, *Seed*, based on a controversial novel about birth control by Charles G. Norris. Since the birth control theme was a little strong for the watchful Hays Office, the screenplay concocted by Gladys Lehman evolved into a banal, somewhat tedious story about a man, John Boles, who wants to become a writer and who is suffocated by the demands of family life, including five kids and a wife, Lois Wilson, who is too sweet and self-sacrificing for words. Eventually he deserts his family, becomes a famous novelist, takes on svelte, smooth Genevieve Tobin as a mistress—and then begins wondering about the folk he left behind, including his now grown children.

Stahl had little trouble filling the roles of the four sons, but the daughter, Margaret, proved a stickler. She had to be wraithlike, vulnerable, sweet yet vital. After combing high schools, drama forums, theaters, restaurants, anywhere and everywhere but the Universal contract list, he finally spotted Davis in the Universal commissary and decided she had the right quality. The monumentally indifferent Laemmles, thoroughly unimpressed with her *Bad Sister* histrionics, acceded readily to the idea of Stahl or anyone else keeping Davis busy while she was still working out her contract option, and Davis landed in *Seed*, where she was hardly seen or heard by audiences. "If you blinked, you missed her, the role was that small," Raymond Hackett, one of her "brothers," later recalled to his wife, Blanche Sweet, who told me:

"Raymond said she was the most pathetic thing he had ever seen— unsure of herself, thoroughly aware she was unappreciated, disregarded by everyone, especially Stahl." The director, having pushed her into the background, proceeded to forget all about her, and Davis practically directed herself through the few scenes she had in *Seed*.

She later recalled, with more than a little bitterness: "There was no makeup man for me, no attempt was made to light me properly, and I felt like a churchmouse next to the soignée Genevieve Tobin, who broke up our dull but happy home . . . but I did my thankless job and kept my mouth shut . . . . if I wasn't dead in pictures already, this appearance was sure to do the trick." She also recalled that up against the vital talents of Tobin, Lois Wilson, Hackett, and Richard Tucker, she felt like a "ghost."

Hackett told his wife, Blanche Sweet, that he was sure Davis had developed a woman-size crush on handsome John Boles, the star, then thirty-seven, fourteen years her senior. Mr. Boles had been in movies off and on for about seven years, alternating between singing leads and romantic foils for such as Gloria Swanson and Bebe Daniels. Gentlemanly and soft-spoken, with all the breeding of a southern aristocrat, Mr. Boles had lit a mighty fire in the heart of the young Norma Shearer, among others, and, onscreen later, was to prove the ultimate *homme fatal* of cinema opposite Irene Dunne, whom he relegated heartlessly to the *Back Street*, and Ann Harding, whose heart he broke in somewhat similar fashion in *The Life of Vergie Winters*. But alas for Davis, Boles was no philanderer or advantage-taker when it came to the susceptibilities of young co-workers.

So little did Universal think of her when the picture was released in May 1931 that she wasn't even mentioned in the advertising, and her name appeared far, far down on the list of credits. When I saw *Seed* in revival some years ago, I found Davis insipid, dull, ZaSu-Pitts-ish. (ZaSu was in the picture as a maid, in fact, and Davis at times seemed to be doing an imitation of the limp-wristed, fluttery comedienne.) The picture itself seemed to lack the courage of its convictions, having been boiled down from a novel that had had more bite and bark, and the plot meandered uneasily. "Lethargic and often dull," said *The New York Times*.

For the third time Davis found herself somebody's sister. In *Waterloo Bridge*, a screen version of the Robert E. Sherwood play, reviewers disregarded her again as she wilted away in a badly written, ill-defined role as the hero's sister who is gracious to the little showgirl with whom he falls in love before going to the World War I front from England. All ends sadly when the showgirl-turned-prostitute, feeling she has forfeited her decency along with the right to her lover's respect and regard, dies on Waterloo Bridge.

Such are the bare bones of this tragic story, which was made twice more, in a vastly superior MGM version of 1940 with Vivien Leigh and Robert Taylor, and as a forgettable 1956 effort with Leslie Caron and John Kerr, retitled, for no good reason, *Gaby*.

Certainly the 1931 version was a slapdash, ramshackle affair, devoid of proper movie underscoring and handicapped by superficial performances from the leads, Mae Clarke (more famous for getting Cagney's grapefruit jammed in her face in *The Public Enemy*) and Kent Douglass, who later, as Douglass Montgomery, was to sparkle briefly in films opposite the likes of Katharine Hepburn and Margaret Sullavan.

Douglass took something of a shine to Davis during the shooting but she found him too fragile and somewhat effeminate for her taste—Margaret Sullavan later had similar reservations about him—and as his burgeoning interest did little for her ego, she promptly discouraged it.

Davis remembered hanging around the set mouthing Mae Clarke's lines and wishing fervently she had the chance to play the role as she felt it *should* be done. Eager, sad, frustrated, disappointed, she was as much a wraith about the set as she was before the camera, as co-workers were to remember, and again she was forgotten, both in the advertisements and in the reviews. "Janet was an insipid part," she later scoffed. "I think I had about four lines in it, and I don't think I had even a change of costume. I was supposed to be nice to Clarke, and in fact I cordially hated her inwardly because she was getting the showcasing I knew *I* could have done ample justice to!"

It is true that Mae Clarke was an actress of distinct limitations, and indeed she wasn't all that pretty. She wound up her career later as a feminine foil for Cagney and others, and eventually was reduced to playing bit parts. Many years later, when I interviewed her, she said, "Gosh, in 1931 I felt I was really on my way, and Bette seemed to be in permanent Loser-Limbo. I hardly remember her from the picture. She seemed anxious to elude everyone's notice. It is hard to believe that this shy stick of a girl within a year or two was to burn up the screen in hot, sexy roles. Of course she wore her hair a brownish ash-blonde at the time and it wasn't very attractive. Nor did she have a clothes sense—not that the studio helped her any. But it must have taken an iron will to get out of the rut she was in when I knew her—certainly she proved she had that, in spades."

There is a story that years later Davis tried to get down-and-out Mae a small part in one of her major 1940s Warner starrers. Davis commented, "I was a nothing also-ran in her picture, and maybe I can help her do just a little more in mine now." But those who knew Davis well at the time felt that she was trying to reestablish a contrast—in petty reverse—with an actress whom she had bitterly envied, considering her frustrating 1931 situation at Universal. Certainly her motivations may have been mixed in this instance.

Waterloo Bridge was received, for the most part, with cool, perfunctory dispatch by the critics. "There are moments when the story has a sympathetic tug," *Variety* sniffed, damning with faint praise.

Davis was, at first depressed when she learned she would be loaned out to RKO for *Other People's Business*, later retitled *Way Back Home*. It was to star Mr. and Mrs. Phillips Lord, who had achieved widespread popularity in a regular NBC radio show called *Seth Parker*. Mr. Lord, a folksy, do-gooder Maine minister, solved his people's problems, comforted them in misfortune, and was a good and uplifting influence.

Jane Murfin concocted a warm, homey, unaffected screenplay based on the radio characters. The plot, what there was of it, had to do with villainous Stanley Fields (one of the movies' favorite heavies of the period), who seeks to pry hapless son Frankie Darro away from the Lords, with whom he has taken refuge. In the course of the story, Fields runs afoul not only of the Lords, but also of local boy Frank Albertson and his girl, Davis, who befriends Darro. Eventually Fields is killed by a train, and all ends happily.

The film was budgeted at $400,000 (a lot for the period) and eventually ran a longer-than-usual 81 minutes. It was full of warm, informal, unassuming Maine touches, and the village life and people are captured without Hollywoodish elaborations and come through as real and human.

Davis was not only pleasantly surprised at the courteous and kind reception she received at RKO from Producer Pandro Berman, who had been struck by her potential in her Universal pictures and had asked for her, but to her delight found, by looking at the rushes, that photographer J. Roy Hunt had shown her to maximum advantage, highlighting her fine eyes and expressive mouth. Director William Keighley, who excelled at light and sentimental romance, understood actresses (he married two of them, Laura LaPlante and Marian Nixon) and took time and care with her scenes. While she was merely a supporting player as Frank Albertson's girlfriend, she appeared in *Way Back Home* to far greater advantage than she had in any previous film.

Soon she had attracted the notice of the screen's leading magazine editor, James R. Quirk of *Photoplay*, who kept his Hollywood staff moving on Davis. One of his writers, Katherine Albert, recalled to me her visit to the RKO set in late 1931, where she found Davis relaxing contentedly with an orangeade in the company of Frank Albertson, who was obviously smitten with her. Now Davis was reading about herself in *Photoplay*.

"She was a shy little thing—almost mousey—in those days," Katherine told me in 1953. "It is amazing, in retrospect, why I didn't sense the fire in her at that time. Maybe it was the part she was playing—a nice, small-town Maine girl—and she was living it on and off screen. She spoke of her love for her mother and sister, and her hopes for the future. I had heard she was very unhappy with the treatment she was getting at Universal, but she seemed hesitant to go into detail about it, at least on that occasion. I guess she didn't want to seem to bite the hands that fed her—though actually they were starving her, both creatively and monetarily. A month or so later, after they let her go, she told me, 'They said I had no sex appeal, and they couldn't imagine any man giving me a tumble. I was regarded as attractive back in New York, and I had plenty of beaux; in fact, turned down several proposals of marriage. If they had paid more attention to me, if they had photographed and directed me differently, and had given me parts I could have shown my mettle in, they might have felt respect for me. But that is all water under the bridge now, thank goodness.'"

Director William Seiter said of her in 1960: "I found her a cooperative and delightful actress, and the Lords were like parents to her, concerned and hospitable. Universal had handled her very stupidly, of course—they didn't realize what they had in her, and it didn't say much for their perspicacity. She claimed that *Way Back Home* was the first film in which she felt she had been properly showcased, and that it gave her hope for the future. Everyone liked her, and she worked hard with what slight material she was given. She was graphically agitated, I remember, in a scene where Stanley Fields, the drunken father of Darro, is menacing her, and her love scenes with Frank Albertson were tender. Frank was obviously in love with her, and she handled him very gently, onscreen and off."

Frank Albertson, who began as a prop boy in movies at thirteen in 1922, was twenty-two when he made *Way Back Home*. In 1960, he was in New York on vacation when *Psycho*, in which he had a small part, premiered, and reminisced about his career in general. He had played many leads and such outstanding character parts as Katharine Hepburn's brother Walter in *Alice Adams*, in which he had really shone with critics and public. While his career in 1960 was on a decided downslide, he was mellow and philosophical while we talked.

He said he had most enjoyed acting with Katharine Hepburn, among the many stars he had supported, but reserved some affectionate words for Bette Davis and *Way Back Home*.

"It was a really warm and homey little picture. The Lords, whom I felt I already knew from their radio program, created a family atmosphere on the set, and yes, I did develop a crush on Bette. She was very warm and sweet. I know people think of her as a fussy, man-hating, dynamo and termagant but she wasn't like that then, not at all. I really *felt* the love scenes but I could tell her romantic interests were elsewhere; I believe she married Harmon Nelson some months later. But we were always friendly when we met in later years."

Davis always defended *Way Back Home* as a warm, genuine film, but the January 1932 critical opinion was mixed. "Unbelievably bad," sniffed *Weekly Variety* but *The New York Times* called it "real and mellow."

After *Way Back Home* finished filming, Universal kicked Davis over to yet another studio, Columbia, for *The Menace*. In later years Davis said of *The Menace* (the original title had been *The Feathered Serpent*), "It was a monstrosity; my part consisted of a great many falls out of closets. The picture was made in eight days. I knew I had obviously reached bottom."

The director, Roy William Neill, accorded the hapless Davis scant attention, and the love interest to whom she was assigned, Walter Byron, drank heavily, smoked incessantly, and though only thirty, was obviously on the downgrade, which accounted for his strangely aged and bloated appearance. He also had the foulest breath of any man she had ever met, and this made the love scenes with him a particular trial for Davis.

After several heavy woo-pitching scenes, Davis couldn't stand it anymore and asked Byron, "Do you ever brush your teeth or use mouthwash? You show a shocking lack of consideration for me when you forget about such things!" Roy William Neill told a *Photoplay* writer ten years later that "when she lit into Byron like that, I knew there was more—much more—to her. It's no wonder to me that by now [1942] that little girl has battled her way to the top like a champ!"

Natalie Moorhead, a well-groomed and handsome blonde actress also in the picture, was some years Davis's senior and was obviously jealous and insecure in her scenes with the visitor from Universal and tried to upstage her. Her tactics—moving upstage away from the camera, forcing Davis to turn around and face her, and so on, prepared Davis for combat with another egotistical star, Miriam Hopkins, some years later. "Natalie was a cold egotist," H. B. Warner, also in the cast, said. "She was very self-conscious and self-protective about her looks and general appearance and I am afraid she gave the little Davis girl a hard time."

The plot was some trivial nonsense about Byron's fleeing England after being falsely accused of murdering his father. He is disfigured in the oil fields of the southwest United States, returns to England to learn who killed his father, and finally pins the murder on his stepmother, Moorhead, and her cohort. Disguised by the plastic surgery that his accident had necessitated, he pretends to be a prospective buyer for the ancestral estate, fooling both his stepmother and his former fiancée, Peggy, played by Davis. Davis and he are reunited at the unconvincing fadeout.

Byron, who had made a glittering start as Gloria Swanson's leading man in *Queen Kelly* in 1928, told an at first sympathetic but finally bored and irritated Davis during on-set tea sessions that he felt he was all through in America and perhaps should return to his native England. "You're full of self-pity and that is destructive," she told him. "Stop the drinking and smoking and watch your health and looks, and maybe things will get better." She always expressed regret in later years that this very handsome man and good actor obviously hadn't taken her advice. Byron took a small part in what turned out to be his last film in 1939, and then lived on in total obscurity until 1972.

The Menace was a hopelessly bad film in all departments, from Roy William Neill's perfunctory get-it-over-and-done-with style of direction to the careless photography, which did nothing for Davis, to the screenplay by Dorothy Howell and Charles Logue, which never got off the ground.

Some of the photographs the still department dreamed up were the silliest and most inappropriate possible. One that is often reprinted shows Byron and Davis staring up at an obviously pâpier-maché "monster." They were so poorly posed by the photographer that they don't even look frightened—just bored. As well they might have been. The reviews of the time shrugged it off with "just routine melodrama without menace or perceptible suspense." *Weekly Variety*, though, delighted a certain someone with, "Bette Davis has to take a decided second to Natalie Moorhead." Another sniffed: "Filled with absurd situations." When I saw it many years later, I felt the original reviewers had been too kind.

Hell's House, shot in 1931 and released in early 1932, was certainly the nadir of Davis's early Hollywood career. "It took two weeks to shoot and looked like it had taken a day and a half," the witty Irish-American actor Pat O'Brien later said of it. It was his first picture with Davis, and they became, in his words, "a mutual consolation society of two." Later Davis and her mother became excellent friends with Pat and his wife.

Davis once said of O'Brien, with whom she would work again, "He was very vital and sexy looking and acting and, I thought, a handsome man in his Irish-looking way, but playing around was not his thing. I don't know if it was Catholic guilt or what, but Pat always went home to the little wife; no womanizer was he." When kidded by his friends about his fidelity to his marriage vows, Pat always gave an unprintable rejoinder along the lines of Paul Newman's remark decades later about the reason for his fidelity to wife Joanne Woodward: "Why should I go out looking for quick hamburgers when I have steak at home?" Frank McHugh later said, "Pat could talk dirty with the best of us, but the funny thing was he never put his cock where his mouth was"—meaning action never followed the words.

Davis needed all the reassurance she could find in co-star O'Brien's friendship, for *Hell's House*, originally known as *Juvenile Court*, was a real horror. The last of the quickie films for which she had been haplessly shunted around by the Laemmles, it displayed her as Peggy, the girlfriend of flashy bootlegger Matt (O'Brien), who takes advantage of hero-worshipping teenager Jimmy (Junior Durkin) by letting him take the rap for one of his own offenses. Junior winds up in reform school (Hell's House, of course), where the goings-on are as Dickensian as poverty-row producer Ben Zeidman and fly-by-night director Howard Higgin could make them. At the horror-pit, Jimmy befriends frail Shorty, (played by another young actor named Junior—in this case Junior Coghlan) who is dying, in properly bathetic style, of a heart ailment. A crusading newspaper publisher, Morgan Wallace, exposes conditions at the reform school, and all turns out well when the cowardly O'Brien, egged on by indignant girlfriend Davis, finally acts like a man and accepts the responsibility for the crime he had foisted on the innocent Junior Durkin.

Junior Durkin was sixteen when he made *Hell's House*. A promising young juvenile with a sensitive face and manner, he had been a hit in *Huckleberry Finn* earlier in the year, but after that found himself a "has-been," and made only a few films after *Hell's House* before his death at twenty in a car crash of which his good pal, the famed child star Jackie Coogan, was the only survivor.

"Junior was an unlucky kid," Pat O'Brien later said of him. "He was too boyish and innocent to graduate into leading-man status, and of course that early death was tragic. But he was so down, so disappointed over failing to make it when he loved acting so, that maybe death came as a mercy, terrible and sad as that sounds."

O'Brien remembers young Durkin developed a tremendous adolescent crush on Davis, who, on and off the screen, adopted a big-sisterly, protective attitude toward him. "I think Junior, who could be very winsome and sweet, was the brother she had always wished she had," O'Brien remembered. "She and her mother went out of their way to be nice to him, and I think it came as a real shock to her when I tipped her off that the poor kid, all of sixteen, no less, had fallen hook, line, and sinker for her!"

While the picture was shot on peanuts in less than two weeks, producer Zeidman and director Higgin found it necessary to cut one scene in which Davis puts her arms around Junior to comfort him. "And they hated to cut it," Pat O'Brien later laughed, "because even two minutes of film loomed large in their budget, but for Christ's sake, the kid had a hard-on in his pants when Bette hugged and kissed him, and the camera caught it!"

Junior Coghlan and some of his pals, according to O'Brien, rescued the few feet of film from the cutting room wastebasket and for some years enjoyed showing it at their stag parties. "It so embarrassed Junior Durkin," according to O'Brien, "that he got into some fist fights trying to recover it. He came to me about a year later over it. 'What do I do?' he wailed. 'Laugh about it, and go around congratulating yourself. So you got a hard-on with Bette Davis in a movie—great—proves you're a man!'"

O'Brien couldn't resist passing the news about her young co-star's "humiliation" on to Davis, who found it amusing, in a self-deprecatory way. "Hell," O'Brien remembered her saying, "it isn't as if I were Jean Harlow or Connie Bennett or Lombard. Why, I was still a virgin then! If I got the poor kid excited, I guess I have to take it as a compliment. But I hadn't even dyed my hair a provocative blond at that time—I can't imagine what he saw in me!"

O'Brien laughed that a lot of adult males later would have commended adolescent Junior Durkin's taste circa 1931. "They were calling her a drab, sexless wren over at Universal, couldn't wait to get rid of her," O'Brien chortled, "but that horny kid saw what nobody else saw— no flies on him!"

Hell's House languished on the second- and third-bill poverty-row circuits but, unaccountably, got a New York release in early 1932. *New York Times* critic Mordaunt Hall wrote: "The direction of the film is old-fashioned. Pat O'Brien gives a forced performance. Young Durkin's playing is sincere and likewise that of Bette Davis." *Weekly Variety* dismissed the proceedings thus: "It merits only the attention of the second runs—the lesser ones. . . . [It] projects as having been put together in a slipshod manner." O'Brien's summation of *Hell's House* was: "The only thing solid about it was Junior's hard-on—and that was cut!"

Back at Universal they had news for Davis. With her latest option expired, she was let go.

4

Warner, Zanuck— and Arliss

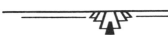

I T IS ALWAYS darkest just before the dawn, as the hoariest but most enduring of clichés has it, and the end of her thankless Universal and loanout year was to usher in, for Bette Davis, the beginning of a bright new career at that most vital and enterprising of studios—Warners.

In the new year, 1932, she would encounter three men who would greatly change the direction of her career.

The first, Jack L. Warner, one of four brothers of Polish-Jewish ancestry, had emigrated from Canada to New York. With his brothers, Harry, Albert, and Sam, Jack struggled up in the film business from the nickelodeons he ran circa 1910 to the short films he began producing in 1912. In 1917 the Warners produced their first successful film, *My Four Years in Germany*, and by 1925 they had amalgamated with First National Pictures and Vitagraph. After experimenting with sound in the John Barrymore film *Don Juan* in 1926, they revolutionized the industry in 1927 with the first film that blended songs with lines of dialogue—*The Jazz Singer*, starring Al Jolson. This put them in the forefront of film production, and they led the way into the Talkie Era. In the early thirties Harry became the president of Warner Brothers, Albert the treasurer, and Jack head of production at the Burbank Studios in Hollywood (Sam had died in 1927).

Jack was a hearty, bluff man who ran his studio with an iron hand. He kept the schedules tight, the salaries low, and his underlings turned out lean, snappy, unadorned pictures that usually ran only a little over an hour. He had a gift for hiring talent, and Darryl Zanuck (and later Hal Wallis) helped him put Warners solidly on the map in the 1930–1933 period with a series of gangster films and taut social dramas that appealed to a Depression audience. Even the musicals for which Warners came to be noted had a snappy, hard edge, featuring struggling chorus girls and male entertainers pushing for the big break.

Jack Warner considered his actors children and ruled them like a despotic, disciplined, but fair father. Like the other greats of his time— Mayer, Thalberg, Laemmle, Cohn, Zukor—he built personalities through steady exposure, and the plethora of mediocre films he forced on them was compensated by the fact that he turned many of them into household names. Noted for his raffish, unsubtle humor—there is a story that when he was presented to Madame Chiang Kai-shek he made a crack about having forgotten to bring his laundry—Jack also had a shrewd, instinctive taste and a feel for prestige values when he felt the time for them had arrived. He was to hold the talents of the distinguished George Arliss in high esteem, as he later did those of Paul Muni and Edward G. Robinson, among others.

In 1932 the brilliant Darryl Zanuck was his chief production aide, and Zanuck contributed fully to the lurid but well-made gangster melodramas that made Cagney and Robinson stars, as well as to the social consciousness and musical films. All were fast-paced, hard-edged, snappily plotted, and modestly budgeted, but with Zanuck less was more, and the product, unembellished by lavish production values (except in the musicals), was smoothly professional.

Zanuck, born in Nebraska in 1902, had served in World War I, then drifted into writing after a series of odd jobs. A screenwriter at Warners from age twenty-one, in 1928 he was made studio manager after successfully merchandising Rin-Tin-Tin pictures, and in 1929 was made head of production. Restless, inventive, and oversexed (his specialty was exposing his heavy endowment to various lovelies on the lot), he gave Warners a tremendous charge with his creative dynamism. In 1933, he left to form Twentieth Century and later to preside over Twentieth Century–Fox, but when he and Davis crossed paths in 1932, he was the Big Gun (figuratively and literally) at the Warner lot.

Murray Kinnell, a talented character actor from Broadway who had appeared with Davis in *The Menace*, was struck by her potential and mentioned her to his friend George Arliss, who was preparing a picture at Warners called *The Man Who Played God*.

At that time (late 1931) George Arliss was the foremost character star in films. In his sixties, a thin man with a skeletal face and piercing eyes, by no means handsome or even distinguished-looking, he was not at all the type one would expect Hollywood, and American movie fans, to take to their hearts. In 1886, when he was eighteen, he first appeared on the English stage. Then he came to the United States on a tour in 1902 and stayed to reign on Broadway for decades, eventually moving into silent films and later talkies, where his distinctive voice and manner won him an Oscar for *Disraeli* (1929–1930). His reputation continued to grow in classy, literate films like *Old English*, *Alexander Hamilton*, and *The Green Goddess*. At the time Davis encountered him, he was Warners' most valued and prestigious star.

Davis was just about to leave Hollywood, had in fact already booked her tickets and was packing with her mother for the return trip to New York, when Arliss phoned and asked to see her. He was immediately impressed with her appearance and manner, and, acting on his own trained intuition as well as Kinnell's recommendation, hired her for the role of Grace, a young girl who is in love with his character of Montgomery Royale, a famous pianist deafened by a bomb meant for a king who was on hand for one of his Paris concerts.

Back in America, deeply depressed by the fact that he may never hear again, Royale has taken a philanthropic interest in strangers he observes through his binoculars in Central Park; by reading their lips, he learns their problems, and in a number of cases becomes their anonymous benefactor. When he later observes Davis in the park telling the young man she loves that she feels it her duty to remain with Royale, whom she reveres and adores but is not physically in love with, he releases her from their engagement and takes up with an older woman, Violet Heming, who has waited for him patiently.

The screenplay, by Julian Josephson and Maude Howell, adapted from a short story by Gouverneur Morris and the play *The Silent Voice* by Jules Eckert Goodman, was directed by John Adolfi in a somewhat posturing, old-fashioned manner that makes the picture seem dated and falsely sentimental today. While the other actors are competent and Arliss is his usual expert, magnetic self, it is Davis who is the revelation of the picture with her sincere, honest, and vibrant playing.

At the interview, Arliss asked her how long she had been on the stage. To her answer, three years, he replied, "Just long enough to rub off the rough edges." He thought her vibrant and personable, but it was not until they got on a Warners sound stage for their first scene together that the full impact of her tremendous potential hit him.

In a Bette Davis career study I wrote for *Films In Review* in 1955, I quote the effect she produced on Arliss, as recalled in his second autobiography, *My Ten Years in the Studios* (1940).

"I think that only two or three times in my experience have I ever got from an actor at rehearsal something beyond what I realized was in the part. Bette Davis proved to be one of those exceptions. I knew she had a 'nice little part' important to me—so I hoped for the best. But when we rehearsed she startled me; the nice little part became a deep and vivid creation, and I felt rather humbled that this young girl [Davis was then twenty-three] had been able to discover and portray something that my imagination had failed to conceive. She startled me because quite unexpectedly I got from her a flash that illuminated mere words and inspired them with passion and emotion. That is the kind of light that cannot be hidden under a bushel, and I am not in the least surprised that Bette Davis is now [1940] the most important star on the screen."

Davis impressed Arliss not only with her talent, but also with her dedication and professionalism. She was no silly ingenue marking time, primping for the cameras in the hope of exciting the romantic sensibilities of her male audience and the envy of the females. She was already, at twenty-three, a maturely dedicated artist who was determined to give her best at all times. She saw herself surrounded by seasoned performers like Violet Heming, Louise Closser Hale, and Ivan Simpson. She realized that cameraman James Van Trees and director Adolfi were working for a "class" effect in all departments, and in this class setting she was determined to be a class act herself.

Davis always regarded *The Man Who Played God* as a significant turning point in her career. She said, "It is probable *The Man Who Played God* was my most important picture. I did others that I liked better, and which were more significant, but there was something about appearing as Mr. Arliss's leading lady that gave me standing."

There were two things about Arliss she did not know at the time. One was that he had ordered completely private screenings of every picture she had done since coming to Hollywood. He winced at the neglect she had suffered, at the lack of attention, the way the bushels of mediocrity had hidden her exceptional light. The other was that he had formed an immediate attraction to her personally, one he would never reveal to her. Though sixty-four years old when he met Davis, Arliss fell in love with her. He was an unabashed ladies' man whose romantic adventures had long been tolerated by his patient and understanding wife of many years, Florence, who appeared in several of his films, usually as his spouse and supportive sidekick. Right up to the gates of old age, Arliss's attention continued to wander, but it was Florence who held his eternal devotion and loyalty. When her eyesight failed in 1937, he retired permanently from the screen to give her his undivided attention. Their son, Leslie Arliss, later became a talented and accomplished director.

When Arliss plays the scene in which he lip-reads Davis's frustration over her thwarted love for handsome young Donald Cook and her determination to stand by a man, himself, who is forty years her senior, he plays it with utter conviction. For as events proved, he proceeded to make the same personal sacrifice offscreen.

Arliss and Davis enjoyed long conversations on the set between takes, and he often served her his favorite tea and scones. Davis recalled that he made her feel like a true lady, like a talented person worthy of the respect of her colleagues. The atmosphere on the set of *The Man Who Played God* was so different from the casual, knockabout, helter-skelter set atmosphere at Universal that she found herself caught up in the sheer wonder of it.

It was Arliss who suggested she lighten her hair to a more vivid shade of blond to help her appearance match the vividness of her personality. It proved wise advice. After wardrobe had provided her with a set of dresses and gowns that were carefully fitted, and that, for the first time, gave her a truly glamorous aspect onscreen, she consulted with Perc Westmore, Warners' makeup genius, who saw to it that her hair was carefully bleached, that a chic, slickly conceived new hairdo was designed for her, and that her makeup played up her assets and deemphasized her liabilities.

As Davis put it years later: "According to the standards of the world I came from [Broadway], I was a blonde—technically, an ash blonde. According to the Hollywood standards of the 1930s, when bright, bleached hair reigned supreme, my hair was nondescript. [Perc] was wise enough to know [as Arliss did] my photographic appearance would be heightened by the blonder hair. He was right. In *The Man Who Played God*—for the first time—I really looked like myself. It was for me a new lease on life. As a matter of fact, I was compared to Constance Bennett.

I was very flattered. I had always liked so much the way she looked on the screen."

Over the year that followed, she was to find the alleged resemblance to Connie Bennett a mixed blessing. It all added up to good publicity, however, as she readily understood.

Skillfully applied makeup and careful lighting by Jimmy Van Trees (with angles often suggested to him by Arliss himself, who understood them as well as anyone) completed the effect the New Bette Davis produced in *The Man Who Played God*.

Weekly Variety was among those publications picking up on the New Bette, with its reviewer rhapsodizing: "A splendid production. . . . Bette Davis, the ingenue, is a vision of wide-eyed blonde beauty."

George Arliss was to reappear in Bette Davis's life on several more crucial occasions. She always revered him, and when he died in 1946, at seventy-eight, she said: "I owe Mr. Arliss more than I could ever have repaid. In a crucial, important way, he was like a father to me, the first major fosterer of my creative life. His death, moreover, is not just my loss—it is the world's."

After seeing rushes of her performance in *The Man Who Played God*, reportedly at the insistence of George Arliss himself, Jack Warner signed Davis to a five-year contract, with one-year options. Wasting no time, he rushed her into two new pictures at once, and she was kept busy going from one set to the other. Both roles were supporting performances in films highlighting major stars, but she had good material to work with and managed to shine onscreen despite limited footage.

So Big, the Edna Ferber novel, had been made before, in 1925, with Colleen Moore. Now Barbara Stanwyck, whose contract Warners shared with Columbia under a new arrangement, was starring in the role of Selina Peake, one of those intrepid women that Ferber enjoyed glorifying. A schoolteacher in the farming country of the West, Selina has the respect of all who know her and has placed her hopes in her son, Hardie Albright, whom she would like to see become a great architect. He has other ideas, however, including womanizing and stockbrokering, but later Selina has the satisfaction of knowing that she has inspired her friend's son, George Brent, to become an acclaimed sculptor. Davis plays Dallas O'Mara, a young artist in love with Albright. When she comes to know Selina, she understands and appreciates this simple woman's essential greatness of spirit, and Selina is left with the hope that Dallas will influence her son to nobler pursuits.

Davis delighted in the role of Dallas, despite its brevity. In later years she claimed that Dallas exemplified the affirmative womanliness that she liked to think of herself as possessing. Her identification with the idealistic yet practical Dallas may have been one of her illusions about herself, for Dallas in actual fact bore little resemblance to the egoistic, hard-driving, self-centered, and neurotic Bette Davis of 1932. "Tennessee Williams was later to tell us we all needed illusions and that was one of Bette's," director William Wellman later said, recalling that he had a time of it toning down Davis's endless squirming and her particularly bad habit of squinting when under harsh, tough close-up lighting. Davis and Stanwyck, who, though but one year her senior, had already achieved major starring status, mixed like oil and water in their few scenes together. "Bette was supposed to be inspired by Barbara's character's example, but it was evident she was jealous because a contemporary had achieved stardom so quickly while she had to grind through small roles and [to date] bad pictures," Wellman later recalled. Barbara sensed her jealousy and reacted in typical Stanwyck style. While not an overbearing person with set workers and fellow actors (on the contrary, Stanwyck was noted for her friendly, informal relations with co-workers), she didn't take nonsense from anyone, having struggled up from Brooklyn in the toughest of show-business circumstances. Davis's tense mannerisms and constant wiggling struck her as affected and designed to hog and, if possible, steal scenes. In one shot, Davis blew her lines and lit a cigarette nervously. "It all makes me so jittery, the pace of this scene," she complained to Stanwyck, who barked back, "You make *yourself* jittery! Try to fit into things!" After that Davis never liked her, and the atmosphere was frigid. "She's an egotistical little bitch," Stanwyck told Wellman. "Why doesn't she relax, for Christ's sake! She'll get her turn. There's plenty of room at the top for talent in Hollywood."

In later years, when I interviewed Stanwyck, I asked for her opinion of various co-workers. About most of them she was warm and cordial. When I mentioned her brief appearances with Davis in *So Big*, her eyes hardened. "She was always so ambitious you knew she'd make it. She had a kind of creative ruthlessness that made her success inevitable," Stanwyck said. Her voice got across the two-edged quality of her remark.

The New York Times critic opined: "Bette Davis, as a young artist who sees into the complicated story of Selina's life, is unusually competent."

It was in *So Big* that Davis first worked with the actor who would be one of the great loves of her life. While their scenes in *So Big* were fleeting, she was to have a more intimate juxtaposition with him in the other picture in which they were appearing simultaneously, *The Rich Are Always With Us.*

George Brent, twenty-eight years old in 1932, had a checkered and fascinating career. Born in Ireland, he had come to America in 1915 at age eleven, after his parents died. Later he returned to Ireland, where he did bits and walk-ons with the Abbey Theatre while carrying on, at seventeen, subversive activities against the British as an Irish revolutionary. In 1921, after a narrow escape from the British, who had a price on his head, he was smuggled back to America via freighter to Canada. Odd jobs were followed by an acting debut in Canadian stock, followed by Broadway, where he was regarded as one of the theater's most attractive young juveniles in the late 1920s. Signaled by Hollywood in 1931, he began a long career as a suave, sexy, but hardly inspired actor who specialized in playing romantic foil to the likes of Garbo, Loy, and others.

The Rich Are Always With Us starred Warners' most glamorous actress-of-the-moment, Ruth Chatterton, who had come over from Paramount with a high-salaried contract after conquering the talkies in such women's-picture fare as *Madame X* and *Sarah and Son.* Given the deluxe treatment all the way for as long as her Warner reign lasted (a scant two years, after which her box office fell off), she was designated in her picture credits as MISS Ruth Chatterton and was dubbed by the fan magazines "the Queen" and "The Screen's First Lady." By no means pretty, Ruth had flair, poise, and authority instead, and as one of her admirers wrote, "could sweep in and out of a drawing room with an imperial aplomb that was classy as all-get-out!" A Broadway star for fifteen years prior to her 1928 screen debut, she had been adored by producer Henry Miller, who called her "Miss Peaches."

It was this formidable figure Davis faced on her first day on the set of *The Rich Are Always With Us.* Having been given the business by Stanwyck on *So Big,* Davis found herself speechless in a scene with Chatterton, and the star, sensing her confusion, took her aside and assured her that she was, after all, a fellow human being and co-worker, and if she would relax, all would go well.

Charmed by the democratic approach of Queen Chatterton, who proved big sisterly in comparison to aloof Stanwyck, Davis relaxed and proceeded to give a fine performance. When I interviewed director Alfred E. Green in the 1950s, he recalled that Davis seemed to fit like a glove the role of Malbro, a flighty society girl in love with the handsome foreign correspondent (Brent) whom the married Park Avenue matron (Chatterton), has appropriated for her very own. The film, written by an ex–Mr. Miriam Hopkins, Austin Parker, was frothy nonsense about Chatterton's persistent loyalty to an aberrant society scamp of a husband (John Miljan), a womanizer and rogue par excellence. Brent grows impatient with her masochistic loyalty to Miljan, who she is in the process of divorcing, but they somehow blunder their way through to a happy denouement, of sorts.

As it turned out, Davis was outmaneuvered in the pursuit of the irresistible Mr. Brent by Chatterton, both onscreen and off. Both ladies fell madly in love with him during the shooting of *The Rich Are Always With Us,* but it was Chatterton who whisked him off to the altar off-screen as soon as her divorce from her current husband, actor Ralph Forbes, was final.

Oddly enough, being beaten by Chatterton in the Brent Cupid Sweepstakes did not turn Davis against her. Bette always remembered Chatterton's kindnesses to her during the shooting, and she designated her one of the premier actresses of her time.

Davis's memories of Chatterton in later years may also have been sweetened by her knowledge that Chatterton's star set as hers rose, and by the fact that Chatterton's and Brent's marriage lasted barely two years (1932–34), after which Davis was to have more than a few cracks at him, both on and off screen.

George Brent was an erratic fellow, disdainful and sharp-tongued. He seemed to have a realistic approach to women and made them dance to his tune rather than the reverse. "No woman will ever own me; I own myself!" he told producer Hal Wallis once, and no woman ever did establish permanent rights to him through many romances and some six marriages, including those to actresses Constance Worth (it scarcely lasted a year, 1937) and Ann Sheridan (who also had a one-year marital turn with him in 1942–1943).

Yet for all his rueful realism, sophisticated awareness of the female psyche, and a feet-on-the-ground cynicism doubtless born of his stark and brutal experiences during the Irish rebellion, Brent had a steadying influence on the ladies in his life and met their problems with a kind of rough compassion that they found healing—while it lasted. Davis was to benefit hugely from these qualities of his in the not-too-distant future.

Orry-Kelly, who had been born Jack Kelly, began his career as a clothes designer at Warners about this time, and he and cameraman Ernie Haller worked overtime to photograph and dress Davis to flattering effect. Davis thought of herself as striking rather than beautiful at the time (most who knew her agreed) but the Haller-Kelly combine did succeed in doing wonders with her appearance in *Rich.*

The New York Times thought little of *The Rich Are Always With Us,* stating that it "unfortunately savors more of Hollywood than it does of fashionable New York society." Chatterton was called "charming" and Davis was pleasantly dismissed and/or patted on the back with "Bette Davis also serves this film well."

Darryl Zanuck kept his eyes open for a good lead for Davis, and found *The Dark Horse.* With a presidential election coming up, this story of a gubernatorial campaign had "the right stuff," Zanuck felt. And the role of the intelligent, enterprising Kay Russell seemed right up Davis's street.

While *The Dark Horse* will never go down in cinematic history as a classic of the first, or even the second, order, it is a lively and witty political comedy-drama that showcased Davis most effectively.

The plot has her and campaign manager Warren William trying to sell a gubernatorial candidate (Guy Kibbee) of monumental stupidity and oafishness. Davis and William scheme their way through to an election-night success for their candidate, meanwhile following the usual leading man–leading lady pattern of falling solidly in love.

The New York Times liked *The Dark Horse,* and Davis in her first solid leading part of the year found herself described as giving "a splendid performance." Of the picture itself, the *Times* critic wrote: "A lively comedy of politics . . . filled with bright lines and clever incidents and never a word or an action is wasted."

Photoplay had referred to *The Dark Horse* in its review as a "grand political satire, which comes at the most opportune of moments," adding "[it] will give you enough chuckles to tide you over a flock of gloomy days."

Meanwhile the magazine's editor Jimmy Quirk was answering the flood of "Davis looks like Connie Bennett" letters with articles and gossip notes that called attention to the highly distinctive individuality of both actresses, but which favored Bette. When Connie Bennett was in New York for a visit, she met Quirk at a party and protested. He told her: "You've already made it—you're a big star. But she's just coming up and needs any and all kinds of inventive publicity. Be a sport, Connie. You can afford to be generous!" Bennett agreed she could indeed afford it, and no more on the matter was heard from that quarter.

Meanwhile, Davis was having problems with Warren William, a notorious ladies' man who reportedly had an erection ninety percent of the time and had to wear special crotch supports to disguise the fact—not always successfully. She had dodged his passes all through *The Dark Horse*, and then, to her horror, found that Warners expected her to go to New York with William on a personal appearance tour. She suspected that Zanuck had cooked this up as a favor to William, who was his friendly rival in the cocksmanship sweeptstakes. William made no secret of the fact that he found Davis the cat's meow sexually, and she had to complain to director Alfred E. Green when William turned their on-screen smooching sessions into grope parties.

As for Zanuck, he admired Davis's talent and potential but found her "too New England staid" for his tastes. "If William has the hots for the dame, I'll make it easy for him," he told Alfred Green. And presently Davis found herself on a train bound for the East with William and a Warner contingent of publicity men and administrative aides.

In 1932, Davis hated personal appearances and publicity tours. She did not think she was sufficiently well known as yet, and it wounded her vanity to face the prospect of people asking, "Who is *she*?" To her pleasant surprise, she got maximum recognition. Jack Warner later said, "I don't think she realized the enormous exposure Warner films give to even supporting players. The Stanwyck and Chatterton films paid off for her."

In later years Davis gave full credit to this hyperefficient Warners publicity machine for speeding her to stardom. "The disadvantage of the contract system was that we were treated like serfs and forced to take roles that were not always suitable. The advantage was that one got maximum exposure to the public in picture after picture, churned out regularly in those days, and wonderful concentrated publicity."

William did not seem to care that Davis was seriously involved with Ham Nelson, whom she would marry that August. "Ham has a bad temper," she hinted. "I know he'll take apart any man who tries to take liberties with me." She also let it be known to one and all that she would go to her marital bed a virgin, all of which elicited coarse laughter from the horny William. "I can't believe a woman as passionate as that waited twenty-four years to find out what a guy had in his pants and what he did with it!" he snorted to Zanuck. "She's giving out a lot of horseshit. She was probably into the boys' pants back in high school!"

Zanuck to his surprise found himself a lady's defender for a change. "She didn't go to a high school, she went to an academy," he rejoined, "and I don't know any guy who *has* made her, but you can try your luck if you want!"

Warren William, once ensconced in New York with his wary prey, dreamed up, with Zanuck's approval, a sketch for him and Davis to do at the Capitol Theater. Called *The Burglar and the Lady*, it portrayed a robbery that later turns out to be a skit depicting a movie scene, with the director yelling, "Cut!"

But "cut" it was not to be back at the hotel, where Davis and William (again thanks to the inventive Zanuck) had rooms on the same floor. When Davis heard the patter of little feet once too often out in the corridor and heard the inimitable, sexy Warren voice calling out, "Room service!" she phoned Ham. "I think I'm in imminent danger of getting raped. Do something about it!"

Within ten minutes Mr. Warren William heard an irate Ham's voice on the phone. "Who do you think you are, trying to make time with MY woman?" was the least of what Mr. Nelson had to say to Mr. William, and after that all was peace at both hotel and theater—or relatively so. "I couldn't escape Warren's looks, at any rate," Davis later said. "They say looks can kill. Well, looks can undress, too, believe you me!"

Bette Davis has said that her favorite of all her film lines is the one from her next 1932 film, *Cabin in the Cotton:* "I'd love to kiss ya, but I just washed ma hair!" spoken, of course, in the southern accent she adopted for the film, which starred a rather washed-out-looking Richard Barthelmess. The great silent star was slipping in 1932; his career would end a few years later, his vogue as the well-meaning innocent forced to express his manhood under pressure having passed during the sophisticated Depression era of gangsters and men who kicked women around and made them like it.

Michael Curtiz was the reluctant director. He had not wanted Davis for the part of Madge, the sexy planter's daughter who seduces sharecropper's son Barthelmess against the background of a planter-sharecropper dispute. During the filming he embarrassed Davis any and every way he could, calling her, within earshot, "a no-good sexless son of a bitch" and harassing her with such insults while she was making love to a camera without Barthelmess on hand to play to.

Darryl Zanuck had insisted that Davis could generate the steamy sexuality necessary for the part. Even when he knew he had been proven wrong during the filming, Curtiz lacked the grace to admit his mistake.

Davis knew Madge was a breakthrough role for her, and she gave it all she had. In a famous bedroom seduction scene, Davis undresses in a closet, then emerges obviously naked, though the shots are filmed at shoulder height. She advances on Barthelmess, who is suddenly aroused by her come-hither steaminess and brokenly whispers her name as the scene dissolves in a passionate embrace.

The scene—and Davis's performance in general—is all the more remarkable in that Davis was still a virgin, her marriage some weeks away. Possibly it was her frustration over that state, her determination to be free of it, that lent such emotion and such sexual kineticism to the scene.

I talked to Richard Barthelmess in 1960, a few years before his death from cancer, and among the topics covered was Davis's emergence as seductress supreme in *Cabin in the Cotton.* "I felt she was emerging from some kind of chrysalis, that true womanhood had somehow eluded her up to then, that family pressures, her mother, her puritanical upbringing, had somehow kept her in delayed adolescence," Barthelmess said. "There was a lot of passion in her, and it was impossible not to sense it. She was twenty-four at the time, and one got the sense of a lot of feeling dammed up in her, a lot of electricity that had not yet found its outlet. In a way it was rather disconcerting—yes, I admit it, frightening."

Barthelmess added, "I was thirty-seven or so at the time, and had forgotten a lot more than she was in the process of discovering—and I don't mean acting. I admit I was never noted—onscreen or off—for being a hot lover-boy. That was not my thing, not my gift, if that is the word for it, but she was so exciting and seductive that she would have aroused a wooden Indian.

"More important, she was an excellent actress who, I knew even then, required only the right director and the right script to shine along with the best of the stars of the time. When *Of Human Bondage* came along a couple of years later, I was not at all surprised at the sensation she made. It was all there in *Cabin,* but the story and the director were not right for her."

Barthelmess recalled that Curtiz had gone out of his way to be cruel to Davis. "He had fought Zanuck over her casting—probably thought Ann Dvorak or some other directly sexual type would have been more right for it—and he couldn't admit it when he saw he was wrong. Mike Curtiz was a mean one. I was the star of the film so I could walk away from him and hole up in my dressing room but Bette was a contract player and had to put up with him, and put up with him she did. Indeed she would taunt him in return at times. She knew Darryl Zanuck believed in her and that Curtiz couldn't remove her. And she gave that performance all she had."

Cabin in the Cotton was indeed a breakthrough performance for Davis. When the picture was released in late September of 1932 the critics picked up on Davis's fresh incarnation at once. Regina Crewe in *The New*

York American raved about "that flashy, luminous newcomer Bette Davis,
who romps off with first honors, for hers is the most dashing and colorful role." Crewe wound up her rave review with, "The girl is superb."
Richard Watts, Jr., of *The New York Herald-Tribune* noted, with some surprise, "Miss Davis shows a surprising vivacity as the seductive rich girl."

She could have used that support, and badly, for Warner and
Zanuck did not build on what they had in her. In her next picture, *Three
on a Match*, she appeared perhaps a total of 15 minutes out of the 63-
minute running time. Moreover her nemesis, Warren William, was on
hand again to annoy and pester her. "I should think you would be flattered by Warren's attentions," Ann Dvorak, one of her co-stars, told
her. "If you like him so much, he's yours on a silver platter," Davis
snapped back. Joan Blondell was also in the film about three girls, one a
former reform school inmate (Blondell) who turns entertainer; another a
wealthy matron (Dvorak) with a little son she adores—and the third,
Davis, a drab secretarial-school graduate who works as a stenographer
(Davis—a stenographer!) and is given no story line (she seems to be on
hand only to join the other two in lighting from the same match in a
restaurant scene, hence the title). Superstition has it that the third person to use the match will die and that turns out to be Dvorak, who
wrecks her marriage, and destroys herself with drink and drugs. Blondell
inherits the husband and the son. As for Davis, after serving as a sort of
companion to the kid while all the melodrama gets sorted out, she proceeds to disappear without a trace—a thankless role in a thankless film
for the erstwhile steamy siren of *Cabin in the Cotton*. Warren William was
less rakish and more respectable than usual as the husband who finds
eventual consolation with Blondell, and since his scenes with Davis were
almost nonexistent, his advances were infrequent—on set at least.

Davis was enraged at being shunted into *Match* after shining so con-
spicuously in *Cotton*. She told one and all that it was a perfect example of
the pernicious contract system under which a player had to take what
was assigned, or face suspension. She was particularly angry because the
screenwriter, Lucien Hubbard, had given her no juicy scenes to play and
had even deprived her of a romantic interest! Nor was Mervyn LeRoy
any help as director, absorbed as he was in making Joan Blondell and
Ann Dvorak look as exciting as possible.

Davis recalled years later with biting irony that LeRoy had let her
know—tactlessly, she felt—that he believed Joan Blondell was going to
become "a great star" and that Ann Dvorak's future was "unlimited."
"Great for them—but what about me?" was her reaction at the time. "It
wasn't that I didn't wish the other girls well," she added, "but I didn't get

a crumb out of that script!" The ultimate irony was that neither Dvorak nor Blondell ever approximated the great stardom Davis was to enjoy. The critics were not slow to pick up on Davis's *Match* mistreatment. The critic of *Hollywood Filmograph,* among others, noted that "Bette Davis is ravishing in appearance, but had very little to do."

But she was about to co-star in real life—a major role. Ham Nelson was back—to stay.

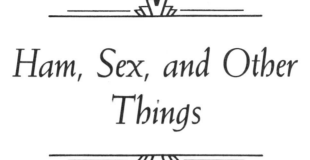

5

Ham, Sex, and Other Things

"I WAS HOPELESSLY puritan! Helplessly passionate!" This was how Bette Davis, in her memoirs, described what she was like during the hot summer of 1932. Still a virgin at twenty-four, still repressed, she had taken on her mother's sublimational attitudes and threw all her sexual energy into her work, playing out scenes in movies that in sophisticated terms were far ahead of the mother-and-sister-preoccupied life she actually led.

Then Ham Nelson reappeared. After working in night clubs in the East as a trumpeter, he had come to Hollywood to play in a band connected with the Olympics held in Los Angeles that summer. Soon he landed a job with the Colony Club, where he played trumpet with the jazz band.

Ham had not changed much from the sixteen-year-old kid she first met at Cushing Academy. Eight years had gone by, he was now twenty-four, but he was still the same shy, insecure, gangling introvert he had always been. He found his release in his music, attacking the trumpet like a man possessed. Ruthie looked on Ham with favor. He would, she decided, make the ideal son-in-law. His family and his New England roots were equal to the Favor and Davis backgrounds. He and Davis liked each other, there was some physical chemistry there, he was gentle and serious, and he had taught Davis a lot about music, not just jazz but classical also.

Ruthie began pestering Bette about being twenty-four and in danger of becoming a bachelor girl transformed into old maid if she waited any longer to marry. Davis listened half-mockingly, half-receptively. It was true that she found her virginity a burden. She had played all those hot love scenes for four years, on stage and screen, and with a variety of men, yet she had not known a man in the biblical sense, and her curiosity and physical needs were mounting. She continued to joke that all she really knew of a naked male was what she had been reluctantly forced to address when she diapered the boy in that early movie. At home, she and Bobby pored over medical and anatomy books and were well acquainted with the "facts" of male-female intercourse. But what did it *feel* like—that was the sixty-four-dollar question. And did it feel differently with a man one loved as against a man one was merely attracted to?

Ham was on hand, subject to daily inspection—with his clothes on, of course—so Davis had plenty of opportunity to think about his potential as husband and lover. She liked his sensitivity and his musicianship and the shy, tentative way he had. She found it remarkable that a man who had knocked around with so many orchestras in so many locations did not project more feisty, extroverted toughness and heartiness. She decided that Ham had become even more handsome with the years. She knew he didn't think himself so—he had described himself as "a big, gawky loon"—but she found his tallness and still-adolescent awkwardness charming and sweet. He told her he thought his nose was too big and his mouth too thick, but she felt these gave his face character and interest.

She and Bobby speculated about Ham's sexual experience. Had he ever had a girl? They read that young males who were not married masturbated frequently—that is, if they weren't lascivious lady chasers. Was Ham, perhaps, a male virgin? He wasn't telling—and she wasn't asking. What had happened to Ham in eight years? Why were young men's lives such mysteries to women? Why did it have to be that way?

Finally, egged on by Ruthie, who stated firmly that it was time she functioned as a woman, Davis asked Ham if he was ready to marry. In future years she was never willing to admit that she had done the proposing, but in fact she had, with Ruthie prodding away in the background. Ham accepted immediately.

Ruthie, as usual, suggested the time and place and terms of the wedding, which took place on August 18, 1932. Still tentative and unsure, aware that Ruthie was rushing things to keep her from changing her mind, she set out with Ham, her mother, and Bobby for Yuma, Arizona. They had decided on Arizona because California insisted on a six-week waiting period. There were to be no romantic airplane flights for Davis—fashionable as they were already becoming in 1932. They set out along the dusty pre-freeway roads in a beat-up Auburn that threatened to conk out at any moment.

The heat of the desert was murderous. Gas stations were few and far between. The clothes stuck to them as they sweated profusely in the heat. Davis drove while Ham sat, languishing and miserable, beside her, and Ruthie and Bobby perspired and complained in the back. When they finally pulled into Yuma after a miserable journey of many hours, they checked into a second-rate hotel, dried their clothes, and Ham went out to buy a suit and wedding ring—a cheap one, since Yuma's few stores were hardly a class act, even by 1932 standards.

The next morning, an Indian mission minister married them. As Ruthie later recalled, Ham misplaced the ring twice; one time it went through a hole in his pocket; another time it fell into a floor crack and he had to grovel to find it. Right after the uninspiring, perfunctory ceremony, they headed straight back to California and Zuma Beach, where Davis was living.

In her memoirs, Davis has waxed rhapsodic about what happened after she and her bridegroom had perfumed and lotioned themselves to the nines, got rid of Ruthie and Bobby, closed the door of their room, and got into bed to face one another as husband and wife for the first time. In Davis's words: "This was Ruth Elizabeth's golden moment. The proper bliss of a wedding night was here. The union under God and everything between a man and an honest-to-goodness maid was hers; and her joy was boundless. . . . Passion formalized, love ritualized, sex smiled upon by society."

Growing more specific, if still restrained (for her), Davis gushed on: "I was able to shower an object with the unnamed joy that lay simmering beneath my humorless drive without a trace of guilt, with no fear of disapproval."

Many years later, Davis described the night in more realistic terms to Jerry Asher, when she lamented that she had not had any affairs before marriage and expressed her envy of young women in the 1960s who could "try a guy out, see if he fit for size." If she had been a virgin that night of August 18, 1932, she found that Ham had been a chronic masturbator, was given to premature ejaculation, was shy and awkward and even unsure of what orifices were correct for penetration. She said that as the years went on she wondered about Ham's sexuality, wondered if he had had relations—however brief and tentative—with other male musicians during his national tours. Bobby told her later that men often indulged in casual relations when thrown together—was that a factor in her bridegroom's past, she later wondered.

She complained that despite her inexperience, *she* had to be the aggressor sexually, that, thanks to the medical and anatomy manuals she and her sister had examined, she brought Ham to climax, but she couldn't get him "properly trained" to satisfy her until some months after they were married. She even admitted that Ham's tall, rangy body, well muscled and well endowed in the crucial spot, had so excited her that she had not hesitated to masturbate and even fellate him—practices considered, and not just by puritans like her mother—perverted in the extreme in 1932. Later she recalled his thorough, abandoned enjoyment of these practices as suspicious, indicative. . . . But she admitted also that once she had encouraged and trained him in more penetrative techniques of the missionary-position kind, he performed creditably.

But along the lines of you never know anyone till you're married to him, she refered to Ham in primarily negative terms years later. There was his tendency to whine, his passive willingness to do the dishes and make the beds instead of protesting that was woman's work, his moodiness and sulking, his inability to act the man's role. She craved a decisive, forthright, masculine man, one she could lean on, defer to, one who would dominate her, set a direction for their lives. Ham, she said, failed her miserably there. There was the inequity in their earnings, which humiliated him. And the difference in their hours—as Ham went to bed after playing in a band all night, she got up to go to the studio. Because of his silences, his withdrawal, his inability to stand up to Ruthie and Bobby, who had taken their own quarters behind the house she and Ham rented, his tendency to walk away from a fight, his almost feminine languors, Bette slowly began to lose respect for Ham Nelson.

In the 1932–1935 period, Davis gradually discovered that she was married to three people rather than one. There was Ham, who fluctuated between whining self-pity and sudden aggressiveness. First he would cry, then he would hit her. When he was on tour with his band, she camped out with him in auto courts and cooked for him—that is, if she was not on a picture. Her attempts to play the little wife only annoyed him. His attempts to tidy up and wash dishes made him seem weak and feminine to her. Then he took up boxing to become more assertive. But he overcompensated and became too combative, knocking around other men, such as Ross Alexander, who showed an interest in his wife. He saw himself as a cuckold and imagined rivals around every corner.

His boxing gloves and macho posturings notwithstanding, Davis sensed weakness in Ham. Slowly she lost respect for him, even came to despise him—but she was unwilling to admit she had failed in what she regarded as a woman's most important role—marriage. Ham was the symbol of her commitment and as such he must be sustained, he must be borne with.

Frantically, Davis tried to recapture the first year or so of their marriage, the romantic love they had known fitfully amidst all the sex education and shy, insecure bumblings of her boy-man spouse. Believing firmly in his musical talent, she deplored the fact that his drive didn't begin to equal hers. He lived from paycheck to paycheck, showed no initiative in getting better band spots. Whatever did come, came, it seemed, by happenstance rather than because of any strong motivation on Ham's part. One of his few merits by default was that he was to all indications faithful to her. "But then, what other woman would want him?" Ruthie scornfully observed. The marriage limped on through 1933, 1934, 1935, and beyond because there seemed no compelling reason to end it.

And then there were those *other two* "wives" to whom Davis was married, Ruthie and Bobby.

Davis often meditated on her inveterate habit of casting herself as the "husband," the "man of the house," to her three. Always she came back to the same conclusion. She had assumed the role that Harlow Morrell Davis had abdicated when she was seven years old. It took no psychoanalyst to figure *that* out, she reflected bitterly.

Now that she had the money and the resources, she kept Ruthie in handsome homes, handsome clothes, servants, expensive furbelows. Davis allowed herself one servant, the faithful Dell Pfeiffer, a loyal, long-suffering, kindly black woman who adored Davis and even enjoyed her angry outbursts and frequent attacks of temperament. Dell thought little of the Three Wives. Ham she avoided. Ruthie she was quiet around. And Bobby terrified her.

Now that Davis had "arrived," Ruthie took the attitude that as Bette Davis's mother she was entitled to the best there was. Davis had to do without in order to keep her mother living in luxury. Ruthie walked before Davis at premieres and other public appearances. "You'd think she was the movie star and Bette just the also-ran relative," Bobby once remarked.

And then there was Bobby. Consumed by sibling rivalry, Bobby announced, circa 1932, that she too wanted to be an actress, but because she lacked the discipline to train and the talent to act, doors were closed to her despite Davis's admittedly half-hearted efforts to pull strings. Bobby then embarked on a series of marriages, all of which turned out badly. She suffered from a severe self-image problem. In childhood her attitude had been: Bette is the favored one. Now, it was: I want what Bette has; I want to *be* Bette.

It was at the point when Bobby realized that not only would she never be Bette, she would never come within a mile of her in any respect, that Bobby began to sink into emotional troubles that in time became frightening, all-out mental illnesses. She moaned that the only positive thing she had brought to the world was her only child, Faye, a sad girl who lived in the shadow of her unstable mother and a series of short-term stepfathers. Bobby began moving in and out of a series of expensive private sanitariums that drained Davis's resources considerably. Bobby had joined Ruthie as parasite supreme. It was a role she was to play over the next forty-odd years. Bette and Ruthie alternated in taking care of Faye when Bobby was "indisposed."

Sometimes during those years, when Bobby was feeling better, and especially after new drugs kept her relatively in balance, she came to work as housekeeper for Davis. Angry at the drain her sister and her mother represented, Davis often used Bobby as a butt for her ever more fierce frustrations and rages. At other times Davis would shower love and apologies on this sad sibling, who found being the sister of Bette Davis an unbearable psychological burden.

Davis found her visits in earlier years to Bobby's mental homes an intolerable strain. Often she would find her in an open ward, sitting alone and forlorn. Doctors would recommend state hospitals, telling her in confidence that they gave better care than the private sanitariums for which Davis was paying inordinate, gouging fees. Bobby's husband Robert Pelgram, Faye's father, had fled to the divorce court. It was all more than this modest, retiring man could take.

Davis never forgot one visit to "the Bobby Bughouse," as she called it. She was sitting quietly, encouraging Bobby to eat a cupcake from the box of goodies she had brought, when up sashayed three female inmates straight out of *The Snake Pit*. Shocked and excited by the sight of Bette Davis Herself in their midst, they proceeded, half-flatteringly, half-derisively, to give manic imitations of Davis to her face, swishing around with swiveling hips and holding imaginary cigarettes at odd angles, and popping their eyes outlandishly. "They were silent performances," Davis said later. "At least they didn't yowl, 'Petah—the lettah!'"

Such were Davis's three wives.

Meanwhile, the "husband" continued to work at her movies with manic concentration.

Darryl Zanuck felt that Davis could do ample justice to the role of Fay in 20,000 *Years in Sing Sing* opposite Spencer Tracy. Tracy was borrowed from Fox for the role of Tom Connors, a cocky mobster who is sentenced to Sing Sing on a felony conviction and imagines his powerful underworld friends will spring him via a fast parole. As his girlfriend, Davis was portraying a girl who seemed hard and enterprising on the surface, yet had her own areas of vulnerability.

Davis was enthusiastic about the role, which she sensed had more dimension than most, and she threw herself into the part of Fay. True, she had martinet Michael Curtiz jumping on her again, but since he now sensed her ability after her reviews in *Cabin in the Cotton*, he tended to give her more respect—and less attention, since he was directing one of those hard, tough, brutal "men's dramas," which he mightily enjoyed and with which he excelled.

Largely left to her own devices, Davis fulfilled Zanuck's hopes for her by making her characterization real and vivid—her accomplishment being all the more striking since she found herself awash in a sea of melodramatic "men's stuff." Davis had always been in awe of Spencer Tracy, who, incidentally, shared her birthday, April 5, though he was eight years her senior—at the time, thirty-two to her twenty-four. She had seen him on the stage and in his early films, and it had long been her ambition to work with him. Quiet and unassuming in his underplaying acting style, Tracy could pack tremendous conviction via his "art that concealed art," and Davis stole every opportunity to watch him work when she was not acting with him.

"Tracy was one of those men she thoroughly respected from start to finish," Louis Calhern, who had a part in the film, said later. "It was not so much a sexual attraction as the admiration of one strong spirit for her counterpart. And the admiration was fully returned."

Tracy thought Davis a great talent, with unlimited potential, and they engaged in mutual-sympathy morale-instilling talks off the set. Neither of them, as of late 1932, was getting the parts their talents warranted, and Tracy traded his stories of Fox miscastings in cheap, badly done films with hers, sympathizing especially when she raved on about being "shunted aside in a nothing role" in *Three on a Match*—a film she never let the Warners powers that be forget about.

Michael Curtiz, asked years later why no romance ensued between Tracy and Davis during the making of 20,000 *Years in Sing Sing*, replied, "They were too much alike, did too much identifying with each other. I think Tracy, much as he admired her, was put off by her masculine aggressiveness and feistiness, and as for her—well, he was a rather plain man for all his dynamism and I felt she liked 'em better-looking—like George Brent, for instance."

But, as friends, they carried on in first-rate fashion, talking about the great movies they would do together when they were "rich and famous." Oddly enough, they were never to do another film together, though they did do a radio show—of one of her greatest hits, *Dark Victory*.

20,000 *Years in Sing Sing* was based on the book about prison conditions by Warden Lewis E. Lawes, played by Arthur Byron in the film as Warden Long. It was a hard-hitting, realistic book and it made a hard-hitting, realistic picture. Tracy, cocky at first, is humbled by his tough prison experiences, which include weeks of solitary confinement. Later his adjustment to prison life improves and when he hears that Fay, the Davis character, has been in an automobile crash, he is given a brief parole in order to visit her, with the promise he will return at a stated time under his own recognizance. He gets into a scuffle in Fay's bedroom with the gangster (the Calhern character) who sent him to prison, and accepts the blame for Fay when she shoots his rival. Later he is sentenced to the electric chair. (Of course, under tougher Production Code rulings instituted a year later, in 1934, Fay would have been obliged to pay for her own crime.)

Mordaunt Hall of *The New York Times* liked the Tracy-Davis co-starrer well enough, writing, "In this rapidly-paced film there are some extraordinarily interesting glimpses of prison routine. . . . Spencer Tracy . . . gives a clever and convincing portrayal." He added, "Bette Davis does well as Fay."

Seen in recent years, 20,000 *Years in Sing Sing* does not hold up too well, its plot devices maudlin and unbelievable by current standards, though the cast, including Warren Hymer, Grant Mitchell, and Louis Calhern, does well, and Curtiz keeps the action moving despite the illogic of some of the situations.

Louis Calhern, a fine actor with a splendid Broadway reputation who later became an eminent character star in films and played Shakespeare's King Lear on the stage to acclaim, told me in 1954 that 20,000 *Years in Sing Sing* was typical of the fast-paced Depression dramas of the early thirties. "None of us was meant to shine in our roles—the material defeated us. We were there to serve the plot situations, there was no opportunity for solid characterization, and action and movement and excitement were everything—and that was where Mike Curtiz and the writers came in.

"Mike was a fine director for this kind of hurly-burly action stuff, but he was a difficult and temperamental man to work with. I know Bette found him a pain in the neck, and for that matter, so did Tracy. Of course he didn't dare treat Tracy disrespectfully—at least not beyond a point—or Tracy would have hauled off and hit him. Not that Bette was timid either—she'd scream back at him and snarl and even spit at him if he went too far. I suspect Mike sort of enjoyed egging her on."

Davis was next rushed into a picture with Douglas Fairbanks, Jr., called *Parachute Jumper*. It was to be the one and only time they ever acted together (though many years later he would be involved as a producer with one of her cinematic ventures).

In his recent autobiography, Fairbanks sloughs off both Davis and the picture in few words, all dismissive. Davis thought him conceited because he was "Pickfair royalty," being the son of the famed swashbuckler Douglas, Sr., and the stepson of Mary Pickford. He was also Joan Crawford's husband, though their marriage was coming apart in a welter of mutual infidelities—hers with Clark Gable, who was married himself at the time—not that anyone cared.

Humiliated at home, Fairbanks in early 1933 tended to be indifferent, cynical, and supercilious about Hollywood and Hollywood people. Later that year he would fall in love (by his own later admission in his book) with Katharine Hepburn when they did *Morning Glory*. For his pains he got no response from the lady. His infatuation with Hepburn is notable in a number of scenes in which he listens to her troubles with a manner so sympathetically concerned that even at the time it aroused speculations about his feelings for her. Within a year he would be off to England, where he would stay for some years, becoming, as Davis later sniffed, "more British than the British."

While many years later they would become friends—of a sort—Fairbanks and Davis found their chemistry lacking in simpatico in 1933, and their scenes together demonstrate their mutual indifference all too clearly. "Those love scenes between them were the stiffest kind I ever had to deal with," director Alfred E. Green later recalled. "I always laughed because the picture was based on an original story called *Some Call It Love*. All I can say is that the way those two played it, no one would ever have mistaken it for love!"

In her circa-1933 discontented and frustrated style, Davis was unhappy with everything about *Parachute Jumper*. She didn't feel that photographer Jim Van Trees lit her properly or highlighted her best angles; she felt Green neglected her for the male actors; she found the talented Leo Carrillo irritating and claimed he tried to pinch her; she and Claire Dodd, a supporting player of the cut-rate femme fatale kind, rubbed each other the wrong way—especially when she noted that Claire got better clothes to wear and better photography. "The damned cameraman must have had a crush on her—at my expense!" she later snorted.

Frank McHugh, saddled with the ridiculous name of "Toodles" as Fairbanks's sidekick, later recalled that the atmosphere on the set was tense and unhappy, and everyone was anxious to get it over with, especially Green, who had to keep them all out of one another's hair.

"Bette was going through a tense and miserable period, and I understood why," McHugh later said. "She was being knocked around in one "man's picture" after another, and wasn't getting the right opportunities to shine. And it frustrated her and made her ornery." She and McHugh reminisced on the set about their stock days.

Fairbanks had an irritating habit of letting Davis's tensions and snappishness roll off his back. Often, as Green recalled, he treated her as if she weren't even there. "He regarded her as the standard 'love interest' necessary to the plot line for, in his view, some idiotic reason, and she was someone to be tolerated and disregarded whenever possible."

The picture is a piece of nonsense about pilots drafted to fly narcotics into the United States, with Fairbanks, originally a marine flier, exposing the villainies of drug lord Carrillo and eventually turning him over to the authorities. Davis plays "Alabama," a southern girl "gone wild in New York," and she worked overtime to attain the correct accent. She was rewarded by *Weekly Variety*'s observation: "A Southern accent that gets across." The doubtful *Times* critic ambivalently stated "[Miss Davis] . . . speaks with a most decided Southern drawl" but failed to indicate his approval or disapproval.

To her delight, Davis found herself cast again with the great George Arliss, her old mentor and career catalyst, in a picture called *The Working Man*. Arliss noted at once that her self-assurance and self-possession had increased tremendously in the short year since *The Man Who Played God*. "My little bird has escaped her cage and found her wings," he told her after their first scenes together.

Later she discovered that Arliss had expressly requested Warner and Zanuck to cast her in his film. Always sensitive to her troubles and concerns, he had continued to take a fatherly interest and wanted to check for himself her progress in cinema technique. He took photographer Sol Polito aside and asked him to favor Davis in as many shots as possible, and even took it upon himself to discuss her costumes with Orry-Kelly who, talented man that he was, sometimes tended to overdo, overshadowing his actresses with his creativity. Arliss also worked with director John Adolfi to highlight Davis's best qualities, and she is sleek and authoritative and feisty in the final product.

"I always sensed that Mr. Arliss was one hundred percent in my corner, as he was in that first film, and I shall always be grateful to him," Davis later said. She added that Arliss had taught her "something wonderful" relating to film acting—something she never forgot, which in essence was: "Films are not shot in situational continuity, so always keep in mind the action in the scene just before and after, at least as they appear in the script progression." She added, "This was the annoying film technique we all had to weather—it would be so aggravating and disconcerting, this shooting out of sequence—a light comedy scene coming just before a big dramatic moment when I was required to spill my emotional guts out. Mr. Arliss's tips were life-savers, believe you me!"

Arliss, an Academy Award winner who was as prescient in directing as he was in his primary pursuit, acting, gently warned her not to give too much of herself in scenes of relative inconsequence. "He was right about that, too," Davis later recalled. "I went into each and every scene, at least in that period, on all cylinders, sometimes lending them an intensity and an attack beyond the merits of the situation."

The Working Man was a trivial effort, unworthy of Arliss, Davis, and the other talents involved. In it Arliss is a retired shoe manufacturer who takes a job incognito in a rival firm because he is bored and wants to help the scions of his dead competitor shape up and fly right before they lose their inheritance via their frivolous lives. Soon he is competing with the stuffed-shirt nephew (Hardie Albright) whom he had left in charge of his own business—and of course the miscreant heirs, Davis and Theodore Newton, see the error of their ways.

Davis had her problems with handsome young Theodore Newton, who played her brother. Newton refused to accept her protestations that she was a "settled married woman and therefore now beyond the pale" and took to following her around, bringing her coffee on the set, and otherwise waxing, as she put it, "uncomfortably attentive." She mentioned this to Arliss, who scoffed, "Oh the boy has a crush—and let him work it out by being nice and understanding. He's not going to harm you." "I don't know about that—you haven't seen the glint in that kid's eye," she snapped back. At her request, Adolfi and Albright had some words with the frustrated would-be swain, who proceeded, as best he could, to cool it. "Thank God he plays my brother and there are no love scenes," she sighed in relief to Albright, who laughed, "He may surprise you with some incest ideas yet!" But, as it turned out, a word to the wise was sufficient, and Newton kept his distance.

Thanks to all the care and attention Arliss had assured for her, Davis got some nice critical pats on the back. "Good work," said the *Times*. "Scores strong," wrote the *Film Daily* reviewer.

In early 1933, Bette and Ham were given a honeymoon for free, but an odd one. They were sent out with the *Forty-second Street Special*, a round-the-country train trip that covered all major cities, where the premieres of the lavish new musical, *Forty-second Street*, were held. Warners and General Electric shared the cost of the elaborately fitted and staffed Pullman train, which wound up in Washington for the March 1933 inauguration of Franklin D. Roosevelt.

They covered thirty-two cities in thirty-two days. Among those accompanying Bette and Ham, who felt rather lost among all the famous names, were Glenda Farrell, Laura LaPlante, Joe E. Brown, Olympics star Eleanor Holm, Tom Mix and his horse—who had a car all his own—Leo Carrillo, and Preston Foster. Also on hand were a dozen gorgeous chorus girls who elicited wolf whistles at all the stops. Fans gawked at them wide-eyed, and some hooted at all the glitter—it was, after all, in the depths of the Depression, and the new president Roosevelt would shortly close the banks. In Boston they made do with the money substitute—scrip. In Washington Davis and Ham met members of the Roosevelt family—she was a firm, devoted admirer of the new president—and then it was New York and yet another caravan, with much smiling and waving to many ragged, forlorn people. Davis recalled that it was then she realized Hollywood made even secondary players national names—those trashy films she had weathered were not to be written off as total losses after all.

She remembered that during all the excitement and the bumpy train rides, sex was the last thing on her and Ham's minds. Then, once back in Los Angeles, with domestic habits reestablished, Ham's sexual idiosyncrasies served their usual purpose—for him. In retrospect, Davis realized that his masturbatory habits, which she knew he continued in solitude, were being adapted for other purposes, among them the prevention of any possible pregnancy. Coitus interruptus was one of Ham's specialties, to her annoyance and frustration, along with his failure to "hold his fire" until her orgasm approached or matched his own. He would pull out at the last second and shoot his sperm on her leg—it was sticky, but it worked. At first she thought it was accidental, part and parcel of his still gauche sexuality. Then she realized he was doing it on purpose. She finally talked him out of pulling out, but then he took to wearing condoms. She told him they irritated her vaginal lining, tricked him into doing without them a few times, and got pregnant.

Having gulled Ham into potential fatherhood without really thinking the question through, Davis was confronted with some hard questions. Did she really want a baby, at age twenty-five, with her career in high gear? Could she take the time out? Her craving for motherhood was at war with her intense careerism. Ham and Ruthie promptly took advantage of her ambivalence.

When she confronted Ham with the news that she had conceived, his reaction was dour and glum. She was too busy to have a baby, he said; her career might be derailed. Nor would he be "humiliated" because she would have to pay the hospital bills. If he wasn't successful enough financially to pay for his own child's birth, then it was better to postpone. An abortion was a must! Then Ruthie, in the East attending Bobby during one of her recurrent nervous breakdowns, wrote that she agreed with Ham. It was bad for her career, too "cluttery," too ill-timed.

Resigned outwardly, torn and miserable inwardly, Davis went with Ham to a scruffy little quack in a dusty little house in a drab little town fifty miles from L.A. Ham waited outside in the car. It took less than an hour. She drove home with him in stoic silence, but later retreated into the bathroom and cried for an hour. In 1933 there was a stigma on abortion even for married people. And with the medical dangers—infection, blood loss—more than a few women died from it. Davis aborted twice, escaping the worst.

6

Battling Toward the Big Break

I N HER AUTOBIOGRAPHY, Davis has some cutting words for her next
film, *Ex-Lady*. She says of it:

"Darryl Zanuck [egged on by critical and popular support of Davis's
recent efforts] decided that it was time to give me the glamour-star
treatment. It was a great mistake. I wasn't the type to be glamorized in
the usual way. In an ecstasy of poor taste and a burst of misspent energy, I was made over and cast as the star of a piece of junk called *Ex-
Lady* which was supposed to be provocative and provoked anyone of
sensibility to nausea.

"As an avant-garde artist, my lover was Gene Raymond, whom I
discarded, *au fin*, for the marvelously corrupt Monroe Owsley. One disgusted critic [from *Hollywood Reporter*] announced that Warner Brothers
could have saved a fortune by photographing the whole picture in one
bed. It is a part of my career that my conscious tastefully avoids. I only
recall that from the daily shooting to the billboards, falsely picturing me
half-naked, my shame was only exceeded by my fury." Robert Florey's
pedestrian direction was no help either.

It seems strange that Davis, who longed for stardom, should have objected to getting her name above a picture's title. And the plot of *Ex-Lady*, a rehash of Barbara Stanwyck's 1931 film *Illicit*, was not only stimulating and refreshing in those pre-Production Code days, it was decades ahead of its time. Davis played a freewheeling soul who believed in living with her guy without benefit of marriage, which she felt only killed the romance and encouraged all kinds of sterilities and boredoms.

It is true that the plot details, as rehashed by David Boehm with fresh dialogue and situations, from the Stanwyck picture, were cursory, unbelievable, and too neatly telescoped and tied up. Then there is reason to believe that Davis deeply resented being handed a revamped version of a Barbara Stanwyck star vehicle; since *So Big* she had disliked Stanwyck.

Also, column items hinted that she and Gene Raymond, her handsome, sexy co-star (later the longtime husband of Jeanette McDonald and a breezy, blond charmer who was great with the ladies), seemed to enjoy each other's company unduly and exclusively on the set, and she had not even been married six months.

But what really set her against the film was the advertising; one of the full-page ads that Warners ran in fan magazines and other national publications displayed her ostensibly naked from the breasts up, heavily made up, and staring outward with brazen provocativeness. Above her face was the legend: WE DON'T *DARE* TELL YOU HOW *DARING* IT IS! To the side were the words: "Never before has the screen had the courage to present a story so frank—so outspoken—yet so true! Get set for a surprise sensation!"

Some of the critics exasperated her by declaring she had been starred over the title prematurely; she wasn't ready. She felt they missed the point that had she been starred in a worthy vehicle, her stardom would have been eminently justified.

In the story, Davis and Raymond are advertising agency co-workers—he a writer, she a commercial artist. She is dead set against marriage as (in her view) a stultifying, unromantic institution, and he reluctantly goes along with her until career pressures force them to marry. Money troubles follow, and attempted infidelities—he with Kay Strozzi, she with Monroe Owsley. Eventually they settle for a copout reconciliation in which 1933 middle-class illusions are soothed via an implication that marriage is okay after all.

Davis told one of her biographers, Whitney Stine, in 1974: "A more unsuitable part in a cheaper type film I don't think could have been found to launch me into stardom. It was a disaster."

The "marvelously corrupt" Owsley was one of the picture's chief assets as Davis's would-be seducer. He presented, in his sinister, sickly, rat-faced persona, an almost refreshing contrast to superwholesome yet sexy, all-American blond Gene Raymond. Owsley, who died prematurely in 1937, was a strange, tormented man offscreen, having much in common with another oddball, Colin Clive, who played with Davis in a later film. All manner of sinister stories went the rounds about Owsley, from reports of homosexual seductions which he conducted with utmost intensity, to scandals involving drug use, alcoholism, and gambling. Whatever the misfortunes of his private life, Owsley was one of those rare actors who managed to present his entire self, dark as it was, onscreen with theatrical flair and panache. Davis, while she admitted that "this rat-faced rodent gives me the shivers," was the first to concede that whatever he projected, it was consummately effective on camera. The circumstances of Owsley's death remain mysterious, and there were reports that the studio hushed up the more sensational elements surrounding it.

Typical of fan reaction to Owsley was one letter published in a fan magazine: "He's a slimy toad, a no-good rat up to trouble—and you feel he's like that *off*-camera, too!" It was significant that Owsley did not sue the magazine for libel—he probably agreed with every word of it!

The New York Times review is worth quoting at length:

"Bette Davis, a young actress who has shown intelligence in the roles assigned to her in films, has had the misfortune to be cast in the principal role of *Ex-Lady*. What that somewhat sinister event meant to her employers was that Miss Davis, having shown herself to be possessed of the proper talent and pictorial allure, now became a star in her own right. What it meant to her embarrassed admirers at the Strand on Thursday night was that Miss Davis had to spend an uncomfortable amount of her time *en déshabille* in boudoir scenes, engaged in repartee and in behavior which were sometimes timidly suggestive, then depressingly naive, and mostly downright foolish."

Gene Raymond told me many years later, "I felt the film was ahead of its time and that Bette looked just wonderful in it. Certainly she had a good photographer [Tony Gaudio] for that. I had a lot of fun with the fellow actors on the set—Frank McHugh, Claire Dodd, and Bette were great to play with—though Bette was so serious and intense she made us all feel like amateurs by comparison. I did resent some silly copy in the press implying we were stuck on each other—especially as she was married—I needed an angry husband breathing down my neck like I needed a head cold, but we tried to laugh it off as just flak designed to sell a movie."

Frank McHugh recalled, "I know Bette was unhappy with the film—
she told both Pat O'Brien and me she was—but it wasn't all that bad,
and there was some snappy dialogue in it, though maybe I'm looking at
it from my angle since I had a lot of it to speak!"

Robert Florey and Davis did not get on well—possibly because neither had much faith in the material. Florey later told Adela Rogers St.
Johns: "If they decided they wanted her to be a full-fledged Warner star,
they could have showcased her in something better than that." Davis
couldn't have agreed more.

The only thing Davis honestly enjoyed about her next Warner
quickie was her reunion with Pat O'Brien, who with his wife had become one of her warm friends and supporters. They continued to have
laughs on the set, as in their earlier film, and on weekends Davis and—
when he was in town—Ham went to the O'Briens for dinner.

The picture in question, *Bureau of Missing Persons*, was replete with
what one writer has called the "calling-all-cars, follow-that-cab" situations. It dealt with the missing persons bureau of a metropolitan police
department, where O'Brien is assigned because he has proved too handy
with his fists as a regular cop. His boss, Lewis Stone, thinks he will cool
off by tracing vanished folk in what he calls the department's "kindergar-
ten."

Soon O'Brien is involved with a mysterious woman, played by
Davis, who wants him to find her missing husband, Alan Dinehart. She
is later implicated in her husband's death. She disappears, and O'Brien
runs a report that she has been found dead and will be buried at public
expense. Lo and behold, she shows up at her own funeral with Dinehart, who, it turns out, murdered his insane twin brother. Davis, declared innocent, and O'Brien resume the romantic attraction they had
only just commenced.

As the plot shows, it was standard Warners keep-it-moving, keep-it-
exciting stuff, and among its other problems *Bureau of Missing Persons*
couldn't seem to make up its mind, under a harried Roy Del Ruth's
direction, if it was comedy, drama, melodrama, or a combination of all
three.

For added insurance, *Bureau* was packed with good character players,
including cynical, wisecracking Glenda Farrell as an ex-wife who drops
in periodically to ensure O'Brien's alimony payments to her, and addled-
as-usual Hugh Herbert, a bureau employee eternally preoccupied with
finding a woman who, it turns out, works right in his office. (Ruth
Donnelly, in one of her half annoyed, half wryly amused portrayals, did
ample justice to this character.)

In fact, the character players were the best thing about this so-so film, with a screenplay by Robert Presnell based on a book, *Missing Men*, by John H. Ayers and Carol Bird. Davis, upon viewing the finished product, was mightily incensed with photographer Barney McGill, who made her look like two different people in mismatched shots. In some she looked almost matronly—at twenty-five yet!—and in others seemed eighteen and just out of high school. Del Ruth gave her little attention, leaving her to her own creative devices. Given the ramshackle screenplay, the character stars stealing the scenes, and the fact that she had half a dozen scenes to play at most, it is small wonder that a more than usually exasperated Davis gave one of the more notably uneven performances of her career.

O'Brien came off well in the picture since his character followed the linear dramatic pattern—find the murderer. He recalled to me in 1965 the unhappiness from which Davis suffered   with the picture, with her role, with the treatment the Warners were giving her.

He said: "*Ex-Lady*, with her name above the title, had been her first official starring film and it flopped, through no fault of her own, and now, in *Bureau of Missing Persons*, she was back among the cast—not even 'first among equals' but, shall we say, 'equal among equals,' and it galled her no end. 'This picture is lousy as hell,' she said to me more than once while I tried to kid her into a more mellow mood on the set. I remember that she really blew her top when some stupid fan magazine published an item that she and I were 'that way' about each other—and we were both married, and moreover, thought of each other only as friends! Oh, it all got to her all right—and I am surprised, in retrospect, that it took her three more years to walk out on the Warners!"

Oddly enough, Davis might have made the cinematic big leagues as early as 1934 instead of having to wait until 1938 and *Jezebel*, for to her surprise and excitement, she heard that Emil Ludwig, the author of a much-praised and well-publicized biography of Napoleon, was negotiating with Jack Warner for the film rights. Reportedly he would even write the screenplay with help from one of the Warner hacks, in order to give it what Warner called "the requisite cinema interest."

Robert Florey, the director, was also involved in the negotiations, which consumed the early months of 1934. Ludwig and Florey were determined that none other than Warners' "Little Giant," Edward G. Robinson, would essay the Little Corporal, with Bette Davis leading all comers for the role of the empress Josephine, whom Napoleon eventually deserts for a more advantageous alliance with the Austrian archduchess Marie Louise, who gives him his heir.

George Arliss was also enthusiastic about the project, though there was no part in it for him. He had intimated he would not be averse to the role of Talleyrand, Napoleon's great minister, but later changed his mind because he felt the part was not of starring stature. During the shooting of *The Working Man*, Davis had talked with Arliss of her desire to do a prestige costume drama, and the sympathetic and concerned Arliss reportedly planted the idea of Davis as Josephine into the minds of Ludwig, Florey, and Warner, who expressed his doubts about Davis in such a project.

"Is she up to costume stuff—I think of her as a modern girl," he growled to Arliss and Florey, who promptly offered arguments to the contrary. But the surprise element in all these plans and alarums was the reluctance of Edward G. Robinson to take on the role of Napoleon. Here was another case of a Warner star who would later shine in major costumers (as would Davis) possibly delaying his "prestige period" unnecessarily for some years.

Robinson's reasons for refusing the role of Napoleon remain obscure. Possibly he felt his fans wouldn't accept him in the role, as Florey later intimated, and preferred to keep playing it safe with gangsters and assorted mountebanks. Davis was deeply disappointed when the negotiations for *Napoleon* faltered, as she had looked forward to playing with Robinson.

Napoleon—at least in his Hollywood incarnation (there had been a notable silent film by Abel Gance covering aspects of his life)—had to await Charles Boyer's excellent portrayal in the 1937 drama at MGM, *Conquest*, opposite Greta Garbo, as his mistress, Marie Walewska. (In that version, Josephine was nonexistent, as she harked back to an earlier era in the Little Corporal's life.)

Arliss sought to console Davis by persuading Warner to lend her to another studio for his 1934 *House of Rothschild* but Warner refused, giving as his reason that the ingenue role in that was too slight and unsuited to Davis's personality.

In retrospect, Davis's loss of Josephine opposite Robinson's Napoleon may have been all for the best, as the empress was not that colorful or dynamic a figure, and screenwriters who handled her (to wit, the Merle Oberon impersonation in Marlon Brando's 1954 *Desirée*) never succeeded in bringing her fully alive.

But in 1934, pre–*Of Human Bondage*, Davis was extremely depressed and disappointed over the loss of the role. And Jack Warner was to be proved wrong in spades within a few years about her unsuitability for costume roles.

As it turned out, it was not the last time her wise mentor George Arliss attempted to come to her rescue. His admiration for her continued unabated. Meanwhile Warners was determined to keep Davis planted firmly in Depression 1934, though sporting its most expensive fashions and acting with the very 1934-ish William Powell.

As I noted in my *Complete Films of William Powell*, the Davis-Powell chemistry distinctly did not work in *Fashions of 1934*, later known simply as *Fashions*. Powell is a "fashion pirate," always trying to swipe Paris designs for cheaper sale in America. He and his assistant, Davis, go to the City of Light to do more pirating, with Frank McHugh along sporting a hidden camera on the head of his cane. Hugh Herbert contributes a goodly share of the laughs as an entrepreneur from California who hopes to promote the use of feathers on Paris gowns. All achieve their objectives with the help of phony duchess Verree Teasdale, an old pal of Powell's from Hoboken, and crusty, snobby fashion emperor Reginald Owen is brought to heel, with all ending in an elaborate Busby Berkeley–choreographed fashion show, after which Powell and Davis return to America and, presumably, marriage.

"I had great respect for Mr. Powell as an actor but at the same time was not particularly motivated to co-star with him again. Likable as he was, we just weren't right for each other before the camera, and I think the onscreen results prove it," Davis said years later.

William Dieterle, who directed, later opined that Davis was very much in Powell's shadow and resented it. Moreover, Perc Westmore and Orry-Kelly saw to it that she was made up and gowned to the extravagant nines, with long, blond Garbo-esque hair, thick pancake makeup, the longest, falsest eyelashes they could create, and slinky, overstylized gowns. "That kind of thing was for Harlow or Crawford—never for me," Davis said later. "In that picture I was frightfully ill at ease, and even felt embarrassed at times."

Davis was also annoyed at having to play onlooker to some protracted funny business between Frank McHugh and Hugh Herbert in the back of a car, and as the scene plays today, she is obviously impatient and annoyed beneath her tight smile and forced attentiveness. "I've spent so much of my life being second fiddle—will it ever end?" she asked the producer, Henry Blanke.

Powell, sensing her reservations concerning him, tended to keep his distance. He was winding up his career at Warners that year, and was soon to go on to MGM and even brighter stardom.

Mordaunt Hall in *The New York Times* wrote: "The story is lively, the gowns are interesting and the Busby Berkeley spectacles with Hollywood dancing girls are impressive. Instead of a stereotyped narrative about the enchantress who becomes an overnight queen of the Broadway stage, there is in this film something original." Another critic called Davis "letter-perfect," an observation she considered double-edged.

She told Kathryn Dougherty, editor of *Photoplay* at the time: "I can't get out of these awful ruts. They just won't take me seriously. Look at me in this picture—all done up like a third-rate imitation of the MGM glamour queens. That isn't me. I'll never be a clothes horse or romantic symbol." Dougherty tried to tell her that she might have more potential in those directions than she thought, and that in some shots photographer William Rees had even made her look quite beautiful. Davis's retort was, "Beautiful never. Striking, sometimes, if I'm lucky!"

She still hated to look at herself on screen. "Everyone comes off better than I do!" she lamented to Dieterle. "Verree Teasdale has more sophistication and wears clothes better, Powell is center stage in a flattering role, McHugh and Herbert steal all the laughs. I just stand around—like an afterthought!"

Even the romantic addresses of handsome young Phillip Reed, who plays a songwriter in love with her, proved scant consolation. "He's cute, but too boyish for me," was her slough-off for the disappointed young Reed, who offscreen was one of many who got "crushed" on her. *Fashions* was a film she obviously wanted to forget.

Davis next found herself cast opposite Charles Farrell, who had won fame in the silent era as the leading man in *Seventh Heaven* opposite Janet Gaynor; they played a waifish couple languishing in a Paris garret, and the world had taken them to its heart. Farrell went on to do other films with Gaynor, and his career prospered, with her and other co-stars, into the talkie era, but by 1934 Farrell found himself on the downgrade, and for him, *The Big Shakedown*, about a counterfeit drug racket, was a B picture and a "Big Comedown." Davis sensed his depression during the film and tried to comfort him as best she could. While there was no romance, he did later recall her kindness and sympathy. "She's a gentler, sweeter, more understanding person than her publicity and reputation would lead one to suppose," Charlie Farrell said years later, after he had made a fortune as owner-manager of the Palm Springs Racquet Club. Later he was mayor of Palm Springs and found a second career on TV with *My Little Margie* and *The Charlie Farrell Show*. Not a peregrinative man romantically, he was for many years the husband of actress Virginia Valli.

"Charlie was a really sweet person," Davis told Katherine Albert years later. "He was certainly no womanizer. In his manly, quiet way he had more self-confidence than many men I've known, and didn't think he had to prove anything—and he didn't."

Katherine Albert also recalled Davis's telling her that "Charlie was a real gentleman in his love scenes—never took advantage of the proximity to get fresh." She recalled Davis getting annoyed when she rejoindered that maybe that was why the picture emerged so dull and also-ran—Charlie hadn't put enough moxie into his onscreen lovemaking!

In *The Big Shakedown* Charlie is a druggist and Davis his hapless wife. They get involved with a racketeer (Ricardo Cortez at his slimiest) who talks Charlie into a cut-rate prescription-drug racket. When Farrell realizes what is going on, he tries to drop Cortez but is beaten and threatened. For fear Davis will be harmed, Farrell continues to go along with it. Meanwhile wife Davis loses her child after a premature delivery. Cortez eventually meets death at the hands of a business rival, Henry O'Neill, winding up in a vat of acid. One critic commented, "If only the acid had shown up earlier, it might have kept the audience from falling asleep."

The reviews were devastating. "Far-fetched, over-acted and unbelievable" was the kindest of the reactions. When the film was shown many years later, I watched it appalled. John Francis Dillon's direction was sloppy in the extreme; he died soon after the picture's completion, so possibly his declining health was a factor in this poor showing. Sid Hickox did not give the required photographic attention to Davis; though she looks sweet, she is not given the subtle lighting that highlights her true individuality as it was evolving by early 1934. The screenplay by Niven Busch and Rian James is confused, lacking in cumulative impact, and the editing is jerky and tenuous.

Character actor Allen Jenkins told me in an interview many years later: "I was in that film, and Bette's unhappiness with it was a depressing thing to watch. We'd have coffee sometimes. She was very democratic with her crew and her fellow actors, and I remember her saying that Glenda Farrell had the meaty part as a shady lady and she'd rather have two minutes on screen in a character with bite than an hour and a half simpering and cooing, as she did in this. She was really p———— off with it all, and I didn't blame her."

Davis and Jimmy Cagney—Warners' other stormy-petrel rebel—had become friends, and they were delighted to be cast together in *Jimmy the Gent,* (formerly *Always a Gent*), based on an original story, *The Heir Chaser,* by Laird Doyle and Ray Nazarro, who had Jimmy—and nobody else—in mind when they wrote it. Jimmy had just come off one of his numerous Warner suspensions and he characterized *Gent* as "crapola—but slightly better-class crapola than usual." Davis, who adored Jimmy and felt he was one of the best actors in Hollywood, had lamented through the years that they had not gotten a better vehicle in which to play; they later did one other, with equally unfortunate results.

Jimmy the Gent is about an opportunist (Cagney) who specializes in tracking down heirs to missing estates, then sharing in the take. His secretary-girlfriend, Davis, deplores Jimmy's corner-cutting business practices, and leaves him in disgust, allying herself with his business rival, Alan Dinehart, whom she believes to be honest, upright, conservative, and a gentleman.

Jimmy then sets out to emulate Dinehart, polishing up his speech, sporting more conservative apparel, holding "tea parties" for his staff of mugs, etc. Davis is unimpressed, so Jimmy then decides to show up Dinehart for the crook he is, with predictable results.

The film ran what was, for a 1934 Warner product, a typical 66 minutes, and Michael Curtiz directed at his usual frantic, slam-bang pace, which emerged on the screen as fast, furious, riveting, and highly entertaining to the fans who lapped up fast action stuff with no regard to quality dramatics, of which *Jimmy the Gent* had none.

Jimmy Cagney always felt highly simpatico with Davis, whom he recognized as a fellow striver for quality. At that time he was in a better position to give the stubborn Warner bosses what-for as he made a bigger salary than Davis and his box-office clout was something to be reckoned with.

A tough street kid from Manhattan, Jimmy had struggled up in vaudeville and had had success on Broadway, doing things the hard way all along, and he was more than a match for the Warners. He was the perfect Depression-era hero, not only as a gangster but in various incarnations of the feisty, enterprising common man buffeted by fate who always lands on his feet, four-square. He told me about Davis in 1961:

"You know, Bette came from old Yankee stock, pretty patrician background, but was she a fighter! Working with her in *Jimmy the Gent* was like baking in a hot oven—it got pretty humid in there but you couldn't wait to see how the cake turned out! She was a really wonderful talent, and I don't know how she stood all those second-rate parts—some of them a cut above bits—that for years they inflicted on her. I think it was the Warners' way of disciplining her for her hotheaded complaints but she was such a trouper that she delivered on each and every assignment no matter how lousy the lines and situations. I was lucky in that I was a lead, later a star, from almost the beginning, so I understood her exasperation better than most. She had the current on from the moment she arrived on the set and she never let up. The vitality of that woman! Words can't convey it."

As did Davis, Cagney heartily regretted that neither found a good vehicle to do together—the two they did do being distinctly second- and third-rate.

"Jimmy had a vitality that matched my own, and he had wonderfully unpredictable little twists and catches and surprises in his technique that kept me on my toes," Davis said later. "What a joy he was to play with! No placidity and false hauteur or phony poise about him! He was very much himself, at all times, so real, so true—would that I had had more Jimmy Cagneys to play with!"

In retrospect, Bette Davis seemed to hold *Fog Over Frisco* in higher esteem than some of the other Warner products she was doing at the time. "I loved my part, William Dieterle directed me expertly, I looked fine, and was very pleased with the film," she told fan magazine writer Katherine Albert. Davis's opinion of *Fog Over Frisco* is puzzling in retrospect, for on reviewing it years later I found it standard Warners melodrama at the usual breakneck speed. The film is wholly undistinguished, and Davis isn't on screen much; Margaret Lindsay and Donald Woods, ostensibly her supports, log more camera time.

In this, Davis is a reckless society girl with an obvious death wish who enjoys engaging in illegal bond transactions with an underworld king (Irving Pichel) who runs a night spot. Lindsay, her stepsister, sets out to find out how deeply Davis is involved. It seems that the Davis character has also involved her fiancé, Lyle Talbot, in her malfeasances. When the nightclub operator learns she has attempted to betray him, he kills her, later kidnaps Lindsay, but receives his comeuppance in the end.

These are the bare bones of the plot of *Fog Over Frisco*, and as noted before, there is nothing to distinguish it from a dozen other Warner products of its ilk. Davis's high opinion of the film may be influenced by the fact that Tony Gaudio did photograph her flatteringly, and her wardrobe was becoming, but the Robert N. Lee and Eugene Solow screenplay, based on George Dyer's original story, seem highly unworthy of Dieterle's obviously infinite pains. Margaret Lindsay and Donald Woods come out well in the final result, and when told thirty years later that Davis held *Fog Over Frisco* in relatively high esteem, Lindsay, too, expressed her puzzlement. She told me:

"I never understood why she took such a small part—she just wasn't in evidence that much—and while I know she liked to play bad girls, this particular girl was not, in my opinion, all that interesting. I liked my part and was surprised that I got more to do than Bette, but I, for one, don't look back on it as any landmark for me, her, or anyone else connected with it!"

The critics at the time shared Lindsay's view rather than Davis's. "A veneer of theatricalism prevails throughout," *Variety* said. "The story, in the way it's brought to the screen, never quite strikes a convincing note." Mordaunt Hall of *The New York Times* felt that the basic story lacked credibility.

William Dieterle never held the picture in high esteem, claiming it was one of a series of trivial potboilers foisted on him by the studio in what he considered "that unfortunate era" before he finally won the "big" Warner subjects he felt he deserved.

Even in material he considered drek, Dieterle could be a martinet in a European style that got on Davis's nerves as much as Curtiz's more vulgar, often scatalogical approach. This did not stop her from working well with him in what he called his "big" era later.

Lyle Talbot in 1960 recalled Davis lost in a trance studying her script and practicing nuances of her speech and inflections "as if she had been handed a Shaw or Shakespeare assignment. Her absolute dedication was unnerving. Her self-involvement came on to me as a kind of self-ishness—true, she worked well with other players and the crew, but I always felt her mind was solely on herself and the effect she was producing."

Talbot added, significantly, "I always felt she must be a tough woman to be married to."

7

Of Human Bondage—
and Recognition

T HE PICTURE that was to transform Davis's life and career almost
didn't happen. In early 1934 Jack Warner absolutely refused to
lend her out for the role of the slatternly, sadistic waitress, Mildred, in
RKO's production of Somerset Maugham's novel *Of Human Bondage*. For
six months she begged him for the loanout; as she recalled, she'd show
up at his office every morning "with the shoeshine boy." Meanwhile she
continued on the Warner chain gang with one mediocre role after another in execrable, slipshod, second-rate pictures. Wild with fury and
frustration, she moved sullenly from set to set, doing her job, hunting
frantically for anything in the cardboard characters and scripts that she
could develop into something real and human.

Then, at long last, in the spring of 1934, two things happened that
swung the balance in her favor. Jack Warner wanted RKO to lend him
Irene Dunne for a muscial, *Sweet Adeline*. John Cromwell, who was to
direct *Of Human Bondage*, urged producer Pandro Berman to offer Jack an
exchange: Davis for Dunne. The second factor was Jack Warner's reluctant but still admiring reaction to the rushes he had seen of Davis's
vicious, murderous Marie Roark in *Bordertown*. He told his associates that

he felt Davis could handle Mildred and that while it was a gamble, if she made the grade in the role she would be more valuable to the studio—and so would *Bordertown*. He called her in, and to her indescribable joy, told her the loanout had been arranged. "The role may hurt you—the public may recoil from Mildred, associate her with you, and back off from you—but go and hang yourself if you must!" he growled. Shrewdly, he postponed *Bordertown's* release for six months.

John Cromwell, then, was the first director to showcase Davis in a major, blockbusting role. He had had extensive Broadway experience before he came to films in 1928 as actor, director, and producer, but gradually specialized in directing and by 1934 had built up a solid reputation as a fine technician and sensitive director of actors, as in Lionel Barrymore's *Sweepings* (1933) and Irene Dunne's *The Silver Cord*, made the same year. He had taken note of Davis's unusual charisma in *Cabin in the Cotton* and *Ex-Lady*, among others, and felt she would be ideal for Mildred and would have the courage to play her without inhibition or punch-pulling. Again George Arliss worked behind the scenes to clinch the assignment for her, getting his friend Somerset Maugham to view, via prints shipped to England, the work done by Davis with Arliss. Maugham sent Berman his unqualified approval of Davis as Mildred.

Maugham did not just go out of his way to please his friend Arliss or to get the ambitious young lady at Warners her crucial break. *Of Human Bondage* was a novel as close to his heart as, in a radically different context, *David Copperfield* had been to Charles Dickens. Both had put much autobiographical soul-searching into their books. Maugham, who suffered from a speech impediment from youth, had made his character, Philip, a club-footed cripple. Like Philip, he had undergone—more than once, in Maugham's case—all the humiliations of unrequited love for an unworthy object—in Maugham's instance, another man. It was this evocation of his own past that gave *Of Human Bondage* the bitter reality and authenticity that won it an enthralled readership.

Screenwriter Lester Cohen made the transcription of Maugham's autobiographical agony as accurate and true as the radically different cinematic medium permitted. Considering that he wound up with only 83 minutes in which to get across all the complexities of Maugham's deeply felt novel, Cohen's screenplay emerges commendably workmanlike.

Philip Carey, Maugham's thinly disguised alter ego, has abandoned painting in Paris to study medicine in London; if doomed to be a second- or third-rate artist, he is determined to become a first-rate doctor. In a tearoom he meets Mildred Rogers, a sluttily attractive but illiterate and surly waitress. He develops an obsession for her. Blind to her pathetic shortcomings of character and sadistic flirtatiousness, he pursues her, though she makes no bones about finding his crippled state repellent and rebuffs his romantic addresses. During the course of the action she jilts him for two men, a crass-spirited salesman who leaves her pregnant and deserts her and a more attractive medical student with whom she runs off. Meanwhile two warmly kind young women develop an interest in Philip, though he has been too wounded and distracted by Mildred to reciprocate. Also, his self-image has been so harmed that he does not recognize that their romantic interest in him is authentic.

Still masochistically hung up on Mildred, Philip takes her in when she is down and out, and when he rebuffs the physical advances she makes as a sort of payment for his kindness, recognizing as he does that there is no affection or true commitment in them, she taunts him for his deformities, destroys his apartment, including the bonds that are putting him through medical school, and disappears yet again.

Then two bright things happen for Philip. He receives an inheritance that will assure his future as a doctor, and he begins a wholesome relationship with a decent young woman. But he has not heard the last of Mildred. He learns that she is dying of tuberculosis in a charity ward. Her death frees him of his obsession, and he is able to go on to his real life, personally and professionally.

Such is screenwriter Cohen's boiled-down cinematic version of the Maugham novel which, to Cohen's credit, captured all the psychological essentials of what Maugham was trying to say about the human bondage of unrequited obsession for an unworthy object.

In 1968 John Cromwell, age seventy-nine, told me what he had seen in twenty-six-year-old Bette Davis, some thirty-four years before, that made him as anxious to cast her as Mildred as she was to play her. "Mildred was a role that many actresses of the time backed off from in horror. She was a slatternly sadist, unsympathetic in the extreme, and her clothing and her postures and her general look were all seedy, pathetic, and sleazy-looking in the way no nineteen thirty-four glamour girl would ever deign to approximate. Bette Davis didn't give a damn about any of that! She wanted to give honest characterizations—unadorned, brutally true and honest, if possible—and at Warners they were dolling her up in blond wigs and fancy clothes and drowning her in glitz and schmaltz and gangster-action stuff and all the rest of it.

"There was an actress under all that phony overlay and she knew it and I knew it and, to his credit, my producer, Pandro Berman knew it. So did Maugham. So did George Arliss."

Unhappy in her marriage, dissatisfied and angry about her nothing roles at Warners, Davis tackled Mildred with an intensity that astonished her co-workers. In time, it even astonished Leslie Howard, the film's star. Howard, a major star in 1934, had taken Broadway by storm, played opposite such first ladies of the screen as Norma Shearer and Mary Pickford, and traveled first class all the way. A chronic womanizer, unfaithful to his long-suffering wife, the ethereal, poetic-looking Howard had done some hard living by 1934, when he was forty, but looked ten years younger, Dorian Gray style. He had not been keen on Davis's assignment to *Bondage*. To him, this little blond creature, not very pretty nor sexually appealing (at least to his taste) seemed distinctly an also-ran.

Patronizingly, Howard read books while she acted, feeding her line readings almost as an afterthought. Then he saw the rushes. Startled to realize that he was working with a first-class actress, a vivid original like no one he had ever encountered, Howard snapped to attention. The bored indifference in his eyes changed to concentrated intensity. Driven by professional jealousy, male prima donna that he was, Howard began to play back to her, as one demanding scene followed another. In some of them he was required to react with white-faced, cringing shock to her brutal, vulgar excoriations. What Howard did not realize (or, being a consummate professional, perhaps he did) was that in meeting her halfway, in listening, reacting, and playing back to her on her own level, he was enhancing Davis's performance.

On her end, Davis's ego was affronted by Howard's lack of sexual interest in her offscreen. Aware at first that he considered her just another conveyer-belt blonde nothing from the Warner sausage factory, she decided if the English Adonis didn't want her sexually, she would whip him into respecting her professionally. In this latter aim she succeeded.

Howard had originally been prejudiced against her because she was American. He asked Cromwell and Berman, with so many fine English actresses to pick from, what was so special about *her*? Why all this fuss about dragging this little nondescript creature over from Warners? They set him right on these points. No English actress would appear in a role so unflattering. And Davis, an authentic New England Yankee, was of English descent. *And* she had hired a Cockney servant, who stayed with her for eight weeks while Davis got the nuances down pat—she drove Ham up the wall by speaking in a Cockney accent even in bed.

But after seeing these rushes, Howard needed no further sales talks from anyone.

There is a scene, later in *Of Human Bondage*, that has gone down in film history. An enraged Davis, humiliated by Howard's rebuff of her crass physical advances, taunts him savagely. The dialogue (on her side), complete with her Cockney accent, is worth repeating:

> "Yew cad, yew dirty swine! I never cared for yew—not once! I was always making a *fool* of yuh! Yuh *bored me stiff!* I *hated* yuh! It made me *sick* when I had to let yuh *kiss me!* I only did it because yuh *begged* me. Yuh *hounded* me, yuh *drove me crazy*, and after yuh kissed me, I always used to *wipe my mouth! Wipe my mouth!* But I made up for it. For every kiss I had to *laugh!* We *laughed* at yuh! Miller and me! Griffith and me! We *laughed* at yuh because yuh were such *a mug, a mug, a monster!* You're a *cripple, a cripple, a cripple!*"

In this scene, Davis offered a portrait of concentrated feminine viciousness so startling and electrically malevolent that it struck audiences dumb with shock. Artistically courageous, she refused to give Mildred any redeeming qualities, any phony Hollywood audience sympathy. Mildred was like a force of nature, lightninglike, a demon of hate and malevolence. With her unerring artist's instinct, Davis knew that mature, responsive, sensitive audiences would sense the underlying bitterness, the deprivations, the kicking around Mildred had taken from a series of men, all of which had given her a contempt for the human race.

When Philip first meets Mildred, Davis gets across her weariness from being on her feet all day, her bone-tiredness, her cynical distrust of every man who smiles at her. Confronted with the poetic, sensitive cripple, at first she doesn't know what to make of him. Then her brutalized nature senses that this is a man who's sweet on her, therefore vulnerable and pliable. Here is a man she can dominate, mistreat, humiliate, one who will come back for more. Above all, Davis's Mildred sees in Howard's Philip someone she can pay back, as a helpless, love-castrated symbol of the male sex, for all the mistreatment she has suffered from men all her life because of her poverty, her bottom-step caste. He is someone to use, to take advantage of. She cannot recognize his love as sincere, for he is not like any other man she's met. To Davis's Mildred, male tenderness is weakness; sensitivity, effeminate; decency, tame.

Many have wondered how Davis got Mildred's character across as convincingly. Her life, they reasoned, had always been protected: She had the safety of a contract while others starved at the depths of the Depression; she had a mother who had protected her at every point from the harsher realities; she was safely married, after twenty-four years of prim virginity, to a "nice young man" who seemed harmless. What they failed to see was the enormous reservoir of anger Davis had stored up over many years: anger at the father who had deserted her; anger at the poverty that had forced her mother to work so hard; anger at the Warner overlords who frustrated her best career instincts; and, the year she made *Of Human Bondage,* anger at her husband and her mother, for forcing her to abort two babies "so as not to deflect your career energies, Bette." All that anger she concentrated in Mildred.

She also drew upon her sense-memory—of the hours she had spent as a waitress at school in order to earn money, of her envy of girls who had ample allowances and a solicitous mother *and* father. And as Mildred made Philip pay for all the indignities men had rained upon her, so Davis made Howard pay for the deserting father, the tyrannical studio overlord, the weak husband who had failed in his traditional role.

The result of all this was a performance that debuted at Radio City Music Hall on June 28, 1934, to critical acclaim and audience shock— shock that evolved, in short order, into a half-horrified, half-admiring awareness of an exciting new star, one of an entirely different order and makeup—an authentic original.

Davis always remembered the reactions of Ham and Ruthie when they came home after seeing a preview of the film. They entered the house, she recalled, in stunned silence, and when she pressed them for their reaction they told her the role would either make her or break her.

They didn't have to wait long for the answer to that.

The critics outdid themselves in superlatives. They noted that she didn't care how she looked; her clothes were dirty and torn; her badly applied makeup made her look like a cheap slattern; her walk was a defeated slouch.

One of the most salient examples of Davis's uncompromising realism is a scene at the end of the picture, when Philip discovers her in the last stages of tuberculosis. She looks so horrifying in that scene that children and sensitive adults in the audience put their heads down behind the seats. Her eyes are deeply shadowed, her face gray and wan, her mouth twisted by disease and suffering, hate, malevolence, and frustration. It is a look of corruption and rot, the look of a partially decomposed corpse. Only Davis would have dared to look like that in glamour-silly, conventional 1934. Only a genius could have gotten away with it. And she did.

Some critics missed the point and accused her of overplaying Mildred. John Cromwell told me: "When it came to these final, ultimate, crucial scenes, I let Bette have her head; I trusted her instincts. A director can guide—but the artist has to dredge up truth from within herself. And that is what Bette gave us in *Of Human Bondage*—the truth, which in life is often just that—a brutal, horrible overstatement. Have people not written that life is stranger than fiction—and even more overstated? Well, that's what Bette gave us, in that picture!"

Life said of Davis's Mildred: "It is perhaps the best performance ever recorded on the screen by a U.S. actress." A respectful and surprised *Film Weekly* reviewer wrote: "Few people realized that she had the ability to understand and interpret the role so successfully."

Mordaunt Hall in *The New York Times* topped all other critical aces, writing: "An enormously effective portrayal is that of Bette Davis as Mildred Rogers . . . . at the first [Radio City Music Hall] showing yesterday of this picture, the audience was so wrought-up over the conduct of this vixen that when Carey finally expressed his contempt for Mildred's behavior, applause was heard from all sides." Hall licked his chops over the "climactic episode, which recalls an incident in Kipling's *The Light That Failed*. This sorry specimen of humanity slashes Carey's efforts at art, destroys his medical books and furniture, and even burns his bonds and private papers, leaving the apartment as though it had been struck by a tornado!"

If Davis had expected to get the Ruth Chatterton star treatment back at Warners, she was speedily disillusioned. It was back to the salt mines and the drek, to her continued anger and frustration. Later, when she was being noised about for an Academy Award nomination, the powers at Warners told their people to vote for other actresses—her hit was made outside the home lot, why let RKO get any breaks? The three 1934 nominations—Norma Shearer in *The Barretts of Wimpole Street*, Grace Moore in *One Night of Love*, and Claudette Colbert in *It Happened One Night*—did not include Davis, who reflected bitterly that Columbia had wanted to borrow her for the Colbert role. (Many years later, Davis would triumph in a role that Colbert bowed out of because of an accident. Fate, unpredictable and quixotic as always, made eventual amends.)

There was so much public anger over the slight against Davis that a write-in campaign was begun for her. The result was that, by missing out, Davis garnered more publicity for what many considered the best actress's performance in 1934 than Colbert racked up as the eventual winner. This resulted in Davis getting, for the 1935 *Dangerous*, the first of a series of legendary "consolation prizes"—an Oscar for a performance in a film from a previous year that had somehow been forgotten.

Also, the Academy rules were changed to allow for a more authentic expression of the industry's will at Oscar time, with Price-Waterhouse delegated to assure correct and authentic vote tabulations.

There has been much debate as to whether Bette Davis dubbed the Academy Award "Oscar" because the statuette had a backside just like Ham's, whose middle name was Oscar.

In the course of researching this book a little-known fact has emerged that bears further exploration—an instance that seems not to have appeared in previous books on Bette Davis. In the May 1935 *Photoplay* magazine story, "The Girl They Tried to Forget," Kirtley Baskette reported, "Hollywood championed [Davis] so vigorously [for the 1934 award] that for a while the whole town seemed to be one giant indignation meeting. Editorials, articles, telegrams, telephone calls bombarded the austere Academy until, I am sure, like the bewildered author in *Once in a Lifetime,* its members concluded that 'It couldn't all be a typographical error.'" Even Baskette's postman, he wrote, thought the Academy's slight was "a darn outrage," and that Baskette ought to have *Photoplay* "give 'em the devil!" The little-known fact was Baskette's assertion that by the spring of 1935, the Academy had given Davis a "belated" award, a "special citation." If this is so, then Davis had kept this recognition quietly hidden away somewhere.

Back at Warners from RKO, Davis was handed another "sausage." *Housewife* was a picture that Davis absolutely despised, before, during, and after appearing in it, and for many years thereafter she took the name of *Housewife* in vain, along with director Alfred Green and screenwriters Robert Lord and Lillie Hayward. Her dissatisfaction may also have been due to the fact that the usually dependable Orry-Kelly must have been on mental furlough when he designed her costumes for this, and a cameraman with whom she seldom worked, William Rees, lighted her rather poorly and made her eyes bulge and her jaw stick out more sternly than usual.

Frank S. Nugent in *The New York Times* confirmed her opinion of the hapless *Housewife* as he enraged her with such observations as:

"A characteristic of a poor boxer is that he telegraphs his punches. In *Housewife* the dramatic punches are not merely telegraphed, but radioed. And the most unexpected element of the film is the bewildering regularity with which the unexpected fails to happen. . . . Mr. Brent and Miss Dvorak do as well as anyone might expect, but Miss Davis is a trifle too obvious as the siren."

Housewife, which I reviewed over fifty years later, is every bit the mess everyone claimed it was. It contains a grab bag of every 1934

Warner cliché conceivable. The errant husband (Brent) neglects his wife (Dvorak) for a sexy former girlfriend (Davis). The husband is given his comeuppance when he accidentally injures his little son, who winds up in the hospital. After some suspense, the boy turns out to be okay. Wife is hurt because she has helped her husband to his success and now he is out on the town with swinger Davis. She takes her revenge by seeing John Halliday, one of her husband's clients. Finally, the husband realizes that his ad agency success is due to his wife. All principals end up in court where the husband sees the light. Exit siren, back to the little woman, and so forth.

Davis pours it on thick as the would-be home-wrecker, acting with more careless obviousness than was her usual wont (one wonders where director Alfred Green was during her apparently self-directed excesses). Brent and Dvorak are reasonably on top of things, but the experienced character actor John Halliday steals whatever there is to steal as the fourth member of the romance ring.

George Brent's marriage to Ruth Chatterton came apart the year *Housewife* was released, and Davis seemed to be living offscreen her role of home-breaking siren now that George was about to join the legions of the free. In reality, she did not break up the marriage and Chatterton was certainly not anyone's idea of a housewife!

During *Housewife*, according to Alfred Green, Brent was easing out of the Chatterton marriage as gracefully as possible, and while he continued having affairs with unknowns who could be kept at a distance, the upfront spectacle of co-star Davis following him back to his dressing room and maneuvering herself next to him for lunch in the commissary unnerved him somewhat—especially as he knew Ham Nelson's temper tantrums by reputation. Davis claimed it took her until the late 1930s to get Brent interested in her, so her frustration over his lack of response must have given her psychic overload during the making of the ill-fated *Housewife*.

In January 1935, Jack Warner finally released *Bordertown*, the picture Davis made just before *Of Human Bondage*.

Bordertown stands out among the standard Davis-Warner products of the time because in it she is given the opportunity to *act*. It is the picture that decided Jack Warner, once and for all, to let Davis take the role of Mildred in *Of Human Bondage*, because, along with his executives, he could not help but be impressed with what she did as Marie Roark, the cheap-minded, sluttish, sex-starved wife of a fat, messy casino owner in a Mexican border town.

It is a mystery why *Bordertown* was held for release until six months after *Of Human Bondage*, which debuted in June 1934. According to director Archie Mayo, Jack Warner intuitively knew *Bondage* would send Davis back to his studio a more important name, and *Bordertown*, in which she also had a strong role, would make a worthy follow-up (and this despite the film that fell between, the abysmal *Housewife*).

Bordertown is actually Paul Muni's film, for it showcases him vividly as an ambitious Mexican-American who takes a job in Eugene Pallette's casino—night spot after encountering racial discrimination and ridicule in his law practice. He helps Pallette make the venture a success, and then scornfully rebuffs Pallette's wife, Davis, when she sets her sights on him. In a famous and, at the time, uniquely conceived murder scene, Davis lets the garage door close on her drunken husband, asphyxiating him with carbon monoxide fumes. Later, she falsely implicates Muni in the murder because she is jealous of his attentions to society girl Margaret Lindsay.

In this scene, Davis elected to demonstrate advancing mental illness while on the witness stand with subtle eye movements and facial tension. Archie Mayo, who liked his melodrama hot and hollery, argued with her about this, as did Jack Warner. They wanted her to go all-out hysterical and chew the scenery, feeling it was what audiences expected of a "loony," but Davis challenged them to let the scene stand at a theater preview; if the audience didn't like it, she'd do a retake. The audience liked it, and the scene survived.

Viewed many years later, the scene seems truncated and inadequate. Davis is not given enough dialogue and business to make it effective, partly the fault of Mayo and the screenwriters, Lillie Hayward and Manuel Seff. It seems to be over in a flash, without natural progression or development. A compromise between the two approaches would have been most effective.

It is in the earlier scenes, in which Davis strides about, wild with frustration over Muni's unresponsiveness, sassy to her hapless servant, enraged over his cold contempt when he discovers she has literally killed for him, that she gets across all the manic viciousness that makes her so arresting. The mystery is if Jack Warner was that impressed with her after viewing *Bordertown* that he let her go over to RKO for *Bondage*, then why did he throw her back into gutless drek—with a few exceptions—for the next two years?

This was Davis's first picture with Paul Muni, a brilliant actor of consummate ego and authority. He was a product of the Yiddish stage, and had later triumphed on Broadway. Muni prepared his roles with great care, never hesitating to disguise his appearance and personality in order to create an authentic character. Painstaking, thorough, filled with the genius that best expresses itself by taking infinite pains, Muni was trying to get across the frustrations and strivings of an ambitious Mexican-American determined to rise above his origins and do his people proud.

It annoyed him no end to be up against Davis, an artist of quite a different stripe, hell-bent on impressing her vivid personality and manic intensity on her characterization. In a sense he had met his match, and Muni resented the competition. Worse, she forced him to play second fiddle because of her vivid interpretation. He told Warner he would never act with her again. "She's too hoggy, too egocentric, she doesn't stay within the framework of her role." Warner saw through his jealousy and insecurity and discounted his remarks. *"I mean it—no more pictures with Davis!"* Muni yelled. It was to be five years before their names appeared together above a picture's title, and by then both had ascended to the top rungs of stardom. But they did not appear together in a single scene!

Meanwhile, in January 1935, the picture was playing all across the country, and Muni and his supportive, sustaining wife, Bela, simmered and seethed over such rave reviews as that from *The New York Times's* Andre Sennwald, who wrote, "[Davis] plays the part with the ugly, sadistic, and utterly convincing sense of reality which distinguished her fine performance in *Of Human Bondage.*"

It was Bela Muni who thought up her husband's answer to this. He went in to Jack Warner and asked for more money and better roles. His overcompensative determination in the face of the Davis's "threat" brought him, within two years, an Academy Award.

The grosses from *Bordertown* and the many plaudits for her performance in it having convinced Warners once again she was ready for the "star treatment," Davis was billed above the title for *The Girl From Tenth Avenue.* For the second time, the gesture was premature because the 69-minute vehicle trotted out to support her restored "status" wasn't up to the fine and sincere acting she poured into every frame.

This time she is a girl from the wrong side of the tracks, New York's Tenth Avenue, who encounters a society lawyer, Ian Hunter, when he is about to make a scene outside the church where his former fiancée (Katherine Alexander) is marrying another man (Colin Clive). Several plot twists later, Davis marries him on the rebound, they are living in her apartment, and with the help of her ex—Floradora Girl landlady, Alison Skipworth, she is learning the manners of a lady, in preparation for her move to Park Avenue.

But fickle Miss Alexander tries to lure Hunter back, citing her wedding to Clive as a mistake, and Davis decides to make a fight for him, for she has fallen in love. The picture ends with Clive finally convincing Hunter to stay with wife Davis.

Davis had two interesting leading men in *The Girl From Tenth Avenue*. Ian Hunter was a handsome, if placid, British actor who had fought in World War I, made it on the London stage, then went on to Hollywood. He specialized in dancing attendance on the assorted love problems of such soap tragediennes as Kay Francis, and while Davis liked him and appeared with him in more films, she found him too tame for her tastes and failed to reciprocate his obvious interest, to his continuing chagrin. Hunter took his rejection with civilized restraint, which could not be said for the other man in *Tenth Avenue*, Colin Clive, who also developed an interest in her that was more neurotic than genuine. Davis found his advances harder to repel. Clive, also a former English stage actor, had made a hit in the World War I film, *Journey's End*, but soon found himself relegated to vividly unwholesome roles in such movies as *Frankenstein* and *Mad Love*. In the former he was the scientist who conjures up the monster, in the latter he was the wild-eyed pianist who is given the hands of a murderer after his own are injured and amputated. Roles like these suited Clive far better than soapy romances. He was handsome, but his tense, on-the-edge manner made women in the audience nervous. Like another brother-under-the-skin, Monroe Owsley, he died in 1937, of alcoholism. A tormented and confused bisexual, he had humiliating homosexual episodes which left him demoralized, and as Ian Hunter later recalled, "Colin was a fine actor but he made everyone around him nervous—nervous as hell! One didn't want to be in the vicinity for what seemed an inevitable blowup, breakdown, or both."

While Hunter plied Davis with civilized English tea sessions during breaks on the set, Clive, as director Alfred Green recalled, would go off to a far, dark corner and brood and glower. Davis admitted in later years that she found Clive arresting if physically unattractive, at least to her, and he certainly matched her intensity on screen, "though his," as she put it, "was an altogether different ballgame." Offscreen, his advances left her feeling "creepy."

Later she regretted not ever having had Clive as her chief leading man—in *Tenth Avenue* he was more of a supporting player, and their onscreen confrontations were few. Green recalled her saying that there were very few male performers who could match her own intensity. If some people called her a witch, then Clive qualified as a warlock, and their onscreen chemistry would have been mighty interesting.

Of course during this period Davis was focused on George Brent, but she discussed both Hunter and Clive with Brent and Al Green. As Al Green recalled it, Brent found both men amusing as suitors, and wholly inappropriate, snickering, "One [Hunter] is a milksop who'd bore you to death and the other is a maniac who might cut your head off some night and plunk it on the icebox!" Instead of shuddering in horror at such direct language, Green said, Davis threw her head back and laughed raucously. "Maybe I'd cut his head off—how do you know?" she rejoindered. That same year Clive did another Frankenstein picture at Universal. In this one, *The Bride of Frankenstein*, he creates a monster woman (Elsa Lanchester was a hit in the role) as spouse for his original monster, and Brent and Green kidded Davis that if she'd only pleaded with Jack Warner successfully for a loanout on that, she and Clive could have raised old Satan himself!

The scriptwriter for *The Girl From Tenth Avenue*, Charles Kenyon, tailored the leading role to Davis's full measure. Soapy and trivial as the picture was, it displayed her as a brazen lower-class dame pulling herself up, via sheer nerve and intense address, to the social level where she could vie on equal terms with her rival and win her upper-class guy. Certainly she is given ample opportunity here to stride purposefully about, flash her eyes kinetically, and give the brazen, feisty speeches that by then had become her trademark. The more passive, albeit civilized, Hunter made a perfect foil for all this.

The New York Times felt Davis had given a performance "both truthful and amusing" and *Variety* felt she had gone "high, wide and handsome on the emotions."

8

Grinding out the Warner Sausage

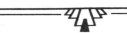

I N LOOKING BACK at mid-1935 when she was languishing in one of her Warner horrors, *Front Page Woman*, Davis said:

"The Warners were quite befuddled by me at this point. No matter what piece of garbage they gave me to do, and no matter how much I scornfully sniffed at it, I did my job—and well. If they wouldn't help me, I'd help myself. Critics and public were making me more important and still they resisted.

"My graduating contract seemed to the studio to be compensation enough for my work, but money was not the question. They were all used to actors who were grateful they had been rescued from diners or from under wet stones and as long as the cash rolled in, were happy. As long as their paychecks weren't shy and their billing was bold, all was right with their world."

During this period she felt that she was being treated "as an intractable child." She recalled meeting Jack Warner at parties where he would patronize her maddeningly, wagging his finger at her like a disapproving parent, using annoying variations on: "Remember, Bette, you have to be at the studio at six o'clock. Get to sleep *soon!*"

This always angered her because she was noted on the set for her promptness and did not like to be made to feel like a five-year-old.

More significant is a reference in her biography to Jack Warner's freedom from adulterous inclinations. "In all fairness," she wrote, "he was singular as a movie mogul. No lecherous boss was he! His sins lay elsewhere. He was the father. The power. The glory. And he was in business to make money. I was aware of this; but I was and still am convinced that the public will buy good work if it is presented in the same packaging that glamorizes the trash."

Katherine Albert told me that Davis was extremely annoyed at Jack Warner's virtue—at least where she was concerned. "God, the man must wear an iron chastity belt," she hissed to Katherine. According to the same source, Davis began making unnecessary visits to Warner's office to try to seduce him. "I just want to see if he's human," she laughed. Once she caught Jack without his pants—he was being fitted for a new suit in his office, having little time to run down to his favorite tailor's.

"Jack, your legs are great," she purred, admiringly.

"Bette—make your exit—pronto!" he rejoindered. His assistant promptly showed her the door.

Still stinging over Laemmle's reference to her having "as much sex appeal as Slim Summerville," Davis was determined to arouse Warner. Katherine warned her that she was flouting the moral turpitude clause in her contract, insisted on by the Production Code and Legion of Decency that ruled Hollywood in 1935, but Davis said she didn't care.

"People are flouting it all the time—look at the way Darryl Zanuck acts," Davis declared defiantly, but, eventually she stopped "trying to get into the boss's pants," as producer Henry Blanke pointedly put it, because of her growing admiration for Warner's wife, Ann, who always treated her graciously. Ann Warner was later to become a crucial Davis ally, so her perspicacity in pulling in her seduction horns might have been instinctive. There was also the factor—quite evident—that Jack Warner had absolutely no sexual interest in Bette Davis.

Writer Jerry Asher, who knew Davis intimately, felt this galled her. "She became quite vain about her alleged ability to get any man she wanted," Jerry recalled. "First George Brent kept her at arm's length, now the Grand Panjandrum himself!"

Jerry also felt that her many quarrels with Jack Warner over the years had their roots not just in her determination to get quality product, but in hurt vanity, which Davis hotly denied.

As of 1935 Brent had been legally free of Ruth Chatterton for a year and was up for grabs, only he was the one doing the grabbing—at the bodies of quite a few attractive Hollywood women, some actresses, some even married, which made Warner extremely nervous, given those eternal moral-turpitude clauses. As Henry Blanke remembered it, Jack called George into his office one day. "George, why don't you get married again?" he began.

"No thanks—like my freedom!" (Brent was noted for his terse responses.)

"Okay, so why don't you give Davis a tumble! You know she's had the hots for you for years!"

"She's a married woman, Jack."

"Since when has that stopped you? Anyway, I'm putting you two in another picture together. Two in a row, in fact. The public likes to see you together. They sense the sexual tension. It comes off real onscreen."

"Maybe from her. Not from me."

"You start shooting Monday at seven. Now get out!"

"Glad to."

In the first of the two 1935 pictures co-starring Bette Davis and George Brent, *Front Page Woman*, Brent is supposed to be in love with Davis, though he feels she is a "bum newspaperwoman. All women are bum in such a job," is ace reporter Brent's ongoing observation. He tricks Davis over a murder verdict, which she reports inaccurately due to his machinations, and she is fired. Then she is forced to restore the balance, and the rest of the fast-paced but surprisingly boring and perfunctory doings have her doing just that.

The fans took notice of Davis's calf-eyed looks at Brent all through the sequences featuring them together. Davis made the mistake of taking hubby Ham Nelson to a screening of *Front Page Woman*, and Mike Curtiz remembered them arguing along such lines as:

"You must be in love with that guy the way you ogle him constantly in front of the camera."

"But Ham, I'm paid to be an actress and you have to look interested in your leading man."

"Horseshit!"

Scriptwriters Roy Chanslor, Lillie Hayward, and Laird Doyle, all replete with sound newspaper backgrounds, made the proceedings, based on ex-newspaperman Richard Macauley's story "Women Are Bum Newspapermen," look authentic. Adela Rogers St. Johns, one of Hearst's premiere newshens, was drafted by the Warners publicity department to give out stories and interviews assuring one and all that Bette Davis's Ellen Garfield went through her paces in the best tradition of tabloid sob sisters. She even got a phone interview with the great William Randolph

Hearst himself, who asseverated that Davis as Garfield was indeed the genuine goods.

Overlooked by the public at large was the fact that, after a rift with Metro-Goldwyn-Mayer over their failure to cast his mistress, Marion Davies, in "stature" roles, Hearst had moved Marion and his Cosmopolitan Productions over to Warners. "I'd hire her any time," Hearst declared. "She can start on the *San Francisco Examiner!*" Jack Warner was delighted with the publicity, and Davis began getting invitations to Hearst's San Simeon estate.

Davis's second 1935 picture with George Brent, *Special Agent*, was no great shakes. Its slipshod direction by William Keighley exasperated her. Photographer Sid Hickox, not one of her favorites, shot her without the care and attention Polito and others had lavished.

Frank S. Nugent in *The New York Times* said succinctly but pointedly:

"The brothers Warner have turned out another of their machine-gun sagas of crime and punishment in *Special Agent*, crisp, fast-moving and thoroughly entertaining . . . . it has all been done before, but somehow it never seems to lose its visual excitement. . . . The Internal Revenue Bureau is personified handsomely in the reflection of contemporary manners by George Brent. Ricardo Cortez is entirely convincing as the racket lord, and Bette Davis manages to fit in reasonably as the patriotic book-keeper who double-crosses her boss for Uncle Sam and Mr. Brent (in about an 05-95 ratio)."

The picture does not hold up well when seen today, and Davis's role hardly seems necessary to the action. The 76 minutes are carelessly edited; Production Code restrictions, running rampant in 1935, forced the reshooting of several scenes which were awkwardly inserted, making for choppy continuity. Screenwriters Laird Doyle and Abem Finkel, working on an idea by Martin Mooney, do not bring the characters into sharp psychological relief, and motivations are not convincingly assigned.

Being without ego or star ambition, Brent usually walked through his parts and collected his paycheck uncomplainingly. Around the studio, he was known as "Apple of Jack Warner's Eye" and "Good Old Mr. Dependable." He said he didn't like most of his pictures, but he had some especially caustic words for *Special Agent*, telling Ruth Waterbury of *Photoplay* that it was "a poor, paltry thing, unbelievable and unconvincing in all its aspects." Ruth later told me that Warners publicity talked her out of using the quotes for fear of affecting the picture's chances. "It was one of those rare instances where George spoke his mind for print," she told me. "He had had early hardship in Ireland, and a decent paycheck went a long way with George. He never thought much of his acting abilities and told me once he was afraid people would find out how lousy he was and fire him—so he seldom made waves."

Waterbury also remembered that Davis had the continuing hots for Brent all through 1935 and that she made no secret of it.

"The chemistry between them onscreen was always exciting," Waterbury remembered. "And the chemistry offscreen even more so! But for years it was more on Bette's side than George's. She finally got her reward—reciprocity—but it took her years! And even then, I always felt she was more emotional about it than he was. Of course, George always kept—at least on the surface—that quizzical, detached attitude toward women that they took to like catnip. Women, whether they admit it or not, don't like to get too sure of a man—Bette was no exception."

During this same period Davis was to weather the unwelcome addresses of a dangerously neurotic young Warner actor who could hold his own with Owsley and Clive—and then some!

Ross Alexander, Davis's fellow contract player at Warners, was a tormented, confused young man. He had gone on the stage in 1923 when he was sixteen (he was a year older than Davis) and had been seduced by several older actors and two prominent stage directors, and "between engagements" had been kept by a series of wealthy men. Opportunistic and self-despising, Ross hated his homosexual side, and later went on a wild overcompensation swing by romancing several prominent actresses. He gravitated toward forceful women and after he came to Warners in 1933, he developed a wild crush (which Jerry Asher called an obsession) on Davis. "He was forever maneuvering to get cast in a picture with her," Jerry remembered. "It was really pathetic, and so self-deceptive when he went on about if he ever held her in his arms and kissed her onscreen he'd kindle a wild response in her. I knew Bette well enough to know that Ross wasn't her type. He was a handsome enough kid, with a good body and a wry, offhand, cynical charm that made him great in certain roles, but she could always spot a bisexual component in a man and that she needed like a hole in the head at that stage. And he wouldn't have been masculine enough for her—not that he was effeminate; that he wasn't, but there was something feminine and feline about the way he put himself across on screen, especially in comedy parts."

It seems that Ross Alexander began writing Davis love letters, which he sneaked under her dressing-room door. "She'd read them, laugh at them and throw them in the wastebasket," Jerry Asher told me. "Ross was a real masochist. He didn't know when he was getting no—a big loud no—for an answer, and the fact that Bette was married to Ham Nelson didn't seem to bother him at all."

Ham tried to stay away from Davis's sets and the studio itself, but one afternoon he went looking for her and found a letter headed, on the envelope, TO MY BELOVED ONE, BETTE. Quick-tempered, jealous Ham tore open the envelope and read the letter. Ross had worded it so that it seemed he and Bette had made love. They never had, of course, but an enraged Ham confronted Davis with it on the set of *Satan Met a Lady*, a movie she was making with Warren William. He dragged her behind a flat and demanded an explanation. Davis read the letter and snickered. "That queer is having pipe dreams," she told her husband. "He's trying to prove his manhood—or something—and he knows I see right through him." Ham clenched his fists, and Davis said, "I've got to get back to the set—deal with him as you like. Just get him off my fucking back!"

Ham went looking for Ross and found him alone in a men's room. He slammed him against the wall and hollered, "It's my *wife* you're writing that slush-and-mush to, and she wants no part of it! If you're any kind of a man, you'll back off!" Ross tried to defend himself by raising his fists, but Ham, taller and stronger, knocked him to the floor.

The resulting black eye prevented Ross from beginning the filming of his next picture. He stayed home, brooded, and drank. Ross's wife, Anne Nagel, a pretty young actress who had fallen deeply in love with him, left him several times when she discovered his half-finished notes to Davis under his desk blotter.

Ross's obsession grew worse. Davis, ever more annoyed, began taunting him when their paths crossed, casting aspersions on his manhood. "She's a merciless bitch!" Ross screamed to Jerry Asher. "No, Ross," Jerry replied, "she just wants you to get off it! Look, you have had some lovely women in your life, including Anne. You can't get them all! Bette is a married woman, and you're just asking for more beatings from Ham!"

Ross began sinking into fits of profound depression. He went out in his car, picked up a male hobo on the highway, and had sex with him. The man made blackmail threats and Ross appealed to the Warners lawyers, who managed to hush the matter up. In January 1937 he killed himself. Jack Warner hired people to get all unsent love letters to Davis out of his house before police and reporters found them.

With her last 1935 film, Davis tried to make a sow's ear into a silk purse, and succeeded—somewhat. "I worked like ten men on *Dangerous*," Davis later said.

One of the most interesting reviews Davis was ever to receive was for *Dangerous*. It came from *Picture Post's* E. Arnot Robertson, who wrote: "I think Bette Davis would probably have been burned as a witch if she had lived two or three hundred years ago. She gives the curious feeling of being charged with power which can find no ordinary outlet."

After the two forgettable, pedestrian duds in which she had languished earlier, *Dangerous*—soapy, melodramatic, and silly as its basic plot was—offered Davis enough material to charge with her individual and unique talent. The story showcases one Joyce Heath, a self-destructive actress down on her luck, who has taken to drink and who feels she's jinxed. She has created such a negative image for herself that no one wants to hire or work with her. The character was modeled on the late Jeanne Eagels, who after her initial 1922 Broadway hit in *Rain* dissipated her fine talent in drink and drugs and a careless life-style, dying in 1929.

A wealthy young architect, Dan Bellows, played by Franchot Tone, who was on loan from Metro-Goldwyn-Mayer, takes an interest in the skidding Joyce, dries her out at his country place under the aegis of a disapproving housekeeper, Alison Skipworth, and gradually restores her sense of self and her ambition. He even finances a comeback play for her, and they fall in love. But Davis has a secret husband, a weakling (John Eldredge) who still loves her and refuses a divorce. Davis proceeds to drive them both into a tree, with the famous lines, "It's going to be your life or mine! If you're killed, I'll be free . . . If I'm killed, it won't matter any longer. And if we both die, good riddance!" He is injured. She escapes with a scratch.

Later, realizing that she is poison for Tone, she sends him back to his fiancée by assuming a heartlessness that wins his disgust, then goes to the hospital to care for her injured husband after witnessing, from across the street, Tone's wedding to socialite Margaret Lindsay, who has been patiently waiting for him to overcome his "dangerous" addiction—Davis. Her comeback, of course, is a smash.

Many critics, and not a few audiences, laughed at this ridiculously contrived ending, to say nothing of the other soapy situations and sappy dialogue, but everyone took seriously Davis's vivid rendition of a driven, complex, self-destructive woman.

During the filming Davis fell in love with handsome, aristocratic Franchot Tone, who had come to movies in 1932 from the stage. For some three years he had lent his superior talents to so-so leading-man roles at Metro-Goldwyn-Mayer and had appeared in pictures with Joan Crawford, whom he eventually married.

The origin of the famous Bette Davis–Joan Crawford feud can be found in this man. By 1935, Tone had already won for himself an *homme fatal* reputation in New York, with a rumor that identified him as the father of a young married stage actress's son—a son who grew up to become briefly a prominent film player before retiring into another profession. The similarities in physical appearance and acting styles were so pronounced that this unacknowledged son quit show business rather early in life. It was also said that when the actress's husband found out the truth, he beat up both his wife and Tone. This was not the first, or the last, touch of melodrama in Tone's life. Joan Crawford's directors were shocked more than once to see Crawford arriving on the set with assorted bruises from quarrels with Tone. She finally divorced him in 1938 when she found him *déshabillé* with a young starlet in his MGM dressing room. In 1951, when he was forty-seven, Tone got his face beaten so thoroughly in a brawl with toughie actor Tom Neal over his third wife, Barbara Payton, that he had to have plastic surgery.

In 1935, when Tone was thirty-one and Davis twenty-seven, she fell very much in love with him. He was not the handsomest actor in town—his head was oddly shaped and his features hardly of the sculptured kind—but he exuded a polished masculine aura and had a voice that drove women to distraction; it "sucked off the consonants and jerked off the vowels," translation being that it was rich, deep, and attractively varied tonally.

Joan Crawford, who married Tone before the release of *Dangerous*, was aware that things were heating up between Tone and Davis over on the Warner lot, but as she was busy winding up a picture at MGM, she was in no position to supervise the goings-on. Davis took full advantage of the situation.

"She was hot for Tone; no question of that!" the film's producer, Harry Joe Brown, later said. "They were all over each other on the set, and later in her dressing room. Davis was so careless (or maybe she was being a showoff) that she would leave the door ajar and one time I came by to talk about the new set we were striking and found them in, well, a very tight (translate that compromising) position. And when they saw me they didn't seem to give a damn! I remember that Franchot just laughed, and told me to shut the door when I went out. I beat it out of there fast. Tone was just about to marry Joan Crawford, and Bette was still married to that jerk Ham Nelson, and, well, it was pretty thick."

Davis seemed to have little regard for the moral-turpitude clauses in her contract. She probably should have, since the Legion of Decency and the Hays Office at the time were riding fierce and high on the better-publicized personalities, and "romantic" episodes carried on too blatantly could mean the finish of a career.

Speculation as to what Harry Joe Brown actually stumbled upon in Davis's dressing room that day has its amusing aspects, as it was well known that one of Franchot Tone's favorite sexual positions was "getting serviced"—or, more bluntly, fellated. In fact, that was what Joan Crawford reportedly found him enjoying when, three years later, she caught him with the starlet—and promptly filed for divorce.

MGM executive Eddie Mannix, who knew Tone well, told me that Tone had confided jokingly that he liked to get fellated more often than not because it was one way to avoid getting a woman pregnant. "I had enough abortions and illegitimate pregnancies in New York to last me a lifetime," Tone laughed. "A lot of truth is, as always, spoken in jest," Mannix chuckled.

Director Alfred E. Green opined that Tone, knowing he was a good actor, one of the best of the MGM stable, "resented being shunted to secondary status and discovered that the only way to be Top Man was in proving his sexual and romantic prowess with one dame after another." Once, over a few drinks, he confided to Green that at Cornell, where he had maneuvered himself into the presidency of the Dramatic Club, he had been known as the "Campus Jack the Ripper." "Of course the only 'ripping' I did was girls' panties in the backseats of cars," he grinned.

So galling did he find the failure of MGM to acknowledge his talent with worthwhile starring parts that, according to Joan Crawford, he worked off his humiliation and despair by beating her up at home. "I put up with the beatings but the dressing-room infidelity was too much," Joan later told Anita Loos.

Luckily for Davis, Tone showed her only his romantic and sexual skills. It was a typical run-of-picture arrangement: For him, when it was over, it was over; for her, it was a keen regret. Going home to spineless Ham after a day of on- and off-screen romancing with dynamic Tone left her deeply frustrated.

"I am positive that the mutual hatred between Davis and Crawford began then and there, with the Tone thing," publicist Jerry Asher, a close friend of all three, told me in 1965. "Joan resented his fiddling with Bette, even after they married, and Bette resented the fact that Joan had established top priority in the Tone scheme of things. Of course nobody thought about the fourth party, poor Ham. What *he* thought was obviously of less than zero import!"

—◊—

BUT THE CHRISTMAS AUDIENCES of 1935 found the Davis-Tone combination in *Dangerous* most kinetic, and quite a few fan letters came into Warners suggesting that they be reteamed. "But Joan was having none of that—she kept him strictly under wraps at MGM and in their Brentwood home," Jerry said, "and Bette seethed, and not in silence, either!"

According to Asher, who often swam and exercised with him, Tone was extraordinarily well endowed where it counted, even in a flaccid state. "His women must have found him a real jaw breaker," Jerry laughed.

9

The First Oscar—and Its Aftermath

Davis ROSE from a sickbed to attend the 1936 Academy Award dinner, at which she received her Oscar for *Dangerous* from the great D. W. Griffith, a special award winner himself on that occasion for his many masterpieces of the silent era.

There was some criticism of her casual attire, considering the sumptuousness of the occasion. The male winner, Victor McLaglen (for *The Informer*) was all done up in white tie and tails, and all the women were in evening gowns, while Davis wore a plain print dress with unbecoming wide lapels. Ill-fitting, the kind of garment one would put on for a casual afternoon of shopping, it aroused the ire of Ruth Waterbury, now the editor of *Photoplay*.

During the evening Ruth took Bette into the ladies' room and let her have it for coming to the dinner dressed the way she was. Ruth told me she had felt Davis was slighting the Academy people for giving her a consolation prize for a picture of which she was not fond in place of one for the earned winner, *Of Human Bondage*. "I think she did it deliberately," Ruth recalled. "It was her way, possibly unconsciously, of telling the Academy it wasn't all that important in her scheme of things." Davis later said her mother, too, reproved her for her attire. She remembered having nothing appropriate to wear, so she elected the print, though her mother was dressed magnificently. One wonders why Ruthie didn't take charge before the event and insist that Davis be dressed as befit a winner, especially since they had dressed together that night.

Davis accepted her belated recognition with modesty, saying the true winner for 1935 should have been Katharine Hepburn for *Alice Adams*. Her admiration for Hepburn's appearance, her acting style, her manner of living, was always unbounded, though decades later, when Hepburn had garnered four Oscars to her two, Davis was to tone down her praise considerably.

Davis opened the year 1936 with another lead opposite Leslie Howard.

In retrospect, it is somewhat difficult to understand why Davis was so enthusiastic about winning the role of Gabrielle Maple in *The Petrified Forest*, the film version of the hit Broadway play starring Leslie Howard. The play also brought Humphrey Bogart, as coldblooded gangster Duke Mantee, into major prominence; he repeated his role onscreen, to added acclaim.

Probably the prestige elements of the play appealed to Davis, who reasoned, most likely that a less-than-strong role in a "prestige" production was still better than a lead in a turkey or an also-ran soaper. The role of Gabrielle, however, could have been played by a number of contract actresses—Margaret Lindsay, for instance, for she is a waitress at an Arizona gas station–restaurant who dreams of a painting career and a sojourn in Paris. It's a dreamy role, free of any really strong confrontational situations. Had Davis not been so anxious for a "big" picture, she would doubtless have refused the part. Jack Warner realized this if she did not and was half-embarrassed, half-scornful when she thanked him profusely for *Forest*. "I think I like Bette better when she's fightin' and fussin'. Gratitude and sugariness are not her thing," he remarked to Hal Wallis.

Howard, of course, was in his element as the dreamy vagrant whose idealism and impracticality have condemned him to outsider status. And Bogart, as the gangster who kidnaps Davis, Howard, father Porter Hall, grandfather Charley Grapewin, and a couple of travelers and holds them prisoner, got more out of the film than anyone else; in fact, it led him to a Warner Brothers contract.

Robert E. Sherwood's rather turgid and pretentious play was revamped for the screen by Charles Kenyon and Delmer Daves. Leo Forbstein's orchestrations helped composer Bernhard Kaun (of whom not much was heard thereafter) get his musical effects across, and the location shooting and realistic gas-station set on a huge Warner stage created the right atmosphere, but there was no denying that the strong Mantee confrontations were a major selling point in both play and film.

Davis sent out mixed signals over the years about her personal relationship with Howard during the making of this, their second film together. Certainly he had gained respect for her since *Bondage*, as she had given a number of striking performances, but according to Dick Foran and director Archie Mayo, he alternated between ignoring her and making crude passes. Davis claimed that in one romantic scene he actually nibbled on her arm while hugging her. She may have confused this with some acting ploy on his part, because Howard told others that she was not his type. Since he was a notorious womanizer (Olivia De Havilland was to have a time of it fending him off during the third Davis-Howard film, *It's Love I'm After*, a year later), one is inclined to believe Howard's side of the story.

The poetic observations about outsiders and insiders aside, *The Petrified Forest*, both on stage and on film, seemed to demonstrate Sherwood's philosophical and dramatic confusion more than anything else, and Davis's evident efforts to bring Gaby Maple alive can be seen in the finished film. This was simply not the kind of forceful role in which she could shine; true, in earlier and later films she would play sensitive, warm women, but these roles had more depth and solidity written into them. Gaby is, after all, a dreamy young girl longing for space in which to actualize her poetic inspirations, and as written, it is a pallid supporting role for the two strongly written male characters.

Davis, as usual, expressed her dislike for Bogart, whom she found crude, overbearing, and sullen, but this might have been a reflection of her annoyance that he had the better role. Dick Foran told me in 1964 that he felt very self-conscious in the role of her rejected suitor, a former football player. "I never felt I was a big-league actor," he confessed, "and I was out of my league with Davis, Howard, and Bogart. I could tell that Bette was not her best self; she was ill a lot, and sustained some injuries on the gas-station set that threw her off form for days, and I just didn't think she was all that happy with the picture. One reason was that she had a real craving to be front and center all the time, and she got shunted aside for the main action, I felt. True, she gets to hold Howard in his death scene after he was shot by Bogart, but he hogged that scene."

The New York Times tried to look at the bright side of Davis's characterizational shift in *Forest*, but there is a strong hint of the patronizing and soothing in Frank Nugent's observation that "Bette Davis . . . demonstrates that she does not have to be hysterical to give a grand portrayal."

Archie Mayo in 1966 remembered that Davis was difficult to direct because she was frustrated with Gaby's essential passivity. "Passivity and sweetness were not that girl's strong cards," he laughed, "and after she got into the picture I think she realized that she was getting short-changed. She tried to blame me for it, but it was the screenwriters she should have gone after!"

Davis found it humiliating that her next film should be called, of all things, *Cream Princess*. She thought the title vulgar and highly suggestive and railed that the Legion of Decency and the Production Code rushed in to censor everything else but didn't raise an eyebrow at that title!

The title was applicable, after a fashion, since it was based on a play by Michael Arlen about a cosmetics heiress (cream, you see) who is actually a waitress masquerading as the heiress because the firm's publicity man thinks her well-publicized romantic adventures will help sales. She is interviewed by a no-nonsense newsman, George Brent, and persuades him to marry her so that he can finish his novel, long postponed for financial reasons, and she can be free of the importunings of such fortune hunters as impoverished Count Gulliano (Ivan Lebedeff). Of course in time her imposture is discovered, but the smitten Brent couldn't care less and whisks her off to his mountain cabin so he can finish that novel and break her in to *hausfrau* ways.

Alfred E. Green, constantly heckled and put-upon by the annoyed and frustrated Davis, made a noble effort to direct things for lively results, W. Franke Harling and Heinz Roemheld poured on a rich musical score that was better than the film deserved, and Charles Kenyon's screenplay tried hard for wit and sass—but to no avail.

Cream Princess eventually retitled by an embarrassed Warners to the more sanitary—but also inexplicable—*The Golden Arrow*, was a monumental dud. Again Davis fans cross-country wrote in to ask why she wasn't given better material. Davis, in one of her characteristic fits of sudden, impulsive temper, even invaded Jack Warner's office with a basket of such letters and dumped them on the floor in front of him. "Later rumors had it that I dumped them right on his desk," she recalled to Ruth Waterbury in 1955, "but it wasn't true. I felt the floor was equally effective. I think he even read some of them, too, not that that did me any good."

What made *The Golden Arrow* and its banal shenanigans even more humiliating was the fact that just six weeks before its release, she had won the Academy Award for *Dangerous*—and here she was, following that signal triumph with one of the most banal, silly, trivial pictures of her career.

"*The Golden Arrow* was definitely one of the deciding factors in my Big Revolt Against Warners later in 1936," she said later. "I figured that if after all this time, *Arrow* was the best I could get, some drastic measures were being called for."

As usual, the Davis-Brent scenes were acted with great bravura and dispatch and a warm simpatico that glowed from the screen. "If only the dialogue and situations had supported them, but they didn't!" the *San Francisco Examiner* critic lamented.

Motion Picture Herald tried to be kind and tactful—to Davis as well as the picture—in its review, but the between-the-lines alarm and concern for the ever-brightening star is apparent: "In her first motion picture since winning the Academy Award for the best performance of 1935, Bette Davis departs abruptly from the dramatic role and undertakes a straight comedy characterization heavily underscored with romance with the same brisk manner and swift utterance that has marked her other work. . . . The story is actionful and swift-moving and at no point approaches the serious."

Davis was also disappointed, during the picture, in George Brent's continuing lack of responsiveness or, perhaps, prudence. His standard putdown, circa 1936, was "You're a married woman, Bette."

In her autobiography Davis refers to the ill-fated *Satan Met a Lady* thus: "When the company scheduled [the film], a Dashiell Hammett remake that was not to achieve any quality until John Huston directed it years later under the title *The Maltese Falcon*, I was so distressed by the whole tone of the script and the vapidity of my part that I marched up to [Jack Warner's] office and demanded that I be given work that was commensurate with my proven ability." Put off—for the time being—by more of Jack's promises, she reluctantly proceeded with the picture.

Satan Met a Lady went through three titles before it settled in: *The Man in the Black Hat, Hard Luck Dame,* and *Men on Her Mind.* It had been made under its original title, *The Maltese Falcon,* for the first time in 1931, with Ricardo Cortez as Sam Spade and Bebe Daniels as the Mystery Woman. (Decades later it was shown on television under the title *Dangerous Female,* so as to avoid confusion with the 1941 version.) In 1936 the Davis-William version, with its endless title changes, was made. Then in 1941, John Huston's masterpiece clinched Humphrey Bogart's superstardom and won added plaudits for Mary Astor, who won a supporting Oscar that year for her role in Davis's *The Great Lie.*

Appearing with Davis and William was Alison Skipworth, who played the role that "Fat Man" Sidney Greenstreet later made immortal—an interesting characterizational sex change. A ram's horn encrusted with priceless gems was the pièce de résistance instead of the legendary falcon that figured in the other two versions. Marie Wilson was given full rein in one of her standard comedy turns as Sam Spade's devoted and protective secretary. Warren William was not too felicitously cast in the role that Bogart later made his own, and his Sam Spade lacks the realistic toughness and cynicism that Bogart so expertly limned. Davis's role was badly written and poorly motivated, and her comings and goings seem erratic and confusing. One bright note for Davis, however: Warren William had obviously lost interest in her and addressed hardly ten words to her throughout the shooting, as she later, half-ruefully, half-relievedly recalled. "Of course I was twenty-eight years old by then," she laughed self-deprecatingly, "and everyone knew he liked them really young and really fresh!"

The plot of the 1936 version is confusing, at best: Valerie (the Davis character) winds up murdering Skipworth's contact man so she can get the ram's horn. She later prevents William's Spade from picking up the $10,000 reward by turning herself in to the train's washroom attendant, in the hope of benefiting herself. When Jack Warner saw the results (poorly directed by William Dieterle, who couldn't make head nor tail of the assorted shenanigans) he found the plot so confusing that he ordered a reediting by Warren Low, which held up the picture's release by some months.

The young *New York Times* critic Bosley Crowther (in later years one of my guides and mentors) certainly spelled it all out clearly and concisely in a pricelessly accurate—and acid—review that is worth quoting at some length, nailing down as it does the assorted ineptitudes of *Satan Met a Lady* and Davis's unjust treatment by all hands. Crowther wrote:

"So disconnected and lunatic are the picture's ingredients, so irrelevant and monstrous its people, that one lives through it in a constant expectation of seeing a group of uniformed individuals appear suddenly from behind the furniture and take the entire cast into protective custody. There is no story, merely a farrago of nonsense representing a series of practical studio compromises with an unworkable script."

Bosley continued: "Without taking sides in a controversy of such titanic proportions, it is no more than gallantry to observe that if Bette Davis had not effectually espoused her own cause against the Warners recently by quitting her job, the Federal Government eventually would have had to step in and do something about her. After viewing *Satan Met a Lady*, all thinking people must acknowledge that a 'Bette Davis Reclamation Project' (BDRP) to prevent the waste of this gifted lady's talents would not be a too-drastic addition to our various programs for the conservation of natural resources."

Bos Crowther was thirty-one when he wrote those words. Years later, a ripe sixty, he recalled the horror he and his critical confreres felt when *Satan* premiered in New York. "God, it brought out the knight to the rescue in all of us males and the protective mother in the female reviewers. We all got together and sent the notices *en masse* to England and Davis."

To Jack Warner's surprise, the Davis-in-rebellion infection spread to others involved with the ill-fated project. Warren William, a proficient actor who had hitherto been a Warner "reliable" (meaning he'd take any piece of garbage thrown him by the studio uncomplainingly), stood up to Jack Warner like a man one day and told him "no more!" Warner could break his contract, put him on suspension, do what he wanted, but he, too, would not see his talent so "monstrously debased and perverted," as he grandiloquently put it. Next, director William Dieterle marched up to the inner sanctum and declared he would join Davis as far away as England himself, if necessary, if the talents he had honed so carefully in Europe and America were not put to more felicitous use. "Christ, that bitch has started an epidemic of rebellion!" Warner groaned.

10

The Great Rebellion—
and the Return

WITH *Satan Met a Lady* finally in the can, Davis went back to
Laguna Beach and waited tensely for Jack Warner's next move. It
came soon enough. She was sent a script called *God's Country and the
Woman*, about a male lumberjack and a female lumberjack who set up
rival lumber companies and spend their time alternately feuding and
romancing. Warner sent a note adding that the film would be directed
by William Keighley, would co-star one of her favorite men, George
Brent, and moreover would be in Technicolor. Since color was still in its
primitive stages in 1936, Davis was unimpressed. She refused the role
and went on an extended strike. Her instinct proved correct. When
God's Country etc. finally debuted on the screen later that year it was a so-
so movie, and one reviewer noted that George Brent's hair, in the
sloppy color process, looked quite purplish!

As an added inducement to do *God's Country*, Jack Warner had called
Davis into his office and mentioned a new novel by Margaret Mitchell,
Gone With the Wind, which he was optioning. Not realizing that she was
turning down one of the future great sellers of 1936, and disenchanted

with Jack's promises and false alarms, she snorted. "I'll bet *that's* a pip!" It was a reaction that she was to regret for years to come.

Back to her fortress on Laguna Beach she went and proceeded to reject several more scripts. Warners finally put her on a three-month suspension, and she began giving out such items to the press as: "If I don't fight now for stronger roles in better pictures, there will be nothing left of my career. I haven't fought my way this far just to gradually fade away in a welter of mediocrity!"

While she sulked in Laguna, off salary and ever more tense and angry, Davis got an offer from a British producer. Ludovico Toeplitz had been born in Italy and migrated to England, where Alexander Korda had discovered him and had hired him as associate producer for such films as the Charles Laughton Oscar-winning smash, *The Private Life of Henry VIII* (1933) and the Douglas Fairbanks, Jr.–Elisabeth Bergner, *Catharine the Great* (1934). Both films had been shown widely in America, and Davis was impressed with them. Toeplitz later went on to produce his own films, including a Maurice Chevalier vehicle, *Beloved Vagabond*. He had watched Davis's well-publicized problems with Warners from afar, and offered her the equivalent in American dollars of $50,000 to star in *I'll Take the Low Road*, which he planned to shoot in England and Italy with Douglass Montgomery as her co-star (thus reuniting her with the one-time "Kent Douglass" of the 1931 *Waterloo Bridge*). Toeplitz promised her top quality, careful direction, solid production values, and above all, script approval.

Davis, who had been turned down in her earnest request to play the Olivia De Havilland role in *Anthony Adverse*—the lavish, tasteful, and expensive costumer starring Fredric March—consulted with Ruthie and Ham about the Toeplitz offer. Anxious to get back to work, excited about making her first trip abroad to new people and new surroundings and what she told the press was "a potential new start, a clean slate," Davis rushed ahead without getting wise legal counsel, signed the contract, and in the summer of 1936 set sail for England with Ham.

Once he had her in London, Toeplitz told Davis that he wanted their association to be an extended one, and offered her yet another $50,000 to follow the picture with Montgomery with the lead opposite Maurice Chevalier in a picture to be made in France. Excited and happy, Davis agreed to this, also. Toeplitz took her and Ham on the town to celebrate. They had a pleasant meeting with Montgomery, and Davis, who had always liked the handsome actor, told him it would be thrilling to play opposite him. This euphoric period of merry socializing and happy plans was presently interrupted by word from Warners' British lawyers.

Davis was informed that she faced an injunction from Warners forbidding her to work for any other company. The terms of her original contract were read to her; she was in a legal straitjacket. Not satisfied with long-distance dealings and anxious for a pleasant European vacation with his wife, Ann, Jack Warner proceeded to join everybody in England, where he intensified his demands. Toeplitz put up a weak bluff at first, declaring to Jack, on advice of his barristers, that Davis was in a foreign country now, and American contracts were invalid. Soon the quarrels grew more personal, as the feisty Toeplitz lectured the bristly Jack Warner on the low quality of most of his films and his "stupid" waste of a "great star's" talents in mediocre fare such as *The Golden Arrow*. The result was that an angry Jack Warner, now really out for blood, went into the English courts hell-bent on forcing Davis to come back home and adhere to the terms of her Warners deal.

Warner hired Sir Patrick Hastings, one of the sharpest legal eagles in Britain, paid him an enormous sum in advance, and urged him to present a watertight case. Davis's counsel, Sir William Jowett, recommended to her by Toeplitz and Montgomery, began preparing her defense, but he was expensive—more expensive than her limited funds could stand. Sir William, who was wealthy, offered to give her a reduced fee or do the work on faith or credit, whichever she preferred. Pride forced her to pay him a fee she could ill afford—$10,000.

Davis settled down on a country estate near London and waited. After remaining with her a while, Ham returned to the United States to grab any musician's job he could find, given the drain on her finances. Davis took long walks in the English countryside, smoked endlessly, and tried to follow as best she could Sir William's hair-splitting legal arguments.

Soon it was time for court, and Sir William proved no match for Sir Patrick Hastings. Flush with the small fortune Warner Brothers had paid him and fully aware there might be more profitable Warner business for him in England if he delivered the verdict Jack demanded, Hastings proceeded to portray Bette Davis as a naughty, spoiled girl who had been raised to fame in America and was being well paid and pampered by a great studio while all around her people were barely surviving during a depression.

Davis countered that it wasn't money she wanted, or rather more of it, as Sir Patrick had snidely implied, but a chance to do roles that would fulfill her acting talents, and in pictures that had at least some pretensions to quality and good workmanship. The battle raged back and forth, and the British press was full of it, day after day. In America the case was also followed closely, and many Hollywood performers awaited the outcome in the hope Bette might achieve a pioneering breakthrough as the first actor to defy a great studio—and win. Of course Jimmy Cagney had been doing variations on this for some years, but he was a big star, so he fought on more equal terms than the contract-imprisoned Davis, who had not yet achieved major stature. Performers in America wanted to know if the average actor could get away with it. The answer turned out to be no.

In presenting his final judgment, the justice presiding over the case declared that Davis had violated her contract, and that Warners had adhered to it. He curtly reminded Davis that she was well paid, had been given a measure of fame many other young women would have envied (essentially parroting Sir Patrick Hastings's and Jack Warner's shrewdly presented arguments) and should stop being naughty and rebellious. He told her to go back to Hollywood and work out her legally binding contract. He brushed off Davis's protestations about the unsuitable roles because he felt that artistic differences over the quality of product were too nebulous and too much a matter of individual opinion to be within the province of the court. As further punishment, Davis was charged with Warners' court fees as well as her own, for having, he implied, made a nuisance of herself and wasted the court's time.

Infuriated, Davis wrote the justice a letter explaining her side but the judge dismissed it as "inadmissible evidence" and cited his decision as irreversible. Photos of Davis taken by the British tabloids as she went in and out of court show a wan, gray, thin young woman with weariness and woe written all over her face. When she contemplated the legal costs, which ran up to forty-five thousand dollars total, her despair was deep indeed.

Then, once again, her good and wise friend George Arliss, asked her to tea. She poured out all her frustrations and miseries to her kind and understanding fellow artist, telling him she was twenty-eight years old and would be "an old woman" by the time her contract ended, and what then? Arliss listened, and then gave her some good advice: "Go back to Hollywood and accept the decision, my dear," he counseled. "Be a graceful loser, a sportsmanlike one. Your prospects may be brighter than you think." Reluctantly she agreed, and set sail for America and Hollywood.

Soon after, Arliss, who was now making films in England and would never again make a Hollywood film, went to see Jack Warner.

Jack, who continued to feel enormous respect for Arliss's great artistry, listened with an open mind to what Arliss said, which was, in effect, that Warner had in Davis a great potential artist who was more than entitled to the prestige treatment. Surely if he could give class treatment to glamour stars like Kay Francis, whose acting skills were limited, he could do the same for a gifted young woman like Davis who had been heavily favored for the 1934 Oscar for *Bondage*, and who had won it in 1935 for *Dangerous*. Build her up gradually, Arliss counseled, find the best vehicles you can for her, and then watch her go! Arliss clinched the argument for profit-minded Jack Warner by reminding him that well-made pictures with prestigious stars *did* make money—lots of it—if the overall approach was right.

That November of 1936 Davis returned to America. Downhearted and tired, unaware of Arliss's earnest advice to Warner and the producer's assurances that he would pay more careful attention to the career fortunes of "a potentially great star," as Arliss had dubbed her, she stopped off briefly in New York, where Ruthie and Ham awaited her. Ham told her he hoped to get more band work and was cutting records that might go over; he felt that for the moment New York was the place for him, especially in view of their tight finances. Ruthie backed him up. Agreeing without protest, Davis made the long three-day train trip across the country, avoiding reporters in Chicago and other major cities. When she and Ruthie arrived back at Warners, she was heartened by the understanding and cordial atmosphere she found on all sides. Then Jack Warner (who had preceded her there) called her into his office, smilingly told her bygones were bygones, that he was assuming the major portion of the legal costs, and that he had a new, stronger picture for her—*Marked Woman*. "In a way I had won," she said later. "Jack had seen my point."

A number of Davis-watchers have been mystified by her enthusiasm over the first picture assigned her by Warners after her return from England. *Marked Woman*, based on the notorious Lucky Luciano case (he was indicted for criminal activities, including prostitution), was just another tough gangster drama, directed by action-genre specialist Lloyd Bacon. Seen fifty years later, it seems hurried, gauche, perfunctory—a sloppy, truncated Hollywood version of the prostitution racket. Due to Production Code restrictions, it wasn't allowed the honesty the subject required, and the prostitutes were depicted as clip joint "hostesses," a pack led by Davis, the most intelligent, enterprising, and outspoken of the lot, which included Lola Lane, Isabel Jewell, Rosalind Marquis, Mayo Methot, and Jane Bryan, a veteran of one picture, in her first of several with Davis.

In this, Davis played Bryan's protective big sister; Bryan comes from a convent school, gets involved in the shady doings, and is killed, causing Davis to turn on gang boss Eduardo Ciannelli, whose henchmen mark up her face with a double cross on the cheek and assorted bruises. Later, Davis and her girls turn state's evidence for special prosecutor Humphrey Bogart, and Ciannelli and his crooked vice operations are brought to bay. Ciannelli is later warned that if he takes revenge on the girls, he will forfeit his chance of a parole later.

Bacon rushed through all of this in 96 minutes. The screenplay by Robert Rosson and Abem Finkel drew heavily on the records of the Luciano trial with its horrific revelations of criminal misconduct and the tyranny of the rackets, but there was a taste of Hollywoodish unreality, and even—horrors—soap!, to the proceedings.

Part of the problem is Davis's performance. She is overemphatic and studied, and talks and comports herself with a literacy and ladylikeness that is out of sync with her crude character. Her class and evident intelligence throw the picture off balance; it is as if she has wandered in from a drawing room exercise or a costume drama, at least in manner and spirit. *Marked Woman* was the most blatant evidence she had yet given in films that her talent and evolving technique far surpassed actioners and gangster epics, and belonged in serious drama and literate, intelligent film fare.

The other girls—notably Jewell and Methot, who was being courted by her future husband, Humphrey Bogart, during the shooting—are more completely in character than Davis is, and convincingly portray their humble backgrounds and the vulnerability of their pathetic circumstances. Ciannelli, who had all but stolen *Winterset* the year before with his vicious portrait of an outlaw, is even more sinister in *Marked Woman*, getting across all the brutality and amorality of the Luciano character with poisonous exactitude.

One other person besides Davis was out of character in *Marked Woman*. Her co-star, Humphrey Bogart, played a virtuous special prosecutor—modeled after Tom Dewey—with a mealymouthed unctuousness and gentleness that went against the persons he had created since his vicious Duke Mantee in *The Petrified Forest*. When Bogart lectures Davis about what a bad girl she is, there is an almost comic sense of

incongruity—he seems to belong on her side, outdoing her in malfeasances.

The scene in which the gangsters mark Davis up to teach her a
lesson has been overrated, because she is not actually seen during the
attack; one of her girls hears her screams through a door. In the next
scene, she is bandaged up in the hospital.

Davis made much of the fact that she went to a doctor to get made
up to appear the way a girl beaten and scarred would actually look. The
director, cinematographer, and Jack Warner himself tried to make her
look prettier so as not to shock cinema audiences, but she went before
the camera as she wished to, and made her point successfully. In actuality, she doesn't look that bad, and many a picture since—and even
before—has presented deformity, scarring, and maiming far more
graphically, so it seems like fuss and feathers and a tempest in a teapot.
But it did, in long-gone 1937, create some excitement among fan-mag
and tabloid writers and even the general press.

Davis had discovered Jane Bryan in a little-theater version of a popular early-thirties Broadway success, *Green Grow the Lilacs*, and had admired
her fresh-faced, individualistic charm so much that she got her signed to
a Warners contract. She treated Bryan as a younger sister from then
on—some said as a daughter, too—and later married one of her husbands at Bryan's house. Bryan was never happy in front of the camera ("I
was in terror most of the time," she later confessed) and though she was
a gifted actress, she eventually married Justin Dart in 1940 and retired
for good. Davis and Bryan were to do even better pictures together after
Marked Woman. In a number of interviews, Bryan talked about how kind
and understanding Davis was to her, encouraging and soothing her and
protecting her from director Bacon, who had a reputation for being
rough on neophytes.

Davis later explained her kindness to Bryan during *Marked Woman*
thus: "I made up my mind that, when possible, I would remember what
it had been like when *I* first started and secure players dared me to crash
the gate of the Establishment. [Bryan] was excellent in the film."

Davis always called *Marked Woman* "a good picture," and "satisfactory
in every respect." Possibly her enormous relief over resuming a steady
career with Warners and Jack Warner's helping her with her British legal
expenses overshadowed her objective appraisal of a poor picture. In
1988, inexplicably, *Marked Woman* was one of a group of Davis films
released to videocassette stores in connection with the celebration of her
eightieth birthday. It acquired some class on that occasion in the com-

pany of *The Old Maid*, *The Corn Is Green*, *The Letter*, *Mr. Skeffington*, and other Davis fare of a later period that far surpassed *Marked Woman* in every respect. Many wondered why *Marked Woman* had been chosen over, for instance, *All This and Heaven, Too* or *The Sisters* or *Old Acquaintance*. The explanation may lie in the fact that *Marked Woman* got more publicity and press coverage than the better films because of the Luciano case.

In 1937 some reviewers overrated the picture and Davis's performance. The *New York Sun* rhapsodized about how *Marked Woman* was "culled right from the front page headlines, a tabloid story come true," and *Variety* gushed about the film's star, "She is among the Hollywood few who can submerge themselves in a role to the point where they *become* the character they are playing." The latter review, in retrospect, seems quite off-base, as Davis, as before noted, comes on more like a haughty society girl slumming than a put-upon prostitute.

For her next 1937 "postreconciliation" picture, Davis found herself co-starring for the first time with Edward G. Robinson. They were hardly a mutual admiration society, and their relations during *Kid Galahad* were professionally correct but cool. In his autobiography, Robinson indicated that he found Davis callow, overly dependent on mannerisms, and insufficiently trained in technique and projection. Davis in *her* autobiography made fun of Robinson, calling him a kind of male prima donna who protested to the director, during his final death scene in *Galahad*, that Davis was doing too much weeping as she hovered over him. According to her, that was precisely the way the character would have behaved; according to him, she was overacting all over the place.

In later years, Robinson's attitude toward Davis had not mellowed, despite her vastly increased fame and many awards. In 1968 he told me: "I guess she improved later, especially after Wyler and Goulding put some discipline into her. But I always felt she had her distinct limitations." Davis's attitude toward Robinson, circa 1962, was: "He always had a high opinion of himself, and last time I met him he had just as inflated a self-estimate as ever!"

Nonetheless they acted well together in *Kid Galahad*, directed by Mike Curtiz, with a script by Seton I. Miller based on a Francis Wallace novel. The story is about fight promoter Robinson, who sponsors a naïve, innocent, and idealistic youngster, Wayne Morris, and grooms him for the boxing championship. Davis, who plays Robinson's torchsinging girlfriend, labels the boy "Kid Galahad" because of his courtly attitude toward women and proceeds secretly to fall in love with him. When Morris wins the heart of Robinson's protected and naïve sister, Jane Bryan, and Robinson finds out about it at the same time he learns Davis is in love with Morris, he sets Morris up in a bout he has promised rival Humphrey Bogart the kid will lose. Later Robinson has a change of heart and helps the kid win the fight via wise ringside tactical advice. Meanwhile Davis has coped with her unrequited and undeclared feelings for Morris by leaving the racket to become a nightclub singer. Bogart guns down Robinson in a fight later, and then Robinson plays the death scene which was the source—or one of the sources, rather—of his long-running fuss with Davis. In the final scene after Robinson's death, Davis walks sadly beneath a poster of champion Morris, and then down an alley.

Inexplicably, Davis seemed to think well of *Kid Galahad*, though she has a knockabout role in a knockabout fight epic which, to be fair, Mike Curtiz directed for maximum excitement and melodramatic impact. She gave out interviews to the press in early 1937 that sounded suspiciously like rationalizations for her appearance in what was essentially just another Warner actioner. In some of the interviews, she went on about the necessity of acting a variety of parts to exhibit her range and claimed that *Kid Galahad* was one of those pictures that won her audiences she might not otherwise have reached. But the unspoken question by interviewers and fans alike was, were these the audiences she was after at that point in her career? Davis never did offer a satisfactory answer to that. Humphrey Bogart, who never got along with her but understood her struggles to get better film fare, opined later that she was probably putting a brave face on the matter, trying to come out as a good sport and a team player—real-life roles unsuitable to the Bette Davis everyone was on to by that time.

It is true that the role of Fluff is a sympathetic one, and that Davis has ample opportunity to demonstrate poignantly and winningly her "unrequited lover" persona. She also may have been trying to cover up in another respect, because she gave an interview to a fan mag in which she said that if she appeared particularly convincing in her love scenes, it did not mean that she was necessarily in love with her onscreen partners.

The interviews caused snickers among those in the know, because it was obvious that Davis had developed a genuine temperature over handsome, muscular twenty-three-year-old Wayne Morris, who became a star after the release of *Kid Galahad*. Morris was perfect for the role, for he was a clean, decent kid offscreen who later became a World War II hero as a Navy aviator, earning four Distinguished Flying Crosses and two Air Medals. Discharged as a lieutenant commander, he went back to films but never recovered his initial flush of fame. In 1959, when he was forty-five, he died of a heart attack while watching aerial maneuvers from a carrier.

But in 1937 Wayne was at the top of the movie heap with *Galahad* and had his pick of eager young ladies, on and off the studio lot. "Bette really fell for him," her friend Jerry Asher remembered. "She was living her unrequited love off as well as on screen; it imparted a particular poignancy to her performance. Jack Warner always said Bette played love scenes best when she was actually in love, and she was overwhelmed by Wayne." Two things saved her, because he was obviously unaware of her feelings. First, she was twenty-nine to his twenty-three, and Wayne, as was well known, liked girls in their late teens or early twenties. Second, she was technically still a married woman, and fooling with other men's wives went against the young Wayne's code. Another factor was also a saving grace; when shooting was over they went on to other films. "And then the fact that she didn't have one kiss, not one clinch with him throughout *Kid Galahad* gave her no memories of what she was potentially missing," Jerry Asher laughed.

Edward G. Robinson was, in his way, as fretful as Davis over his continued assignment to slam-bang action and crime fare. His protest was to result in a costume treatment later on. A distinguished product of the American Academy of Dramatic Arts and the Theatre Guild, Robinson had won his spurs on Broadway and in the Theatre Guild's classical repertory, but found himself in a rut of his own when the smash success of *Little Caesar* in 1930 inspired his Warner bosses to keep him in gangster and action fare.

I recall that when I interviewed him many years later, I asked why his own inability to escape type-casting for so long had not rendered him more simpatico toward Davis's own struggles, and he replied instantly, and with some spirit, that he had come to Hollywood with many years of stage training and seasoning behind him while she had had a bare three years in the theater. "If she had gotten seven to ten years of theater work, like Chatterton and others had, she'd have come to films more prepared," he snapped. That was the last sentence, to my knowledge, that he was to accord posterity on the subject of Bette Davis because he died soon after.

Kid Galahad was to be the subject of no less than two unfortunate remakes. One, *The Wagons Roll at Night*, in 1941, had a circus rather than a boxing setting, with Bogart, this time as the Robinson character, Sylvia Sidney, and Eddie Albert. The other, in 1962, inappropriately cast

Elvis Presley as a singing fighter. Television retitled the 1937 picture *The Battling Bellhop* to avoid confusion with the indifferent but eventually more popular Presley version.

In the reviews, Davis got singled out occasionally, but usually found herself congratulated en masse with Robinson, Morris, and the others. *The New York Times* nailed down *Kid Galahad* aptly enough with the words: "a good little picture—lively, suspenseful, and positively echoing with the bone-bruising thud of right hooks to the jaw."

That Certain Woman, Davis's next film, was notable chiefly for her meeting and working with the brilliant English-born director-screenwriter Edmund Goulding, who would be instrumental in transforming her into one of the screen's superstars in upcoming films. She later said Goulding was one of the "true geniuses of picturemaking, one of Hollywood's greatest directors." On another occasion she said, "He was what we called a 'woman's director' and a 'star maker.' There was a certain amount of progress toward stardom for me in [*That Certain Woman*]. He concentrated on attractive shots of me—in other words, gave me the star treatment. It was the first time I had had this. I was always a member of the cast—a leading member—but not made special in the way Goulding made me special in this film. And in the last scene in chiffon, a large beautiful picture hat, and a glamorous hairdo, I looked really like a movie star."

Her opinion of *That Certain Woman* was not high. "[It] was certainly not one of my favorite scripts . . . there was a falseness to the whole project." In her autobiography she said, "[*That Certain Woman*] tasted a bit of soap and recalled Miss Chatterton's nobility that Barbara Stanwyck eventually inherited."

That Certain Woman was a remake of Gloria Swanson's *The Trespasser*, which her then-lover Joe Kennedy had produced with notable success in 1929. It won Swanson an Academy Award nomination. Goulding wrote the screenplay for the Swanson version, as he did for the Davis remake. His intentions were certainly of the best; he gambled that *Woman* would do for Davis in 1937 what *Trespasser* had done for Swanson in 1929. But times were different. By 1937 the public was sated with this kind of soap opera obviousness, and what had seemed novel and timely in 1929 came off dated and saccharine by 1937, when the vicissitudes of the Depression had made audiences more realistic and less easily carried away. Another factor that Goulding did not take into account was the novelty value of Swanson as a talkie actress; *The Trespasser* was the first movie in which this great silent star spoke for her fans, and this factor was instrumental in its box-office success.

But as Davis had indicated, Goulding was a wonderful director for her. He ranks with William Wyler as a Bette Davis director par excellence, though their styles and approaches to her were radically different. Wyler disciplined her, toned her down, made her realistic; Goulding enhanced her femininity, her capacity to move audiences and enthrall them. She needed both approaches in the years coming up, and, to her credit, took full advantage of them.

Wyler also adopted a masculine approach in his treatment of Davis. He dominated her, delighted the deep-down submissive part of her nature that life and fate had not permitted her to bring to the surface. Goulding, on the other hand, was feminine to Wyler's masculine; he sought not to dominate and direct her energies but rather to coax out of her the intrinsic womanliness with which Goulding empathized. Both directors were godsends to an artist who had struggled for years to express herself fully and completely.

Goulding had been born in England in 1891, and went on the stage at twelve, in 1903. By 1914, at age twenty-three, he was wearing the triple hats of actor, director, and playwright in the London theater. From 1914 until 1918 he saw impressive service in the British military forces, and repressed his homosexuality. He reminisced later to close friends that he had been a celibate throughout his military career, his love for other men sublimated and transformed into one-for-all, all-for-one buddyhood.

After the war, Goulding emigrated to the United States, and his cultured, tasteful, sensitive gifts were soon enlisted in the service of American films. From 1921 on he brought a number of fine dramas to the American screen, and in 1925 he joined MGM, where he won fame for *Grand Hotel* and the original version of *Anna Karenina*, titled *Love*, in 1927 with Greta Garbo and John Gilbert.

Goulding's homosexual sensibility was to foster many a starring career, including Joan Fontaine's in the exquisite *The Constant Nymph* in 1943, and his love for Tyrone Power helped transform that handsome and sensitive bisexual actor into a star, via his performances in *The Razor's Edge* and *Nightmare Alley*, the latter considered, to this day, Power's finest performance.

Though Goulding married (many said in order to have a cover for his homosexual pursuits), his love affairs with men from all walks of life and all types of careers were long the talk of Hollywood's informed, but the studio overlords and his co-workers admired and respected him, especially since he was essentially kind and affirmative. "He had more friends in Hollywood than any man I ever knew," Errol Flynn later said of him. Flynn even had an affair with him, as did, for a time, Tyrone Power, who was overwhelmed by the brilliance and artistry of the director who had coaxed from him his best performance. Goulding later initiated the affair between Power and Errol Flynn which was much discussed in Movietown, while it lasted. The lovers trysted at Goulding's handsome home.

This, then, was the man who changed the course of Bette Davis's career. True, they were not able to make a first-class start, considering the soapy artifices of *That Certain Woman*, whose weaknesses Goulding fully understood but hoped to improve via good acting and photography. The film reunited, for the first time since their youth, Henry Fonda and Davis, who had come a long way from the aloof boy and lovelorn girl they had been in the backseat of a 1924 auto. Fonda had come into films in 1935, and had made an immediate impact opposite Janet Gaynor over at Fox in *The Farmer Takes a Wife*. By 1937, when he joined Davis and Goulding on the set of *That Certain Woman*, Fonda was enjoying a steadily growing reputation as an actor of honest force and humanistic realism, though his greatest days were still a while off. In *That Certain Woman* he definitely has the weaker role, functioning, along with the skilled Ian Hunter, as one of two leading men for a film built around the female star.

The sudsy plot, redeemed in many scenes by Davis's fine acting, has her as a gangster's widow who gets involved with a weakling playboy, Fonda, whose stern and brutal tycoon father, Donald Crisp, considers her unsuitable as a potential daughter-in-law. They marry, but the father breaks them up on their honeymoon by appealing to Fonda's weak, dependent nature, and soon she is pregnant and alone. Her lawyer-employer, Hunter, is a married man who falls in love with her and helps her care for her child, whose existence she conceals from Fonda and his father. The latter finds out about the boy when Davis becomes involved in a scandal after Hunter dies in her apartment and the media sneak out photos of Davis and Hunter's wife at the bedside. Crisp tries to declare her an unfit mother and take the boy from her, but later she gives him up to Fonda and his new, invalid wife. The wife (Anita Louise) later conveniently dies, and Fonda races to southern France where a languishing Davis, in reclusive luxury on the money Hunter has left her, joyfully awaits him.

As this recital of the basic plot ingredients reflects only too blatantly, *That Certain Woman* is a grab bag of the most reprehensible romantic cliché conventions, rendered hoary via repeated use. To his credit, however, Goulding's meticulous direction and his shrewd guidance of Davis's new star persona redeem the result, to a point.

Sometimes Goulding let his enthusiasms—and romantic inspirations—carry him away. He was of the school of directors who like to get up and act out the parts, and when he felt Davis and Fonda were not "pitching the woo" in one love scene with what he felt was the required intensity, he pushed Davis aside and worked up a passionate smooching scene with Fonda that had the latter red-faced and sweating with embarrassment. Gifted with a sense of humor, even about himself, Goulding partook heartily of the ensuing laughter, most of it at his own expense. Everyone liked Goulding; even his more outrageous stunts, as George Brent later recalled, usually elicited the affectionately tolerant "oh that's just Eddie."

Davis appeared in *That Certain Woman* with the great character actor and supporting-Oscar winner (for 1941's *How Green Was My Valley*) Donald Crisp. Crisp, who also pursued a major career in finance, had been an early Griffith actor (*Broken Blossoms, Birth of a Nation*) and in the 1920s a prominent silent film director before finding his niche as a sterling character support. Years later, he rated *The Old Maid* as his favorite picture with Davis and *That Certain Woman* as the worst: "God, the poor girl had fought a losing battle in England the year before to get better pictures, and here we were with her a year later awash in soap! I felt for her, deeply."

Frank Nugent in *The New York Times* summed things up well, writing, "[She] performs valiantly as usual, giving color to a role which, in lesser hands, might have been colorless as the shadows that surround it . . . tragic heroines (Kay Francis included) are invited to move over and make room in their penitential niche for the Mary Donnell whose woes Miss Bette Davis is manfully shouldering [here]. With the hounds of fate baying at her heels, Mary's progress through the film is pretty much of a nip-and-tuck affair with Mary getting most of the nips."

Over the years, Davis has had little to say about *It's Love I'm After*, her third picture with Leslie Howard. A sparkling comedy, well scripted by the talented Casey Robinson, it had a cast that boasted Olivia De Havilland, (her first picture with Davis), the handsome Patric Knowles, Eric Blore, Spring Byington, and Bonita Granville, and while director Archie Mayo wasn't the wisest choice for this sophisticated farce, he gave a good account of himself.

Davis and Howard in this are a famous theatrical couple (modeled on the Lunts) who seem madly in love to their fans but who privately fight and reconcile endlessly. Engaged to be married, their relationship is so tempestuous it threatens to explode at any time. Complications ensue when Knowles asks Howard to disillusion his fiancée, De Havilland, who has a passionate crush on him, by behaving so boorishly as his family's houseguest that she will be cured for keeps. But his fey misconduct only attracts De Havilland all the more—especially when he boorishly flirts with her and she mistakes it for genuine courtship. All is finally straightened out when Davis appears and pretends to be Howard's wife and the mother of his children. Affronted by his "caddish deceitfulness," De Havilland rebounds into the arms of the waiting Knowles.

Aware that a third appearance with Howard spelled prestige, Davis nonetheless felt that her role had a secondary feel, that De Havilland's role had more color—and got more footage—and that Howard hogged the best comedy scenes. Recent viewings of the film do tend to confirm her feeling that she was lost in a crowd, in more ways than one. She was also irritated by the fact that Howard was billed over her. Despite Hal Wallis's earnest protestations that the film was a refreshing "change of pace" for her, that she was in "glamorous" company, that the Robinson screenplay was sparkling and witty, and that the production had all the "gloss-feel" of an MGM or Paramount project, she was not convinced.

Even the inclusion of an early scene in which she and Howard play the potion scene from *Romeo and Juliet* did not impress her, especially as it was done comedy-style with the passionate protestations undercut by hissing antagonisms—some of them comic—between the principals. Reminded that only a short year before, Howard had played this scene seriously with Norma Shearer over at MGM in the elaborate production of *Romeo and Juliet*, Davis huffed: "Norma got the best of it—she got him serious, and in full acting fettle—I got him when he was only clowning the scene! Must I always accept second best?"

The arguments between Davis, Warner, and Hal Wallis over the billing continued after shooting was over. Of her four 1937 pictures she had had top billing in two—*Marked Woman* and *That Certain Woman*—and now was playing second fiddle to Howard, as she had to Eddie Robinson in *Kid Galahad*. She didn't like it one bit, and didn't let them forget it.

"It isn't the billing—it's the picture, the quality of the picture, Bette," Jack Warner kept insisting at one session. Rising to go, she lashed back, "The picture falls short—for me—on both counts!"

Even she was surprised by some of the good reviews the picture got, and which Wallis hastened to show her. "So?" she sneered. "There's more mention of Howard and De Havilland and even Eric Blore than there is of me!"

After calling *It's Love I'm After* "a rippling farce, brightly written and deftly directed," Frank Nugent in *The New York Times* went on to cite the "agreeable change for Mr. Howard and Miss Davis. It fares extremely well at their hands." Still, a dissatisfied Davis found the review cold comfort.

11

Bette O'Hara?

THE REASONS WHY Bette Davis didn't get to play Scarlett O'Hara in *Gone With the Wind* remain complicated to this day. Everyone has his or her own story, including Davis.

In the spring of 1936 Jack Warner told her to be "a good girl" and make *God's Country and the Woman* for him, in return for which he would give her a crack at what he called "a great new book" he had optioned. Davis was unimpressed, snorted, "I bet it's a pip!" and stormed off for London and her lawsuit. The irony in this was that Jack, at long last, was holding out to her a role and a picture that would have been perfect for her, had she only stopped long enough to investigate further. There was, it is true, a solid rationale for her attitude at that moment. But because Jack had sent her so many false alarms about future roles, Davis reasoned that he was hoodwinking her again with another tantalizing chimera—just to enlist her immediate cooperation with the project in hand.

While she was in London, up to her ears in legal difficulties, *Gone With the Wind* had been published to great acclaim, and Jack Warner, in an attack of bad judgment, had sold the option rights to David O.

Selznick. Several considerations may have motivated him—Davis's scorn for it (even though she had not read it and knew nothing about it) and his own feeling that *GWTW* production costs would overstrain the Warner budget, given its length and complexity.

By 1937, Selznick was conducting a worldwide search for the right performer to play Rhett Butler, the soldier of fortune with a sexual magnetism and self-assurance women fear but take to like catnip; and Scarlett O'Hara, the willful southern beauty all men desire. Perverse, ambitious, and a born survivor, Scarlett resists Rhett's love for her until near the end—only to lose it—for a time; tomorrow, in her famous words, being another day.

By mid-1937, Davis had read the novel several times and was vividly aware of all the hoopla Selznick had generated about the search for the "absolutely right" Scarlett and Rhett. She was primed for another chance and determined to get it. Jack Warner knew how badly she wanted Scarlett, and at first, to punish her for all the hell she had put him through in London the year before, told her that no loanouts was one of the conditions she had agreed to. David O. Selznick thought Davis a possibility, but he wondered: Could he get her, and what would Jack Warner's terms be if he did?

Jack came up with a proposition: He would lend Davis for Scarlett if David would accept Errol Flynn as Rhett. Jack reasoned that if he had to lend, why not get two major stars back instead of just one—his shrewd showman's instinct told him *GWTW* would be a star-enhancing blockbuster for all concerned. Davis led all fan polls and thousands during 1937 had written in proclaiming the Fiery Filly from the Burbank lot the Perfect Fiery Filly of *GWTW*. But David had his reservations, and so did George Cukor, the man who, at that time, it appeared, would direct. Yes, she had the temperament, the iron-strong character, the survivalist toughness, the passionate tenacity required to pursue the gentle southern aristocrat, Ashley Wilkes, who would spend the entire picture rebuffing her. No one, indeed, was more equipped temperamentally and creatively than Davis to be arch-unrequited lover, survivor, mover and shaker in rebuilding the commerce of the shattered postwar South. Yes, they agreed, she had it all—except for one element. Did she have the ravishing beauty, the kinetic sex appeal to keep masterful, strong-minded, tough realist Rhett Butler chasing her for ten-odd years? On that matter, there was reason to entertain doubt.

Word of this one reservation got back to Davis at Warners. She was the first to admit she was striking rather than beautiful, but she maintained, in several impassioned calls to Selznick, that she could compensate for that with passion, with fire, with sheer personality force. And, as she later demonstrated in other pictures of her great period, careful camera work and clever makeup could give her an illusion of beauty. Selznick was won over, but George Cukor's verdict was late in coming in.

Davis maintained for years that Cukor had a bias against her; he still saw her as the drab little wren he had known in Rochester a decade before. This argument scarcely holds water, however, as Cukor, a brilliant man who missed nothing, had noted her outstanding performances of the past few years. Davis was wrong about Cukor, who agreed with Selznick that she could make personality seem like "nine tenths of it" and that *this* Scarlett could be no kitten but a tigress-in-the-making who had to telegraph her personality right off the bat, in reel one.

Meanwhile, to keep the publicity mills grinding and the suspense at fever pitch, Selznick kept throwing out leads, hints, and even publicity releases attesting to the fact that he was considering many other actresses. There was Miriam Hopkins, an authentic southerner, even to the state where *GWTW* was set. Born in Bainbridge, Georgia, she would have the accent down pat. But Miriam would be thirty-six or so when they finally got around to shooting—a bit long in the tooth for a character who was to age from sixteen to twenty-eight. Fiery, yes; bitchy, most certainly; a strong character, undoubtedly, but just too old. Hopkins fought for the role. Had she not done the first color epic, *Becky Sharp*, in 1935, and would *GWTW* not be in color? Had she not demonstrated that she could dominate a cinematic transcription of a great novel, so was she not a proven quantity? Again the verdict came in: too old. Jack and George couched it slightly more tactfully when they told her; "mature" was the adjective employed. But this didn't prevent the Bainbridge Bitch from smashing furniture and pulling down drapes in the hotel suite where she had tensely awaited the decision.

Then there was Margaret Sullavan, also a southerner, in this case from Virginia. In 1935 she and Randolph Scott had co-starred for Paramount in *So Red the Rose* from the Stark Young novel, which had a plot and Civil War–period ambience similar to *GWTW*'s. Scott, too, was under consideration for the role of the courtly, elusive Ashley Wilkes— the role Leslie Howard later got. Maggie wanted the role, but, as it turned out, she married Leland Hayward and proceeded to have two children in a year and a half, which left her at the time looking somewhat worn and pudgy.

Katharine Hepburn, a favorite of Cukor's, was in the running for a while, but she was not beautiful in the way Scarlett would have to be, and her angular, New England aura did not fit into *GWTW*'s ambience, as Cukor finally conceded. Tallulah Bankhead also got a shot at it, but again, as in the case of Hopkins, she looked, at thirty-five, too old and worn. Alabama-born, she could have gotten the accent right, but that was not enough to carry the day for her. Then things got ridiculous, with Joan Crawford stating she would like a crack at it (Selznick and Cukor groaned and sent her a tactful no). Susan Hayward, only eighteen at the time, was tested, but found too immature. And on and on it went, with Selznick's suspenseful "search" reaping maximum publicity, to his continued delight.

Norma Shearer was next in the running. The great MGM star would prove, with *Marie Antoinette*, that she could dominate a lengthy period picture, complete with lavish costumes and settings. Selznick seriously considered a deal with MGM by which he would borrow her and Clark Gable as a Scarlett-Rhett package. Shearer was beautiful, authoritative, emotionally compelling—but she had two strikes against her. Born in 1900, she, too, would have seemed somewhat mature at thirty-seven for Scarlett. When her fans got wind of her flirtation with the role, they wrote in so many letters to MGM and Selznick to the effect that their idol was "too ladylike," "too nice a person" to play bitchy, sexy, vixenish Scarlett that Miss Shearer gracefully withdrew.

Meanwhile Clark Gable was leading all these polls for Rhett hands down, a mile ahead of such competitors as Fredric March (at forty too old and not sexy and insolent enough for Rhett), Ronald Colman (too long in the tooth at forty-five and too civilized and British), Warner Baxter (again, too old and insufficiently forceful). Gary Cooper was considered, but again the chemistry and personality qualities didn't seem quite right.

Which brought David and George back to Errol Flynn again—as one half of the package with Davis, courtesy of Jack Warner.

In his heart of hearts, Jack knew that Errol, handsome, rakish, and charming, and sexy as he could be, lacked the "X" factor for Rhett. But he was thinking of how *GWTW* would send the money-making Errol back to Warners an even bigger moolah-producer. It was Davis who did not want Flynn as Rhett. She told Jack Warner that Errol might be dashing and charming enough in schlock adventure like *Captain Blood* and *Charge of the Light Brigade*, but a commanding, dominating figure like Rhett called for a man, not a boy, and to her that was what Flynn was: a charming, flirtatious, sexy, cute boy. What she didn't tell Jack was that she had had a yen for Errol since he had first shown up in late 1934. Charismatic, sexy, winning, yes, but treacherous, untrustworthy, and a teasing tormentor of women, that was Davis's personal evaluation of Flynn. She had seen what he did to other women—he wouldn't wind *her* around his little finger.

The result was that Davis flatly refused to do Scarlett if Flynn did Rhett. It is hard to believe, after all these years, that she would have given up a role practically written for her just because of Flynn. She later said several times over the years that his inevitably inept, light-weight performance would have pulled down the quality of her own performance—but would it have? The future would reveal that in the two pictures Jack Warner (with his sense of consummate, if crudely implemented, irony) was to cast her in opposite Flynn, she pulled him up rather than the reverse—so why didn't it occur to her in 1937 that she could have done this for Flynn with *GWTW?*

Possibly she was not sure, in 1937, that she could carry two people through one picture. *Jezebel*, though imminent, was still in the future. She had not yet ascended to major clout with critics and public and full self-awareness of her powers. Or possibly, she was falling in love even then with Flynn, (who, like herself, was married), and didn't want the emotional overkill or strain or whatever she imagined the risk would entail.

And then there was Gable, who was practically set for Rhett, under a loanout deal from MGM. Davis's feelings toward him were likewise ambivalent. She knew he was totally right for Rhett, but she still held against him a statement he had made in 1935—that his co-star Claudette Colbert was a far better loanout choice for *It Happened One Night* than Davis would have been. "Claudette has the comedy timing, the expertise," he had told Frank Capra "Davis is too heavy, too intense; let her stick to drama; she's no comedienne. And she isn't sexy enough to get an audience imagining I would chase her around the country on a bus, as I do in the picture." Davis had also heard that Gable had reservations about her as Scarlett. "Would Rhett Butler knock himself out for the likes of her?" he laughed to Cukor and Selznick. "Rhett Butler—a man who could command the most beautiful women around to do his bidding?"

George Cukor, who loved fights, saw to it that Gable's opinion got back to Davis, with predictable results. The King had hit a sore spot—her alleged lack of beauty. Hadn't she been putting the less-talented "beauties" in their place for six years in Hollywood? she screamed. Just who did that big-eared ape think he was?

In her counterattack, Davis didn't stop with the legendary ears. A defiant Gable had refused to pin them back, but they still made him self-

conscious. She also made fun of his teeth. He had had them fixed early
in his MGM career, but under the caps they had rotted clear out of his
mouth, so he had the leavings extracted, and since 1931 had sported
dentures, top and bottom. Sometimes one or the other slipped, and his
speech took on an odd slurry-slurpy quality, which some of his women
fans even found sexy. If Franchot Tone had sucked off his consonants
and jerked off his vowels, Gable was now doing the same in his own
style.

The ears, the teeth. Davis continued to gather ammunition against
MGM's top romantic heartthrob, the idol of millions of women. Davis
picked up more information from Carole Lombard, later Gable's wife. It
seemed that Gable had a form of mild phimosis which he refused to
correct—his cock, like his ears, he held sacrosanct. The phimosis rendered the foreskin of his uncircumcised cock so painful when he pulled
it back that he left it alone most of the time. Inevitably smegma odor
accumulated unduly. Lombard, noted for her scatological vulgarisms and
flippant obscenities, had even blithely informed a press conference that
Gable was not only uncircumcised but that his bedmanship left something to be desired—premature ejaculation being implied. Also, as Carole told Ruth Waterbury, "Pappy's pee-pee isn't all that big, whether up
or down!"

Since Davis did not feel any particular sexual attraction to Gable, it
was consequently all the easier for her to use her accumulated arsenal of
retaliatory weapons against a man who, she believed, had shunned,
downgraded, and dismissed her qualifications for the role she wanted
above all others.

She proceeded to give Ruth Waterbury of *Photoplay* and Katherine
Albert and others variations of the same on-set interview, with Gable as
its subject. Since her remarks were unprintable for family or even general publications, they weren't put down in cold black print. They were
widely circulated among the Cinemaland Cognoscenti, however. After
pointing out that she had no regrets about missing out on Gable as a co-
star, she spit out, "I can't stand a man who has fake store teeth and
doesn't keep his uncircumcised cock clean under the foreskin," adding, "I
hear he shoots too soon and messes himself all the time. Great Lover?
Great Fake!" Word of this, as Adela Rogers St. Johns and Ruth Waterbury both told me, got back to Gable, and as Adela put it, "Clark didn't
find Bette any laughing matter after that!" But, as it turned out, Gable
escaped the worst. George Cukor could have told Davis that his being
fired from *Gone With the Wind* came about not only because Gable felt he
was favoring the female stars, but because Cukor knew that Gable had

given his famous uncircumcised cock to gay wolf William Haines back in the 1920s when Haines was a star and Gable a bit player, in an effort to get Haines's backing in his upward climb. Accordingly, it made him nervous to work with Cukor, especially when Cukor lapsed into calling him "dear" and "honey" on the set.

According to Jerry Asher, one hilarious story, very likely true if one knew George, had the scorned director sending Gable a birthday present in 1939, which contained a cake of Lifebuoy soap and a small bottle of Listerine. The accompanying note, according to Jerry, read: "Clark dear—the soap is to clean out the cheese beneath your foreskin and the Listerine is to take away the smell." Neither George nor anyone else has, it appears, gone on record as to how the voraciously oral Billy Haines coped without Listerine or Lifebuoy. Some secrets remain sacred in Hollywood to the end.

Through the years, Davis continued to rave and storm in interviews and on talk shows and in private and not-so-private conversations about having "missed out on Scarlett—the role of my life!"

In her autobiography she wrote: "I only argue with their eventual choice [for Scarlett] because it was not I. Nor do I detract one whit from Miss [Vivien] Leigh's beautiful performance when I say that I still wish I had gotten my hands on it!"

But, after a fashion, Bette Davis was to have the last word—and the last laugh—after all. Her next film, *Jezebel*, from the Owen Davis play, gave her not only an equally strong southern vixen role, but won her the 1938 Academy Award—which was announced smack in the middle of the shooting of *Gone With the Wind* in early 1939.

An elated Davis was to say later: "Julie Marsden, the Jezebel in question, was a blood sister of Scarlett's. Willful, perverse and proud, she was every inch the southern belle. She had the same cast-iron fragility, the same resourcefulness, the same rebellion. Julie was the best part I'd had since Mildred."

12

Jezebel, Oscar II, and Wyler

*J*EZEBEL WAS THE PICTURE that transformed Davis's life and career—
and she almost didn't get to do it. It seems Miriam Hopkins, who
had done it as a Broadway play in the 1933–1934 season, was hell-bent
on doing the film version as well, and moreover she owned joint rights
to it with producer Guthrie McClintic. She was jealous of Davis and still
fighting the initial lesbian attraction she had felt toward her a decade
before in Rochester. The idea of Davis taking over Julie Marsden, the
strong-minded southern belle who learns humility and self-sacrifice the
hard way, filled her with fury.

Davis wanted *Jezebel.* And Warners, spurred on by her, tricked
Miriam into surrendering the rights by promising that Julie's stage originator would be the first to be considered for the role if and when they
ever got around to producing it. Grabbing the $12,000 offered, Miriam
failed to read the fine print of the agreement—it didn't state absolutely
that she would get the role, just promised her top consideration.
Miriam's oversight in this regard, given her tenacity and determination
where matters of crucial importance to her were concerned, remains a

mystery. Since she was forever on her financial uppers, she may have needed the money up front. But the role was now Davis's.

Davis meanwhile worked her way through *Kid Galahad* and *That Certain Woman* more cheerfully than usual, knowing, as she did, that Hal Wallis and his associate producer, Henry Blanke, had writers Clement Ripley and Abem Finkel hard at work on the script. When Ripley's and Finkel's best inspirations fell short of the solid, tight, flowing script Wallis wanted, he brought in Walter Huston's writer son, John, who helped shape up the continuity and sharpened the characterizations. With *It's Love I'm After* finally out of the way, Davis looked forward to her first costume picture—and her first chance at a quality production—the kind she had always longed for and had never gotten in all her six years at Warners.

Jezebel is the story of Julie Marsden, a willful New Orleans belle, circa 1852, the orphaned heiress to a fortune who demands her way in all matters great and small. In love with stuffy, play-by-the-rules Preston Dillard (Henry Fonda), a rising bank executive, she keeps him maddeningly off balance with her assorted perversities and rebellious quirks. Genuinely in love with Pres, but unable to control her egoistic ways, Julie alienates him fatally when she wears a red dress to the all-white Olympus ball. Taking his stern revenge, Pres forces her to dance alone with him to a waltz from which the others withdraw in shock and disgust. Then he deserts her.

Playing second fiddle to Pres is Buck Cantrell (George Brent) who is also in love with Julie but is more realistic and tolerant about her foibles. Devastated by Pres's withdrawal, Julie holes up in her country place and later gets her hopes up when he returns—but with a new wife, a northerner (Margaret Lindsay). Enraged and frustrated, willful and perverse once again, Julie precipitates a duel between Buck and Pres's brother (Richard Cromwell) in which Buck is killed, defending what he thinks is Julie's honor. Julie's protective and loving Aunt Belle (Fay Bainter), saddened and disillusioned, tells Julie she is "thinking of a woman called Jezebel, who did evil in the sight of God." Later Pres falls ill of yellow fever, and Julie rushes to nurse him in New Orleans. When he is being taken off to a quarantine island, Julie persuades Amy, his wife, to let her go with him, because without her toughness and tenacity he will surely die. Julie Marsden becomes "clean" again and redeems herself.

Jezebel has many scenes that only Davis could play.

In her first scene she is wearing a riding outfit, shocking the conventional ladies gathered at her house for tea. Flamboyant and defiant, she establishes Julie's character straight off. She enters the fateful ball brazen and arrogant, flouncing her red dress in everyone's face. But then as Pres humiliates her by forcing her to dance, she falters, descends into frantic mortification—a wonderfully delineated midscene character shift. In the scene where she learns Pres will be returning, her depression is superseded dramatically by hopeful energy as she orders the servants to prepare the house.

In scenes where she is playing the men against each other, and brazenly making advances to Pres, she is electric, willful, perverse, determined. She presides over a dinner party, ironic, detached, embittered. And in the final scene, as she selflessly concedes to Amy that Pres loves his wife, not her, but that she is the only one who can save his life on the quarantine island, her passionate feelings are controlled and indeed transcended by the self-immolation that is new to her—and strangely exalting and fulfilling. Later she rides through the streets in a cart with Pres's head in her lap, a look of sacrificial determination and ecstasy on her mobile features—as bravura an ending as any star could wish.

For the rest of her life Davis credited William Wyler with helping her achieve the performance she gave. At first, when told that he would direct the picture on loan from Sam Goldwyn, she was annoyed, remembering the little man at Universal years before who had said, "These dames who think they can show their chests to get jobs." She asked for an interview with Wyler and confronted him with his ancient malfeasance. He told her he didn't even remember the occasion, that six years had gone by and he—and she—were different people, seasoned Hollywood veterans now. His honest, direct rejoinder won Davis over, and soon they were working together on the set of *Jezebel*.

William Wyler was like no man Bette Davis had ever met. He was born in Germany in 1902, where he had initially been interested in studying the violin. A distant relative of Carl Laemmle's, he had traded on the connection to come to America in 1922, at age twenty, and functioned in a variety of studio jobs—publicity writer, casting director, grip, and assistant director—but was dismissed scornfully for some years as "just another of Carl Laemmle's parasitical relatives." Since Laemmle's nepotism was a running joke in the industry, this was a cruel designation indeed.

Presently, however, Wyler demonstrated that he was very much his own man. He became a production assistant on the epic *Ben-Hur* at MGM, soon began turning out two-reel Westerns, and then in the early thirties graduated to directing dramas. After working successfully with John Barrymore in *Counsellor at Law* (1933) and with Margaret Sullavan (for a while his wife) in *The Good Fairy* (1935), Wyler truly came into his own creatively with the acclaimed *These Three* and *Dodsworth* (1936) in which his painstaking, meticulous method enhanced enormously the already considerable talents of actresses Miriam Hopkins in the first and Ruth Chatterton and Walter Huston in the second.

The latter pictures were produced by Samuel Goldwyn, who, despite his often ridiculed malapropisms, was a man of shrewd and instinctive taste. Wyler had just completed Goldwyn's *Dead End* when he was assigned *Jezebel* over at Warners in 1937.

At first he and Davis fought bitterly on the set. As usual, she was testing her director's mettle and his manhood and spirit as well; she found Willie Wyler a fine brand of tempered steel, and her initial aggravation at being checkmated and outmaneuvered gave way gradually to an overwhelming respect for his methods. She realized that at last she had found the director who could discipline the best out of her. He told her to stop moving her head, to stop wiggling her pelvis. He convinced her to scale down her mannerisms and refine her acting ploys without sacrificing any of the energy that gave her performances distinction. He made her do a scene over and over until he got the distillation of her emotion that gave the scene its impact. He drilled her and rehearsed her and drove her mad—and kept her coming back for more.

Here, she realized, was the one man to whom she could surrender her entire being. All her life she had been haunted by a longing for a man whose mastery over her could fulfill her completely as a woman. But then there was the masculine side of her personality—her willfulness, egoism, and strength. She fought her new mentor tooth and nail but finally rejoiced in the submission he forced upon her. Soon she was in love with Willie Wyler.

Certainly, the object of her deepest, most profoundly felt passion was no pretty boy. Small, chunky, homely, Wyler was so unprepossessing in appearance that actor Charles Bickford later called him "the Golem"—a singularly unattractive creature in one of the German horror films of the 1920s. Yet under all the ugliness and blunt incivility and brutal directness and unbending will was a supreme ladies' man. In the final analysis, Wyler possessed in full measure the supermasculinity that many of the pretty boys and lotharios could only assume on the surface. Wyler had *substance*. He made her husband look whiny and adolescent by comparison. She and Wyler became lovers. Guilty and frightened, knowing that a full knowledge of her flagrant infidelity could drive the high-strung Ham to violence or worse, Davis was in a state of constant schizoid tension during the filming of *Jezebel*—the ecstasy of her passionate affair with Wyler was countered by the ominous specter of Ham's possible retaliation if he discovered the liaison.

The guilty lovers did not spend all their time in bed. Over coffee, over dinners she hastily prepared, Wyler went over and over her role with her; again and again he drilled and rehearsed her. She recalled that he was the first to point out that she had not fully matured as an actress because, up to 1937 her playing had been too intense, too overwrought, too undisciplined, that often she had "made too much of a good thing." He gave her insights into her creative processes that gave her a new perspective on her talent.

There was one fly in the ointment, however. Wyler's painstaking measures, his endless confabs with photographer Ernie Haller, his determination to showcase his now willing and pliable Galatea to maximum effect was taking the picture way over schedule and over budget. While pleased with the few rushes Wyler made available to him, Jack Warner began to find the protracted shooting schedule outrageous. He threatened to fire Wyler and bring in William Dieterle. Davis went to Warner personally. She told him that Wyler was ekeing out, slowly but surely, protractedly but purposefully, a great picture that would give her a whole new persona. "All that is all very well, Bette," Jack Warner told her, "but what good is it if the costs mount to the point where we lose money?"

Davis saved Wyler's and her neck at that point. She offered to work until midnight to finish the film—midnight every single night. She offered Warner everything but the kitchen sink to keep Willie Wyler on the picture. Warner grudgingly acceded, and Wyler stayed. But the problems proliferated.

Henry Fonda presented quite a few of them. His wife, Frances, was having a baby, and he wanted to be back in New York by Christmas week. The picture had been dragging on for months. Now Fonda wanted his role shot out of continuity so that he could get the hell out and back home. Davis's already frayed nerves were exacerbated by having to defer to Fonda's schedule.

Then the willfulness and perversity and odd attacks of self-destructiveness, so characteristic of Davis at times, caused her to make a stupid error. Worn ragged by Wyler's perfectionist demands, she quarreled with him. She convinced herself that since he had had her physically, he was beginning to take her for granted. So she decided that a nice, juicy, hell-raising flirtation with Fonda was in order. She sensed that Fonda, sexually frustrated, three thousand miles away from his expectant wife, was responding to this new Bette Davis. She and Hank had never made it in the long-ago as kids, and nothing had happened during *That Certain Woman* either, but now Bette Davis was coming into her own, and she felt that Fonda was a prize long overdue her.

As curious as the next man, unaware that part of Davis's strategy was to keep masterful Wyler from taking her for granted, Fonda fell into a brief affair with his dynamic, irresistible co-star. They began meeting secretly. She stood Wyler up after hours. It delighted her to see the Golem suffer and sweat it out on the set each day, guessing as he did that she and Fonda had gone wild at the latter's apartment the night before. Soon she was playing each man against the other, and it amused her that Wyler was particularly tough with Fonda during the famed ballroom scene, making him dance and dance and dance to his tune until Fonda was ready to drop from exhaustion. Wyler began muttering about "these pretty boys who can't take the heat."

Meanwhile, the fateful December deadline on which Fonda had insisted was fast approaching. One night, forced to go home to Ham, who had just arrived in town after one of his out-of-town engagements, Davis got a long-distance call from New York. It was Frances Brokaw Fonda. Frances, who had a society background but knew how to roll with the bitches when necessary, let her have it. "I know what you're doing with my husband, you bitch," she screamed at Davis. "I'm going to have his baby shortly, and you're keeping him out there for your own sluttish purposes. Now finish up that shooting and let him go, or, baby or no baby, I'll take the first train and scratch your bug-eyes out!"

Davis had always had a good instinct for worthy feminine rivals. Something about Frances's intense hysteria and unbridled anger told her to pull in her horns (her instincts turned out to be right, for Frances Brokaw Fonda was to prove unstable in the years to come; the mother of Jane and Peter wound up committing suicide and became the subject of lurid headlines).

After a few days off the picture with one of her standard psychosomatic ailments, Davis went back to the set, was putty in Wyler's hands for the remainder of her scenes in *Jezebel*, kept the puzzled Hank Fonda at arm's length, and got him back to New York and Frances in time for Jane Fonda's birth on December 21, 1937. Many years later, when Jane Fonda was on hand for an award given Bette, Bette reminded her of how her imminent birth had wreaked havoc on the *Jezebel* set (she didn't reveal the other aspects) and Jane, amused yet somehow uneasy, tendered her an apology for arriving so unpropitiously.

All the fuss and feathers resulted, however, in the finest picture

Davis had done to date. It won her the 1938 Academy Award (to Miriam Hopkins's manic anger and despair—she threw chairs around her New York drawing room the morning after the award was announced). Fay Bainter, so touching and eloquent as the understanding Aunt Belle, won the Best Supporting award. Davis regretted heartily that William Wyler did not get a directorial Oscar (he made up for it later with signal honors from the Academy) and gave him full credit for the film and everything and anything in it, including her own performance.

In her autobiography, Davis said of Wyler: "The thrill of winning my second Oscar was only lessened by the Academy's failure to give the directorial award to Willie. He made my performance. He made the script. *Jezebel* is a fine picture. It was all Wyler. I had known all the horrors of no direction and bad direction. I now knew what a great director was and what he could mean to an actress. I will always be grateful to him for his toughness and his genius."

Davis received the 1938 award in company with her old friend and former co-star Spencer Tracy, who won his own second Oscar for his performance as Father Flanagan, the priest who rescued homeless boys, in *Boys Town*. It was a proud moment for them both. "We've come a long way since 20,000 *Years in Sing Sing*, Bette," he smiled. "A long way indeed, Spence," she smiled back. "And it wasn't just luck. A hell of a lot of hard work brought us here tonight."

As for Ruth Waterbury's injunctions of 1936 concerning the proper attire for a star on Academy Award night, Davis made sure that there would be no screams from the formidable Ruth that time around. "[She] must have been delighted," Davis later reported, "because I was dressed to the nines for the Academy dinner this time—a brown net dress with aigrettes at the neckline. It was the beginning of the halcyon years. The proof of the pudding would be the scripts to follow—and the directors. I was never surer of myself professionally than at this moment."

Of Fay Bainter she said "[Her] contribution to the film and to my performance was enormous. It just wouldn't have been the same picture without her." Many years later, Fay Bainter said, "No woman ever worked harder for that award than Bette. Wyler was tough, and he made her sweat it out, but the results, as she admitted, were worth it. And how was she to work with? I've heard all those stories about what a termagant she was supposed to be, but she never showed me her claws once—in fact she was a perfect lamb."

Her involvement with Wyler, while it developed through two more admirably executed films, turned to ashes by 1939. They were to part, then reconcile, then part again for keeps. After what he had gone through in his short but tempestuous marriage with wildcat Maggie Sullavan, Wyler had no taste for new variations of feminine neurosis. He was excited and stimulated by Davis, by the enormous creativity he had found in her and had brilliantly tempered and released, by the spitfire unpredictability and passionate sexuality, but he knew he couldn't live with it, day by day, with any semblance of peace or even rationality. Between the two strong natures there was constant friction. On a movie set their disparate inner fiercenesses blended admirably; off set they proved destructive—in permanent terms. Writer Ruth Waterbury later said of the Wyler-Davis duo:

"That was the contradiction in her. She longed for a strong man to take charge of her life but when she found him, she couldn't scale down her own temperament in order to be comfortable with him." Still, Wyler and Davis almost married once she was free of Ham. One day, after a fight, she found a note from him in a sealed envelope on her hall table. Angry and perverse-spirited, she left it there for days. When she did open it, she learned that he had given her a twenty-four-hour ultimatum: Marry him or forget about it for keeps. Since she hadn't answered, he went off with actress Margaret Tallichet to the nearest available marriage mart. At first she regretted the lost chance; later, more philosophical, she realized it wouldn't have lasted any longer than his marriage had to that other fiery filly, Margaret Sullavan.

After his experiences with her during the *Jezebel* shooting, Henry Fonda, too, had written her off. In the years to come, he would refuse, several times, to act with her again. Her penchant for playing men against each other, her willfulness and perversity that had made her so perfect for Julie Marsden, her fierce temper and manipulative bitchery were elements he needed like a hole in the head. He immersed himself in marriages—several more of them—and fatherhood—and all Bette Davis was accorded was a friendly nod and a polite word when their paths crossed. Not that she cared. She had seen all the rabbits in Fonda's hat, and to her he was past tense.

Davis did not like the advertising campaign on *Jezebel*—featuring her in a low-cut gown and the screamy legend, "She's meanest when she's lovin' most!" "I *hate* that line—it cheapens the picture's theme," she told George Brent—who had been an also-ran among Davis's men in *Jezebel*, and, as usual, couldn't have cared less. "Yes, Bette," the imperturbable George shot back, "but ain't it the truth about you!" For this he was rewarded with a drink in his face, but he only laughed. Shortly she was laughing with him.

The critics, as expected, went wild over Davis and *Jezebel*. Typical of the response to the film was that of *Film Weekly*, which enthused:

"The performance is Bette's decisive victory. She handles it as though, having brought her enemies to their knees, she has decided to be merciful. By the pure power of imaginative acting she gives a performance as vivid and inspiring as any star display of personality—and on an infinitely deeper layer of truth. Never before has Bette so triumphantly proved her point that a woman's face can be appealing and moving even when not preserved in peach-like perfection. Never again can her claim be denied that it is possible on the screen for acting to transmute personality."

Davis now stood on an eminence that filled her with deep satisfaction. Had she but known it, there were even greater eminences to come. But for the moment, she rested content. Not so Miriam Hopkins. They could hear her teeth grinding clear out to Pacific Palisades.

Davis always keenly regretted that Harlow Morrell Davis did not live to see her reach the uppermost heights. He died in January 1938 in Boston while she was still struggling to finish *Jezebel*. This, above all, was a picture she had particularly wanted him to see, given its superior workmanship and the disciplined performance Wyler had forced out of her.

To the day of his death he was snippy, distant, patronizing. When her father had visited California some years before, he had condescendingly dismissed her husband Ham as "a nice young boy." His references to the early films she had done were usually along the lines of "fleeting, careless exercises." *Of Human Bondage* he had thought "hysterical" and "excessive," her Oscar-winning *Dangerous* "trashy, tasteless." He implied—strongly—his Yankee, starchy disapproval of her "garish blon-dined hair," her "low-cut, unladylike clothing." When a friend at his Boston office had shown him a June 1936 copy of *Photoplay*, with Davis highlighted in a "glamour pose," he had tossed it into the wastebasket. "A *stage* career would have been more dignified," he tartly observed.

Work was all that mattered to him—work and his papers and his legal reading. An efficient and well-paid patent attorney, he withdrew from social life, nursed his asthma, and finally collapsed and expired suddenly, at fifty-four, of a heart attack. Davis bitterly recalled him as loving but one creature in the world, his vicious, sharp-toothed Chow dog, whom he enjoyed setting on people to shake them up, frighten them. That was Harlow Morrell Davis's idea of uproarious fun.

Davis threw herself into the remaining shots of *Jezebel*, feeling little regret that the schedule prevented her attending the Boston funeral.

Later, with the picture done, she cried for days—cried for the father who might have been, the father whose coldness and rejection of her had affected her so strongly.

With *Jezebel* completed in late January 1938, Davis had her doctor tell Warners that she desperately needed a couple of months off. She had lost weight and her nerves were ragged. While on temporary medical leave in February and March, she was sent several scripts she thought were inferior and refused to do. One, about a successful theater star who rejoins her unwanted husband when he leaves prison, was called *Comet Over Broadway*. Davis considered it soapy and superficial— just the kind of thing she had been trying to escape. It was later assigned to Kay Francis, whose fortunes were slipping at Warners because she refused to negotiate her expensive contract downward. Kay eked out the remainder of her term at Warners in B pictures. (Years later, Davis visited Francis when she was doing stock in New England; they reminisced about the Warner days. "I wanted the money," Francis told her. "I wanted the career," Davis rejoined.)

Davis's judgment concerning *Comet Over Broadway* was vindicated when the picture, upon release, got poorly reviewed. The other script she thumbed down was a trivial affair called *Garden of the Moon*. A capsule review of this programmer read as follows: "Nightclub owner Pat O'Brien and bandleader John Payne have a running feud. There is time out for numerous Busby Berkeley numbers." Margaret Lindsay played O'Brien's girlfriend, the part Davis refused. "It would have been nice to work with my friend Pat again, but not in that!" Davis said. *Garden of the Moon* also got forgettable reviews.

For refusing to work in *Comet* and *Garden*, Davis was put on suspension. Her father's death had shaken her, and her affair with Wyler was at a temporary impasse. She was exhausted and depressed, and Ham was increasingly getting on her nerves with his lack of career drive and his passive torpors that alternated with anger. Suspensions were hard in those days. They meant loss of salary—one of the studio's ploys for keeping actors in line. Davis showed determination and courage in holding out for something better, however, and eventually, it came.

After four months of idleness, Davis began shooting *The Sisters* in June 1938. The film was in production through August. Anyone who doubts that Bette Davis could be as warm, supportive, womanly, tender, and sympathetic as any actress one would want to name should see her in this. *Life* magazine's October 31, 1938, review says it as well as any, commenting as it does on the "extraordinary grace, sensitivity and distinction" of her performance.

Davis later said, "I was delighted with this part because it was a change of pace. My ambition always has been . . . for variety in the kinds of parts I play. My career has proved this. I was always challenged by a new type of person to play."

In this she is one of three sisters in a Montana town—the eldest and most stable. Henry Travers and Beulah Bondi are her parents. Jane Bryan (in her second film with Davis) is one of her two sisters, who marries a conventional hometown boy, Dick Foran. The other sister, Anita Louise, is a pretty, flighty type who marries a middle-aged man, Alan Hale, for his money, finally finding happiness with a younger man after Hale's death. Davis falls in love with and marries an improvident, emotionally immature San Francisco newspaperman, Errol Flynn, who is a disappointed novelist, and in a burst of self-hate Flynn ships out for the Orient, leaving wife Davis pregnant. After refusing the romantic attentions of businessman Ian Hunter, Davis returns home, helps her sisters in their various adjustments, and is later followed by a repentant Flynn, whom she still loves, and whom she readily forgives.

These are the bare bones of the plot, but Davis's fine, vital acting, supported by a bevy of fine character actors (Travers, Bondi, Donald Crisp, Lee Patrick, Laura Hope Crews) turns *The Sisters* into a major dramatic event.

Davis later maintained that she was glad to be in an Errol Flynn picture (he made twice as much money as she did, $4500 to her $2250 per week) because she knew that he had the box-office clout to put the picture over big. Handsome and extremely popular with the public, Flynn had excelled as adventurers and heroic figures, and his *Robin Hood* film was one of the big grossers of 1938. In private life, married since 1935 to actress Lili Damita, he was unstable, hard-drinking, and a compulsive womanizer and rake in all areas, later adding drug abuse to his repertoire.

A mountebank adventurer from his youth in Australia, he had been expelled from many schools, had sailed the seas in his own boat, had sampled many vocations, including gold prospecting, and after a few bit parts had fallen into stardom, with a minimum of effort on his part, in the 1935 *Captain Blood*, in which he was a derring-do adventurer who set women's hearts fluttering from coast to coast.

Sexually insatiable, Flynn had also gone the bisexual route, and it was rumored that several young men he had seduced had killed themselves over him after his subsequent desertion. Many young women, too, were in his thrall, but the woman he reportedly loved most deeply, his co-star Olivia De Havilland, eluded his advances to the end.

Determined to prove his attractiveness to any and all comers, men and women, Flynn tried to proposition Davis as soon as shooting began, but was summarily turned down. A number of Davis's friends and career associates have maintained that Davis was physically and romantically attracted to Flynn, always had been, but knew his reputation as arch trifler and heartless narcissist and had heard her fill of the stories of suicides, broken hearts, and assorted agonizings that this *beau homme sans merci* had left in his wake. Pride in her was stronger than passion, and just as she had refused to surrender to Wyler's stronger personality, so she refused now to surrender to Flynn's rakish but compelling charm. But the stories that she was secretly in love with Flynn date from their work together in *The Sisters*. And she acted her scenes with him with a compelling sincerity and sensitivity that surprised everyone viewing the rushes, including martinet director Anatole Litvak, then the husband of temperamental Miriam Hopkins.

Litvak, a Russian refugee whose biggest hit had been *Mayerling*, the 1937 French film starring Charles Boyer and Danielle Darrieux as the ill-fated Archduke Rudolf (the Austrian crown prince) and Marie Vetsera of the famed 1889 suicide pact, was a sadist on the set, demanding thorough rehearsals and endless setups and retakes. His fussy efforts, however, were not always justified, as Wyler's were, and did not always achieve the same felicitous results. He drove Davis mercilessly through the two- to three-minute San Francisco earthquake scene, which turned out to be Warners' somewhat pallid and inadequate answer to MGM's more tumultuous and detailed rendition of the same famed 1906 event in *San Francisco*. By refusing to allow her a double in the sequence where the walls and ceilings of her apartment collapse around her, he endangered her life. Her usual stubborn pride and perfectionism drove Davis to stick out the dangerous shots, and when she played them with steely determination, Litvak's sadistic glee turned gradually to reluctant, then ever more fervent admiration, which before the year was out would lead to an intense, albeit brief, liaison between them.

Flynn, who knew women, knew instinctively that Davis was attracted to him, but was refusing to be his game-of-hearts patsy. His initial cavalier approach to his scenes with her, in which the devilish, amiably contemptuous gleam in his eye was readily apparent, gave way as shooting progressed to a serious, concentrated performance as he found himself playing back to her the intensity of her banked passion for him. "He was certainly one of the great male beauties of his time," Davis later said, "but a terrible actor—not because he didn't have the basic talent, but because he was lazy, self-indulgent, refused to take his work seriously, and tended to throw away his lines and scenes."

Davis resented that Flynn was more popular with the 1938 fans than she was and making twice as much money. In her view, she worked hard and carefully while he sauntered through his stints, and to her that was unjust. In addition, Warners had exacerbated her attitude by at first telling her the billing would be "Errol Flynn in *The Sisters*, with Bette Davis" because her contract up to that point did not provide for her above-title billing in all instances.

She managed to dissipate one nagging humiliation by standing firm on the matter of billing, so that eventually it read "Errol Flynn and Bette Davis in *The Sisters*." Considering that Warners knew *Jezebel* to be an enormous hit as of the summer of 1938 (the box-office returns since March were already in), it is amazing that they did not have the foresight to co-star her above the title without her urging.

In a 1964 interview with me, Hal Wallis, the film's producer, explained Warners' anger with Davis's high-handed refusals of other scripts and her walkouts, absences, endless temper tantrums, and myriad demands. "That was their way of punishing her; for instance, keeping her on tenterhooks about the co-starring billing with Flynn. In my opinion, their business instincts would have dictated their giving her that top billing before the picture went out to theaters, but meanwhile they enjoyed giving her a dose of her own medicine."

Hal Wallis recalled Jack Warner saying of the attendant fuss over the billing, "That dame needs to be brought up short now and then; she's an egomaniac and I like to get her sweating at times." Wallis also opined that Davis's friendship with Warner's diplomatic and kindly wife, Ann, who more than once went to bat for her, was as responsible for Davis's getting the last word with Warner as her own feisty determination was. But Wallis added, "To be fair, all Ann's protective friendship and help would have gone for nothing if Davis hadn't had the requisite fighter instincts on her own, and boy, did she have enough of that to spare!"

Davis's essential femininity and nurturing womanly spirit shone through *The Sisters*. It is one of her most affirmative parts, and she is admirably convincing not only in the love scenes with Flynn but in her efforts to help her sisters and in her gentleness with her unrequited lover and boss, Ian Hunter.

Jack Warner, so often cast as Davis's arch antagonist, is credited with a most perceptive remark about Davis. "She always acts better when she's in love, and though she'd have killed me for saying so, I felt she was in love with Flynn all through the shooting, but she'd be damned if she let him or anyone else know it!"

But revival prints of *The Sisters* demonstrate Davis's feeling for Flynn only too clearly. All through the picture he is the naughty boy, childish, contrary, and unreliable; he deserts her when she is pregnant to ship out to the Orient; his self-hatred over his career failures triumphs over his need for her character's maternal nurturing and wifely devotion. With self-loathing, he leaves her to what he thinks is a better fate with a stronger, more prosperous man, but eventually he returns to seek again her loving ministrations and enduring concern.

In actual life that is how Davis saw Flynn, and that is yet another reason why their scenes together are ultimately convincing. She loves him, yes, but has no illusions about him. She surrenders to his boyish parasitism in the film, and even takes him back after his desertion—but offscreen she secretly loved but overtly scorned Flynn, derided and avoided him. She sensed the vulnerability he had aroused in her, and she resisted it with all her might. But the fact she was drawn to him as an onscreen vis-à-vis is attested to by her willingness to co-star with him again the next year.

Davis garnered some fine reviews for this, her second period film, (set in 1904–1909). *Variety* called her "scintillating" and the film "superbly made." "Her acting is a joy," said *The Hollywood Reporter*. And by mid-1938 there was to be yet another man in her life—an eccentric original if ever there was one!

Howard Hughes was thirty-two years old in 1938, the year he and Davis met. He had won fame as the producer of the aviation film *Hell's Angels*, which launched Jean Harlow into stardom in 1930. At age eighteen, in 1924, he had inherited the Hughes Tool Company, founded by his father, which manufactured oil drilling equipment. Canny, shrewd, and workaholic, young Hughes guided the firm to even greater successes, and at twenty, in 1926, he went into the film business, his first production being *Everybody's Acting*, a silent directed and acted by Marshall Neilan. Mickey Neilan, who knew Hughes well and worked with him for some years, described him to me in 1952: "Howard was a shy, strange fellow. He lived deep within himself. He was handsome but he didn't think he was. He saw himself as a great gangling buffoon of a guy. He was very self-conscious of his height. I tried to assure him that height was the most attractive thing a man could have, that women liked literally to 'look up' at a swain, the higher the better, but he told me I was just trying to make him feel better about himself. With the girls I introduced him to, he was very insecure. He would be courtly and considerate, but he wouldn't follow through. I took him to a madame one time when he was about twenty-one; I figured a good hoedown in a classy whorehouse with gals who knew how to make a guy happy would loosen him up. But he told me prostitutes disgusted him, that he was afraid of catching diseases from them. Howard was not a happy guy. He didn't know how to enjoy life. We had a falling out at the time of *Hell's Angels*. He'd promised to let me direct it, then reneged after I had done a lot of work on it. We drifted apart after that."

Mickey failed to mention that his chronic alcoholism, which was interfering with his work increasingly, had been the real cause of his dismissal from the *Hell's Angels* project. He did other films after that but his career went steadily downhill. His wife, Blanche Sweet, who divorced him because of his drinking (and also because Mickey had spent her fortune extravagantly), told me that she always liked Howard. He was, she said, "so very serious for so young a man. He didn't like drinkers and irresponsibility, and he was very cautious and shrewd about hanging on to and building further the fortune his dad left him." Blanche always felt that Howard "was nursing some secret sorrow, some hidden wound." She remembered him at parties, age twenty-two or so, staring with intent melancholy into the distance, oblivious to all around him. Howard's uncle, the writer Rupert Hughes, called him "the family oddball."

In the early 1930s, Howard Hughes's interest in Hollywood cooled for a time, and he put all his energies into aviation. Soon he was winning fame and respect as an aircraft designer and builder, and as a pilot and developer of advanced airplanes. He broke speed records in 1935 flying a plane of his own design, and then broke his own record two years later.

The year Bette Davis and Howard Hughes met, he had won the Congressional Medal of Honor for flying around the world in a little over ninety hours. In a few years he would return to films, making the sexy and sensational *The Outlaw*, more famous for the young Jane Russell's cleavage than for its cinematic qualities. His life was a combination of aircraft designing and testing, erratic film production (he would delay his film releases for years, as in the case of *The Outlaw*), and temperamental, eccentric reclusiveness that was not, as his detractors claimed, a male Garbo act but rather the result of his increasing hearing problems, his "loner" idiosyncrasies, and something else—a homosexual side that filled him with guilt and self-hatred. His tastes ran to handsome young airline mechanics and garagemen whom he often took flying—disappearing with them to one of his many retreats for weeks on end. Unable to be faithful to any one young man for long, he would tire of them, pay them off, sometimes set them up in businesses—then move on, satisfying his endless curiosity with other males in an endlessly compulsive manner that only added to his guilt, confusion, and self-rage as the years went on. He managed to avoid overt scandals or blackmail, and was well liked and respected by the men who had been his lovers.

He was also given to "front" involvements with women, and had acquired a reputation as a Hollywood lothario, being seen with its most beautiful women. He married several times, most notably to lovely actress Jean Peters, but his sexual orientation continued along confused bisexual lines, with frequent forays into homosexual involvements.

Hughes also suffered from impotence, especially with women. In forcing himself to live up to what was essentially a false macho image, he tended toward premature ejaculation and was a chronic masturbator, often finding it necessary to masturbate his way through sex with his female partner. If women were halfway attractive and found him attractive, he was always able to gratify them, after a fashion, though narcissism drove him on rather than heterosexual desire for the woman as sex object.

The only actress up to 1938 with whom he felt at all at ease was Katharine Hepburn, a woman with an unorthodox, individualistic approach to life. They were a heavily publicized off-and-on "romance," though many of her friends felt that she functioned solely as good pal, good listener, fellow eccentric with whom he could identify comfortably. Hepburn liked to wear pants, too, which appealed to Howard. It fit his buddy image of her.

The occasion for his meeting with Davis in the summer of 1938 was an event for the Tailwaggers, an organization for stray, lost, and abandoned canines, for which dog-lover Davis did much fund-raising. Invited to be guest of honor at a Beverly Hills Hotel Tailwaggers event, he found himself sitting next to Davis at dinner, and a spark was ignited. Davis later described Hughes as "extremely attractive and one of the wealthiest men in the West—or East for that matter . . . his influence and cooperation were a great help to me, but this interest proved to be directed toward me rather than the cause at hand."

Hughes and Hepburn were temporarily apart, mainly for geographical reasons, and he was lonely and rootless—and manless—when he met Davis. She, too, was in a state of emotional flux. Her marriage to Ham Nelson was winding down, more with a whimper than a bang. Her loneliness had driven her into an intense but short-lived affair with Anatole Litvak. Litvak was married to Miriam Hopkins, but it was an on-again, off-again thing, temporarily off, so he and Davis comforted each other for a time. "Loneliness—pure and simple loneliness—drove me into *that*," Davis later said.

By the time Hopkins was on to the liaison, it had already subsided, but she did not forgive Davis for seeing her husband. The two were divorced the next year, and Hopkins felt that Davis had trifled with Litvak just to spite her. In fact, Davis had gotten the impression that Hopkins's marriage was winding down and headed for the exit door, just as hers was.

So the Litvak thing was over conclusively (though he and Davis would work together again), and now she was bedding down with Hughes at her Coldwater Canyon home. "She was like a greedy little girl at a party-table who just had to sample other women's cupcakes," Hopkins later screamed. "First she wanted my husband and then she wanted Hepburn's boyfriend, and her own husband was all but forgotten!"

What Miriam did *not* noise abroad was her own increasing lesbian attraction to Bette. The fact that instead of reciprocating, Davis trifled with her *husband* galled her. Shortly she would share close quarters with the woman she found so disturbing, but only in a professional context. Even on that level, the fireworks were to be Fourth of July-ish.

Meanwhile Davis was discovering that the tall young man she had naked in bed with her was more complex sexually than she had imagined. She had taken on more than she had bargained for. During their intimate sessions he confessed to her his homosexual leanings, and when his premature ejaculations and impotence became too pronounced, he begged her to perform fellatio and swear and use scatological language so that he could close his eyes and imagine she was a man! Since there was a lot of the masculine and the aggressive in Davis, and since she could summon the language of the locker room regularly and didn't hesitate to use it, she managed to give the harried Howard his illusion—and his properly timed and executed orgasm. Then, after providing him with his homosexual fantasy, the feminine would come out in her, as per his request, and she would make hot milk for him and hold him in her arms until he fell asleep.

Matters progressed along these lines for some months—until Ham Nelson returned from the East, where he had been for months. Aware of the Hughes involvement, Ham sneaked in one day while Davis and Hughes were out taking a drive, and thoroughly bugged the living room and bedroom. After obtaining his evidence, the disillusioned and harried Ham, feeling despised and unwanted, knowing that his marriage was coming to an end, broke in on Hughes and Davis while they were in bed and proceeded to blackmail Hughes for a cool $70,000. At first Hughes, humiliated and frightened by the personal revelations in the recordings, planned to hire the 1938 equivalent of a hit man to kill Ham, until Ham informed him that he had notified the police to pick up Hughes if he were found dead. Hughes forked over the $70,000.

The result of all this was that the coup de grace was applied once and for all to the six-year marriage between Bette Davis and Harmon Oscar Nelson, and it also spelled kaput for her liaison with Hughes, who counted himself lucky not to be named corespondent in the divorce complaint filed by Ham against Bette. Anatole Litvak also heaved a sigh of relief.

Davis brooded over the $70,000 that Ham had cost Hughes, and borrowed the money and paid him back. Hughes felt great respect for her for doing this, and their friendship survived, even though he high-tailed it back to good pal Katharine Hepburn in short order.

In a deposition filed in December 1938, Ham Nelson charged, among other things, that Davis had been casually indifferent to him, had refused to perform her wifely duties (read "in bed"), curtly ignored the friends he brought to the house, and gave her mother, sister, and other relatives, professional associates, and even the servants, the time she should have given him, her husband. He then went into detail about how she told him she didn't want him around anymore and had spoken to him "bitingly, caustically, cruelly." All this and much more along the same lines.

The property was divided down the middle, including the bank accounts, as per the California equal-property law. Ham then left quickly for New York, where he had been offered a position with Young and Rubicam, the advertising agency. Despite the lurid and hurtful parting, they remained long-distance friends—of a sort.

As a lifeguard in her teens—already taking charge (*Collection of Douglas Whitney*)

—◇—

Even as a baby those eyes popped. (*Collection of Douglas Whitney*)

—◇—

With sister Bobby—the two had a lifelong love-hate relationship. (*Collection of Douglas Whitney*)

—◇—

Carl Laemmle, Jr.'s, "little brown wren,"
1931 (*Collection of Douglas Whitney*)

———◇———

The drab sister comforted by Emma Dunn
in *Bad Sister* (her first movie), 1931 (*Collection of Douglas Whitney*)

———◇———

Blond and glamorous, Warner-style, 1932 (*Collection of Douglas Whitney*)

—◇—

George Arliss, with Davis in *The Man Who Played God*, 1932, accelerated her rise. (*Collection of Douglas Whitney*)

———◇———

Davis fell in love with George Brent, center, in *The Rich Are Always With Us*, 1932, but star Ruth Chatterton, left, made him her hubby for a while. (*Collection of Douglas Whitney*)

———◇———

Caught between sexy Gene Raymond and creepy Monroe Owsley in *Ex Lady*, 1933 *(Collection of Douglas Whitney)*

Getting together with William Powell her one and only time in *Fashions of 1934 (Collection of Douglas Whitney)*

TOP: Leslie Howard was afraid she'd steal his picture, *Of Human Bondage,* 1934. She did. *(Collection of Doug McClelland)*

BOTTOM: Unprettily realistic in *Of Human Bondage* (that's Reginald Denny propping her up), she made her starring mark. *(Collection of Douglas Whitney)*

—◇—

She shot off so many sparks in *Dangerous*, 1935 (here with Pierre Watkin), that she copped her first Oscar. *(Collection of Douglas Whitney)*

—◇—

With first husband, Harmon "Ham" Nelson, at the 1936 Oscar event. Ham was humiliated by her achieving greater success than he. *(Collection of Douglas Whitney)*

—◇—

The famous ball scene in the naughty red gown in *Jezebel*, 1938, with a disgusted Henry Fonda and white-garbed debutantes looking on *(Collection of Douglas Whitney)*

—◇—

She patronized the young actor she called "Little Ronnie" Reagan, here with her and Geraldine Fitzgerald in the famed *Dark Victory*, 1939. *(Collection of Douglas Whitney)*

—◇—

Donald Crisp, Brian Aherne, Davis, and Gilbert Roland sense trouble in *Juarez*, 1939. *(Collection of Douglas Whitney)*

—◇—

Davis put down Errol Flynn as an actor, but they did very well together in *The Private Lives of Elizabeth and Essex*, 1939. Years later she admitted he was a better actor than she had thought. *(Collection of Douglas Whitney)*

The sparks flew between Davis and Miriam Hopkins in the famous wedding-gown scene in *The Old Maid*, 1939. *(Collection of Douglas Whitney)*

LEFT: Divorced from Ham, she tried a second marriage to Arthur Farnsworth in 1940, with sister Bobby in attendance. He left her a widow in 1943. (*Collection of Douglas Whitney*)

BELOW: Rumors about a relationship between her and co-star Mary Astor in *The Great Lie*, 1941, were unfounded, or so she insisted. Here she shares a cigarette with Astor. (*Collection of Douglas Whitney*)

—◊—

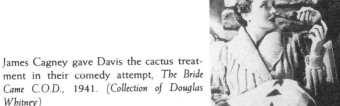

James Cagney gave Davis the cactus treatment in their comedy attempt, *The Bride Came C.O.D.*, 1941. (*Collection of Douglas Whitney*)

—◊—

Up the staircase—and up to no good—in *The Little Foxes,* 1941 *(Collection of Douglas Whitney)*

TOP: In her superhit *Now, Voyager*, 1942, she tells John Loder, right, that "the world is a small place, but Boston is a large one." That's Ilka Chase in the middle. (*Collection of Douglas Whitney*)

BOTTOM: The famous flashback scene from *Now, Voyager* with handsome Charles Drake (*Collection of Lawrence J. Quirk*)

—◊—

Don't be fooled by this cuddly shot on the set of *Old Acquaintance*, 1943. Davis and Hopkins hated each other. *(Collection of Douglas Whitney)*

Giving them Bette Davis–style hell at a bond-raising event during World War II. Her blunt but effective calls for patriotism got results. *(Collection of Douglas Whitney)*

Made up as a woman famed for her beauty in *Mr. Skeffington*, 1944 *(Collection of Douglas Whitney)*

—◇—

With Jack Carson and Jane Wyman in *Hollywood Canteen*, 1944. Davis had an eye for the cuter servicemen, who reciprocated her interest. *(Collection of Douglas Whitney)*

—◇—

During one of her brief truces with Jack Warner in 1945 (*Collection of Douglas Whitney*)

———◊———

13

1939: The Great Year

NEW YEAR 1939 brought Davis to an all-time high professionally, with four films that were moneymakers as well as artistic successes. Privately, the year began miserably for her.

Davis had begun *Dark Victory* (released in early 1939) with physical health depleted and emotional health prime fodder for a psychiatrist. Ham was divorcing her after blackmailing her lover, Hughes. Anatole Litvak, whose continental charm and vivacity and love of partying had revived her spirits, was put off by the grim, drab offscreen life Davis led, as she pinched pennies to cope with Ruthie's extravagance and Bobby's sanitarium fees. Her frequent spells of depression, her psychosomatic complaints, her fear of press exposure, all combined to affect her nervous system disastrously.

Her woes were compounded when Miriam Hopkins, as always seething with jealousy over Davis's preemption of *Jezebel*, phoned to remind her that *she* was still the wife of Litvak. After threatening to name Davis corespondent in her divorce suit against Litvak, Miriam, still ridden with lesbian hankerings for Davis, was calmed down by Jack Warner, who signed her to a new contract. She had been off the screen for over a year, and was raring to go. Jack promised her top vehicles, possibly a co-starrer with Davis herself. "If I get into a picture with that husband stealer," Hopkins raged, "I'll show her what acting is *really* about!"

Apprised of Miriam's carryings-on, Warner and Wallis only laughed. "If the Hopkins dame wants to work up an ongoing bitch feud," Jack Warner chortled, "let her! It'll make for great publicity if we pair them in a picture" (a prophesy that was to come true). Meanwhile Hopkins prepared to divorce the only-too-willing Litvak without naming Davis, as per Jack Warner's express plea. Litvak later said, "Marriage with Miriam—an affair with Bette—I've had enough of crazy, temperamental women to last me for years—now I need a rest, no?" All agreed he did.

Davis was so overwrought and ill during the first weeks of *Dark Victory*'s schedule that she begged Wallis to release her from the assignment, claiming she was sick and wasn't doing justice to the role. But Wallis had just seen the first rushes. "For God's sake, *stay* sick, Bette," he said, "you're doing just wonderfully!"

Jack Warner, Hal Wallis, and Hal's associate producer, David Lewis, then held separate conferences with director Edmund Goulding and leading man George Brent. "It's up to you guys to keep the lady on an even keel," Hal announced. "Eddie, you work with her—and George, you *play* with her—and it'll keep her excited, amused, and on the ball!" As it turned out, neither man needed much persuasion; they had gotten the same idea on their own.

This was Edmund Goulding's second picture with Davis. She had responded well to him in *That Certain Woman*. Now, convinced that her role of the dying heiress Judith Traherne would bring her to the fullness of her talent and the public acclaim she deserved, he worked with her carefully, soothingly, planing down her overacting, keeping her gestures and expressions controlled and on target. Goulding worked differently from Wyler; as in *That Certain Woman*, his approach was gentle, feminine, empathetic. Instead of threatening and yelling and dominating as Wyler had done, he worked along with her, giving her the benefit of his intuition, making her laugh gleefully at his clowning—acting out with the leading man the impassioned lovemaking he expected from Davis. By subtle indirection and gentle persuasion he got from Davis a performance every bit as disciplined as Wyler could have.

The two directors' styles varied widely. One persuaded and guided gently; the other drove and disciplined—both worked equally well. Even so, Davis took careful handling. If driven too far too fast she went haywire and stomped off to her dressing room. But finally, as the weeks went on, she began to lose herself in, Judith Traherne, and from then to the end of shooting, work for her was a delight, and an escape from her overwhelming personal concerns.

George Brent did his bit offscreen as well as on, complementing Goulding's professional mentoring admirably: During the shooting of *Dark Victory*, Davis won a prize she had sought for six years—a reciprocation of Brent's feelings. The deep sympathy and concern that he came to feel for Davis as he watched her offscreen disasters accumulating broadened into a love for her that eventually became sexual as well. The two became lovers. The soothing romantic and physical addresses from a man she had always felt deeply for, acted out night after night at his place or at her Coldwater Canyon house, gave Davis an emotional release and sensual catharsis that added greatly to her portrayal of Judith. Delighted that she was in such good hands, Jack Warner and Hal Wallis swore columnists Louella and Hedda to secrecy regarding the romance, since the moral turpitude clauses that Hays and the Legion of Decency might have insisted be implemented could have ruined Davis's career.

Dark Victory had originally been a Tallulah Bankhead 1934 Broadway play that ran only fifty-one performances before closing. But David O. Selznick had been intrigued with it and bought it for $50,000. He toyed with pairing Garbo and Fredric March in it, along with other potential stellar combinations, but eventually lost interest, and in January 1938 sold it to Warners, which at first considered it as a vehicle for Kay Francis. But Kay was superstitious about playing a dying woman, and while it lay around, Davis found a script, fell in love with it, and pressed hard for it.

Jack Warner had his doubts—who wants to see a picture about a woman who kicks off? was his reaction. "When you're just getting into high gear, why go morbid on your audience?" he told Bette. "All those women out there want to see you making love, fulfilling their dreams vicariously. Then you conk out on them!"

But Davis kept pushing at Warner, repeating over and over that at that point she needed something she could put her heart into, and finally Jack, admitting the role itself was juicy, even if the theme made his flesh crawl, told her, "Okay, go hang yourself!" and the role was hers.

Casey Robinson, the premier purveyor of strong feminine-interest scripts, really whipped up a pièce de résistance with *Dark Victory*. The plot is so well known after over fifty years that only a cursory recapitulation is necessary.

Judith Traherne, a fun-loving heiress on Long Island, likes horses, booze, and men in roughly that order. Sybaritic and shallow, she rides the nags, swills the champagne, romances the guys, and butterflies about her social circle with a hollow indifference tinged with a great love of life and adventure. Then she learns that she is dying of a brain tumor. After the operation she thinks she is cured, falls in love with the doctor, George Brent, who doesn't have the heart to tell her she has less than a year to live. But when she learns by accident of her death sentence, she turns brittle and bitchy and cynically peregrinative, then valiantly faces reality, marries the doctor, who has fallen in love with her, and gives up her former life to assist him in Vermont with his research. When death comes, she faces it without self-pity. Her affliction and eventual death redeem her spiritually and bring out her best aspects, and hers is truly at the end a victory over the dark.

Dark Victory, thanks to the script, Goulding's guidance, and Davis's concentrated application of her finest artistic instincts, emerges as a triumphant cinematic blending of acting, direction, scripting, and Ernest Haller's photography. And Max Steiner comes through with one of his more poignant scores, aptly underlining, as only he can, Davis's emotional crises and eventual catharsis.

The picture is full of fine scenes, such as Davis's panic when she realizes the seriousness of her condition: She stares into a mirror, pushing back her chair, rubbing her forehead. When her maid asks her if she had a headache, she barks, "Yes, a BIG headache! Bring me some champagne!" And her expression gets across tellingly the wonderfully mobile synthesis of horror, panic, and emotional devastation that she is feeling at that moment. When she realizes Brent has lied to her about her condition after the first operation, she is scornful, contemptuous ("Having fun with the knives lately, doctor?"), and heartbrokenly disillusioned by what she thinks is only his pity when she thought he had given her his love.

Then, when she and Brent have reconciled and marry, she is bright, breezy, and busy on the farm in Vermont where, via mutual agreement, they've promised not to think of the Great Inevitable due in months or weeks. Just prior to Brent's departure for a medical conference in New York (he is researching her disease), Davis is planting hyacinths in the garden with best friend Geraldine Fitzgerald (wonderfully sympathetic and sensitive in her role of Greek Chorus–style supportive) when she recognizes the sudden dimming of her vision that she has been told will precede her demise by only a few hours. The sun is bright but she thinks it has darkened, then recognizes its warmth on her hands. Sudden horror and dismay are shortly superseded by a valiant determination that Brent shall not see her die; she sends him away, mounts the stairs, and to a Max Steiner alarum of angel sounds, prays, then lies on the bed—to a gradual blurring of the film's focus.

Throughout, Davis's technique is sure and strong. She lives the role of Judith Traherne; into it she puts all the struggles and disappointments of her career, all the turmoil and horror of her romantic and marital disasters, all the newfound resignation of a spirit that has transcended adversity through wisdom and serenity. Judith Traherne is one of the screen's most vivid creations, as filtered through the intense yet disciplined creative gifts of one of the screen's prime artists.

The reception of *Dark Victory* by the critics when it debuted in April 1939 was ecstatic. James Shelley Hamilton in the *National Board of Review Magazine* (predecessor to *Films in Review*) wrote, "It's [Davis's] show, her special kind of show, all the way through . . . she has never before seemed to be so entirely inside a part, with every mannerism and physical aspect of her suited to its expression." Frank Nugent in *The New York Times* wrote: "Miss Davis is superb. More than that, she is enchanted and enchanting."

Nugent added, "Admittedly it is a great role—rangy, full-bodied, designed for a virtuosa, almost sure to invite the faint damning of 'tour de force.' But that must not detract from the elequence, the tenderness, the heart-breaking sincerity with which she has played it. We do not belittle an actress to remark upon her great opportunity; what matters is that she made the most of it."

Dark Victory was to bring Davis yet another Academy Award nomination. She lost, however, the Best Actress of 1939 accolade to the actress who had won the role she so desperately wanted, Vivien Leigh for Scarlett O'Hara.

Dark Victory was also the one and only time she ever appeared with Ronald Reagan. He is strictly a supporting actor in this; a weak, alcoholic, aimless but amiable young playboy who listens to her troubles with a light, wryly expressed sympathy, and who even indicates a possible romantic interest, which in the script is given short shrift. Then twenty-eight years old, Ronald Reagan was at the height of his youthful all-American boy romantic appeal. Two years an also-ran Warner player after a period as a Midwestern sports announcer, he had a fine voice, looked great in swimming trunks, and was much sought after by various ladies, most of them actresses.

His role as written by Casey Robinson was merely that of a thoughtless, aimless, mildly likable young playboy pal of Judith Traherne's, but Edmund Goulding, with his eye ever out for the manly charms of attractive studs, took a shine to Reagan, then developed a crush on him which clean-cut, solidly heterosexual Reagan uneasily sensed. Things got tense when Goulding began coaching Reagan in his role, insisting that he put effete, gay nuances into his playing. Reagan resisted, and Goulding, bitchy and feeling subtly rejected, proceeded to give him a hard time. Reagan later recalled that Goulding made him feel inadequate and shallow and ungifted. Certainly the feyness that Goulding wanted Reagan to convey in his character was wrong for Reagan the man and Reagan the actor. His instincts told him that the role should be interpreted as just another spoiled-brat bubblehead on the way to alcoholism, with too much money and leisure for his own good. In the end, his will prevailed over Goulding's—for which Goulding never forgave him.

George Brent was to continue his protective, forbearing attitude toward Davis for a full year; he became her shoulder to cry on and to lean on, and she was always grateful to him for it. Being only human, Brent found himself often impatient with his lover's high-strung, over-emphatic, and superelectric approach to matters great and small—and eventually even he tired of the emotional wear and tear. As Davis had herself admitted, she wanted desperately to marry Brent, but he didn't think marriage would work for them—a wise attitude, in retrospect. In the period after the Chatterton divorce, Brent—except for two very short excursions to the altar with Ann Sheridan and Constance Worth—was on a sabbatical from marriage, doubted it suited his temperament. This devastated Davis, and compounded her feelings of rejection.

Geraldine Fitzgerald has spoken well of Bette Davis right down to the present. In 1971 she told Rex Reed: "I've remained friends with Bette to this day. Not long ago, we both had to travel to Hollywood for something, so we decided to catch a train and catch up. In every town, crowds would gather around her, and she was like a queen, pretending not to notice all the excitement. She'd keep talking, asking about every man on the old Warners lot, and I'd say, 'Well, I never had an affair with him,' and she'd roar, 'Well, you're the only one who didn't, Fitzie!'"

In 1976 Geraldine was telling Doug McClelland: "We used to sit around the [*Dark Victory*] set and say, 'I don't think it's going to work.' A great deal was improvised, and Eddie Goulding rewrote much of it. In fact, he invented my whole character—she was not in the original stage play—as a kind of Greek chorus for the dying heroine so she wouldn't have to be complaining a lot."

Recalling to Doug the famous scene when she and Davis are gardening and Davis feels blindness coming on and realizes her death is imminent, Geraldine said Goulding asked her, "What would you do in real life under those circumstances?" She replied that she had always been frightened of death and that in all likelihood she'd probably run away. "He told me to do just that; I did, and it's in the movie." (Geraldine's memory of this was somewhat inaccurate, for Davis's character insists that she leave in order to spare her the drama of a heartrending parting.)

Geraldine insisted to Doug McClelland that Davis was not difficult to work with—not with her, anyway. She remembered that at the close, when it came time for her to mount the stairs to die quietly and resignedly in her bedroom, she asked Eddie Goulding, to everyone's amusement, "Well, Eddie am I going to act this or is Max?" "She adored Max Steiner, whose music complemented her performances so excellently, and in this instance she was joking," she added hastily, continuing, "She always played fair with her fellow actors, never tried to turn your face away from the camera, as so many did. [Was Geraldine thinking of Miriam Hopkins at that point?] She would not have thought such behavior a moral thing to do. And she knew it would be better for the film if everyone was in there pitching."

Defending some of the roles Davis accepted circa 1976, Geraldine sharply observed: "Some people today say she takes any role—but I can tell you, although maybe I shouldn't, that she supports *armies* of people."

As late as 1987 Geraldine was defending her friend to anyone who would listen. "Her life has been a gutsy and heroic one—she's the most resilient, toughly elastic person I know. And almost eighty at that! Other people are settling back to relax long before that age—but not Bette—nor me, for that matter! Maybe I took a page from her book. She'd inspire anyone!" Between directing scenes in one of her recent plays, Geraldine told me, "*Dark Victory* will always be imprinted on my memory as one of my most sublime experiences—thanks to her. When you acted with her you were caught up into something bigger than yourself—that was Bette—larger than life—and in the best sense of that now-clichéd phrase. That's one of the secrets of her long-pervasive, widespread artistic influence!"

Casey Robinson, who wrote the screenplay for *Dark Victory,* said in 1979, forty years later: "[The film] is about two things, love and death, and I decided [when writing the film] that these two elements should be kept apart as long as possible; that when there was a scene about love, it wasn't about death; when there was a scene about death, it wasn't about love. That is on the surface. So when there was a scene about love, death was underneath it; when there was a scene about death, love was underneath it—all the time, until the very end, when one would reunite them into a sort of requiem."

In the second of her blockbuster 1939 pictures, *Juarez*, Davis was seen to maximum advantage as Carlotta, empress of Mexico and consort of the ill-fated Emperor Maximilian, the Austrian archduke who is inveigled by Napoleon III into accepting the crown by means of a rigged plebiscite in order to further Napoleon's machinations for collecting Mexican debts to France.

Paul Muni is Juarez, the intrepid Indian who is the legally elected president of Mexico and who fights the foreign intruder ruthlessly until Maximilian is defeated and executed, Davis's Carlotta, always emotionally unstable and superintense, goes to Europe to plead with the perfidious Napoleon to help her husband put down Juarez's resurgent forces, but Napoleon, intimidated by the post–Civil War United States' determination to invoke the Monroe Doctrine with force if necessary (the period of the film is 1864–1867) and determined to cut his losses in Mexico, coldly refuses her. This gives Davis the occasion for one of her most classic angry scenes, in which she denounces Napoleon before his wife and ministers, later falling into the faint that presages her gradual descent into madness. And this time around, in a harrowing scene later in the film, Davis goes mad with a colorful vengeance far surpassing her mad scene in *Bordertown*. She is wild-eyed and pitiable indeed as she insists to Metternich (Walter Kingsford) that the "evil" Napoleon is haunting her, and that "they" are out to destroy her. In this and other scenes Davis gives a colorful, compelling delineation of a woman never physically or mentally strong to begin with who summons manic energy (which eventually consumes her) in her determination to rescue the life and fortunes of a beloved husband.

Though Paul Muni and Bette Davis are co-starred (his name took precedence) in this colorful and impressive historical drama, they never meet throughout. His story, and hers and her husband's, are told contrapuntally, with clever intercutting and parallel action techniques. Some have maintained that it amounts to two separate scripts, but a careful analysis of the film indicates only too clearly that one cannot exist without the other—for both dramas are poignant explorations of character and motivation that feed upon each other, both to highlight contrasts and illuminate the tragic human motivations and drives that impel one, Juarez, to eventual victory, and the other, Maximilian, to defeat and execution.

Juarez is a rousing, colorful historical drama, beautifully directed by William Dieterle, a sensitive artist with a great feel for sweeping mate-

rial such as this. It is compellingly scored by the great Erich Wolfgang
Korngold, who masterfully blended Mexican and Austrian themes for
heartstopping results. *Juarez* is cinema at its baroque best, with all the
finest technical appurtenances that the various artisans of the screen had
learned as of 1939. Beautifully acted by the principals, touching in its
intimate scenes, deeply moving in its pageantry and intense evocation of
conflicting national ideals—monarchist versus republican—it is one of
the great masterpieces of the screen and has been unfairly downgraded
through the years by people whose political obsessiveness overshadows
their esthetic appreciation. Certainly *Juarez* celebrates the democratic
process eloquently, as in the scene where Muni's Juarez explains to the
impulsive but well-meaning young general Diaz (John Garfield) the difference between a monarchy and a republic. Muni throughout, heavily
made up to approximate the stolid Indian features of the legendary
Juarez, is magnificent, giving his role strength and solidity and iron
purpose.

In their respective autobiographies, both Davis and John Huston
have tried to blame Muni for "hogging" the picture, with Davis claiming
that he added "fifty pages to the script," and Huston, who wrote the
screenplay along with Aeneas MacKenzie and Wolfgang Reinhardt, insisting that Muni's ego impelled him to force changes in his favor, even
assigning his brother-in-law, the screenwriter Abem Finkel, to carry
them out. But the final result seems to belie this. Carlotta and Maximilian in their half and Juarez in his seem to dine quite equitably at the
banquet of fine drama, pageantry, and human poignancy that this great
picture offers. The final cut is 125 minutes, but thanks to the fine pacing
and riveting drama, it seems to fly by in half an hour.

Brian Aherne as Maximilian gives the finest performance of his career. An excellent actor who had won fame in 1931 as Robert Browning
to Katharine Cornell's Elizabeth Barrett in *The Barretts of Wimpole Street*
when he was only twenty-nine, Aherne, a veteran of the London stage
and Broadway, had made an initial splash in films as Marlene Dietrich's
sculptor-lover in the 1933 *Song of Songs*, and had followed this up with
solid leading-man stints opposite such great ladies of drama as Helen
Hayes, Joan Crawford, and Merle Oberon. His Maximilian is a most
touching piece of acting, sensitive, kind, yet conscious of his monar-
chical destiny and determined to rule justly in the interests of all his
people. He, too, is affecting when it is his turn to explain to Garfield's
Diaz the proper functions of a monarch in a just society as he conceives them

All three stars get their innings, and to compare the qualities of

Aherne's, Davis's, and Muni's delineations is to differentiate between apples, oranges, and pears. Of the three, Davis's is perhaps the most vivid characterization. Her Carlotta is intense, passionate, hysterical, poised always on the thin, sharp edge of the instability that leads eventually to catastrophic madness. She subtly suggests her eventual fate in her wild-eyed, intensely articulated pleas to Claude Rains's Napoleon, and even in her grief-stricken, self-denying speech to her husband in which, barren irrevocably, she offers to go away to give him a chance to find someone else who will give him an heir. Since he loves her intensely, he refuses the offer in a tender, deeply felt love scene. Later they adopt a boy of Mexican blood as their "crown prince," to ensure the dynasty's continuance. But all is for naught, with Napoleon's determined withdrawal from his abortive Mexican adventure leaving Maximilian and his few devoted followers and ragtag "Imperial Army" at the mercy of the ever-advancing forces of native Mexicans under the implacable Juarez.

If any fault is to be found, it is in the tacked-on ending in a cathedral, in which Muni, looking down at Aherne's executed body in a coffin, asks forgiveness. It is totally unreal and unmotivated, despite Muni's and the audience's recognition that Maximilian is a good man with the most noble of intentions.

Davis remembered the picture as her introduction to the actor she held forever after in great awe and admiration—Claude Rains. She recalled that imperial study scene in which she excoriates him for his betrayal of his treaty with her husband and shouts, "Murderer! Murderer!" Rains's Napoleon looked at her with such poisonous hatred as he scornfully refused her that she was sure he was expressing a real-life contempt for her acting efforts. Such, of course, was not the case, as Rains held Davis's abilities in the highest regard, and they derived great enjoyment from working together in three more pictures.

Claude Rains came to Hollywood in 1933, after triumphant years on the London stage and on Broadway, especially in characterizations in which he shone courtesy of the Theatre Guild. In that first role, the 1933 *Invisible Man*, he wasn't seen through most of the picture, but the bandaged figure was, nonetheless, unarguably Rains, given the matchless voice and the characteristic bravura stance. An intense, unhappy, driven man, the often-married Rains cut a wide swath in the Hollywood of the thirties and forties, giving even character roles of limited footage the force of a star appearance. Davis and Rains became great personal friends through the years. After his death, when asked by a TV talk-show host if Rains were a "happy" man, Davis made an eloquent rejoinder to the effect that no complex artist was ever happy in the ordinary sense of the word, that those who felt and thought deeply could find release only through art—or words to that effect. Certainly in her understanding of the complex gifts of the inimitable, irreplaceable Claude Rains, Davis demonstrated her understanding of the artist's psyche and esthetic.

Rains's Napoleon is the best rendition ever of that upstart nephew of the original Napoleon, who began as a revolutionist, then became president of the French Republic, and finally the head of the Second Empire. Rains makes him proud, vain, crafty, elusive, and cowardly. His scenes are relatively few but Rains makes them vivid.

There was some criticism, then and since, of John Garfield's Porfirio Diaz, the chief complaint being that Garfield's persona was too modern and New York—naturalistic for historical roles, but actually his fine acting and strong personality triumph over any anachronistic flavor. *Juarez* is full of fine actors: Montague Love, Gale Sondergaard (wonderfully sly and serpentine as the manipulative Empress Eugenie), the sterling and solid Harry Davenport as the emperor's doctor, and John Miljan, the vital Joseph Calleia, and Irving Pichel as revolutionary types.

Gilbert Roland is touching and stalwart as a loyal Mexican officer devoted to the emperor. In 1964 Roland spoke to me about *Juarez* on the set of a movie he was making. "There was a feeling of importance, of excitement to it," he said. "Even while we were shooting it, William Dieterle guided us all so expertly and with such flow and movement in the scenes that when I saw it complete, with Korngold's score and all, in a movie house, I got identically the feeling I had in the hurly-burly of acting in it." Of Davis, Roland said, "She looked so beautiful in that film, in her black wig and period costumes; people keep saying that Bette Davis was never a beauty, but at that time, and especially in that picture, she was as lovely as any woman I ever saw or could name."

Though Davis and Brian Aherne act beautifully and convincingly the deep and profoundly committed conjugal love that Maximilian and Carlotta in actual historical fact felt for one another, they got along in real life like oil and water. Both took cracks at the other in their respective autobiographies. It is obvious that they were not chemically and mentally simpatico. Davis claimed that he was haughty, self-involved, and touchy, and that when she told him he should always wear a beard (she meant it as a compliment, she maintains), he looked down at her with hatred and told her *she* should always sport a black wig.

Aherne spoke slightingly and dismissively of Davis in the several interviews I did with him in the 1960s and 1970s. "She was gifted, but she coasted on her natural talent too much," he said frostily. "It took a strong director who knew what he was about to rein her in and teach her discipline and control. She tended to overdo everything, she tore emotions to shreds. She didn't seem to appreciate the value of subtle understatement, of indirection." Since Aherne, as Davis herself always maintained, was certainly not averse to hamming it up grandiloquently when it suited him, his observations did smack of the pot calling the kettle black. Always intimidated and affronted by aggressive ladies, Aherne wound up marrying the shy, reserved (or anyway she was at that time) Joan Fontaine, who, circa 1939, was in real life much like the insecure, frightened girl she portrayed so effectively in her starring breakthrough film, *Rebecca*. (Later Fontaine evolved into a fiercely independent, combative personality, and her remarks about the masculine supremacy—inclined Aherne were not kind.)

Davis's only recorded comment about the ill-starred Aherne-Fontaine marriage was, "I don't know how she stands his uppity, supercilious ways."

It is interesting to speculate on how Davis and the redoubtable Paul Muni would have played off each other had they ever appeared in the same scene in *Juarez*. Both had come a long way since *Bordertown*. Like Davis, Muni had gone on to costume vehicles of monumental prestige such as *The Story of Louis Pasteur* (for which he won the 1936 Oscar) and *The Life of Emile Zola*. The Warners held Muni in awe by 1939, and he was "Mr. Muni" to everyone but his closest friends and his watchful, strong-minded wife. Even Hal Wallis and Jack Warner himself felt more comfortable communicating with the Great One through messages and intermediaries. John Huston, who always resented Muni's brother-in-law's interference with the *Juarez* screenplay, described him as tough in arguments, winning out not so much intellectually or logically as via sheer stubbornness. When bested in an argument, Muni simply pulled rank and threatened to quit the project, which, according to Huston, "sent everybody scurrying and conciliating to beat the band."

Still, there is no denying the monolithic strength of Muni's *Juarez*. His tendency to lose his real personality behind the makeup, mannerisms, and general mystique of the man he was portraying in *Juarez* gave him a reality, a verisimilitude, and a convincing force of character that were riveting and irresistible to audiences. In one of his most majestic scenes, Muni arrives in a town square alone in his carriage, enemy forces all around him, and a populace in thrall to his traitorous rival. He goes to the door of the palace, forces his cowardly opponent out, and harangues the crowd, winning, against all odds, their fresh allegiance and the murder of his rival. And he is very touching as he mourns the death of Abraham Lincoln while exiled in a mountain enclave surrounded by his few followers.

Juarez reflects well on everyone concerned with the making of it. Donald Crisp, who played Bazaine, the commander of the French forces in Mexico, felt that *Juarez* was one of Hollywood's most underrated pictures, and commented on its epic sweep, on its wonderful human variety and colorful ambience.

"William Dieterle," Crisp recalled, "was a really gifted director who could capture the essentials of an historical film; he blended the characters, the action, the atmosphere into a colorful, authentic overall look that reminded me of Griffith at his best." Crisp, who had worked with Griffith in the early movie days and had played General Grant in *Birth of a Nation* and the villain in *Broken Blossoms*, knew whereof he spoke. "Dieterle made you feel for the characters in *Juarez*; he kept you siding with one, then the other, it was a triumph of deeply felt empathy. He made those people come alive, even beyond what was written of them in the script. It was a privilege to work in a Dieterle picture."

James Shelley Hamilton, always a perceptive critic, wrote of *Juarez* in *The National Board of Review Magazine*, "Most of the acting is on a superlatively high level. Paul Muni as the stolid Indian and Brian Aherne as the elegant and refined Emperor are remarkably effective contrasts in appearance, manner and speech."

Of Bette Davis, Hamilton declared, "[She] subdues her strikingly individual characteristics to a portrayal of the Empress Carlotta that is not only touching but overtoned with premonitions of her eventual tragedy, and her finally flitting away into the darkness of madness is the most unforgettable moment in the picture."

14

The Old Maid *and Elizabeth:* Davis at Her Zenith

I N March 1939 Davis began work on the picture in which, in my considered opinion, she gives her all-time best performance. Her Charlotte Lovell in *The Old Maid* is a role of sweeping range with strong and colorful emotional contrasts. Moreover, as Charlotte, Davis undergoes a complete change of character, aging from twenty-three in 1861 to forty-three in 1881. Playing Charlotte gave her an opportunity to demonstrate the steady, relentless, dramatically compelling progress from vivacious, hopeful, romantic youthfulness to disillusioned, embittered, desiccated middle age. She had never before had such an opportunity.

The Old Maid was a pivotal film in Davis's career in that it showed her capable of playing strong characters of a kind never before associated with her. With few exceptions she had played contemporary young women with various love problems or melodramatic dilemmas. True, she had been evil in *Of Human Bondage,* petty and spiteful in *Jezebel,* even psychotic in *Bordertown* and *Dangerous,* but *The Old Maid* provided her with a character so different from any other she had done that it startled her audiences and her producer into recognizing that here was an actress with far greater potential than had hitherto been suspected.

The Old Maid began as a novel by Edith Wharton—a novella, actually, part of a grouping called *Old New York.* Later *The Old Maid* was published on its own, and it came to the attention of playwright Zoe Akins, who dramatized it for Broadway. As one of the outstanding plays of the 1934–1935 season, it proceeded to win the Pulitzer Prize.

Presently it was picked up by Paramount and assigned to Virginia Van Upp, who prepared a screenplay. The Paramount executives worried about its viability for cinema, however, so it was eventually sold to Warners.

Judith Anderson and Helen Mencken (one of the earlier Mrs. Humphrey Bogarts) had made great personal successes on Broadway and at first there was concern about finding two cinema actresses who could equal their ensemble chemistry and force. Hal Wallis knew from the start that only Bette Davis could plumb and dissect the complex depths of Charlotte Lovell, the young Philadelphia aristocrat who has a secret love child by a man killed in the Civil War and who, obsessed with her guilty secret, loses out on a promising marriage and gradually becomes an embittered old maid while her child grows up not knowing Charlotte is her mother. But who would play Delia Lovell Ralston, Charlotte's cousin, who rejects the man Charlotte loves and loses in favor of a Philadelphia millionaire? Later Delia, mother of two, is determined to usurp the love of the child of the dead man she also loved, and alienate her from Charlotte. Kay Francis was seriously considered for Delia, but her contractual quarrels with Warners ruled that out.

Miriam Hopkins had made a picture-to-picture deal with Warners, and it was decided by Jack Warner, Hal Wallis, and the screenwriter, Casey Robinson, that she would make an excellent foil for Davis, and vice-versa. Both were fine actresses with the bravura-style theatrical flair called for in the screenplay. Shortly Hopkins was cast for the film, creating a juxtaposition with Davis that was to be fateful—and full of fireworks.

Casey Robinson has recounted his difficulties with the screenplay. He took on the assignment when pressed by Wallis, but refused to read the Van Upp treatment, returning instead to the original play. Literate as it was, it seemed too saccharine and sugary to him to the exclusion of more complex emotions. The screenplay he prepared mixed equal portions of salt and sugar. Director Edmund Goulding picked up on this bittersweet love-hate tone.

Robinson also recalled that the many weddings in the film posed structural problems that he could only overcome with photographer Tony Gaudio's help, with clever montaging and by contrasting elements within the weddings themselves.

Bette Davis has never looked more beautiful than in some of the early sequences of *The Old Maid*, thanks to Gaudio's careful lighting and astute angling. In her wedding gown scene, when she is torn between hope for her imminent marriage and the memory of the man she loved and lost and of her illegitimate child, who is hidden in a home she has founded for orphans of the war, her face registers wild and agonized changes of mood. The picture seems to come to a dead stop, a deep stillness, in this beautiful scene. And later in the same scene, when Hopkins discovers that Davis's illegitimate daughter is the child of the man she once rejected but still loves, the scene turns diabolical; her sweet concern is superseded by jealous rage ("You and Clem! You and Clem!" she hisses at the terrified bride, who rejoinders, "You still love him!").

Terrible is Hopkins's anger as she screams, "You hypocrite—twenty children to hide one child!" and a spirited Davis answers, "Yes! *His* child! I should have known that was something you could never forgive!" Intent on evening the score, Hopkins rushes downstairs and lies to the bridegroom about Davis's health, forcing a cancellation of the wedding.

Later, in another riveting scene, Davis, finds out from the man she almost married that Hopkins lied (pleading Davis's sudden ill health rather than revealing the truth about the child) and confronts Hopkins with her hurt and hatred. "You lied to him so I wouldn't have a chance, didn't you!" Davis is left, frustrated and enraged, to face the camera, a look of terrible anger and furious bewilderment on her mobile features.

Davis and the love child go to live with Hopkins, who proceeds to steal the child's love away from Davis, who, over the next fifteen years, withers into the sour and strict old maid, "Aunt Charlotte." The girl, Tina, grows to adulthood believing she is an orphan from Davis's institution, loving the motherly Hopkins and hating the grim old maid, who disciplines herself never to show softness toward the child for fear she will reveal the truth of her maternity.

Soon Tina is in love with Lanning Halsey, a handsome young Philadelphia aristocrat (William Lundigan was most personable in the role), but his family disapproves, given her unknown parentage, and plans to send him away to forget her. Hopkins inveigles a reluctant Davis into allowing her to adopt Tina, so she will have the benefit of a good family name. On the night before the subsequent wedding, Davis almost tells Tina (winningly played by Jane Bryan, in yet another of her appearances with Davis) the truth, but finally surrenders her to Delia. "You're the mother she needs and wants tonight," Davis says. "She was never mine, perhaps because her father was never really mine either. He loved you. She loves you, too. Go to her, Delia."

Hopkins later tells Tina that Davis is an old maid because Davis had refused to give Tina up to marry a man "who would have given her everything." She asks Tina to "give the last kiss" to Aunt Charlotte just before her carriage sets off after the wedding. This she does, and in the final scene, arms linked, the mellow widow and the at-last-peaceful old maid walk arm in arm through the mansion's front door to join the other wedding guests.

The film is full of poignant scenes, such as the one in which William Lundigan and Jane Bryan are making love, communing as only the young can, while Davis listens forlornly behind the drawing room door; slowly she draws up her shawl in unconscious protection against the cold within as well as without. And when she senses the dangerous abandon of Tina's love for Lanning, she is petrified by the thought of history repeating itself and goes into the hall to confront the couple and order Lanning from the house. Davis cringes as Bryan castigates her for being a sour, ugly, withered old maid who hates her because she is young and in love, while she "knows nothing about love."

Earlier in the picture, Davis looks down on happy young couples dancing at Hopkins's daughter's wedding. Wistfully she goes into a bedroom and begins dancing to the music. Suddenly she is overwhelmed by her loneliness, and slowly she sinks to a couch, brokenly whispering the name of the one man she had truly loved, who had been taken from her by the long-past Civil War.

And perhaps the finest, most eloquent, most dramatically compelling scene of all: Davis stops Hopkins on the stairs, the night before the wedding, as she is about to go up and give the bride-to-be motherly advice on her wifely duties. The hatred between them flares up bitterly. "You made me an old maid," Davis hisses, "you divided his child from me; you taught her to call you Mother! Well, tonight, just for tonight, she belongs to me!" And when Hopkins protests that she "hasn't thought of Clem Spender in years," Davis declares: "Oh yes you have; you've thought of him when you've thought of her—of him and no one else! . . . a woman never stops thinking of the man she loves; she thinks of him for years, in all sorts of unconscious ways, in thinking of all sorts of things—a sunset, an old song, a cameo on a chain."

The Old Maid is infused with a tension rare in dramatic films—the hatred between the women, often layered over with civility and politeness, is a tangible thing, and it lends the film a diabolical force and a riveting, compelling fierceness. While many of these qualities are due to the fine acting of the principals, the real-life bitterness, tension, and professional rivalry between Davis and Hopkins bring them alive in a truly unique way.

Hopkins had relished the chance to co-star with Davis. Here was her long-sought opportunity to put her down, upstage her, humiliate and madden her. She was still seething with rage because of Davis's brief but intense affair with her husband, Anatole Litvak, whom she would divorce later in 1939, not naming Davis as corespondent only because her pride could not have stood it. Her professional jealousy of Davis knew no bounds. Here her hated rival had won an Oscar and vastly augmented fame for a role in *Jezebel* that she had played in a flop Broadway play four years before! And she brooded that only ten or so years back, she had been the star and Davis practically a bit player in the Rochester group! How their positions had reversed, how intolerable Hopkins found it. Davis was queen of the lot; Hopkins was an intruder on a limited contract. Davis's name alone could carry a film; Hopkins's box-office clout was so limited that producers could not star her in a major way, let alone carry her name singly above the title.

For all these reasons Hopkins went into *The Old Maid* primed to make her rival miserable at every turn. In her autobiography, Davis expressed amazement at the inventive turns Miriam's upstaging took— moving backward in a couch scene to capture the most flattering camera angle while Davis had to turn to face her; creating business with her ever-fluttering hands while Davis delivered a key speech; appearing on the first day of shooting in a replica of a gown Davis had worn in *Jezebel*, as if to say: I was there first, and years before you!

Hopkins, carried away by her spiteful rage and jealousy, adopted other stratagems that only boomeranged on herself. Judith Anderson had played Delia as a harsh, forbidding, revengeful woman—Hopkins couldn't stand the idea of the audience disliking her, so she played Delia for more warmth and sympathy; while this made for a plus in subtlety of a sort, it muted her characterization and helped hand the picture to Davis.

Davis frustrated Hopkins by not reacting to the overt and subtle attacks made on her. She later admitted that she went home at night and screamed for an hour. She marveled at how Hopkins, an excellent actress in a fine role, could blur her cinematic impact in pursuing upstaging stratagems.

Whatever Hopkins thought she was doing, it only succeeded in enhancing Davis's truly majestic and deeply felt performance. Full-bodied, wide in range, Charlotte Lovell was a role that called for the full complement of Davis's considerable histrionic powers. As the young girl she is loving, vulnerable, hungry for union with the man (George Brent) she loves, and determined to win him on the rebound after Hopkins rejects him to wed another. And when she has her man pinned down, she is aggressive about it, too. "Don't you know that what happens to you means more to me than anything?" she whispers passionately, in one of the most tender and intense love scenes the screen has ever boasted. Tenderness, warmth, womanly steadfastness, and the vulnerability that dares to win its objective despite all odds and risks, that is the young Charlotte Lovell, as Davis limns her. Later, caring for her child in the Charlotte Lovell Home for War Orphans, she is the very essence of motherly nurturing and tender sustenance. And later, in the famous scene in her wedding gown, Davis conveys most affectingly her never-ending mourning for her lost lover: "He didn't come back. He never will. . . ."

That is the magic of *The Old Maid* for Davis. And the magic that Davis brings to *The Old Maid*. Given the power and literacy and splendid acting and utter taste of this film in all departments, it remains a mystery to this day why it doesn't rank higher among the great films of that great cinema year 1939. We hear endlessly of *Mr. Smith Goes to Washington* and *Stage Coach* and *Wuthering Heights* and, of course, the definitive film of the year, *Gone With the Wind*, but *The Old Maid*, which won rave critical notices and made more money in 1939 than *Dark Victory* or most other films, is strangely neglected.

Yet it had a magical, wondrous effect on audiences that year—certainly on me, at age sixteen. Right after the Warner shield, the credits of *The Old Maid* appear, and the screen is infused with a fierce white light. Max Steiner's inspired score—perhaps the finest he ever wrote—encapsulized in the short credit running time, tells the entire story of the film—its initial youthful and romantic promise; its grim, disillusioning, and poignant midsection; and its final portion, a form of catharsis and resolution, but tragic and sadly unfulfilling.

Edmund Goulding, who had guided Davis through two previous films most creditably, surpasses himself in his direction of *The Old Maid*. Enthralled and stimulated by the intense, neurotic quarrels of frustrated, heart-wounded women, he fills *The Old Maid* with his special sensibility. This is a picture that even William Wyler could not have handled so truthfully, so sensitively, and so presciently. He who had weathered World War I, who had known so many disappointments in his gay love affairs, who harbored closeted secrets and fears in homophobic 1939 and in a bitchy, gossipy Hollywood—who would have understood more than Goulding the black secrets, the mourning for departed loved ones, all the repressions and displacements that give *The Old Maid* its own special brand of nuclear fission? And so it all comes together—the gay sensibility of Goulding expressed at its finest hour; the anger and jealousy and frustration of Hopkins; the instinctual recognition of Davis that in Charlotte Lovell is a many-faceted, richly-hued role of stark contrasts and unlimited characterizational range. The picture, like all works of true art, reveals something new with each viewing; the remarkable contrapuntal fusion of love and hate, tenderness and iciness, combat and surrender, the inner in combat with the outer, the yang with the yin, it is all here.

Davis never really liked *The Old Maid.* In her autobiography she said she was never mad about the role, but admitted it proved most popular. Her jaundiced and highly subjective attitude toward the best role and best film of her entire sixty-odd-year career was doubtless influenced by the hateful memories of Hopkins's spite and perfidy, which kept her constantly on edge. But this infused her performance with yet another dimension of tension and superb dramatic attack, toned down and disciplined by the sensitively watchful and delicately persuasive Goulding.

Heading a gifted list of character players is the admirable Donald Crisp as the understanding and compassionate family doctor who knows how to keep deep, dark secrets. "Ever since Tina turned instinctively to you as a mother," Crisp intones in his keynote speech to Hopkins, "you have watched Charlotte grow into a bitter and frustrated woman—and no woman like that was ever easy to live with." In her final film appearance, the lovable and funny-sad Louise Fazenda, in private life Mrs. Hal Wallis, wife of *The Old Maid*'s producer, is deeply touching as the loyal maid who witnesses the passage of the years and their effect on the mistresses she adores. "It's going to be a happy day, a very happy day for you," she whispers to Davis as she stands desolate in her bleak bedroom on the night before Tina's marriage, following up with a warm pat on the arm. Jerome Cowan is also excellent as the second "man who got away" and in 1964 he told me that *The Old Maid* was the finest picture he had ever been privileged to appear in. "It was quality from the word go," he said. "Edmund Goulding was so fine and sensitive, knew exactly what he wanted from all of us. And Bette surpassed herself in that. Playing with her was exquisite creative tension—I caught fire from her—I hope I did justice to her in other films we did, but never so much as in that one."

The art direction by the gifted Robert Haas caught the 1861–1881 ambience with an aptitude that was as perceptive as it was scholarly and period-sensitive. Special attention should be called to the montage effects. In the first portion, the years 1861–1866 are tellingly illustrated with battle scenes (supplemented by Steiner's rousing alarums), a shot of the dead lover's grave in a military cemetery, followed by renditions of Lincoln's second inaugural ("With malice toward none, with charity for all"), dissolving into the quiet, fluid musical nuances of Steiner that accompany the sign announcing Charlotte's home for war orphans. The second montage sequence is even more creative, with the growing Tina's feet skipping and jumping, then practicing at the piano pedals, then dancing a waltz, then being fitted for young ladies' silk shoes with bows.

George Brent, as the lost lover Clem Spender, who dies in the war, has few scenes, all in the film's first half, but he makes them count. In fact, this stoic, passive actor is more alive than usual here: telling off Delia for jilting him; compassionately tender when Charlotte confesses her long-standing unrequited love for him; gentle and understanding as he promises her at the train station that he will try to come back to her. In real life, during the spring of 1939, Brent was serving as protector, consoler, and tender bed partner for a Davis who was considerably off kilter and often hysterical as a result of the disasters of 1938 with her by-then-ex-husband Ham Nelson, and her by-now-erstwhile lovers Wyler and Litvak. Brent gave her his love, but he could not, would not, give her marriage, feeling he was not cut out for "an imprisoning institution" as he called it, but there is no question that he carried her through a period so emotionally wounding and upsetting that it might have unhinged her otherwise.

Frank Nugent in *The New York Times* had lavish praise for Davis's "poignant and wise" performance in *The Old Maid*, and James Shelley Hamilton wrote, "She has never touched the popular heart so effectually as she has apparently done here, and that without the slightest abatement of the sincerity and histrionic integrity that is one of [Davis's] strongest characteristics."

Contemporary feminists still find *The Old Maid* timely, despite its period setting, in its depiction of women's roles and their fates being so unfairly dependent on men and marriage in that period. It was the sweeping range and surprising depth of Bette Davis's performance in *The Old Maid* that decided Jack Warner and Hal Wallis to star her as Queen Elizabeth in the film version of Maxwell Anderson's *Elizabeth the Queen*, in which Lynn Fontanne and Alfred Lunt had had a stage hit some years before, with Lunt as the queen's lover, Lord Essex. Warner, Wallis, and his associate producer, Robert Lord, watched the rushes of *The Old Maid* carefully, and were deeply impressed with Davis's ability, at only thirty-one years of age, to suggest the bitterness, rueful wisdom, and mellowness of middle age. Her authoritative performance here, they assured themselves, more than qualified her for the complex character of Elizabeth, who would be in her sixties. In *The Old Maid* Davis used, courtesy of makeup artist Perc Westmore, a wan, grayish, ashen base for her skin with no lipstick or eye makeup, and it had effectively aged her without leaving her looking grotesque, as overemphasized "wrinkle, line, and bulge" makeup then so popular would have. Elizabeth, of course, being theatrical by nature, with elaborate costuming of an exaggerated design and a profusion of vivid red wigs to cover her balding gray pate, could be given an even more vividly "aged" look, but highly theatricalized and bizarre, again without conventional wrinkling or bulging.

Noting also, from the rushes of *The Old Maid*, that Davis could convey the authority and self-contained precision of a woman along in years, Jack and Hal commissioned Aeneas MacKenzie and Norman Reilly Raine to fashion a screenplay in which Davis could cut loose along those lines, and in grand queenly style. It was decided that the film should be photographed in Technicolor (Davis's first) and Sol Polito and W. Howard Greene worked in close collaboration to assure that Davis aged vividly and compellingly. Perc Westmore later had another inspiration: Since color would highlight every detail garishly, he shaved Davis's hair back two inches, thus underlining the reality of baldness under the red wigs and hairpieces. He then applied white, pasty makeup and shaved off her eyebrows, replacing them with thin lines that, in Robert Lord's words, "made her look like a baby in a Halloween mask and costume."

Davis spent much time studying portrait reproductions provided by the research department, seeking to approximate Elizabeth's actual appearance as accurately as possible. Her own appearance meant nothing to her—only historical accuracy. "Make me up horribly, and dress me outlandishly—I don't care, so long as you get the essence of the original," she told Perc Westmore and Orry-Kelly. When fussy, bossy director Mike Curtiz demanded that the overblown, full-skirted costumes be cut down to fit set requirements, Davis, knowing they were authentic, accurate reproductions, tricked him by doing tests in the cutdown versions and actual shooting in the originals. Having taken Curtiz's measure from long and bitter experience, she knew he would be too tied up with other details to even notice. "He had his ego field-day jumping on the costumes," she told Orry-Kelly cynically. "I doubt he will bother repeating himself."

Davis worked herself up and even threatened to walk off the picture because of the title. First it was *The Knight and the Lady*. This she hated; it cheapened the project, she wrote Warner. Warner then changed it to *Elizabeth the Queen* (the original stage title), then to *Elizabeth and Essex*, because Davis had insisted that she be favored in the title, and finally, in deference to box-office considerations, to *The Private Lives of Elizabeth and Essex*. Having won her case with the title, Davis then insisted on top billing. She had put up with "Errol Flynn and Bette Davis" billing the year before in *The Sisters*, in deference to Flynn's box-office clout at that time, but by mid-1939 she herself was a formidable ticket lure and she felt she didn't have to cater to Flynn anymore. Flynn did not like the switch but eventually agreed to "Bette Davis and Errol Flynn" because he knew he was in a prestige project made from a play whose verse language (courtesy of Maxwell Anderson) had been partially incorporated into the film—verse he did not feel qualified to handle with his usual jaunty dispatch.

Davis had not wanted Flynn as Essex. She had done everything she could to get Laurence Olivier, who, like herself, had won a great stardom submitting to Willie Wyler's strictures during *Wuthering Heights*, released just as *Essex* was getting under way. Olivier, too, had chafed under Wyler's direction; like her he had quarreled bitterly with the intrepid little man and walked angrily off the set. And again like Davis, he had sat in wonder at the results that Wyler showed him in the projection-room rushes. Eventually he, also like Davis, credited Wyler as the man who had made his international renown possible. Davis dreamed of Olivier as Essex, the euphonious and musical Maxwell Anderson verse delivered eloquently by a master of the spoken English word. She was to say for years afterward that Olivier as Essex to her Elizabeth would have taken the film to a new level of prestigious literacy and glamour—but it was not to be.

Jack Warner, to please Davis, tried to land Olivier, but there were contractual and other problems, and moreover Olivier felt his fortunes would thrive better in the hands of Alfred Hitchcock. His instincts proved correct, for *Rebecca* made Olivier an even bigger star, clinched by his Darcy in *Pride and Prejudice* at MGM with Greer Garson and his Nelson in *That Hamilton Woman* opposite his by-then wife, the brilliant and beautiful Vivien Leigh—she who had overshadowed Davis's Oscar-nominated *Dark Victory* with her Scarlett in *GWTW*.

Resignedly, Davis settled for Flynn when Jack Warner insisted that he had the period flair and swashbuckling aplomb necessary for the daring and adventurous Earl of Essex—and moreover he would supplement her own box-office clout. Though still being comforted intimately by the forbearing and patient George Brent, who had been with her in two of her four 1939 films, Davis admitted that she still responded to Flynn's dashing good looks and romantic aura. But she was determined to repress these feelings this time around. She succeeded only partially. Her romantic attraction to Flynn is more than apparent in their love scenes, and while there were many stories of the humorous incivilities and ingenious teasing Errol inflicted on Davis during the shooting, his response to her poorly suppressed admiration is apparent in the picture's more intimate love scenes. In fact his eyes widen with respect and an almost humble appreciation of her feelings in several sequences, and he plays back her impassioned words with understanding and sensitivity.

As current viewings of the now fifty-year-old *Elizabeth and Essex* make apparent, Errol Flynn was actually a much better actor than was realized at the time. Davis always admitted he had a fine latent talent that he should have disciplined and refined had he not been obsessed with women, wine, and various forms of devilish diversion.

Davis continued to find Michael Curtiz grating, annoying, and exasperating. Feisty and peppery as ever, replete with vulgarisms and abuse, Curtiz nevertheless had to respect the formidable figure Davis had become by 1939, so there was more uneasy truce than open combat in their on-set collaboration. Still, he would occasionally get out of line and lapse into shouting at her, but this time around, the Queen of the Warner Lot sent him into slinking, albeit sullen, retreats with acidly delivered, staccato-sharp variations on, "Shut up, Mike! Shut up and let's get on with it!" In short, on the set of *The Private Lives of Elizabeth and Essex*, Bully Curtiz had met his match at last.

Early in the shooting, Davis asked Warner why he had assigned Mike Curtiz to such an elaborate historical drama—certainly Anderson free verse was not a Curtiz forte—and he had replied, with irrefutable logic, that Curtiz was the studio expert in guiding rousing historical pageants and romances along quickly and surely. "He may not be up to the drama and the artistic stuff, Bette," Jack Warner told her, "but he will keep the pageantry and the historical spectacle moving at a fast clip." Then, in an affectionate barb, Jack told her, "Anyway, you can direct yourself—and you probably will. And Errol and everyone else along with you!"

The plot, such as it is, surrounded by the high-powered acting and historical sweep, has Essex the beloved of the queen, but headstrong and rebellious. He has enemies at court who want to undermine his influence and his hold over the queen. Eventually he is caught in what appears to be treason, and is sent to the Tower. Elizabeth, in a last-minute attempt to save her beloved, promises him his freedom if he will only be satisfied to live as a loyal and therefore passive subject under her rule, but he insists, with an honesty that costs him his head, that he is himself a leader born to rule, and that as long as he lives she would wear her crown uneasily. Since, in the final analysis, Elizabeth prizes the glory and prosperity of England and her crown above all other things, she brokenheartedly sends her beloved to his doom, sitting alone on her throne in the Tower as he descends to his death via trapdoor to the floor below.

Erich Wolfgang Korngold had been assigned to the Elizabeth project, and his inspired musical motifs contribute greatly to the film's overall flavor. Korngold subtly worked in medieval-sounding motifs and Renaissance-flavored melodies for a wonderful blend of superbly apropos mood music. Certainly the skillful Curtiz keeps the film moving at a fast clip, despite the Anderson verse passages and the love scenes and sequences involving Elizabeth with her entourage.

Olivia De Havilland, fresh from shooting her triumphant performance as Melanie in *Gone With the Wind*, had returned to Warners hoping for some starring parts, but instead found herself relegated to what was essentially a supporting role in *Essex* as a lady of the court enamored of Flynn. She plays something of a saucy minx, and with a sophistication and sexiness one does not usually ascribe to De Havilland. As usual Flynn pressed his suit, and as usual she informed him that his addresses were tiresome and unwanted. Olivia was a fortress that Flynn, to his lasting sorrow and frustration, was never successfully to storm. Though Davis always remained on excellent terms with De Havilland, whom she greatly respected and admired, she couldn't help being irritated with Flynn's continued pursuit of Olivia, and on occasion she outdid the real Elizabeth with some regal snappishness and dyspeptic cantankerousness on the set. These outbursts were only intensified when Flynn would suddenly pinch Davis's lavishly accoutred behind or even imitate the heavy walk she assumed to approximate how Elizabeth had moved. Davis threw a heavy candelabra at Flynn one day when he said that as Elizabeth she walked "like she had defecated in her panties," adding, "Shall I help you to the special porcelain throne awaiting you in your dressing room, Your Majesty?"

The supporting cast again featured Davis's dependable old standby

Donald Crisp as Sir Francis Bacon, who tries to temper Essex's self-destructive restlessness. Vincent Price was his usual flamboyant self as Sir Walter Raleigh, and Henry Daniell is in top form as a treacherous courtier, as is Alan Hale as a warring Irish earl. Henry Stephenson as another of the queen's noble advisors adds characteristic solidity to the proceedings.

Jack Warner, knowing Davis's deep disappointment over missing out on *Gone With the Wind*, had his private little joke co-starring her, twice in one year, with the man she had deemed unfit for Rhett Butler. But he also felt sympathetic to her feelings about *GWTW*, and this was one of the factors influencing him to give her four blockbuster films during what was to be her greatest year, 1939. He carefully arranged to release *The Private Lives of Elizabeth and Essex* in December 1939—the very month that *Gone With the Wind* debuted—feeling that this impressive costumer in color, with its lavish budget, solid historical ambience, and top production values, would somehow allay and soothe her regrets.

While Davis's performance is well thought out in most respects, she did have an annoying habit of squirming around both while sitting and standing. Certainly Willie Wyler would have caught her on this one, had he been in charge, because the movement detracts from her otherwise regal performance. It is worth remarking that she did not repeat this blunder when she played Elizabeth again sixteen years later. Frank Nugent in *The New York Times* felt that Davis's Elizabeth was "a strong, resolute, glamor-skimping characterization."

One day Charles Laughton, who had won *his* Oscar for the 1933 *Private Life of Henry VIII*, appeared on the set.

"Hi, Pop!" Davis shouted, advancing toward him in full costume and with a queenly insouciance.

"Ah! It's my favorite daughter!" he replied smartly, falling in quickly with her mood.

They went to a corner of the set and talked for a long while during a complicated lighting operation. Davis recalled confessing to him that she felt she had bitten off more than she could chew in essaying the role of Elizabeth when she was only thirty-one. She never forgot Laughton's reply:

"Never stop daring to hang yourself, Bette!"

Davis felt a real kinship with Laughton. Like herself he had been plagued with feelings of physical inferiority; he felt fat, ungainly, blighted—indeed deformed. As he had believed himself not handsome, so she had always felt herself not beautiful. While she was not homosexual, she could identify with his struggles over his essential femininity as she had struggled with the disparate masculine impulses in her own nature that had given her an aggressiveness and tenacity so often disconcerting to her overlords. She had heard of his homosexuality and its humiliations; the grapevine never seemed to let up on the unfortunate Laughton, whose marriage to Elsa Lanchester was largely regarded as one of convenience and friendship, while he pursued his true romantic objectives—handsome young men—with a manic intensity that frightened him as much as them. Hurt deeply by their assorted reactions—they either used him or recoiled from him—Laughton had become a deeply embittered and distrustful man whose wild rages reportedly matched her own when he was thwarted or frustrated or rendered despairing by his unfortunate bents. Davis, circa 1939, did not have the deep and sophisticated understanding of the gay temperament that she was to develop in later years despite the fact that she had been awash in gay and bisexual actors through much of her stage and film career, but Charles was one man with whom she sympathized—and empathized—deeply. While her brand of outsiderism was not his, as she knew, there were many points at which their psyches met. She was always among Laughton's firmest defenders.

One time at a party, shortly after their meeting on the *Elizabeth and Essex* set, she heard a cruel joke about him—one Elsa Lanchester was to elaborate on when she reminisced about Charles after his death. It seems Elsa had come home to find Charles ready with a confession. He had picked up a man in a London park, and had brought him in. They had had sex on the living room sofa. The young man later demanded money and threatened to bring the police in. Elsa, as the story went, took all this in stride but was much more concerned that the sofa where the liaison took place should be sent out to the cleaners!

The party guests thought this hilarious, but Davis faced them all down. "The man is a great artist," she declared firmly, "and you people demean yourselves, not him, by relaying such unkind stories." Years later she would come similarly to the defense of another great actor she fervently admired. According to Jerry Asher, as of 1939 her attitude toward homosexuals was, "We all carry some variety of infirmity or sorrow with us—let's treat each other kindly. None of us is getting out of our human condition alive!"

The year 1939 was to bring Charles Laughton one of his greatest roles—the pitiful, grotesquely deformed Quasimodo in the remake of *The Hunchback of Notre Dame*. (Lon Chaney had been memorable in the silent version.) Davis saw the film and told Jerry Asher: "Charles is a great artist—he understands the depths of the human heart. Only a man of sorrows could play Quasimodo like that man did!" Jerry relayed her words to Laughton, who responded with an affectionately grateful telegram of thanks.

15

The Fourth Warner Brother—and Farney

AFTER COMPLETING *The Private Lives of Elizabeth and Essex* in mid-summer 1939, Davis decided she needed a vacation—a long one. Despite the fact that she had completed six pictures in a row with little or no vacation between assignments, Jack Warner wanted her to go immediately into another picture, *'Til We Meet Again*. A soapy, saccharine remake of *One Way Passage*, the 1932 Kay Francis–William Powell hit dealt with a condemned criminal and a dying woman who meet on an ocean liner and vow to meet again though both are fated to die. It was a big hit with the matinee ladies in Depression 1932. Warner, however, failed to see that the material was worn and outdated and that it too closely resembled *Dark Victory* and was thus anathema to Davis, who had had enough dying for some time to come, and kept pressing it on her, to her annoyance and distraction.

She lit off for the East and told the studio in no uncertain terms that she wanted four or five months off. Considering that *The Old Maid* was just going into release that August of 1939, and that the Elizabeth-Essex picture would not premiere for four months, Jack Warner's desire to keep Davis on the treadmill does seem greedy and demanding—two qualities for which he was well known both before and after 1939.

But Davis, fed up, proved elusive as she wandered the New England states, trying to reestablish old ties in Massachusetts with people she had outgrown and no longer had anything in common with. She drove up through New Hampshire and stopped off at little inns along the coast, walking beaches for hours. At this point she knew she was the first lady of the screen, although her salary was still inadequate. Artistically, she had achieved all her major objectives, with one film, *The Old Maid*, playing to enthralled audiences and winning critical superlatives— and another due out in some months, in which, as Queen Elizabeth, she would be placed on a par with Lynn Fontanne.

But none of this gave her any satisfaction. What did it mean to be dubbed Popeye the Magnificent, the First Lady of the Screen, or the Fourth Warner Brother when at thirty-one she was feeling old and emotionally depleted. She had lost Ham via a bitter, recriminative divorce; her romances with Wyler and Litvak had gone nowhere, and Wyler had married Margaret Tallichet, closing the door on her for good; George Brent had been nurturing and sustaining and understanding, but only to a point. She was lonely and rootless, and the future that should have looked so bright seemed instead to offer only downhill journeys and ever grimmer vistas.

Was it true what her relatives and friends said of her, that she insisted on wearing the pants, being the "man of the family" as she had had to be for Ruthie, for Bobby, for eight years now—for longer than that, really, since the day in her early youth when Harlow Morrell Davis had taken himself out of their lives and forced her to fill his shoes. Her ruthlessness, assertiveness, and will to win, triumph, and dominate were ever at war with her need to lean, the longing to look up to a strong, noble, decent, independent-spirited man whose career—in his own sphere—would match hers.

It was in this mood of inner conflict that her lonely journey ended at Peckett's Inn in Franconia, New Hampshire—a place Ruthie had fondly recommended as soothing, rustic, yet warm and hospitable.

There she met Arthur Farnsworth, a handsome, thirty-four-year-old assistant manager at the inn. Kind, manly, hospitable, soothing, understanding, Farnsworth came from an excellent old Vermont family. He had a little money and would some day inherit more. He had been a professional flier until he was hurt in an accident which he would not discuss. In 1939 his divorce from Boston socialite Betty Jane Aydelotte, (who also had an airline pilot's license,) was finalized. He didn't want to talk about *her* either.

Like Davis, Farnsworth in 1939 was in a state of life-pause, trying to find himself. The position at Peckett's Inn was on the menial side, but it was undemanding, and it gave him time to think. Davis fell in love with him almost at once. She chose to ignore the facts that gradually emerged about him, such as he was something of a mother's boy, mother being a dragon from one of Vermont's most aristocratic families, who would have given Gladys Cooper's brutal Boston dowager in *Now, Voyager,* a run for her money. His father, it appeared, was a milquetoast dentist very much henpecked by the mater familias, and his siblings were unimaginative, unremarkable, soft types from all appearances.

But Davis saw only what she chose to see—the chunky, well-developed body, the clipped Yankee accent that bespoke his aristocratic lineage, the quiet, unassuming man's-man aura. Farney actually had little to say but she chose to believe that it was the laconic attitude of a true man. Though well educated, Farney was a being of passive intellect, with no capacity for self-analysis, with no strong moral sense, and, had she been able to realize it, he was something of a high-class hustler—though gigolo was the term more in fashion then.

He told her he was still intensely interested in flying. He would later take a good position with Minneapolis Honeywell and would serve as liaison during World War II between aircraft plants and the government. He had sustained some head wounds while flying, making him subject to periodic epileptic seizures that would keep him out of World War II service.

Determined to cast him as the Man She Had Always Sought, Davis took Farney to bed within a week—and there found him most adept, expert, and far superior to gangling, bumbling, masturbatory Ham—or even the Messrs. Brent, Wyler, Hughes, and Litvak.

Handsome, muscular, beautifully endowed, always ready, accommodating—pliable yet manly Farney—who could ask for anything more, given her mood?

Next she began to feel the need to put down roots, so she bought a run-down old house called Butternut near Littleton, New Hampshire. She called in a moonlighting crew of Warner carpenters from Hollywood to fix it up (Jack Warner was fit to be tied when he heard) and began planting and painting and becoming the rooted New Englander she had decided to be, totally and completely and unstintingly—for a few months.

And there was Farney to play house with her; sitting in a big arm-chair by the fireside, pipe in mouth, striding about in sexy, manly boots, helping her lift things, sawing wood, planning rooms. It was a movie fantasy come true, and though she didn't realize it, that was what she was after—a perfect Bette Davis movie. Setting: Butternut. Leading Man: Farney. Director: Bette Davis, who else? Screenwriter, too. Only Max Steiner's appropriate motifs were missing; in lieu of them she played classical music, which Farney also loved.

Meanwhile Jack Warner came calling. In surprisingly lèse-majesté style—indeed his wife, Ann, thought it déclassé—Jack came to New York and stooped to following her all the way to New Hampshire. He was desperate to get her into a new picture. What would it be? What did she want? Davis airily and frostily discussed ideas for new pictures while the studio tycoon worked up an unaccustomed sweat. Despite herself, she felt contempt for him for coming to her; she had always gone to him before. She liked him haughty, disdainful, argumentative. Now she looked him over with a critical eye—a middle-aged, paunchy, soliciting creature who bargained with her, to his disadvantage, as if his life depended on it. He had still one card to play—or rather not play—to keep her continued respect. He would not raise her salary. She had to be satisfied with the lousy $3,000 a week. "We'll wait and see on that," he repeated over and over.

She toyed with several ideas. One that intrigued her, oddly enough, was a remake of Garbo's 1930 *Anna Christie*, with, of all people, James Cagney opposite her in the role Charles Bickford played. The Garbo talkie had been too primitive, she told Jack, too strained. It had been a hit only because it was Garbo's first talkie appearance. She would do it better, she said; she would make the points O'Neill had intended.

Soon the talk moved to the best-selling *All This and Heaven, Too*—about a governess in an aristocratic household in 1847 Paris who becomes involved in a scandal. This intrigued her somewhat. Jack Warner went back to Hollywood with the understanding that, come January 1940, *All This and Heaven, Too*, provided the script measured up, would be *it*.

She and Farney continued to play house at Butternut and then back in Hollywood, where they began redecorating and refurbishing River-bottom, a house in Glendale that her real estate agents, knowing her taste for all that was redolent of New England, had found for her. Farney began commuting back and forth on his aircraft assignments. Suave and undemanding and weak, he left her pretty much on her own.

Davis opened the new year 1940 with *All This and Heaven, Too*, a lush, romantic costume drama that co-starred her with Charles Boyer. Davis always praised him unreservedly, calling him at various times "that romantic, beautiful actor" and "a joy to work with, professional to the core." Certainly in the elaborate film version of the best-selling Rachel Field novel about her great-aunt Henriette DesPortes's involvement in a famous Parisian murder scandal of 1847, the Davis-Boyer combo, supported by such sterling performers as Barbara O'Neil (fresh from her role of Scarlett's mother in *Gone With the Wind*), Jeffrey Lynn, Harry Davenport, Helen Westley, and Walter Hampden, exuded star glamour at its zenith.

The story is about Davis's term as governess in the Parisian mansion of the duc and duchesse de Praslin. When Davis wins the four children's affection and the love of the husband, the pathologically jealous duchess dismisses her and is then murdered by the duc when he discovers that she has refused the governess a letter of recommendation, with the result that she is living in abject poverty.

This handsomely produced story ran up a budget of $1,400,000, a respectable sum for 1940, and ran, before cutting, for 23 reels—cut down to 143 minutes for general release in July 1940.

Boyer returned Davis's compliments in a 1966 interview, and his comments about her are worth repeating at some length. He told me:

"She was, in my opinion, the most gifted American actress on the screen. She had enormous reserves of emotion, a splendidly disciplined technique, and could convey so much with gestures and expressions. I felt a little guilty when we started *All This and Heaven, Too* because my role as the amorous, eventually murderous, husband was much more flamboyant and impassioned, whereas Bette had to be restrained and subdued through most of the action. As befit her depiction of a reserved, disciplined governess who did not dare call her feelings her own, she had to maintain an outward restraint. This was indeed a feat of tightrope walking for an actress who had won her much-deserved fame portraying passionate, electric characters. I told her of my feelings of guilt over having what in my opinion was the showier, hence easier, role, and she brushed them aside. I remember her telling me that it was a privilege to appear with an actor (I repeat her words, certainly not mine) so accomplished and distinguished, and that it meant so much to her to work with performers who could play back to her, on their own level and in their own style, the feelings she was attempting to convey."

Boyer added, "I had heard much about her temperament, and how difficult she was supposed to be. I found none of that. We worked together amicably and harmoniously from start to finish. I know she and

Tola [director Anatole Litvak] had their artistic differences, but I always felt both of them were concerned for the good of the picture, and even though their concepts were different, they were sincerely expressed. All in all, it was a most happy blending of talents."

Barbara O'Neil gave a superb performance as the neurotic, possessive, paranoid, and obsessively jealous duchesse de Praslin; hers was the most bravura part of all, and she gave it the full juice, indeed out-Bette-ing Bette in their scenes together. Davis confessed that she regretted not having the role of the duchesse herself, as it was a very showy role, but she decided on the quieter, more repressed Henriette, in the final analysis, because it gave her a chance to showcase yet again the warm, womanly, self-contained persona that was also very much a part of her (as in *The Sisters*) and she felt that this had not had much airing in her four most recent roles—a dying heiress, a mad empress, a bitter old maid, and a flamboyant queen. It was time to remind audiences yet again that this other Bette Davis incarnation was still in good working order.

The sterling actor Harry Davenport, a veteran of the stage and numerous fine character performances, was seventy-four in 1940 but still forceful and magnetic as the old servant who tries to warn Henriette of the hideous danger hanging over her in the aristocratic house of jealousy and hate. He is eloquent indeed when he ripostes Davis's denial that any word or action of love had ever passed between her and the duc with the words, "And your feelings—could they also be shared?"

Casey Robinson, the sensitive screenwriter who understood the Davis mystique so well, wrote a literate, intelligent screenplay with much scope and solid characterization. He stuck closely to Rachel Field's novel, even using much of her dialogue, and Field visited with Davis on the set, where they became fast friends discussing the character and motivations of the original Henriette. Had she indeed been a harlot and homebreaker who had seduced the duc and wrought havoc leading to murder? Field felt she was an innocent victim and that there had been no physical affair between her and the duc. Davis shilly-shallied on this; at one time she thought they had committed adultery, at another she felt Field—and Robinson—had told it as it was.

As shooting progressed, Davis began to understand that she was giving one of her more subtle, restrained, disciplined performances. Boyer, fine artist that he was, expressed tension with his entire body, and the wildest passion in his brooding, expressive dark eyes. She found herself catching fire from the finely honed technique of a co-star who was, for once, her equal in talent and technique. She felt the joy any artist can know when his or her projections are met and reciprocated with creative understanding and esthetic perception. She did not act with performers of Boyer's quality often—and it meant much to her, as she was often to state.

Her problems with Anatole Litvak were something else again. She and Tola had, briefly but intensely, been lovers; in bed he was a tender, responsive, sensitive lover; as a director he could be a martinet, demanding, rude, and as insulting and abrasive in his way as Mike Curtiz. He had a heavy-handed, literal directorial style that got on her nerves no end. Tola was also a man for putting it all on paper, going by the book, by the letter, even when some degree of spontaneity and flexibility were called for. And often her instincts were more true than his. When she played the courtroom scene in which she denies her complicity in the murder, she felt she should pull out all the stops, weep passionately, sink down on the railing, gesticulate bewilderedly, like a trapped animal. Tola accused her of trying to make up for her many repressed, restrained scenes by going overboard on that one. He failed to understand that her grief and fear for the duc had caused her normal restraints to give way. Davis finally called Hal Wallis and associate producer David Lewis in to look at the rushes in which she had played it her way. They overruled Tola, and ordered the scene to remain as it was.

Naturally, this caused further enmity between Litvak and Davis, and soon Boyer, O'Neil, and the other cast members were retreating discreetly beyond earshot as star and director argued out every scene toe to toe and eyeball to eyeball. Finally Litvak learned the lesson the hard way, that there was no arguing with Davis when she had her mind firmly and finally set. She threatened to have him fired, and the credit for such a major picture was something the still insecure Litvak desperately needed. He threw up his hands, gave in, and Davis did things her way for the rest of the shooting. The root of the problem was that Davis didn't have the confidence in Litvak's directorial instincts that she had in Wyler's and Goulding's. She found too often that his directions ran counter to her own instincts as to how a scene should be played. The finished result with Henriette played as Davis thought she should be proves her right in this instance (she was not always to be).

Certainly *All This and Heaven Too* displays Davis at one of the summits of her achievement, and one of the proudest moments of her life came when she was able to take her mother to the lavish premiere at the Carthay Circle Theatre.

In her autobiography, Davis wrote: "There is no question that the

Hollywood premiere, so often satirized, is an exciting affair. If you are in a picture being premiered, it is difficult not to feel like a queen. Certainly it was not difficult for Ruthie to be the Dowager Empress. We giggled quietly at the change that had come over our lives since our arrival in Hollywood seven [*sic*] years before."

There was much praise for the winning youngsters who played the Praslin children, Virginia Weidler, borrowed from MGM; June Lockhart, talented daughter of Gene; Ann Todd, a winsome charmer; and especially little Richard Nichols, a pale, waiflike little fellow straight out of Dickens who was the only performer to outplay Davis herself in some of their scenes together.

In his July 5, 1940, review, the *New York Times* critic Bosley Crowther wrote: "Alert to the opportunity, Miss Davis and Mr. Boyer put all the 'soul' they possess into the playing . . . under the slow-paced direction of Anatole Litvak, they carry through mainly on one somber key—Miss Davis with her large eyes filled with sadness and her mouth drooping heavily with woe; Mr. Boyer with his face a rigid mask, out of which his dark eyes signal pain."

In a prologue and epilogue, Davis has to win her spurs with some witchy schoolgirls in America who learn about her past; when the teacher tells her pupils about all the hurt and horror she endured, they cry over her as a heroine—it is a saccharine but somehow effective touch.

THE ROLE OF LESLIE CROSBIE in Somerset Maugham's *The Letter* had already been played by a bevy of distinguished actresses by the time Davis finally essayed it in 1940. Gladys Cooper had originated it in a London play in 1927. Later Katharine Cornell had played it in New York. By 1929 it was a Hollywood movie with the great Jeanne Eagels, who died soon after its release.

One of Maugham's more trenchant and biting stories, it deals with the wife of an English plantation manager in Malaya who murders her lover while her husband is away. She is tried for the crime but pleads self-defense, saying the dead man was a mere acquaintance who had made sudden advances. Her defense attorney is suspicious of her, and later his assistant brings him a copy of the letter she had written the deceased, in which she begs him to see her. This throws a different light on the case, and the attorney is forced to spend the unknowing husband's life savings—$10,000—to recover the letter from the murdered man's bitter and revengeful Eurasian wife.

Later, Leslie Crosbie is exonerated at the trial; her defense attorney, who has suppressed the letter out of friendship for the husband, is guilt-ridden and bitter. When the husband asks about the missing money, with which he had planned to buy property, Leslie is forced to tell him the truth. He forgives her, but is deeply hurt. Later, under stress, she confesses that "with all my heart, I still love the man I killed!" He leaves her, disgusted and appalled, and she goes into the garden to meet her doom at the hands of the murdered lover's wife.

Such is the plot of *The Letter*, and it is melodramatic and lurid. But in the 1940 film version it was admirably scripted by Howard Koch, photographed to wonderful atmospheric effect by Tony Gaudio (on whom Davis had insisted), and directed by William Wyler with a painstaking, multiple-take thoroughness that had by then become his trademark, and that won the picture, and Davis, Academy Award nominations for 1940.

The Letter contains one of Davis's greatest performances. She played Leslie Crosbie not in the emotional, throat-clutching way Jeanne Eagels had in the earlier picture but in a tense, taut, controlled manner that heightened the tension enormously. And in this second picture with Wyler, she submitted, despite the usual arguments, to his ideas and came through with a polished, disciplined, subtle performance that could not have been bettered.

Her romance with Wyler was several years in the past by 1940, so they worked together as professionals who thoroughly respected each other. She still found his methods nerve-racking and annoying, and there were a number of shouting matches on the set, but when she saw the rushes, with their flattering camera angles and shrewd highlighting of her best features, as well as the sterling characterization Wyler had forced out of her by his usual endless retakes and demanding methods, all she could feel was a profound gratitude.

Davis was later to pay tribute to Wyler as one of the very few directors whom she could trust completely, and to whom she would subordinate her own instincts and judgment. "That is a very rare quality in a director; I had so few of them I really respected and trusted. I had implicit confidence in Willie in that picture. In our last picture (*The Little Foxes*) we might have had creative differences, but in those first two I allowed his will to prevail and later blessed him for handling me with such disciplined firmness."

James Stephenson, the English actor who had been playing small supporting roles in Warner films, including Davis's *The Old Maid* and *Elizabeth and Essex*, came into his own under Wyler's guidance in *The Letter*, and in his role as the doubting, disillusioned defense attorney he wound up getting critical acclaim almost equal to Davis's own. Unaccustomed to Wyler's methods, Stephenson, a product of London theater training, at times revolted vociferously (as had another English actor, Laurence Olivier, from whom Wyler forced a performance that made him an international star). Several times he walked off the set. Davis later recalled that each time he did that, she went after him, promising that if he returned and submitted to Wyler's methods, it would mean the great breakthrough he had not yet found in America. Later, Stephenson tendered Davis heartfelt thanks for her support.

Herbert Marshall is very fine as Davis's deceived husband, loving and loyal throughout the trial of someone he loves and believes innocent, heartbroken, disillusioned but still forgiving when he finds out the sordid and pathetic truths of his wife's infidelity. In the 1929 Jeanne Eagels film version, Marshall, curiously enough, had been the murdered lover. In the 1940 version, he was played by a hapless young actor named David Newell, who is seen only momentarily stumbling out onto the porch to die in the dirt below the steps of the plantation house.

In the London play, the action had ended with Leslie's words, "With all my heart, I still love the man I killed," a fitting curtain on a stage production free of censorship, but the Hollywood Production Code people demanded that Davis be punished for her sins. Accordingly, Howard Koch had to write a scene in which she goes out to meet her death at the hands of the Eurasian wife of the victim. Then, something had to be done about "punishing sufficiently" murderess number two, so as Gale Sondergaard, who played the role, leaves the scene with a confederate, she is accosted by a policeman. Davis recalled later that there was great concern at the studio that such bowdlerization might injure the realistic approach Wyler was trying to achieve, but the feared minus turned into a plus, when it was revealed that the haunting camera effects, the dramatic play of light and shadow, and the musical inspirations of Max Steiner had added, in Davis's own death scene, an exciting new dimension to the proceedings.

The Maugham story proved so popular that it was remade several times—each time with inferior results. A rather hasty, slapdash, melodramatic version called *The Unfaithful* appeared in 1947, directed by Vincent Sherman with, of all people, Ann Sheridan in the Davis role. (Ann, likable as she was, in no way measured up to Davis's interpretation; she lacked the depth, passion, and technique for it.) As late as 1982, a telemovie version, directed by John Erman, featured Lee Remick in yet another of the roles that were beyond her depth. To this day, the Davis version stands as the definitive one—and deservedly so.

In one breathtakingly sinister scene, guided by Wyler from start to finish with painstaking professionalism, Gale Sondergaard receives Davis at her dwelling. She has demanded that her husband's murderer come in person to get the letter in exchange for the $10,000. As Wyler directs the scene, Davis advances toward Sondergaard, who is standing on an elevated level. The widow's eyes glitter with hatred; they stare at each other for what seems an eternity; Davis, eyes widening, fearful yet determined, waits for the evidence that would potentially damn her. Sondergaard slowly extracts the letter from her sleeve and contemptuously throws it on the floor, forcing Davis to stoop to retrieve it. This is a salient example of the excruciating tension Wyler could inject into a scene, editing out of it anything extraneous or superfluous.

In future years, whenever she spoke of *The Letter*, Davis mentioned the enormous contribution Stephenson and Sondergaard had made. "It always meant so much to me," she said more than once, "to have fine actors playing opposite me; they gave me something sterling to play against, and enhanced my own performance accordingly."

At this point Davis was still "between husbands," and though her romance with Farney was catching fire despite the three thousand miles that separated them most of the time, she was not immune to the manly charms of one particular actor named Bruce Lester, who was, as she later recalled in somewhat sugary terms for her, "the essence of winsome sweetness." Lester had several good scenes with her—he was an assistant to the defense attorney who commiserated with her, being ignorant of her guilt—and she went out of her way to put him at ease and ensure that he would give a creditable performance.

Soon they were seen lunching together and leaving alone in her car after the day's shooting ended, and rumors of a Bette Davis–Bruce Lester romance began circulating. Lester, of whom little was to be heard thereafter, was a very sincere, decent young man who was not at all sure that acting was what he really wanted. Later he praised Davis for her encouragement and concern at that point in his life. The romance, such as it was, seems to have come to nothing. "She found Bruce attractive and sweet, but he was a bit tame for her speed," Jerry Asher later said.

The New York Times reviewer extolled *The Letter*, when it opened in New York on November 22, 1940, as "a superior melodrama, compounded of excellent acting, insinuating atmosphere and unrelaxed suspense," with Davis described as "a strangely cool and calculating killer who conducts herself with reserve and yet implies a deep confusion of emotions." Stephenson came off as "superb," and of Wyler the review stated, "His hand is patent throughout."

* * *

Davis could be generous, helpful, and sympathetic to co-actors she really liked and admired. The British actor James Stephenson, who had given such a sterling account of himself in *The Letter* as her defense attorney, was one of them.

A courtly gentleman to his fingertips, Stephenson had come over from England several years before, after languishing at Warners' Teddington Studios near London, which had produced a string of cheaply made and badly done programmers (films) for the British market exclusively. Davis took note of him when he played a very small part as Miriam Hopkins's husband, James Ralston, in *The Old Maid*, and felt that his finely honed talents were being wasted. She was instrumental in casting him in *The Letter*, over Wyler's initial objections. Stephenson, he told her, was too staid and British to play the intense defense attorney. Later, after Stephenson gave an excellent account of himself, Wyler uncharacteristically admitted he was wrong.

Due to Davis's pleas to the front office, Stephenson was then given a good role with Ronald Reagan in *International Squadron*, about Royal Air Force heroics, and then, again via Davis's wire-pulling, he wound up as the lead in *Shining Victory*, a 1941 drama about a Scottish doctor conducting psychiatric research in a Scottish sanitarium, whose love for Geraldine Fitzgerald complicates his life.

Shining Victory represented a first in the directorial career of Irving Rapper, a talented jack-of-all-trades who had been born in London in 1898 and came to New York at age eight. After directing the Washington Square Players, Rapper moved on to Broadway as both actor and director, and then went to Hollywood, where he was an assistant director and writer and dialogue coach, working, circa 1939, on Davis's *Juarez*.

Shining Victory, based on A. J. Cronin's *Jupiter Laughs*, was Rapper's first directorial assignment, and he was determined to make the most of it. Crediting Stephenson, Geraldine Fitzgerald, Donald Crisp, Barbara O'Neil, and other fine players with cooperating "magnificently" with him, as he later told me, Rapper went on to direct top Warner films, even directing Davis in some of her more notable future vehicles.

Davis had had some interesting conversations with him on the set of *Jezebel* (he had served as dialogue director) and thought him creatively gifted and personally stimulating (both denied a romance).

As a good-luck gesture to Stephenson and Geraldine Fitzgerald, Davis appeared in *Shining Victory* made up as a nurse for a bit part in which she delivers a letter. There are three versions of this incident.

Rapper claims he didn't recognize her at first, but allowed her to re-
hearse the scene anyway. Davis claims he was in on the joke from the
beginning. Hal Wallis claims the whole thing was a gag and the scene in
question was never photographed, only rehearsed. Some claim to have
seen Davis in the finished film; others look for her in vain. But there is
proof the scene exists, whether or not photographed. A studio still
shows Davis, coiffed severely, in a starched, bibbed, and white-collared
nurse's uniform, sporting what appears to be a pince-nez with a string
attached around her neck, handing a letter to actress Hermine Sterler,
who looks severe and mannish in a jacket and tie. Whether her bit in
Shining Victory, photographed, merely rehearsed, whatever, belongs in
the Bette Davis canon is still being debated.

To Davis's and his other admirers' great grief, James Stephenson, still
only in his forties, died suddenly in 1941, just as his Warner career was
getting into high gear. "All that struggle, and just as things were breaking for him—this," was Davis's terse but deeply felt statement to the
press at the time.

In October 1940, with great reluctance, Davis accepted a project
Hal Wallis had proffered. It was based on a popular novel by Polan
Banks called *January Heights*. The title was later changed to *Far Horizon*,
and finally to *The Great Lie*. Lenore Coffee was assigned to write the
screenplay, with Edmund Goulding directing and Hal Wallis and Henry
Blanke doubling up on the producing duties.

Davis was disgusted with the screenplay. "It's soap-opera drivel and
it stinks in all departments!" she complained to Goulding, Wallis, and
anyone else who would listen. Writer Lenore Coffee, a nervous, reclusive, high-strung person, had a time of it coping with Davis's late-
night phone calls and screaming entreaties to make the script more
"human, presentable, decently playable!"

Davis's instincts about the story were right. In this one she is a "nice"
society girl with a Maryland plantation. She is in love with playboy flier
George Brent (who also thought the script stank, but couldn't care less
as long as he was paid on schedule), who jilts her to marry high-strung
pianist Mary Astor. When Mary finds out her prior divorce wasn't final,
so they're not married, she decides she is too busy to go through the
ceremony again because a concert is coming up in Philadelphia.

A disgusted George walks out and back to Bette, who forgives and
marries him. Then he goes to South America on an air survey and is lost
in the jungle, presumed dead. Astor then discovers that she is to have
Brent's baby—but it will interfere with her career and image, so Davis
tells her she wants the baby, offers Mary an annuity, and suffers with

her through the pregnancy out in the Arizona desert, where Mary retreats so her public won't know she's *enceinte*. When the baby is delivered, Davis takes it home, Mary resumes her career, and presto chango!
Brent isn't dead after all. He comes back to Davis, who lets him think
the baby is hers—her great lie.

Restless Mary gets the idea that if George knows the child's hers,
she will get him back. So she shows up at the plantation and goads
Davis into telling him the truth. But George makes it plain it is Davis he
loves and offers to let Mary take the baby. Mary doesn't, parades in to
play Tchaikovsky (unaccountably) for arriving guests, and all is joy and
peace.

Davis's agitation and disgust with the script were apparent from the
first day of shooting. Astor thought it was her she was mad at; she was
wrong. Davis had wanted her for the role from the beginning, not only
because she was a skilled pianist who could make the concert shots look
believable, but because she had the hauteur, spitefulness, egomania, and
bitchiness to make Sandra, the pianist, thoroughly believable. Astor had
had a checkered career in films up to this time. She had been married a
few times, one of which had ended in a nationally publicized scandal.
Her diary had been found in 1936 and headlines had yakked about its
alleged detailings of wild lovemaking with well-known men, among
them the ugly but supersexy playwright George S. Kaufman. Astor's
husband, Dr. Franklin Thorpe, had attempted to use all the publicity to
rob Mary of her daughter. During that time, she was appearing as the
"good" woman opposite Ruth Chatterton's bitchy, philandering wife of
Walter Huston in *Dodsworth*. The press made hay pointing out the contrast between the good onscreen Mary and the naughty offscreen Mary.
Oddly enough, it didn't hurt her career; her notoriety sold tickets. "So
the Astor dame got in a scandal—they'll want to see her, cluck about
her, wonder about her," realistic Jack Warner told his minions. "If there's
a part up her street we'll use her some time."

Mary had never been a major star. From 1936 to 1940 her career
had schlepped along in pictures with such apropos titles as *Paradise for
Three, No Time to Marry, There's Always a Woman, Woman Against Woman*,
and similar drekky soap. Fans viewing her in more sophisticated fare like
Midnight, with Claudette Colbert, found it hard to believe that this chic,
ruefully sophisticated world-weary brunette had ever been a virginal
leading lady to John Barrymore when he had played dashing Don Juans
in the 1920s. Rumor had it he had seduced her despite her watchful
parents, and that had begun her checkered career as siren par excellence.

This, then, was the woman confronted with Davis, who had chosen her over a field of candidates including Anna Sten, Sylvia Sidney, and even Miriam Hopkins. One day on the set Davis let loose with a whoop of disgust, threw her script down, told director Goulding and photographer Tony Gaudio to hold everything, and called Astor into her dressing room for what the latter thought would surely be a dressing down. Instead Davis said she wanted to work with her on the hopeless script and juice it up by injecting some wild, bitchy, realistic woman-to-woman rivalry. Together they went over the story line by line and between them worked up situations so lively and compelling that Eddie Goulding commended it as "material that only women could have thought up—but it plays, oh how it plays!"

One outstanding example was the tug-of-war the girls act out on the forbidding, isolated ranch where Astor goes to have her baby. Davis has to keep her eating right, playing double solitaire with her to quiet her nerves, slapping her when she becomes hysterical. Spoiled, selfish, and a prima donna to the core, Astor hates all the nasty, messy details of pregnancy. Used to her booze and her smoking, she has to do without both, and in one hilarious scene (a Davis-Astor inspiration) in which she begs for a drink, Davis tells her the doctor will allow but one ounce of brandy and Astor growls, "Who ever heard of an *ounce* of brandy?" Another time watchdog Davis catches her gorging in the kitchen, and disciplines her amusingly. Finally, while Astor is being delivered, Davis, in mannish attire, strides up and down outside the ranch house in a perfect imitation of an expectant father. This scene made Goulding nervous. "It's too—well, lesbian in tone, Bette," he protested. "The Production Code people and some of the more bluenosey public may pick up on it." Davis drew herself up to her full height, threw away her lighted cigarette (six crewmen jumped to put it out when it fell near flammable material), and spit out at Goulding, "Are you implying that I have lesbian tendencies, *Miss* Director?" But Goulding, who could be as bitchy a queen as anyone, hissed back, "The audience might think so, *Mr.* Davis!" "Well let them!" she screamed back. "There's enough strangling, nitpicking censorship as it is, and if it adds a little paprika so much the better!" *Miss* Goulding and *Mr.* Davis glared at each other for a full minute, and then burst into laughter.

In one of her two autobiographies, Astor gives Davis full credit for helping her get an Academy Award (Best Supporting Actress of 1941) for her role of the temperamental pianist. "I didn't take that picture from Bette, she handed it to me on a silver platter! Sandra was one of the best roles I ever had, and she built it up and made it real and I can never thank her enough!" On Oscar night in 1942, Astor thanked two people in her acceptance speech: Tchaikovsky and Davis.

Thanks to her years of piano study, Astor gave her concert scenes a reality that won the approbation of José Iturbi, who was on the set. She eschewed the "spaghetti arms" technique of other actors who couldn't even play, and did it the right way, practicing so assiduously at home that, even though she was working on a dummy piano before the camera, she seemed completely authentic in her movements.

George Brent was, of course, the man left behind the parade in all this. In fact, he was missing from the middle third of the picture, being presumably dead in a plane crash. "I'm used to playing second and third fiddle," he complained to Goulding one day, "but this takes the cake!" The director, who had long cherished a secret passion for George, hugged him and purred, "Well, *I* still love you, George!" "That's what I'm afraid of, Eddie," George laughed, disengaging himself from the Goulding embrace and lighting a cigarette. But Goulding had the last word. A few setups later he had Davis and Astor in stitches as he demonstrated to George how he should play a love scene—with Eddie in the female part, of course. Red-faced, George told everyone present he had to take a leak and would be back later. "And don't follow him to the john, Eddie," Davis laughed, "or he'll give you some of that Irish Republican Army rubout stuff he was trained in as a kid!" As always graceful, witty, and ready with a return quip under fire, Eddie Goulding put his hand to his heart, cocked his head sidewise, and purred, "Ah, but some things are worth dying for!"

Stung by his previous allusions to lesbianism, Davis brought him up short with, "You superintend the action, Eddie, I'll make the love!"

Most critics felt *The Great Lie* was pretty silly and superficial goods when it opened in April 1941. Bosley Crowther in *The New York Times* wrote, "The story is such a trifle that it hardly seems worth the while. However, the women will probably love it, since fibs are so provocative of fun . . . . the only excuse to be found for this thoroughly synthetic tale is that it gives Miss Davis an opportunity to display her fine talent for distress, to be maternal and noble, the 'good' woman opposed to the 'bad.'" When a Cleveland critic rhapsodized (in rather ornate language) that "Edmund Goulding has such a miraculous, uncanny talent for deciphering the mysteries of the feminine psyche," there was some hilarity at WB.

DAVIS SPENT ALL of her free time in 1940 dreaming about Farney. Since his work kept him in the East, and later at Minneapolis Honeywell in Minnesota, their fairly infrequent reunions were very romantic. Absence, it seemed, made the heart grow fonder. He was just enough of a factor in her life for her to keep romantic illusions intact. But he wasn't right on top of her, either, as Ham had been. He didn't whine, he didn't complain, he didn't have to be weaned away from masturbation, as Ham and Hughes had been. His technique was expert and sure as always; he satisfied her deeply, played back to her all the mature passion she had by then developed with a vengeance.

She took a brief trip to Hawaii in early 1940. On the way back she met a dynamic publicity man, Bob Taplinger. He, too, was masculine, though more dominating and self-confident a personality than Farney. He was good in bed, too, but she sensed in Taplinger, even as the ship neared the California coast, an impatience with her, a rejection of her assertiveness. The romance was soon cold, and she was back to mooning over Farney again. Then, in late December of 1940, with *The Great Lie* drawing to a close, she made a decision. She and Farney would marry. He made no objection—so long as the interstate arrangement continued, with nestings when feasible at Riverbottom on the West Coast and Butternut on the East.

She deliberately timed the wedding to keep the media at bay and got married on December 31, 1940—when the newspapers were on vacation time—at her dear friend Jane Bryan's handsome ranch in Rimrock, Arizona. Jane had deserted her promising career, to Davis's great regret, to marry superentrepreneur Justin Dart.

Davis, mightily amused that the next picture scheduled for her in the New Year 1941 had been titled *The Bride Came C.O.D.*, waited until the day after the wedding, January 1, 1941, to send Jack Warner her fait accompli telegram, leaving him and his publicity department, to say nothing of the Hollywood press corps, stymied. It read:

ARTHUR FARNSWORTH AND I WERE MARRIED AT EIGHT O'CLOCK TUESDAY EVENING (DECEMBER 31) AT THE RANCH OF MR AND MRS JUSTIN DART IN ARIZONA [She purposely omitted the town.]

On hand for the living-room ceremony, conducted by a Methodist minister at Farney's suggestion (and his stern Methodist mother's insistence), were sister Bobby and her current husband, Robert Pelgram; Ruthie; Perc Westmore and his girlfriend, hairdresser Margaret Donovan; Davis's cousin John Favor; and a few others.

After spending their wedding night in a room at the Darts, Davis and Farney returned to Riverbottom the next day, as *The Bride Came C.O.D.* was due to start January 7.

Fearful that marriage might lessen Farney's sex appeal in her eyes, Davis found her trepidations unfounded; each bed session continued to be romantically and sexually enthralling. Davis also found his frequent absences through 1941 very much to her taste. Passive and preoccupied, wrapped up in his work, Farney did not interfere in her career in any way, nor did he express any desire to. His salary, true, did not match hers and she found herself paying all the important bills, but he took care of his own needs on his own pay so could not, she reasoned, technically qualify as a parasitical Mr. Bette Davis. Except for a week or so late in 1941, when his attack of pneumonia in Minneapolis caused her to fly to him, upsetting her shooting schedule on a picture, Farney proved to be an undemanding marital presence.

The Bride Came C.O.D. was one of Davis's less felicitous assignments. Her newfound happiness in her second marriage probably impaired her judgment in this instance. It had been decided by the powers that were at Warners—especially the anxious Hal Wallis—that Davis needed a change of pace from heavy drama and soap, and that a fast-paced, lively comedy would meet the bill. Ignored was the fact that the bulk of Davis fans paid to see her emote with a vengeance—comedy had never been her forte, nor was she particularly adept at it. The decision, in retrospect, was unfortunate, to say the least. Jack Warner was not keen on the project, but Wallis convinced him otherwise. "She'll get stale if she is doing high drama all the time—she needs a rest," Wallis told the boss. "Let's see just how good she actually can be in comedy, and she can romp through it in no time."

Then Wallis had another brainstorm. He decided to pair James Cagney with her in this silly story of a runaway heiress and the pilot who kidnaps her (he's in the pay of her millionaire oil-tycoon father) to prevent her from marrying a buffoonish band leader. Father and bandleader were, respectively Eugene Pallette and Jack Carson, fine comedians both, but defeated in this case by the silly material, as were all on hand. Pilot and heiress land in a ghost town on the California-Arizona border, where they encounter a lovable old hermit (Harry Davenport), go through all manner of misunderstandings, and finally wind up in each other's arms. Screenwriters Julius J. and Philip G. Epstein were not at their best here, desperately conjuring up monumentally silly situations: Davis gets several dozen cactus spines in her derriere after jumping from a plane that has been forced to land; Cagney hits the same derriere with a sling-shot; Cagney imitates a coyote-howl to get Davis to move nearer him when they bunk out in the desert—then he inanely repeats the howl on their wedding night. And so forth and so on. Watching the somewhat overweight forty-one-year-old Cagney making like a fey, coy swain was one of the chief embarrassments of the picture. As for Davis, she revealed a lack of light comedy timing and overplayed the silly misunderstandings and false alarms as if she were working herself up to high tragic denouements. If ever a picture demonstrated that comedy— or at least this brand of screwball comedy—was not her forte, this one does. A farce that Carole Lombard could have larked through took on monumental weight with Davis in the role—so weighty and leaden in fact, that the picture died on her hands.

The critics were cool to the film when it first appeared in 1941, which is to their credit. *The New York Times* said, "[It] is neither the funniest comedy in history nor the shortest distance between two points . . . . a serviceable romp." *The Times* was unduly kind.

Seen many years later, the picture alternates between the frenetic and the pathetic. The desperate Epsteins concocted desperation situations—confusion as to California-Nevada wedding rules, unnecessary wrangles between the secondary characters—that defy all logic. The wonder was that Cagney, who like Davis had fought Warners tooth and nail for more money and better roles, had ever accepted it—even with brother Bill on the production team. And why no one had advised him to lose weight is a cinematic mystery. He looks lined, fat, tired, and confused in many situations that an actor like Cary Grant could have carried off with jaunty aplomb. Davis, in addition to looking ridiculously inept with cactus spines in her behind and stuffing herself with food after a starvation episode in a mine, was for once badly photographed by Ernie Haller (the hot 100-degree Death Valley locations did not help, to be sure) and looked haggard and even sweaty in many scenes—sweat on a star, even in the desert, being one of the standard no-nos onscreen circa 1941.

Not far into the shooting, everyone began to get depressed and disgusted and with great relief they went back to the Burbank studios for the interior shots.

One of the few bright aspects of the picture was the fine performance of veteran Harry Davenport, who got a seventy-fifth birthday party on January 19 from cast and crew. Davis, who greatly admired Davenport (one of the truly great players of all time, she called him) went to him several times for consolation when the script was driving her up the wall. "If you only knew the clinkers I had to do on the stage, and after I was a star, too!" he reassured her. "This, too, will pass." Davis later told director William Keighley, "After the fine dialogue Harry got with me in *All This and Heaven Too*, I feel like apologizing every day for this drivel." The Epsteins were asked to recast some of the situations, but the substitutions were even worse.

In later years Davis admitted that *Bride* was one of her chief mistakes of the period. She called it "truly ridiculous" and on another occasion noted "We [she and Cagney] both reached bottom with this one." It is regrettable that she and Cagney had not exercised in advance the judgment and foresight that they had applied in other instances, and gone on suspension before agreeing to this.

Director William Keighley later said of the atmosphere on location and on the Burbank set: "It was funereal, and that is an understatement. You should have seen the long faces just before I called 'action' and the sighs of relief when I called 'cut!' The happy faces they made on-camera were hollow ones—only Harry Davenport, who was such a good actor he could get into the spirit of anything, and liked his larger-than-usual part, seemed reasonably content. I didn't really want to do the picture, and I don't feel Bette or Jimmy did, either. They got talked into it when they were off their guard—which was seldom, I might add. It was all Hal Wallis's fault. He thought he was being creative in asking Bette and Jimmy to do something offbeat. He was stupid, in my books."

16

Popeye the Magnificent

I N 1941 BETTE DAVIS won a signal honor. She was elected president of the Academy of Motion Picture Arts and Sciences, succeeding the producer Walter Wanger. As the first woman ever to receive this honor, she was naturally flattered and gratified. But before the first official meeting, determined to take her duties seriously, she read the bylaws, researched the past fourteen years of the Academy's history, and arrived at the session full of plans and suggestions.

Shortly she realized that she was supposed to preside as a sort of charming, public relations–enhancing figurehead. Having won two Oscars, plus nominations, plus numerous citations and tributes from all sides, she would enhance the Academy's prestige, it was reasoned. That was all very well, she told her cohorts, but a president must preside, give advice, recommendations, initiate policy. In an atmosphere of tense silence she put on her glasses and read her list of proposals. First she felt the awards should be presented in a large theater rather than at a dinner. Then she expressed her dissatisfaction about extras voting, telling the board bluntly that many of them had no taste and no culture, and couldn't even speak English in many cases.

When the board protested that they had been considering putting off Oscar dinners until after the War, she barked "Nonsense!" and said they were excellent for Academy public relations, especially if held in large theaters. The board met all of her suggestions with frigid silence. Disgusted, Davis resigned shortly thereafter. "If I couldn't function, if my suggestions were disregarded, why should I bother?" she told the press, Darryl Zanuck threatened she would "never work again in Hollywood"—a ridiculous statement, considering she had the security of a long-term Warners contract, plus enormous prestige and clout. When the new president, Jean Hersholt, was installed, all the ideas she had proposed, ironically, were eventually adopted!

Samuel Goldwyn had purchased the movie rights for Tallulah Bankhead's hit Broadway play of 1939, *The Little Foxes*. He assigned William Wyler to direct it, and Wyler decided that no one but Bette Davis should play the lead, the ruthless Regina Giddens, for which Bankhead and Miriam Hopkins, both southern born, had also been considered. Bankhead was deeply offended when she was not asked to do the film, but Goldwyn's New York representative had to tell her bluntly that she was not box-office, at least where film audiences were concerned, and had not done a film in eight years. She had had a fling at movies in the 1931–1933 period, when she was under contract to Paramount, but she did not photograph well—her hooded eyes seemed lifeless, for one thing—and the moviegoing public of the time had not taken to her. Goldwyn and Wyler reasoned, correctly, that if the movie fans hadn't cottoned to Tallulah in 1933, they certainly wouldn't cotton to her in 1941, when she was pushing forty.

Angry and frustrated, knowing she was the ideal person for the part and had created it by her own instincts and talent, Tallulah went about New York taking the name of Bette Davis in vain. "She'll ham it up, she'll put all those damned second-rate oglings and twitchings into it; she'll never be able to lose herself in the role as I did," Tallulah raged, while she drank gin from a bottle in heavy, deep swigs and threw bric-a-brac about until, as her onetime husband, character actor John Emery, reported, "Her apartment looked like the London blitz had hit it!" John was also famous for his bon mot about what life was like as Tallulah's one and only husband (briefly). "It was like the rise, decline, and fall of the Roman Empire!" he reported.

Bankhead continued to seethe for months. Finally she got a chance to meet her hated rival—at a party. Guests gathered around, some of them making bets as to which grande dame would emerge the winner. The exchange went something like this, according to Davis. Tallulah hissed, "So you're the woman who gets to play all my parts in the movies. And I play them so much better!" "I couldn't agree with you more, Miss Bankhead," Davis said sweetly, and turned away. Stunned and open-mouthed, subdued and puzzled, Bankhead asked for a cocktail and repaired quietly to a window seat. The ones who had bet on Davis collected.

The truth was that Davis greatly admired Bankhead. Initially, she did not want to see the theater version of *The Little Foxes* because she wanted to work out her own interpretation of Regina. But eventually she went and wound up so admiring of the Bankhead portrayal, which she saw again, that when she and Wyler got together to discuss the film, she insisted that it could be played no other way. Wyler disagreed vociferously, and for once she refused to submit to his judgments and opinions. This led to constant screaming matches on the set and in his office, but she was adamant, and once even walked off the set, her nerves shot, her emotions in tatters.

Davis pulled her weight with all comers where *The Little Foxes* was concerned. Sam Goldwyn, who had once dismissed her as a film prospect when she had tested for the Colman film in 1929, paid through the nose—some $385,000—to borrow her. Jack Warner had not wanted to lend his valuable star, whom he was still paying a niggardly $3,000 a week, and that was what he proposed to pay her for twelve weeks of *Little Foxes* shooting at the Goldwyn lot. Davis marched into Jack's office and icily informed him that he was pulling no "David O. Selznick pocket-the-money-and-pay-the-star-a-pittance" stuff with *her*, and left him open-mouthed, but eventually compliant, when she demanded his share of the $385,000 deal for herself, no strings attached.

One of the main reasons Jack Warner lent Davis was so that he could get Gary Cooper (for *Sergeant York*) from Goldwyn. He had chuckled initially to himself, delighted with the money; as it evolved, it was Davis who did the chuckling—she had put two top producers in their place. Revenge was sweet, she found.

Meanwhile Miriam Hopkins, who had been the other choice for Regina, was still smarting because Davis had fobbed off her romantic addresses. When she heard that Davis and Wyler were arguing and that Davis had walked off the set, she was gleeful. "That part I was born for!" she told one and all, and hung close to her phone, awaiting a call from Goldwyn and/or Wyler. The call never came. Davis, after calming her nerves and listening to her physician's advice to take it one day at a time, went back to finish her work. Determined to be as tough on Wyler as he had so often been on her, she told him the role would be played her way or else. She was too powerful in 1941 to refuse; Wyler and Goldwyn knuckled under. When Goldwyn, somewhat lamely, tried to interfere with the costumes, Davis brushed him off curtly.

Davis had decided, especially after seeing Bankhead's interpretation, that she would have to play the part as written by Lillian Hellman (who also did the screenplay), to wit: icy, heartless, venomous, formidable, unyielding, and ruthlessly cold. Regina has spent her life competing with her crass, business-oriented brothers, Oscar and Ben (Carl Benton Reid and Charles Dingle). They have always disregarded her because she is a woman, and she is out to even the score. Married to a kind and gentle man, Horace Giddens (Herbert Marshall), who has a heart condition, she is disillusioned with his lack of ruthlessness, and when her nephew Leo steals $75,000 worth of bonds to use in a business deal her brothers have cooked up, she is enraged when her husband wants to claim he lent Leo (Dan Duryea) the bonds. In a scene noted for its passive viciousness, Davis lets her husband die on the stairs after refusing to get his heart medicine.

Davis then blackmails her brothers into giving her two thirds of the deal they are making in exchange for her $75,000 input. Her daughter, Alexandra (Teresa Wright), a good-hearted girl who loves her father, overhears the conversation and flees her mother's house in anger and disgust, with boyfriend Richard Carlson, a town newspaperman who has tried to enlighten her on "the little foxes"—the Giddenses—"who spoil the vines." In the final shot, Davis is seen behind the curtains on the second floor, watching Wright's and Carlson's flight. She knows she is alone, despised, and feared—with a corpse in the nearby bedroom. As she withdraws from behind the curtains, her face registers the sure awareness that she is on her own henceforth, in every respect. But one somehow feels she will survive and prosper. Her cold words to Wright as she is about to leave telegraph this: "I'd like to keep you with me, Alexandra, but I won't make you stay." She even seems glad to note that her hitherto sweet and passive daughter is not, after all, "made of sugar water."

Davis's most famous speech in the film is addressed to her husband, when her plans have been thwarted. "I hope you die! I hope you die soon! I'll be *waiting* for you to die!" This is a woman who has been kept down for many years—first by her rapacious brothers, then by a loveless marriage to a man she thought "would give me the world" and who turns out to have all the limitations of "a bank clerk." Adversity has made her cold, monstrous. Money and power alone, she feels, bring security. Trust no one. Davis's character has also been disillusioned by watching how Oscar has treated Birdie (Patricia Collinge, in a masterly portrayal), a sweet, sensitive southern gentlewoman driven to drink by the boorish crassness of the people around her. Unlike Birdie, Regina, a woman of more spirit and ruthlessness, has decided that if she can't lick 'em, she'll join 'em—and better than that, lick 'em again.

Oddly enough, William Wyler, usually so preceptive about characterization, missed the point of Regina's character—her dehumanization at the hands of her environment, her single-minded, hate-motivated, self-protective ruthlessness. Willie thought Regina should demonstrate some womanly, vulnerable, sympathetic elements, that she should even be somewhat sexy. Davis tried to point out to him that if her character had had sex appeal her manless life would be inexplicable to audiences. And had she been vulnerable or sympathetic in some aspects of her character, her murderous, stop-at-nothing ruthlessness would not have rung true.

Davis played the role as Bankhead had played it—hard, cold, intent only on money and power. In trusting her own instincts (which turned out to be right), in forcing her will on Wyler, she alienated him professionally and to some degree personally—for keeps. He never again invited her to appear in one of his films. (In 1949 Hopkins appeared in *The Heiress*, a Wyler film, but in a supporting role.)

Davis had many objections to the picture while making it. She felt that the Giddens home (pre-financial breakthrough) should have a seedy, worn look to it, and that went for her clothes too, but Goldwyn managed to have his way on that—the home looked Hollywood rich. Neither he nor Wyler liked her rice makeup, which caused her face to look fortyish. "But that's what I am, in this picture!" Davis told Goldwyn. "I'm the mother of a grown daughter, for Christ's sake!" Goldwyn backed down on that one.

"Sam Goldwyn had good taste in some ways," Davis said later. "He knew good stories, but he did tend to want to gloss up pictures where gloss was distinctly not called for." Davis enjoyed regaling friends with a particularly hilarious sample of the far-famed Goldwynesque tendency to malapropisms. When one of his money men had warned him that *The Little Foxes* might be too caustic to appeal to the film public, Sam had rejoindered, "I don't care what it costs—I want it!"

Many of the performers who had appeared in the stage version were on hand for the film version—an added burr in the Bankhead posterior. They all went on to major character-player careers in movies, including Carl Benton Reid and Charles Dingle (Regina's brothers), Dan Duryea (who was to have a nice career playing variations on the sleazy Leo), and Patricia Collinge.

Years later, Richard Carlson told me that the tension on the set had been "bloody murder. Bette and Willie really went at it. Teresa [Wright] asked me one time if anybody'd survive the carnage. I wondered myself, for a while." Carlson, who had appeared earlier in 1941 in *Back Street* with Margaret Sullavan, compared Maggie and Bette thus: "They were both strong, tempermental ladies, but Maggie tended to underplay more. Bette went for the big effects. But they came out even, in my books!" Teresa Wright recalled bursting into tears one day on the set while Willie and Bette yelled scatological insults at each other. Later Bette comforted her with the words, "This, too, shall pass. Keep calm."

Davis had the satisfaction of knowing she was right after all in the way she chose to interpret Regina. Even the not easily pleased Bosley Crowther of *The New York Times* sat up and made nice for her in this. "The Little Foxes will not increase your admiration for mankind," he wrote. "It is cold, cynical. But it is a very exciting picture to watch. . . . [Davis's] performance is . . . abundant with color and mood." Howard Barnes of *The New York Herald-Tribune* really warmed the cockles of Davis's heart, and redeemed the decision she had made over Wyler's objections, when he wrote, "Bette Davis matches Miss Bankhead's splendid portrayal in the play."

The Little Foxes won equal approbation abroad. The British critic Dilys Powell wrote, "[*The Little Foxes*] is enormously helped by its chief player: Bette Davis has never given a finer performance than as the cold murderess."

The Little Foxes silences, once and for all, the frequent over-the-years carpings that Davis was limited to personality extensions, and could not lose herself in a characterization. Her Regina is well thought out, beautifully controlled, wisely conceived, and artistically disciplined in a manner that would make any first-class actress in any medium proud. It is regrettable that Davis had such difficulty in finding roles and characterizations truly worthy of her range and unique gifts. Often in the future, when she did find them and wanted to put them on the screen, the overlords of the studio nixed them as "too costumy," or "too expensive," or "too counter to the current public taste."

As she often stated, Davis believed throughout her career that the public would pay to see good, intelligent, subtle work done with creative conviction and artistic discipline. It is a wonder that she got so many good pictures into the theaters, despite front-office obstructionism. Hal Wallis told her that he couldn't stand the pictures she particularly prized and was proud of doing, "but as long as the public pays to see them we'll keep grinding them out."

Back at Warners after her Goldwyn-Wyler ordeal, Davis found herself confronted with one of Jack Warner's ironic inconsistencies. He refused to let her do Cassie, the mentally ill, forlorn creature of *King's Row*, because the part was too short, even though she and Ida Lupino both craved it. Then he readily agreed to cast her in another secondary part in *The Man Who Came to Dinner*, knowing she'd help sell it.

Davis had desperately wanted John Barrymore to play with her in *The Man Who Came to Dinner*. She had seen the play in New York and felt it should be a movie. Warners purchased the George S. Kaufman–Moss Hart play for a record $250,000, and though she was told her role was distinctly secondary, she said she didn't care and wanted to be part of the proceedings.

The real reason for her enthusiasm was her fervent hope that she would get to act with Barrymore. Davis had never played with any of the Barrymores, and here was her big chance. At her insistence, Warners tested John extensively for the role, but his health had failed badly by then, and he couldn't remember his lines, reading them from a cue card.

Davis was appalled at this development, but for a time refused to admit defeat. But when Jack Warner and director William Keighley showed her some of the Barrymore rushes, and she saw for herself how pathetic he looked, how wan and ill, and how devoid of his usual spark, and the way his eyes wandered to the off-camera blackboard on which was written his dialogue, she cried, out of sheer vexation at having her will thwarted and out of pity for a once-great actor now heading obviously for the exit door, in life as in his career. Barrymore would be dead within months, succumbing to a multiplicity of ailments at age sixty—four months after the January 1, 1942, release of *The Man Who Came to Dinner*.

Davis gave up her fight for Barrymore for good when her dog bit her on the nose, resulting in much bloodiness and swelling. Terrified, she fled Hollywood for the East, where she rested at Butternut until she healed. Taking advantage of her preoccupation with her nose, Jack Warner quietly dropped Barrymore and took on Monty Woolley, who had played Sheridan Whiteside on the New York stage. A distracted Davis did not immediately object to Woolley—not *immediately*.

Back in Hollywood with the famous nose back in shape, Davis began fussing in her usual manner over the script and the photography and everything else connected with *Dinner*. Monty Woolley, as she well knew, was giving a fine performance as the hysterical, egoistic Sheridan Whiteside, modeled, as everyone knew, on the effeminate, individualistic, brazen critic Alexander Woollcott (who even played the role himself in one production).

The cast was good: Ann Sheridan as a flighty actress, Jimmy Durante for comic relief, and a handsome new actor, Richard Travis, as the male foil for the romantic competitiveness of Sheridan and Davis.

Contrary to rumor, there was no bitchy Davis-Hopkins flak between Davis and Sheridan. To begin, Annie Sheridan (one of George Brent's wives—fleetingly) was a rather hearty, uncomplicated, friendly woman offscreen, with a minimum of ego and temperament and a talent that was sparkling and flashy—but distinctly limited, as Davis well knew. Result: No sense of competition from the Sheridan quarter, hence Davis could relax on that score. "Annie just didn't rub her wrong—in fact, flattered her by asking advice on the timing of her lines, stuff like that. Davis ate it up; she loved playing God," as Keighley put it later.

The role of Maggie Cutler, true, was secondary, and Davis as a quiet, self-contained secretary made a rather drab contrast to the flamboyant, dressed-to-the-nines character played by Sheridan, but this aspect Davis didn't seem to mind. "Funny that," Hal Wallis told me in 1962, "because it was like her first film, *Bad Sister*, in a way—here she was the drab wren up against the flashy peacock! Bette was full of surprises, and her not minding her status on this picture was one of them. Of course we were all grateful to her for helping hype the film at the box office. Any picture with her name on it at that time was bound to sell—and big!"

Some of her friends, circa 1941, were of the opinion that Davis was more given to handing soapy trash to fellow actors like Mary Astor, as in *The Great Lie*, and playing second fiddle to Woolley in *Dinner* because of her newfound felicity with Arthur Farnsworth. It was a relatively serene period in her life.

Bosley Crowther of *The New York Times* handed Davis a critical posie in his review, writing, "One palm should be handed Bette Davis for accepting the secondary role of the secretary, and another palm should be handed her for playing it so moderately and well." A saddened John Barrymore, reportedly heartbroken over losing a role that might well have let him exit from life with flying colors, congratulated both Woolley and Davis with a gracious telegram.

During *The Man Who Came to Dinner*, Davis worked with someone from her distant past. Best known for her Aunt Pittypat in *Gone With the Wind*, Laura Hope Crews had had a small role (as a whorehouse madam) in Davis's *The Sisters* in 1938, but the two had barely worked together. When Crews was hired for *The Man Who Came to Dinner* (in a small role that was later cut) she was in decline at sixty-two, and in fact would die within the year.

Since she had some scenes with Davis in the picture, Crews was somewhat nervous, considering the reversal in their fortunes, and feared, as she told friends, that Davis, noted for her temper and arrogance, might pull the "star bit" and take revenge for the slap-and-pushing that then-star Crews had given ingenue Davis in stock thirteen years before.

But Davis showed she was above such tactics, and that she harbored no ill will; rather, she went out of her way to be kind and considerate, made sure that a chair was provided for her, along with refreshments, and even let her lie down in her own dressing room on one occasion when Miss Crews felt faint.

Asked about this at the time by a fan book writer, Davis said, "I want that kind of consideration when I am old and sick—those times come to all of us."

At the end of shooting Miss Crews came to Davis's dressing room, silently pressed a box into her hand, and was gone. In it Davis found an exquisite, jewel-encrusted watch.

"BETTE FASCINATED ME. There is something elemental about Bette—a demon within her which threatens to break out and eat everybody, beginning with their ears." Thus spoke John Huston of Bette Davis in his autobiography. He added, "The studio was afraid of her, afraid of her demon. They confused it with overacting. Over their objections, I let the demon go."

Huston's final sentence is ambiguous—until one views the picture he directed her in, *In This Our Life*. Then it is obvious that he did indeed let the demon go—*berserk!* Davis overacts all over the place in John Huston's second film as a director, made on the heels of his triumph in the noirish Sam Spade melodrama *The Maltese Falcon* (Warners' third try at the story; Davis had been in version II). *In This Our Life* is a melodramatic mélange indeed. Neither he nor Davis liked the script. She claimed that the Pulitzer Prize–winning novel by Ellen Glasgow, on which it was based, had been cheapened and vulgarized, emphasizing phony melodrama at the cost of the carefully written character delineations Miss Glasgow had created. Glasgow, who met Davis after seeing the picture, couldn't have agreed more. In fact, she out-Davised Davis in her angry excoriation of the picture. Davis, who was used to bullying writers, met her match in

Glasgow. Trying to weather the onslaught of temperament from the outraged authoress, she ventured, "You should have been an actress, Miss Glasgow—you're so volatile!" "If I had chosen acting over writing," the authoritarian Glasgow retorted, "I wouldn't be the overacting ham you are!" As always, when her bluff was called, Davis backed off.

Glasgow was a better film critic than she knew, for Davis didn't realize that whatever the weaknesses of the script, her own overblown, actressy portrayal had aggravated matters. The outraged authoress was one of the few with the guts to tell her so.

The reviewer for *Script*, Rob Wagner, would have warmed the cockles of Miss Glasgow's acerbic and righteously indignant heart, for he wrote:

"Considering the extensive acclaim vouchsafed Miss Davis' past histrionic excesses, it is no small wonder that the lady favors assignments which permit her to bug her eyes, twitch her hands and maneuver the lower extremities as though in performance of some esoteric Charleston. Unfortunately, Stanley Timberlake, as conceived in the Ellen Glasgow novel, provides no legitimate reasons for theatrical hanky-panky. Nothing daunted, the star promptly dismembered the character, reassembled it in the image and likeness of many of her past portrayals. In so doing, the integrity of the Glasgow work disappeared."

Wagner spoke truly, for *In This Our Life* is a catalog of all Davis's most unrestrained acting tricks, idiosyncrasies, and histrionic mischiefmaking. If ever she had needed Willie Wyler, she needed him for that picture. As it was, Huston was a young director (then thirty-five) who was only on his second picture and was still feeling his way along with charts and drawings for every single scene. In addition, he was interpreting a script in which he had little faith but which he did not want to walk out on for fear of offending his pal, the screenwriter Howard Koch. Davis knew instinctively she could have her own way and use her own ideas throughout.

Possibly, from his own standpoint, the harried Huston was right in letting her "go," as he put it. Had he taken her on, in addition to his other concerns, he might not have lasted on the picture, given her studio clout. It is amusing, in view of his countless macho posturings in later years, to discover Huston in the role of pussycat, vis-à-vis Davis. What Wyler, Mike Curtiz, or Goulding would have found intolerable in her, he swallowed wholesale, to Davis's contempt. Years later, when told of his bullying, macho attitudes with other co-workers, she snorted, "Well, the one time *I* had him, the son of a bitch was *putty* in *my* hands!" And so he was.

Granted that the Ellen Glasgow novel was complex, with a host of subplots and subcharacters, Koch had his hands full hacking a main story line out of a novel that should never have been filmed.

To be as brief as possible about the plot, Davis is the bad sister and Olivia De Havilland is the good sister in a genteel but impoverished Virginia family. Davis steals her sister's husband, serious, milquetoasty Dennis Morgan, and later he commits suicide from guilt. De Havilland and dad Frank Craven and mom Billie Burke forgive the errant woman and home she comes. Soon she is off her mourning act, for now she is out to win back the lawyer, George Brent, whom she had jilted for Morgan. Now romantically involved with De Havilland, he spurns Davis, who rushes off and is killed driving too fast. The final scene finds De Havilland and Brent learning of the death and drawing close to-gether—at peace, at last.

All of this might have jelled had the doings not been limned so melodramatically both in Davis's acting and in the hapless Koch's script. Davis and Huston both liked, and later cited, the depiction by Ernest Anderson of a decent, self-educated black man whom Davis tries to pin the accident on and who is later exonerated. Davis always claimed that blacks of the period were gratified to play a decent exemplar instead of the loony Stepin Fetchits and the saccharine servant types so often por-trayed. This point is valid enough, and Anderson's and his mother's (Hattie McDaniel) quiet, poignant underplaying are the best things in the film.

An amusing sidelight, one of the film's rare touches of individuality and imagination: Huston, for fun, put some unbilled "guest stars" into a roadhouse sequence, including his dad, Walter Huston, as a bartender, and John's "gang" from The Maltese Falcon—Bogart, Astor, Greenstreet, Lorre, Ward Bond, Barton MacLane, and Elisha Cook, Jr., as customers. But one must look sharp to see them.

Not all critics agreed with Rob Wagner. Film reviewer and author William Schoell is among the film's defenders, writing in 1974: "[The picture] is a powerful, absorbing drama of sibling rivalry, selfishness, suicide and incest . . . . sometimes it lacks enough depth and impact in its presentation, but it is constantly on the verge of exploding like a powder-keg and many scenes have intrinsic power. . . . Surprisingly enough, much of it is not at all dated. The near-final scene between Davis and Charles Coburn (excellent in his dramatic role as Davis's un-cle here) is brutally effective and brilliantly rendered."

Davis was delighted to be back again in a picture with her good friend, Olivia De Havilland, though for the third time in a row they were cast as rivals in love. Davis had originally wanted Olivia's role, but had been talked out of it by the film's producer, Hal Wallis, who pointed out to her that she had been the passive good girl in *The Man Who Came to Dinner* opposite Ann Sheridan's flamboyant bitch, and now she had to switch roles or her fans would think she had lost her guts. Faced with this challenge, Davis said no more about the good-sister part but instead occupied herself with working up an inappropriate hairstyle featuring wind-blown bangs that caused laughter later at a studio preview and making up her face garishly, the main feature being a Cupid's-bow mouth (a departure) which she thought would give variety but only disappointed fans who whispered—and wrote in—"Why steal Crawford's act? Let *her* lipstick and rouge to the nines!"

De Havilland, too, was relieved that her assignment went uncontested, for she felt that playing a flamboyant bitch went against her established image. If pushed to take it, she would have flatly refused.

De Havilland gave a fine, controlled, womanly, and wise depiction of the decent Roy. (Glasgow had given the women men's names: Davis was Stanley. This annoyed Wallis, but Davis thought it cute and insisted the names be retained.) De Havilland's problems with the picture lay elsewhere, for once again, as in the case of Errol Flynn, she found herself the focus of male passion. John Huston fell head over heels in love with her and made no secret of it. This gave a gleeful Davis plenty of excuses to "protect" Olivia from his advances (Olivia, to be sure, was glad of the protection) and to accuse Huston of favoring Olivia in scenes, especially in close-ups. All in all, Davis kept Huston on the defensive throughout the shooting, driving him up the wall, and bullying Mr. Macho unmercifully. Indeed, it took a war—World War II—to save him from her.

When Pearl Harbor was attacked on December 7, 1941, the film was still weeks away from completion. Huston was suddenly called to Washington on War Department business, and Raoul Walsh was called in to shoot some scenes, including the climactic one where Davis realizes that her uncle, Charles Coburn, has incestuous desires for her. Walsh had no reason to put up with Davis's tantrums and moods, and made it plain. A far more experienced director than Huston was at that time, he was more interested in pleasing Jack Warner, who held his knack for speedy shooting in high esteem, and Davis was told to get off her ass and get with it. She had already held up shooting for various reasons that fall of 1941, including a plane trip to Farney in Minneapolis when her hapless mate had contracted pneumonia. Once back, she kept everybody on edge, and Walsh had had enough of it. By January 1942, the picture was in the can, by hook or by crook, mostly hook. Henceforth, Walsh was never one of Davis's favorite people.

Davis's ill-disguised antipathy for John Huston had other roots. She felt he had traded on the name of his father, Walter Huston, again and again, and that his early roustabout, rootless, wandering existence, punctuated with occasional schooling and acting jobs, had been that of a spoiled, irresponsible brat rather than that of an authentic rebel. "He was a weakling dropout—I was the true rebel who rose above my environment," she once told Wallis. Huston, again thanks to his father's connections, had later gotten writing jobs and had worked on *Jezebel* and *Juarez*. As a screenwriter Huston always worked in tandem with others. "He contributed the sass, his co-authors contributed the substance," was yet another of Davis's nasty cracks about Huston. About his infatuation for De Havilland during the *In This Our Life* shooting, Davis sneered: "He fawned on her like a lapdog. I like a man who asserts his feelings honestly. He is a vanilla ice-cream cone, that man!"

In later years, she said she had felt *The Maltese Falcon* was a one-time fluke, thought that in 1941 Huston was a dilletantish also-ran, and expressed her surprise that he had gone so far as a director, "considering that the man never has had, and never will have, a recognizable style of any kind!" She added that she only accepted him for *In This Our Life* because everyone "was raising so much hell about *Falcon*—I thought I'd see what this so-called boy wonder was like close up. I found out!"

Decades later, on the set of *The Night of the Iguana* (the film version of a play in which Davis had starred), I asked Huston (who had had his revenge by bumping Davis in favor of Ava Gardner for the movie) what Davis had been like to work with in *In This Our Life*. By then all puffed up with success and critical recognition, Huston barked: "She was a hell-raising bitch! I know she's never liked me and all I can say is fuck her!" Which represented the sum total of what I could get out of John Huston regarding Bette Davis.

De Havilland always recalled the picture rather fondly, and when I asked her about it in 1964, when she was doing yet another picture with Davis (*Hush . . . Hush, Sweet Charlotte*, for which Davis expressly requested her) she enthused about Davis, was stonily silent about John Huston, and lavishly praised Charles Coburn, Billie Burke (cast against usual type in a dramatic role as Davis's languishing mother), and Frank Craven ("Such solid, true performers," she repeated several times).

She smiled and laughed in delight when I told her that my favorite De Havilland scene in *In This Our Life* was the one in which, having gone to Baltimore to comfort the melodramatically widowed Davis after

Morgan's suicide, she discovers Morgan's picture among her sister's bed-clothes; with a poignant, understated pathos she gently turns the picture over, the gesture implying sadly that *that* phase of her life is now finally, irrevocably concluded.

Certainly Coburn outdoes himself as the bullying, arrogant uncle who has cheated her father in business and whose incestuous passion for niece Davis is pathetically quenched when his doctor tells him he has only weeks to live. And Billie Burke and Frank Craven, fine actors both, are deeply touching as the downtrodden, defeated, and regretful parents.

BY EARLY 1942 Davis had started to think with her customary hard-headedness about salary increases and a scaling down of her constant work. When *In This Our Life* finally ground to a halt, she prepared to observe her annual twelve-week layoff period without salary.

The publicity department then asked her to do all the usual chores that a completed picture required—interviews with the press, photo sessions. This she was happy to do without salary, as per the agreement, realizing that the publicity people had to do their jobs as she did hers.

When she arrived at the photo gallery, she was informed by a studio representative that she couldn't do the publicity work because she was technically on layoff, and the studio would have to pay her if she did any work at all. After telling the representative that she was doing the work gratis, she raced wildly to Jack Warner's inner sanctum and let him have it in no uncertain terms, claiming that his representative had ordered her off the lot as if she were a bit player, not, as she yelled at Jack, "your biggest moneymaker—and your most underpaid one!" She was a star now, she continued, and refused to be pushed around, especially when she was giving him a day of free work, had been glad to do it, and then was told to leave.

"You'll pay for this disrespect!" she screamed as she left Warner's office. "Oh brother, how you'll pay!" She raced off on a vacation to Mexico, and for weeks refused phone calls, telegrams, or letters from Burbank. Warner was frantic. "What does the woman want now?" he asked her agent. He found out soon enough. Davis wanted a new contract that stipulated a small fortune for each picture, the pictures to be kept to three pictures maximum per year, plus all the star "perks" that "those pampered bitches at MGM [Crawford] are getting!" Frantic to get his biggest asset back from Mexico, Jack Warner, eating humble pie, gave in to every demand.

17

War Bonds, Now, Voyager, and the Canteen

F ROM 1942 ON, Davis was in the forefront of all patriotic activities, especially bond-selling tours. A new program was instituted, with the cooperation of the government and the studios, to take advantage of the tremendous appeal of Hollywood personalities in furthering the war effort. The United States had officially entered World War II on December 8, 1941, the day after Pearl Harbor, when Davis's idol Franklin D. Roosevelt addressed Congress with his famous "a day that will live in infamy" speech. Davis had written Washington at once, saying that, as a popular star with a wide following, she stood ready to do all she could.

She did not have to wait long. When *In This Our Life* finished shooting in early 1942, she was assigned to the "Stars Over America" contingent of personalities who would fan out through every state in the Union, addressing crowds, signing autographs, selling war bonds, and offering film mementos at auction, with proceeds going to the war effort.

Davis worked tirelessly at this, as did many other top stars. Assigned at first to the Iowa territory, she drew such crowds there that she went on at government request to Missouri, where she sold a phenomenal

number of war bonds and got an arm-and-wrist ache from signing countless autographs. Next, she went on to Oklahoma, where the Okies fell
in love with her, and soon she was swinging around at barn dances,
visiting private homes, and speaking endlessly at fairs and rotary meetings and schools all over the state. With her usual asperity she told
reporters, "I think it outrageous that movie stars have to wheedle and
beg people into buying bonds to help their country, but if that is the
way it is, I'm going to squeeze all I can out of everyone!" She won a
mixed reaction for her zeal in an Oklahoma City factory when she gave
the workers a harangue about "doing what you can, to the level you
can—or you're not my idea of an American!" Farney, who had just been
put in charge of training films that Disney made for the Minneapolis
Honeywell aircraft, suggested by phone that a little more tact might be
in order when it came to speeches and dealing with the press, and she
yelled over the thousand miles that separated them, "It lights fires under
their asses! It gets them *reacting* and *acting*! Somebody has got to wake
these people up to the fact that they're fighting for their lives! It's all or
nothing!"

Even Jack Warner, whose business, after all, was to sell Bette Davis
pictures to millions of adoring fans, counseled her that press reports had
her yelling like a training sergeant at privates in state after state. "These
are your fans, Bette," he insisted, "They want you warm, gracious,
kindly, and they want the personification of what they see on screen.
Don't get hateful. Don't get strident. Don't disenchant them!"

"Jack, I know what I'm doing," she shot back. "You and your brother
in New York just sit around and count the money I make for you. I'm
the one who has to deal up front with the public, and I know what I'm
doing! The only way to get them to contribute, to develop enthusiasm,
is to let 'em have it straight, no holds barred!"

Actually, the public seemed to like Davis's patriotic harangues and
pep sessions and rallies. She knew her public better than the Warner
people did. Playing bitches like Mildred, she told her aides, was what
had made her a star, not fluttering, sugar-water roles. They expected her
to be feisty and vivid. They expected to get stirred up. And stir them up
she would.

Jack Warner and others were later forced to admit that her tactics
paid off. She wound up selling a total of two million dollars' worth of
bonds in two days. And over two weeks, she sold many more.

In Tulsa, Oklahoma, as she later reported, her autograph alone sold
to a well-heeled oil man for $50,000. At an aircraft factory she sold a

picture of herself as *Jezebel*—a bitch, not a nice girl, she reminded Warner—for a cool quarter of a million dollars worth of bonds.

IN APRIL 1942 Davis began work on a picture that was to become
one of her most successful and admired. *Now, Voyager* is one of my three
personal Bette Davis favorites and was one of her own great favorites.
The Bette Davis image is given a thorough workout in this fine drama.

Now, Voyager, adapted from a fine Olive Higgins Prouty novel of
1941, her third in a series about the fictional Vale family of Boston, was
directed by Irving Rapper, the talented Warners writer who had moved
on to directing. Casey Robinson, one of the screen's most expert writers
of dramas highlighting women and their concerns, offered his best inspirations here. Hal Wallis produced with his usual energy and taste. Sol
Polito photographed with great technical skill and creative sensibility.
Orry-Kelly was on hand yet again to dress the women with flawless
taste. Robert Haas's perceptive feeling for ambience and locale was in
full flower here. And Max Steiner won one of his many Academy
Awards with a rich, evocative score.

And the brilliant talents of fine actors—Paul Henreid, Claude Rains,
John Loder, the amusing comedians Franklin Pangborn and Frank
Puglia—hold their own against the women—Gladys Cooper's domi-
neering Boston matriarch, Ilka Chase's understanding sister-in-law, Lee
Patrick's incisive ship's passenger, Janis Wilson's pathetic misfit child,
and Bonita Granville's bitchily bullying niece.

And at the center is Bette Davis, in full artistic maturity at age
thirty-four, in the Class-A picture she had so often dreamed of during
her mid-1930s potboiler phase.

The well-known story deals with the repressed, miserable, overweight, and squirrel-spectacled Charlotte Vale, frustrated spinster
daughter of a Boston Brahmin family. She is dominated by starchy, unloving materfamilias Gladys Cooper. Eventually she is rescued from a
lifetime of loneliness and desolation by psychiatrist Claude Rains, who
cites for her the words of one of life's most famous outsiders—the poet
Walt Whitman: "Untold want, by life nor land ne'er granted, now, voyager, sail thou forth to seek and find. . . ."

And so freshly caparisoned, beautifully made up, gorgeously cou-
tured, glasses discarded, but with confidence and self-esteem still lacking, Davis goes, courtesy of a Rains-Chase conspiracy, on a South
American cruise, and meets Paul Henreid, a Prince Valiant unhappily

married to a self-centered hypochondriac. She learns the fulfillment of reciprocal love and returns to the Marlborough Street matriarch ready to do battle. She bests her, inherits all the family money, then helps Henreid's child, Janis Wilson, a blighted thirteen-year-old, toward happiness. Somewhat masochistically self-denying, Charlotte tells Henreid's Jerry that she will take care of the girl and he must stay with his wife, the famous closing lines being: "Jerry, don't let's ask for the moon—we have the stars!"

The universal appeal of *Now, Voyager* has never been commented upon sufficiently. Too much has been made of it as gay camp, feminine wish-fulfillment, fairy-tale unreality. To many, then and now, *Now, Voyager* has pointed the way upward, to a greater self-understanding. Certainly in 1942 it burst as a white light on my nineteen-year-old consciousness. To many women *and* men in movie houses across the United States, it imparted a message of hope; it said yes, you *can* slough off the dross of negative surroundings, futile human associations, defeatist atmospheres; yes, you *do* have the right to search for love.

Bette Davis noted that she received thousands of letters from men and women all over the country after *Now, Voyager* was released, citing similar real-life stories of domineering parents, wounded self-image, frustration in love, disappointments in the search for self-realization. She took deep pride in the knowledge that she and the other artists associated with the film had helped to illuminate the deepest needs and wishes of the human heart. She won the permanent gratitude and respect of many in 1942, including me. I emerged from that Lynn, Massachusetts, theater determined to be *me*, not what others expected of me; to forge my way to the individual fulfillments my destiny had designed for me. If one of the functions of true art is to enlighten, clarify, and inspire, then *Now, Voyager* qualifies for such a designation. Not that the film was perfect. Yes, there was a lot of wish-fulfillment in it; yes, luck favored her with wealth and other opportunities to fulfill herself. But these minor flaws are not important; what is important is the positive thrust of the picture's theme, the buoyancy, the hopefulness of its spirit.

There is a scene in *Now, Voyager* that is one of my all-time favorites (and I've been seeing movies for sixty years). Early on in the picture, Davis, living in a drab, bleak upper room of a great Boston mansion, tyrannized by her pathologically domineering mother, is being driven toward madness by emotional starvation and wounded self-esteem. Her sister-in-law, frightened and concerned for the overweight, unattractive spinster's emotional welfare, has brought the compassionate psychiatrist Claude Rains to the house, and he has persuaded Davis to show him her room. Suddenly she takes a photograph album from her youth out of the desk drawer. Wild-eyed and tense, bitter and sardonic, she forces him to look at it with her. Flipping through the pages, she says, "You wouldn't have known me then—I was twenty, then. . . ." Max Steiner's music swells grandly and suddenly, bathed in cameraman Sol Polito's radiant white light, blurring and rippling montage effects usher in a startlingly dramatic flashback scene in which Davis is making youthfully fervent love on a sunny, windswept deck with a handsome young ship's officer in a white uniform, played by the then twenty-seven-year-old Charles Drake. "It was the proudest moment of my life," her voice-over later proclaims. The young man in the white uniform, now vanished irretrievably into the past, represents lost fulfillment, catharsis, freedom, self-realization, ultimate happiness . . .

Later in the scene, Davis tells Rains of how her mother did not think the man, whom she had met on a cruise up the west coast of Africa, "suitable for a Vale of Boston." "What man *is* suitable? She's never found one!" she cries. She goes on to tell Rains of her mother's assorted tyrannies and cruelties, and he leaves her weeping to go down and castigate the dragon in the Marlborough Street drawing room, countering her fierce and arrogant protestations of "a mother's rights" with, "A child has rights! To make her own decisions! To grow and blossom in her own particular soil."

Later in the film, Davis, liberated by her love for Henreid, but aware that he is beyond her reach because he is married, says, "Shall I tell you what you've given me—first, a little bottle of perfume made me feel so important . . . and then your flowers came, and I knew you were thinking of me. I could have walked into a den of lions. In fact, I did, and the lion didn't hurt me!"

Casey Robinson's literate and tasteful dialogue, much of it from the Prouty novel, is one of the picture's salient features. He argued bitterly in later years with Davis's assertion that she had to rewrite the dialogue as she went along. He insisted, in no uncertain terms, that not a word was changed from his original script. The truth lies somewhere between, probably, as Davis had a notable propensity for meddling with dialogue and situations so they would suit what she conceived to be the most salable and appealing aspects of her mystique. Indeed she was quite a meddler in any and all areas, as director Irving Rapper told me in 1957. When I asked him to sum up, in one word, what it had been like to work with her, he hissed, "Tough!" He then went on to tell of their endless arguments over every detail, and how he went home every night angry and exhausted. Unfortunately, fine talent that he was, Irving Rap-

per did not command her ultimate trust and respect as Goulding and
Wyler did. Something in the Davis-Rapper chemistry prevented her
from falling in with him. In this, as in the other pictures they were to
do, he found her bullying and hounding a misery.

John Loder, who played with great dignity and conviction the
Boston aristocrat, Elliott Livingston, whom Charlotte jilts because, as
she tells her enraged mother, "I don't love him," had some interesting
memories of the film when I interviewed him in 1970. "She put her
whole heart and being into that film. She had a passion and an artistic
conviction I have never encountered in another actress. Going into a
scene with her was like going into a hot furnace—and somehow, instead of getting burned by the flames, you came out of it purged,
cleansed; you felt you had learned something."

Loder felt that Davis had imparted ultimate conviction to her role
because "she had innate breeding. I know she won her initial reputation
as a hellcat, as a shrew, but if you look closely, even in those roles she
achieved the classy effects that only a thoroughbred could manage."

Paul Henreid, who became a star thanks to his role as the lover,
Jerry Durrance, had lavish words of praise in 1964 for Davis. Remarking
more than once that she had remained friends with him and his family
over the many years since, he recounted: "I know she had wanted an
American actor for the role. I was an Austrian, had worked with Max
Reinhardt, was as continental as could be, complete with a heavy accent
that I later toned down with hard work. She was appalled with my test.
They had put me in a fancy smoking jacket, brilliantined my hair, made
me up so thickly I looked like a department store dummy. She asked me
what I thought of it. I said I felt I looked all wrong."

Davis, as he recalled, thereupon ordered another test. "Show the
guy in his natural state," she ordered. The results satisfied her as she
recognized his fine, sensitive acting gift. "She was the soul of kindness
to me all through the shooting, as she was to all the cast," Henreid said.
"I have never understood these stories of how difficult she was to other
cast members. On the contrary, she would fight their battles with the
director."

The oft-discussed scene in which Paul lights two cigarettes, then
passes one to Davis, has been claimed as an original inspiration by
many, including Olive Higgins Prouty, Irving Rapper, Hal Wallis, and
Henreid himself. But it wasn't *that* original. George Brent had done the
same thing ten years before with Ruth Chatterton in *The Rich Are Always
With Us*. Reportedly he picked up the habit in that picture and had done
it for Davis a number of times since. ("It must have been thousands of

times, as she smoked like a chimney!" Jerry Asher later said.) It appears then that it was Davis, tutored years before by Brent, who finally came up with the idea after other cigarette-lighting methods in that scene had been found awkward and cumbersome.

Charles Drake, who appeared with Davis in the famous flashback scene, recalled that he was "just a kid, had only been in films a short time, and I was really in awe of Bette. She was thirty-four or so to my twenty-seven, but damned if they didn't dress her up to look the twenty she was supposed to be—and younger than that! But it wasn't just the way they made her up and dressed and coiffured her. She, being a genius, had suggested herself into the persona of a young girl, and so lifelike she was that I felt I really was with a very young girl!"

Drake also recalled that Rapper had been rough with him because of his inexperience but "Bette was just swell—always reassuring and kind and going to bat for me with Rapper." He snapped "no comment" when questioned as to the rumors that Davis had gotten overly lost in her part and had developed an offscreen crush on him. But his blush and his silence conveyed much.

It has also been rumored that Davis was more than a little interested in Paul Henreid despite the fact both of them were married at the time. He, too, has always refused to discuss this with interviewers. Where Drake barked "no comment," Paul put it with a little more continental suavity. "It is ungentlemanly to discuss personal matters concerning a lady, especially one who has been such a good friend to me and my family," was his rejoinder to me when I ventured upon the subject. A word to the wise, or a sentence, being sufficient, I did not pursue it.

Only a few months before her death in 1971, Gladys Cooper was appearing in London in a version of *The Chalk Garden*. Then eighty-three, her acting style unimpaired, she was delightful in the play, and later we talked in her dressing room. Of Davis she said, "She was and is so gifted. I have always felt sad that the theater was robbed of her talent so consistently through the years. I know she did stage things, but she had a major, unlimited gift, had an inner flame, a gorgeous intensity. Much of what she was given to do in Hollywood was unworthy of her talents. She could have played Shakespeare, Shaw, Ibsen. Some thought her limited; I always felt she limited herself, by agreeing to some most unworthy vehicles. I studied her closely during *Now, Voyager* and there was absolutely no limit to what she could have accomplished. Though she was the star and I the supporting player, she was so gracious, so civilized, so kind—and oddly, so humble. She told me she reverenced my talent, that it was a privilege to play with me. She was a woman who, no matter what Hollywood did to her, always had a great innate breeding. And such strength! More strength than most men I've known!"

It was Jerry Asher, a close friend of mine who had been a studio publicist and had written many fan magazine stories, including ones for my *Screen Stars* and *Movie World* in the 1960s, who gave me a startling "first" that I have yet to see in print and which I have never used until this book. He swore it was true.

At one point, Davis, convinced that only an All-American-boy type would be right for the role of Jerry Durrance in *Now, Voyager*, seriously considered Ronald Reagan for the part! She ordered a screening of the Sam Wood–directed *King's Row*, which had been shot in 1941 but not released until early 1942. The future president, who has always singled out the role of Drake McHugh as his all-time favorite, made a big forward leap in front-office respect and approbation as the result of fan reaction to him in this. His Drake was a touching study of a fundamentally decent young man in a small town in 1900, who loses his inheritance through embezzlement and is forced to give up his loose ways and find a job on the railroad. The doctor-father of a girl he had once loved, who thought him at the time a vulgar womanizer and hell-raiser, deliberately amputates Drake's legs after a railroad accident which has actually left him unscathed. When Reagan's Drake awakens and realizes he has lost his lower limbs, he shouts out the famous words, "Where's the rest of me?"—the line forever associated with him. Director Sam Wood had guided Reagan, then thirty, through a far more sensitive portrayal than he had ever given, and it was much discussed around the lot.

Davis, who admired Reagan's then wife Jane Wyman, also a Warner actress, had come to know them fairly well. In later years she was to speak of Reagan disparagingly, calling him "Little Ronnie Reagan" and expressing her wonder that "Little Ronnie," an "also-ran in the Warner acting ranks," had made it to governor of California—and then president. As in the case of Robert Montgomery, she had disliked his conservative views, and her rock-ribbed Democratic liberalism had resented his eventual conversion from Democrat to Republican. Indeed, it was only after his kind remarks concerning her in 1987 during the Kennedy Center Awards (she was one of the honorees) that she began to speak well of him, commenting on his graciousness that evening.

But in 1942, according to Jerry, the thirty-four-year-old Davis had spotted in the thirty-year-old Reagan many of the solid, decent, manly qualities she felt were required for the character of *Now, Voyager's* Jerry Durrance.

According to Asher, who had an impishly wicked tongue, Davis had also taken full note of Reagan's charms (pictures of him in swimsuits flexing his muscles could be seen as late as 1942 in many a fan magazine) and with her propensity for finding other women's husbands all the more attractive because they were possibly unattainable, she got it into her head that he would be interesting to play to for the months the film would require to complete.

According to Jerry, it was Jack Warner who talked her out of it. "One swallow doesn't make a summer," Jack huffed, "and just because Sam got a good performance out of the kid in *King's Row* doesn't mean he's up to playing your lover in a class-A production like *Now, Voyager!*" Davis asked Warner to test him; he laughed her off. Then she asked Hal Wallis and Irving Rapper about it. They thought the idea was a hoot and a howl. "Bette Davis and Ronald Reagan in *Now, Voyager?* You gotta be kidding, lady," was the gist of their responses. So the idea came to nothing, especially after Davis spotted Henreid. Reagan, who probably heard about it, would doubtless have accepted Jack's putdown with good humor. As late as 1988 he was telling how, when Jack heard he was running for governor, he yipped. "Chuck Heston for governor; Reagan for best friend!"

WATCH ON THE RHINE had been a distinguished 1941 Broadway play about a dedicated undergrounder who counters the Nazi threat, and it brought many honors to that fine Hungarian actor Paul Lukas, who had wasted his talents for years in trivial Hollywood films (Wyler's *Dodsworth* being one of the notable exceptions in 1936).

In 1942 Warners bought the play, and, surprisingly, considering the customs of the time in Filmville, assigned the play's star to the movie. But Jack Warner and his minions worried about Lukas's lack of box-office clout. While he was instantly recognizable to film fans who had watched him partially redeem weak pictures and enhance strong ones, Warner felt none of them would go out of his or her way to plunk down cold cash for a Paul Lukas starrer. Warner thereupon persuaded Davis to take the secondary role of his noble, self-sacrificing, supportive, and loyal wife, who brings her resistance fighter husband and their children to Washington after years of foiling and frustrating the Nazis in numerous European locales.

In Washington, all goes well for a while, the weary idealists rest from their labors, and then George Coulouris, a fellow guest, a Rumanian count with Nazi connections, discovers their secret and threatens to expose them to the German embassy officials. Lukas takes him to the garage, kills him, and before driving off with the body leaves his wife and children to the care of her mother, Lucile Watson, and brother, Donald Woods. The latter, shocked out of their complacent isolationism, wish him Godspeed.

Such is the plot, and as written and performed, Paul Lukas's role is the dominant one. Davis, a fervent Democrat and Roosevelt supporter, fell once again into the trap of agreeing graciously to rescue a picture with her proven box-office appeal, and at first came on so humble as to suggest that Paul Lukas should have top billing, given his prominence in the proceedings; Hal Wallis soon talked her out of *that*.

Soon, as was usual in Bette Davis pictures, there was trouble aplenty on the set. Even though Lillian Hellman (with co-writer Dashiell Hammett) had opened up the play with additional scenes, and had built up for Davis the part Mady Christians had played so well on the stage, Davis soon came to realize that once again she had made the mistake of taking an unsuitable, secondary role (as in *The Man Who Came to Dinner*) after struggling for years to get strong starring parts. She could be heard mumbling that she was being "used and exploited" and tried to enlist a haughty, reserved, and unsympathetic Lucile Watson to her cause. Watson, an excellent character actress who had many years of stage experience and who had performed admirably in pictures with such stars as Norma Shearer and Vivien Leigh (neither of whom had outshone her in their scenes together), felt Davis overacted "like a rank amateur" and enraged Davis further by telling her that "more years on the stage would have benefited you enormously, my dear." When Davis found out, moreover, that Lucile was a rock-ribbed Republican and thought Roosevelt and his works were sheer anathema, the atmosphere froze up even more. The last straw came when Watson, weary of listening to Davis's complaints about her "limited straitjacket of a role" and about how she wished now that Irene Dunne and Margaret Sullavan, who refused the role, had been "suckered into it instead of me," told Davis crisply, that if she "didn't feel she was up to it, then get out of it."

Instead Davis took to arguing with Herman Shumlin, the distinguished stage director brought out to do *Watch* because he had directed the play. Shumlin, unfortunately, knew nothing about camera technique, and tried to direct the film as if it were a play. Davis began screaming at him, and the unfortunate man reacted by disappearing to a corner of the set where he quietly drank tea while the crew waited and the costs mounted. Finally Hal Wallis, apprised of Shumlin's difficulties with cameraman Merritt Gerstad, who wasn't reacting positively to the harried Shumlin's talk of blocking and wanted to hear more about angles and close-ups, reassigned the outraged Gerstad and brought in the more tactful and even-tempered Hal Mohr. The experienced photographer wound up co-directing the picture; he would set up the appropriate camera angles while Shumlin rehearsed the actors theater-style; then they'd all get together for the scene itself. Sometimes the ploy worked; often it didn't. Davis, ever more irritated and annoyed with what she called "unfamiliar, unprofessional methods I'm not used to," began overacting and overemphasizing her line readings, ostensibly, as she told anyone willing to listen, "because this goddamned mess of a picture needs some pepping up to keep the audience awake." Soon she was coming on so strong that she was upstaging and outacting Paul Lukas who, considering it was actually his play and his picture, put up with it admirably. "I was so grateful to her for helping the picture with her box-office following, she could do no wrong," he said years later. "I honestly felt at the time that she was giving the picture some needed excitement."

Davis, done up in plain clothing and with few wardrobe changes, all of them drab except for one evening gown, with her hair coiffed unattractively, groused and brooded through the entire shooting. She even managed in the end to offend the gentlemanly, long-suffering Lukas, for when he remarked over coffee during a scene break that he had heard Charles Boyer had been offered his role on the screen but refused it because of his French accent, Davis snapped: "Charles is a great actor; this is beneath him. I'm glad he stayed out of it." After that, the only allies Davis found on the *Watch on the Rhine* set were her old pal Geraldine Fitzgerald, who played the informing count's wife, and little Janis Wilson, who had been Tina in *Now, Voyager*, and whom Davis had sneaked in as one of her children. She and villain George Coulouris got on well, as Coulouris, a man with a great deal of self-possession and a biting wit, amused and stimulated the restless Davis with his sharp retorts to her needling sallies. Once, when she told him she thought he had overembroidered one of their confrontation scenes, George put her down solidly with, "Overembroidering is your department, Miss Davis!" Laughing raucously at his gall, Davis went to get him a cup of coffee and a bun. "I wish I could get that kind of reaction out of her," the nervous and despairing Shumlin remarked. "Then for heaven's sake talk up to her! If you don't, she thinks you're soft and turns on you!" Coulouris barked.

Unfortunately Shumlin didn't follow his advice and the results show this only too blatantly. Davis throws many scenes off balance with her upfront posturings and standard gestures; it is obvious she resents—too late—her passive character as written and has decided that if she can't be flamboyant and bitchy she'll grab attention any other way she can.

She had gone into *Watch on the Rhine* only a scant ten days after finishing *Now, Voyager* in June 1942, and many of her mannerisms and stances belong more to Charlotte Vale than to Sara Muller, the drab but valiant wife.

Bosley Crowther, who had often commented on Davis's scene-hogging and scenery-chewing, couldn't help giving her a patronizing pat on the back for being a good girl when he wrote in *The New York Times* that "[the] wife, played by Bette Davis, is a model of human selflessness." *The National Board of Review Magazine*, predecessor to *Films in Review*, naively missed the point of the entire thing, praising Davis's overplaying and stage-front hoggings of the action with the somewhat inappropriate words: "Bette Davis subdues herself to a secondary role almost with an air of gratitude [sic!] for being able at last to be uncomplicatedly decent and admirable. It's not a very colorful performance but quiet loyalty and restrained heroism do not furnish many outlets for histrionic show and Miss Davis is artist enough not to throw in any extra bits of it to prove that she is one of the stars." The reviewer must have been asleep or wearing blinders, for that is precisely what Davis did try to do. Only the script and direction (Hal Wallis had frantically begged Shumlin to "hold her down" as tactfully as possible) had forestalled her attempts—and then only partially.

Both Geraldine Fitzgerald and Donald Woods had memories of Davis in *Watch on the Rhine* decades later. Fitzgerald said she knew Davis was unhappy with the picture. "Her intentions were of the best but the role was too subdued and unworthy of, and unsuited to, her great gifts and I know she regretted doing it—but by that time too much film had been shot and it was too late." Fitzgerald added, "I always enjoyed working with Bette and we did a lot of socializing at our respective homes. She and Farney were wonderful hosts; I always have felt that was, on balance, the happiest of her marriages. Not that they didn't have their problems, but she seemed more at peace with him than with the others."

Fitzgerald and Woods both opined that Shumlin should not have been imported from the theater to repeat as director, and that the job should have been given to someone like Irving Rapper (Fitzgerald's suggestion in retrospect) or even Michael Curtiz (Wood's surprise nominee).

Donald Woods, who had worked with Bette back in the thirties at Warners, said, "I have always tried to get along with people I work with; fighting and fussing is not my metabolism. Bette consumed so much energy fighting with people I have often marveled that there was any left to use before the cameras. Yes, she overacted; that was the standard complaint about her; but she always contended that that was what the public paid her for." He remembered her snorting: "If they want some sweet little girl simpering all over the place, let them get Marian Nixon or Jean Parker or someone. That is not for me!" To which Donald Woods intoned, "Amen!"

DAVIS NEXT AGREED to sing a special number in *Thank Your Lucky Stars*, one of Warners' all-star extravaganzas aimed at raising service morale and money during World War II. Jules Stein had suggested that each star be paid fifty thousand dollars for his/her stint, and that it be promptly donated to the Hollywood Canteen. Produced by Mark Hellinger and directed by David Butler, it featured a fast-paced, kaleidoscopic screenplay by Norman Panama, Melvin Frank, and James V. Kern based on a story by Everett Freeman and Arthur Schwartz.

Truth to tell, much of the show was boring, brightened only by several numbers by the talented Dinah Shore, including the title song, and a surprisingly well parodied "Blues in the Night" by John Garfield. Hattie McDaniel and Willie Best were amusing in a bouncy number, "Ice Cold Katie," but Ann Sheridan flopped as a torcher with "Love Isn't Born It Is Made," and Errol Flynn was dispirited singing a pub song in what he thought was a rowdy Irish manner. Jack Carson and Alan Hale in another number came across—for the first time in their careers—as tedious bores, as did Olivia De Havilland and Ida Lupino in a falsely jazzy vaudeville number for which both ladies lacked the zest and wit.

"They're Either Too Young or Too Old," the Bette Davis number, however, was a surprise hit and eventually ended up on the Lucky Strike Hit Parade and other popular song surveys. So the fans and flacks and press all waited impatiently through the more mediocre and perfunctory numbers for Davis's appearance—and she did not disappoint.

Wearing a pink print Orry-Kelly creation and with her hair becomingly coiffed, Davis first appears outside a night spot, looking hesitant. The war has left her desolately manless and she is out on the town alone. She enters the club and finds all the men are either old, one-foot-in-the-grave decrepits or pimply-faced kids. Her song is torched and belted in mock despair with Davis talking as much as singing it, using the throaty inflections and the standard mannerisms her fans had come to expect. Indeed her very faults become sterling assets here—she is no songstress, but the heavy-handed, phonily dignified stance she adopts is perfectly designed for caricature—and then along comes a young kid, played by a jitterbug contest winner and amateur actor, Conrad Weidel, who proceeds to rush Davis into a wild jitterbug, twirling her around and bouncing her up and down in a routine that would have exhausted the most intrepid sixteen-year-old, male or female.

Davis later recalled that young Weidel was terrified of her. "If I hurt you or drop you, Miss Davis, the top guys will probably put me in a cement mixer," he quaked, but she said, "Forget about who I am or who you think I am, get all that out of your mind, let your instincts come to the fore, and just do it, boy!"

This young Weidel proceeded to do, and so expertly and intently that, as Davis later said, "He made me look like the dancer I distinctly was not, never have been, and never will be!"

The number became the hit of the movie and was widely discussed in all the reviews. The Fourth Warner Brother had let her hair down in no uncertain terms, and the public lapped it up. Too heavy-handed to be a first-rate comedienne-chanteuse, Davis had nonetheless triumphed on sheer going-against-type grit. The critics agreed, and one of Davis's most perceptive if candid critics, James Agee, wrote in *The Nation* of "a cruel-compassionate sort of interest in watching amateurs like Bette Davis do what they can with a song."

Davis was very taken with the number, and sang it often in later years.

IN *OLD ACQUAINTANCE*, which began in the late fall of 1942, Davis was reunited with her old rival, perennial nemesis, and unrequited lover Miriam Hopkins. Lenore Coffee did the screenplay based on the John Van Druten play, which had run on Broadway in 1940–1941 with Jane Cowl and Peggy Wood in the leads. In this Miriam is a bitch who writes commercially profitable novels and Davis is a novelist who is high on critical prestige and low on sales. Davis scintillates in *Old Acquaintance* as a bachelor girl with a penchant for loving unattainable men, including her longtime-pal Hopkins's husband, John Loder, and a handsome young man-about-town, Gig Young, who is, she feels, ten years too young for her.

Old Acquaintance was a great hit with the critics and the public when it was released in November 1943. Edmund Goulding, who had guided the girls with great success through *The Old Maid* four years before, had been scheduled to direct, and he had even gotten involved in writing the screenplay. Soon, however, he was caught in the preproduction crossfire between Davis and Hopkins, both actresses on the defensive and wary about appearing once more against a background of tense confrontations, bitchy ripostes, and one-upmanship scene-stealing ploys, chiefly on Hopkins's end.

After Miriam screamed at Eddie Goulding over the phone one time too many, Eddie had a big fat heart attack and was carried off to the hospital, "like Hamlet being carried offstage," as Henry Blanke unkindly remarked. Word got around that, for all Eddie's grunting and groaning and fainting fits in the hospital, his attack was largely psychosomatic; this was proven true enough when, relieved of the Davis-Hopkins assignment, he recovered in rapid order and was soon putting the finishing touches on the Charles Boyer–Joan Fontaine film, *The Constant Nymph*, which he had begun earlier in 1942. In that picture Fontaine, as a shy, sensitive young girl, spends all her time mooning over Boyer, a composer twice her age who is involved with the more full-blown and aggressive Alexis Smith. As director, Goulding was afforded the chance to spend all his time mooning over Boyer, and as he told George Cukor years later, "It was so much more restful contemplating Charles's majestic presence than refereeing Bette and Miriam."

Meanwhile, a search for Goulding's successor was on, and producer Henry Blanke and Jack Warner considered a number of candidates. Irving Rapper was asked about it but he pleaded his imminent entrance into the navy. In actuality, as he told Blanke later, he wasn't up to a double dose of female temperament. Directing Davis, he said, he could handle, but two bitches in one film, no thank you! Blanke next approached Vincent Sherman, a former actor and screenwriter who began directing for Warners in 1939. Jack Warner had been pleased with the way Sherman had handled the Ida Lupino melodrama *The Hard Way*, which was released in 1942 to good box office and considerable reviewer acclaim. Sherman, after some initial misgivings, decided to give *Old Acquaintance* a try, though he wasn't wild over the script.

Davis had never worked with Sherman and knew nothing about him, but when he showed her rushes of Hopkins that he had shot without her (illness had delayed Davis's arrival on the set) she was so pleased with the way Sherman highlighted Miriam's more unsympathetic qualities— her shrillness, bitchery, viciousness, and hysterias—that she forgot about her indisposition and reported for work the next day.

According to Hal Wallis, Davis was not happy about working with Hopkins again. She knew Miriam was ideal for the part of the self-centered purveyor of best-seller trash who neglects husband and daughter in her pursuit of success, but she also was aware instinctively that Miriam still harbored romantic feelings for her and, if thwarted again as she had been in *The Old Maid*, would repay Davis for her rebuffs by trying to take the picture away from her.

Sherman, a man's man who was not gay and who did not enjoy, as Goulding did, the bitchy quarrels of neurotic women, was appalled when Miriam began pulling out her scene-stealing tricks one by one. Unable to get any of the personalized attention off-set that she craved from Davis, she began blowing smoke in Davis's face, using her hands and arms to distract from Davis's speeches, leaning far back in a two-shot that was supposed to favor them both—all the tricks (and a few new ones) that she had employed in *The Old Maid* to sublimate her thwarted love and assuage her hurt pride at being the outsider on a lot where Davis was the Fourth Warner Brother.

Later on, after the picture was released, the lilting, bittersweet romantic leitmotif that Franz Waxman had dreamed up for the picture was turned into sheet music, and Davis was infuriated when she learned that Hopkins had reportedly influenced lyricist Kim Gannon to underline the lesbian aspects of the relationship between the characters of Millie and Kit. When she saw a window display of the sheet music, which featured the girls in a buddy-buddy, affectionate moment, Davis hit the roof. She raised all kinds of hell trying to force the Warner attorneys to kill the sheet music release, but too much money had been invested in it and the studio lawyers refused.

Soon Miriam was accusing the hapless Sherman of giving Davis more close-ups, and he spent hours in her dressing room while she screamed and cried, assuring her that he was interested in the overall result, not in favoring anyone. Then it was time to film the now-famous moment in the movie where Davis, sick of Hopkins's bitchery and false accusations that Davis had filched her husband years before, quietly puts her parcels on a chair, walks over to Miriam, and shakes her thoroughly, throwing her on a couch and exiting while Miriam pounds angrily on the sofa and yowls her lungs out. Everyone knew about the tension between Davis and Hopkins, though not everyone knew all that was behind it, and the press demanded to be on hand when the scene was shot. Jack Warner, to his credit, felt that this would be vulgarizing things too much even for *his* taste, and ordered the set closed. But the crew members and anyone else who was able to sneak on from neighboring sets were on hand, with sweating palms and bated breath. Davis, of course, sick of Hopkins's "sleazy, smarmy overtures" and bitchy, egotistical scene-stealing ploys, proceeded to give the performance of her life, shaking Miriam with a vicious thoroughness and throwing her on the couch with such force that instead of pounding the couch and yowl-ing in the first shot, as she had been directed to do, Miriam just collapsed and cried. She had more than a little of the masochist in her, however, and realizing that she had aroused a sadism in Davis born of the latter's frustration and exasperation with her, Hopkins forced her through five or six takes, her eyes registering the wild enjoyment of Davis's punishing hands.

Sherman, finally on to this, took Miriam aside and told her that she was holding up production and there would be just one more take of the "shake and throw" scene—or else. On take nine, Miriam was perfect, and Sherman printed it with a sigh of relief. As for Davis, she later reported, "I had all I could do to keep from venting my full anger on Miriam. Instead, I went home and yelled for an hour. It was *The Old Maid* all over again!" Farney, who had to bear the brunt of Davis's delayed outbursts of temper, decided that a business trip east was in order, and for the remaining weeks of shooting, Davis wrecked her home after a day on the set, throwing furniture and vases and pounding pillows with fiendish glee.

Davis told Henry Blanke that she had known, of course, that Hopkins would act up throughout the shooting. "But she's perfect for the part, the only one who could do justice to it, and I'll do anything for the good of a picture!" Davis added, "She's an excellent actress; it's a shame she has to bring her private problems into her on-set behavior. She did this with others besides myself, and in time it ruined her career as a star. No one wanted to work with her." There was an element of truth in this, as after *Old Acquaintance* Miriam's screen career went downhill and she never starred above the title again. With the exception of her fine supporting performance in Olivia De Havilland's 1949 hit, *The Heiress*, directed by Wyler, her roles in films from 1943 on were secondary and negligible. Miriam did have the last word in 1949 when *The Heiress* was acclaimed on all sides, and Davis's *Beyond the Forest*, which had opened at about the same time, was soundly panned. Reportedly, she couldn't resist sending Davis a bitchy telegram to the effect that it was better to be number two in a winner than number one in a loser. Again, Davis did her screaming in private.

Davis always felt that the John Van Druten play should have been left as it was; Lenore Coffee had written earlier scenes in the character's lives for the movie, and Davis felt they diluted the impact of the drama. Nonetheless, though Coffee and Van Druten did not collaborate personally (she simply expanded on what she found in the original play script), there were some excellent exchanges that boasted considerable literacy and sharpness.

Hopkins, certainly, had no reason to complain about some of the lines she was given. Reporting on Davis's earlier confidence that she was in love with and planning to marry Gig Young, ten years younger and a naval officer looking resplendently handsome in his uniform, Miriam purrs venomously, "She wants to be a sailor's bride—of forty-two!" In another riotously witchy scene, Anne Revere is a perceptive, sharp reporter (a switch from her severe mother of St. Bernadette that same year) interviewing Hopkins on the success of her latest trashy novel. Davis happens in, and Revere forgets where she is and enthuses, "When you turn out a novel, Miss Marlowe, it's a gem; none of this grinding it out like sausage!" Then, aware of her gaffe, the reporter gasps, "I should cut my throat, I guess!" From the couch Miriam responds, "There's a knife over there on the table!"

Davis has many opportunities to enthrall her audience with supercharged dramatic situations. Her face blanches and her eyes pop out in fine Davis style when her young naval officer, whom she has decided she loves and whose proposal she is about to accept, informs her that he has fallen in love with Hopkins's young daughter. She turns away from him, and Sol Polito's camera zeroes in for a close close shot that practically goes up her nostrils; her distress and frustration are conveyed most intensely. When Davis, just prior to shaking Hopkins, lets her have it verbally, her voice shakes and her octaves warble and the fierceness in her eyes telegraphs the physical mayhem to come.

John Loder, Hopkins's husband in the movies said in an interview years later that the tension on the set was very great, and with the frequent absences of the stars and the constant displays of temperament, he was amazed that the picture ever finished. "I found Bette very warm and responsive in our scenes together; in fact I liked working with her in *Old Acquaintance* better than in *Now, Voyager*, for some reason. To be fair, Miriam was a very fine actress, very stimulating and responsive, but I made the mistake of telling Bette that, and she didn't speak to me for a week!" Of course the picture winds up with the manless friends together by the fireside, calmed and reconciled and Davis's amusing line about there being times in a woman's life when only a glass of champagne will help.

James Agee noted in *The Nation*, "The odd thing is that the two ladies and Vincent Sherman, directing, make the whole business look fairly intelligent, detailed and plausible."

THE YEAR 1943 brought Davis a sudden tragedy, followed by a disillusionment.

For nearly three years the Davis-Farnsworth marriage continued on its steady, long-distance course. But during 1943 Farney had seemed ever more distant and preoccupied. Davis knew his work at Minneapolis Honeywell was top secret, having to do with government aircraft projects. So, back and forth between Butternut and Riverbottom, and occasionally Minneapolis, New York, and Boston, they traveled, trying to keep some of the fire alive in their relationship.

Then on August 23, 1943, after doing some errands for Davis, Farney fell into convulsions on a Hollywood sidewalk. He lingered in a nearby hospital for two days, with Davis sitting tense and worried in the next room, and then died on August 25. Davis was in shock. Farney's bossy mother came immediately from New York, and demanded an autopsy, which revealed a severe cranial injury. Police were brought into the investigation when it was discovered that Farney's briefcase was missing. Foul play was a possibility because of his secret government work. Davis then told an inquest that earlier in the summer Farney had struck his head hard in a fall on the stairs at Butternut. He had not complained unduly, and she had thought little of it at the time. After one funeral service at Forest Lawn, Davis, Mrs. Farnsworth, Ruthie, and a large entourage headed east for Butternut, where Davis wanted Farney buried. Mrs. Farnsworth became hysterical at the grave service, and insisted Farney be laid to rest in the Farnsworth vault in Vermont. Davis, exasperated, put Ruthie in charge of digging him up and shipping him to a third service in Vermont. She went back immediately to Hollywood.

Jack Warner, for once considerate of her feelings, offered to postpone work on her new picture, *Mr. Skeffington,* but Davis told him that work—lots of it—was the best therapy, and within a week she was on the set.

Davis did not sentimentalize Farney for long. His briefcase was found; in it were bottles of liquor. Then she learned that he had been hit over the head two weeks before he died by a cuckolded husband who had found Farney in bed with his wife. This incident exacerbated the earlier head wound and caused the clot that killed him.

Disillusioned, Davis realized that Farney was a drunk. And a weakling. And an adulterer. His finances, too, she discovered, were messed up. It appeared that he had been spending their money—her money— on other women, trips, expensive gifts, when she thought he had been slaving away in Minneapolis.

During 1944 Bette Davis was as fed up with love as any woman could be. She had married two copouts. She thought of times when, during the marriage to Farney, Ham Nelson had come to visit. She had remained friendly toward him in spite of all the trouble he'd caused her. Just before Ham left for the service he had come to say good-bye to her and Farney. The two had gotten along like brothers and should have— she recalled later—because they were in some ways two of a kind. Ham sent her a letter of sympathy from the service when Farney died. She left it unanswered. Yes, she had forgiven Ham; yes, she would always remember their earliest years with fondness, but she wanted to keep him on the back shelf for a while, even as a friend. Like Farney, he had once betrayed her trust; he had been a blackmailer and a whining weakling. Farney had been a two-faced smoothie and an adulterer. Men!

She spent a lot of time in 1944 working at the Hollywood Canteen. The men were attractive and she still, at thirty-six, had physical needs, romantic needs. Fool! she told herself. Sex, she told her friends, was God's joke on mankind. So was romance, for that matter. But if sex and romance were not to be taken seriously, they could still be entertaining.

When gossip began to reach her concerning her erotic encounters with the hunkier servicemen at the canteen, she shrugged. Men were good for one thing only, she bitterly told Bobby. And why should she deny herself? Hal Wallis tried to warn her that she was now Holly-wood's top actress, a figure worthy of respect, with enormous national prestige, and she should cool her activities with the canteen kids. Scorn-fully she rejoined that all men were shits—hadn't her two husbands taught her that? And why should there be a double standard; why shouldn't women enjoy themselves just as men did? At thirty-six her physical needs were approaching their height. Time went fast, she told Wallis and his wife, the motherly and concerned Louise Fazenda, who had developed a genuine fondness for Davis since playing her servant in *The Old Maid*.

"What has happened to Bette?" the Hollywood insiders began to ask. Louella and Hedda and others in the press contingent took to covering for her. They could see she was lonely, restless, unhappy; had they known the real causes of her unhappiness, her determination to use sex to compensate for her emotional disillusionments and deprivations, they might have sympathized even more deeply. But Davis, gentlewoman that she was, at least when it came to public relations, continued to cover up for Farney. In all the interviews she gave in 1944 and 1945, she mourned him; in all her public statements he was treated re-spectfully, as a husband she had loved and lost and missed. She didn't want to hurt Farney's relatives, either, even if she couldn't stand his siblings, even if his mother was an overbearing monster. So publicly she paid her respects, and inwardly she seethed with anger and frustration.

Considering that Davis began the long and complex *Mr. Skeffington* within a month of her husband's death, the energy and dedication she put into it seem all the more remarkable. She always found that work was for her the best possible tonic and palliative for personal troubles, and it is perhaps providential that she had been making wardrobe tests for the picture with shooting scheduled imminently just at the time of Farney's death. Jack Warner told her that she could postpone shooting on *Mr. Skeffington* as long as she wanted—even months (it took a major crisis like a death in the family to spur him to flexibility of this sort)—but she pleased him and earned his reluctant respect by plunging in almost immediately. Davis's perfectionism and temperamental demands and her quarrels with director Vincent Sherman and the screenwriters Philip and Julius Epstein caused the picture to go way over budget and shooting schedule; it ran from September 1943 into March 1944, consuming a full six months from conception to completion. Again the finished product ran impossibly long, and had to be cut to 145 minutes—even that was phenomenally long for a major 1944 production, especially with wartime costs escalating and the restrictions on material and energy.

Davis was intrigued by the role of Fanny Trellis, the spoiled heiress of 1914 New York because, as written by the novelist "Elizabeth" and the Epsteins, she was supposed to be phenomenally beautiful. Since Davis had never considered herself good-looking (nor, as she knew, had many others) it tickled her that she would be playing a great beauty and femme fatale, a sort of man-trap par excellence who gets her comeuppance after age and illness overtake her, and learns the hard way, that, in the film's most famous and oft-quoted phrase, "a woman is beautiful only when she is loved."

The sterling actor Claude Rains had his best opportunity in a Davis picture to date (a better one would come later). Here he is not merely one of the supporting players, but Davis's leading man. As in the case of Charles Boyer and a very few others, Davis was deeply gratified to be playing opposite a talent she considered at least equal, if not superior, to her own, and she and Rains, who had become great personal friends, worked felicitously together as always.

Fanny Trellis, Davis's character, has married wealthy financier Job Skeffington (Rains) in order to save her beloved brother, Trippy (Richard Waring) from jail; it seems he has been tampering with the company's finances, accepting commission fees he has not really earned. Fanny has many suitors; a consummate narcissist and flirt, she is forever dressing up and primping and analyzing her beauty in mirrors.

Skeffington knows she has married him for his money (her own estate is depleted) and to save Trippy. When Trippy dies in the war, Fanny is devastated, and she and the unloved Job drift apart into what today would be called an open relationship. Fanny soon divorces him to be absolutely free to romance as many younger men as possible, and Job, who has given his unloving wife a large settlement, goes to Europe with their daughter, whom Fanny doesn't want because she is a constant reminder that her youth is passing away.

Fanny then chases much younger men and whiles away her time in idle luxury until an attack of diphtheria destroys her beauty while she is in her early forties. Deserted by all but her faithful cousin, Walter Abel, and her servant, Dorothy Peterson, she becomes a recluse until Abel tells her that Job, broke and a victim of Nazi persecution, is back. She agrees to help him out financially but will not see him. Abel urges her to, and she goes down the great flight of stairs to find Job in the drawing room, frail, white-haired—and blind. Realizing at last the depth of her selfishness and aware that to the blind Job she will always be as beautiful as ever, she takes him upstairs with the words to one and all, "Mr. Skeffington has come home" and recalls yet again his words to her of long ago, "A woman is beautiful only if she is loved."

A plot and treatment that verged dangerously on outright, indeed outrageous soap opera is saved in this instance by fine, restrained direction from Vincent Sherman, the literate and intelligent screenplay by the Epsteins that ably depicts various periods from 1914 to 1944, and excellent performances from Davis, Rains, and the rest of the cast.

Davis played this legendary beauty gone to seed with a vicious relish, as if she were getting back, once and for all, at all the actresses whose beauty she had envied. She had often expressed her impatience with lovely ladies who soared to stardom simply because they were photogenic. And she had always resented the cracks about not being beautiful, but rather "striking," an adjective that, she remarked, covered a lot of territory, some of it in the wrong neighborhoods. So here was her chance to get back, and she made the most of it.

Her greatest admirer and sternest critic, James Agee at *The Nation*, said it all concerning her effort. Leading off with the observation that *Mr. Skeffington* was yet another of those films that "demonstrated the horrors of egocentricity on a mammoth scale," he added that Davis had proved her point "to an audience which, I fear, will be made up mainly of unloved and not easily lovable women. Essentially," Agee wrote with his usual understated, acid wit, "*Mr. Skeffington* is just a super soap opera, or an endless woman's-page meditation on What-To-Do-When-Beauty-

Fades." The implied advice, he concluded, "was dismaying: hang on to your husband, who alone will stay by you then, and count yourself blessed if, like Mr. Rains in his old age, he is blinded."

It is true that for all its endless footage, lavish appurtenances, top production values, and powerhouse performances from Davis, Rains, and company, *Mr. Skeffington* exudes soap opera throughout. But there are touches of humor. When Davis's grown daughter (Marjorie Riordan) comes home from abroad, Davis is forced to introduce her to her latest swain (Johnny Mitchell), who is half her age. The kid puts his foot in it neatly by chirping pleasantly to the daughter, "Well I'll have to call you young Fanny and you—" His stuttering confusion as he leaves the sentence unfinished is hilarious, and the look Davis gives him would stop not just a few clocks but London's Big Ben itself.

Jerome Cowan is solid and true as one of her suitors from the great days who disillusions her by proposing marriage, then reneges when she tests him by telling him that she is old—and-unforgivable sin!—also broke. In an earlier scene, when she wafts down the great staircase, the very essence of a 1914 young society beauty, she accepts the adulation of her young admirers with the noblesse-oblige éclat of a princess to the purple born. And her grief and desolation are graphically illustrated late in the picture as she wanders the mansion frantically, aware at last that "the enemy time in us all" has overtaken her.

Mr. Skeffington won fan approval nationwide in 1944, and did well with many of the critics. But behind the facade, it turned out to be a picture fraught with endless quarreling, as well as the protracted shooting schedule that Jack Warner and his minions at first tolerated out of consideration for Davis's recent widowhood. "Keep her busy and engaged, heavily engaged," had been Jack's advice to Sherman and the Epsteins—not that they needed to exert much initiative on a Davis determined to lose herself in her work.

Davis worked hard to create a convincing character. She raised her voice a full octave; at first disconcerting, it was soon apparent that it fit the vain Fanny perfectly. She got hairdresser Margaret Donovan to design beautiful period hairdos for her, and Ernie Haller and Perc Westmore photographed and made her up to the nines. For the ravaged, postdiphtheria, aged Fanny, Westmore came up with rubber pieces which Davis found a trial, as they shut off her pores and clung painfully to her delicate skin.

In other areas, Davis went out of line, forcing rewrites, and then cutting out other dialogue that in her view was unsuitable. The Epsteins were also producers of the film, and Davis began telling them what to do and what not to do. When she gratuitously inserted dialogue without consulting them and told them that she could both write and produce better than they could, they walked off the picture and threatened suit. Davis's attitude was "good riddance!" With the help of fill-in supervisor Steve Trilling, Davis and Sherman blundered through to the finish— months over schedule. Then the first of a series of incidents occurred which indicated that someone didn't like Bette Davis. An eyewash she used regularly turned out to be toxic, and only Perc Westmore's quick action saved her sight in one eye. The liquid was found to have been tampered with. This put the set of *Mr. Skeffington* into a state of ultimate siege, with Battle-ax Bette self-appointed head of her own special security police. Everyone concerned was relieved when *Mr. Skeffington* wrapped up.

WITH MR. SKEFFINGTON finally in the can, Davis found her next film more of a pleasure than a duty, more play than work. Warners had decided to make a movie about the Hollywood Canteen that Davis and John Garfield had founded in 1942 and where, post-Farney, she had been consoling herself.

Davis always gave John Garfield much of the credit for the canteen's success. Garfield, 4-F in the war, felt it was the least he could do for his contemporaries in uniform. Since the Los Angeles area was a prime embarkation point for soldiers, sailors, and marines headed for the Pacific theater, there had been a need for it even prior to 1942 when the draft put a lot of men in uniform. For her part, in her free time Davis met with and enlisted numerous enthusiasts famous, not so famous, and unknown. Everyone got into the spirit and the canteen flourished until the end of the war. It also flourished financially, through the efforts of Jules Stein, president of MCA (Davis's agents) and his wife, Doris, who made wise investments and set up the framework. So wisely in fact did Jules Stein manage the canteen's finances that half a million dollars remained in the treasury at V-J Day. With these funds a foundation was started that continued to benefit servicemen.

Those in the know joked that Davis's extracurricular activities with the men at the canteen, if properly directed and photographed, would have made the Bette Davis movie to end all Bette Davis movies! Meanwhile Davis gave out dignified interviews to the press, telling all the fan mag mavens and the newspapers that she would always be grateful "for the loyalty of those who outlived the first flush of publicity and novelty and continued to work with us."

When Warners got around to making *Hollywood Canteen* in 1944, they marshalled practically every Warner personality not in the service for the film. Joan Crawford, fresh on the contract list, appeared in a few scenes, none of them with Davis. Other luminaries on hand were big guns like Barbara Stanwyck and smaller fry like Alan Hale.

The film, a 124-minute affair directed by Delmer Daves from his own screenplay and original story, had a superslim plotline: Robert Hutton and Dane Clark play two soldiers on sick leave who spend three exciting, star-laden nights at the canteen before embarking for the Pacific. Hutton, lionized as the millionth GI to come to the canteen headquarters, gets to date Joan Leslie, on whom he develops a man-size crush. Dane Clark gets to dance with Joan Crawford but presumably not fall in love with her. (Asked years later to give a contrast between working with Davis and Crawford, Dane shrugged and laughed, "Apples and Oranges—doesn't that take me off the hook?") Then Davis and Garfield get center stage to talk about the canteen and its aims and purposes, Davis as president, Garfield as vice president.

Most of the film is taken up with musical numbers such as Roy Rogers singing "Don't Fence Me In," Eddie Cantor and Nora Martin warbling "We're Having a Baby," Joe E. Brown and Dennis Morgan making a try at "You Can Always Tell a Yank," and Jane Wyman and Jack Carson performing gamely and expertly a number titled "What Are You Doing the Rest of Your Life?" Asked years later if in *Hollywood Canteen* she had been tempted to do yet another hot jitterbug number as in *Thank Your Lucky Stars* the year before (only this time with a hot GI, natch!), Davis laughed and said she knew her limitations and was content to stay within them that time around! LeRoy Prinz got much credit in the reviews for the clever musical numbers, fast-paced and elegant, that he created and directed.

In a 1988 interview for this book, Joan Leslie recalled:

"Bette Davis was a guest star in two wartime pictures I did, *Thank Your Lucky Stars* and *Hollywood Canteen,* but we only worked together in *Canteen.* Of course I had seen her around the lot, visited her sets, and was proud just to be in the same movie with her. We had one scene together in *Hollywood Canteen.* She was a founder of the canteen and, I think, the person who talked Jack Warner into giving the film's proceeds to the canteen and the USO. In the plot, the canteen decides to give the one millionth serviceman to enter there anything he wanted.

"Well, in our scene, Bette, as herself, calls me and tells me about the winner [Robert Hutton] and that what he wants is a date with me—Joan Leslie, movie star. She was required to do most of the talking, leaving me mainly with, 'Oh, of course I'll do it.' Now, at the same time Bette was working on another film, one of her big starring vehicles in which she was, as always, totally absorbed, and she had quite a bit of dialogue in our little scene. So here she was, suddenly thrust onto this strange set, with a totally new crew. She blew her lines a few times. Finally, she exclaimed, 'Oh, I just don't think I can do this. I can't play myself! If you give me a gun, a cigarette, a wig, I can play any old bag, but I can't play myself!'

"Everyone laughed. This broke the tension on the set and allowed the scene to proceed smoothly, as this super, sophisticated lady probably knew it would."

Director Delmer Daves and I talked about Bette on location in Connecticut in 1960, where Delmer was directing *Parrish*. Delmer, a ladies' man par excellence who had had wild affairs with Kay Francis and other lovelies, remembered that Bette had a wandering eye for the many handsome servicemen who showed up at the canteen. "She had been widowed the year before, and it was a very lonely, sad time for Bette," he remembered. "And some of those kids were prize specimens, real catnip for the gals. I'm not saying she disappeared with any of them, but I wouldn't have blamed her if she had. She was in a real tense, uptight mood at times, and some romantic quickies might have filled the bill for her, might have calmed her down."

But according to actor Jack Carson, who appeared in *Hollywood Canteen*, Davis did get "calmed down," and with her fair share of romantic quickies, culled from the embarrassment of masculine riches pouring into the canteen from all branches of the service. As Jack recalled to me on the set of *The Bramble Bush* in 1959, Bette took a special liking to slim but well-muscled young sailors sporting the then regulation thirteen buttons up, down, and across the flies of World War II legend.

"There were some real lookers there at the canteen out to make the service kids happy," Jack laughed, "knockouts like Dolores Moran and Julie Bishop and Dorothy Malone. But Bette was the one they clustered around. As I remember, she was in one of her heavy costume pictures then [*The Corn is Green*] and she would jump out of costume and race from Warners down to the canteen and when she showed up she'd look like something the cat dragged in—hair unkempt, makeup still partly smeared over her face, and with any old thing thrown on, and those guys would drop whatever cutie-pie starlet they had on hand and would make a beeline for her. Within two minutes of showing up, she'd be mobbed by them."

Jack recalled asking one brawny marine what there was about Bette that got them all so turned on. "I hear she screws like a mink," he leered. "I thought that an ungentlemanly remark considering how Bette was knocking herself out night after night for those guys—she'd wash dishes, serve food, do anything and everything—and I was about to call the loudmouth son of a bitch on it, and then it struck me, 'Well ain't it the truth?'"

Jack remembered that there was much laughter among the girls handling the fan mail when more than a few letters came in from guys who had been shipped to the Pacific and wrote, in highly individual, none-too-grammatical, and often misspelled words, how they could never forget the exciting, fulfilling, "wowie" hours Bette had given them.

But as always she continued to be in love with love. Sex was a consolation, but love, her undoing, continued to be a racking need. During the nightly peregrinations and prowlings at the Hollywood Canteen, she had met only one serviceman who aroused her deeper vulnerabilities. He was a ruggedly handsome army corporal named Lewis A. Riley. Riley, some years younger than herself, told her he had seen every movie she had ever made and that she was his goddess. Soon Riley alone was making public appearances with her—no backstairs quickies this time around. As thrilled as a kid with the biggest ice cream sundae in the world, he preened and puffed out his chest when Davis took him to fancy Hollywood places like La Rue and Chasen's. They were photographed, and the pictures appeared in the daily papers and the fan magazines. In short, they were an item.

"He's a nobody, Bette," Ann Warner told her. "You are a famous woman. Why throw yourself away on a good-looking set of muscles in khaki?" Soon she had the good-looking set of muscles in bed, and then she was in love with him.

When Riley was transferred clear across the country to Fort Benning, Georgia, where he was assigned to the 168th Signal Company, Photo Division, of the Second Army, Davis decided that some camp following would be in order. With *Mr. Skeffington* and *Hollywood Canteen* finished, there was nothing to keep her, for a month or so anyway, in Hollywood. Jack Warner, who reportedly had engineered Riley's transfer east to get rid of him, didn't want to give her time off, but Davis gave him one of her ultimatums and off she went to Georgia.

She took a rented house in Phoenix City, Alabama, just across the border from Columbus, Georgia, Fort Benning, and her corporal. The amorous corporal continued his corporeal activities whenever he could get away from his duties. Davis had her sister Bobby along as a cover-up. Bobby's emotional health had improved; she was even feeling chipper. Davis and Riley kept her even more so by arranging dates with the sexiest servicemen that Fort Benning could provide.

While in Alabama, Davis got a chance to meet her idol, Franklin D. Roosevelt. She had often crossed swords in his defense with the more conservative Hollywood residents who hated his liberal reforms and his determination to put the government to work helping the less privileged. Now, in 1944, he was leading a world war to its successful conclusion. She wrote asking to meet him in Washington, and then found herself standing in line at a public tea. Shocked to find one of the most famous women in the country willing to shake his hand under such plebeian circumstances, he asked her to come to his house in Warm Springs for an evening of dinner and socializing. Since Warm Springs, Georgia, was fairly near Fort Benning and her corporal, Davis arranged to go there. She always recalled the wonderful evening she spent with the president.

Shortly thereafter (Jack Warner pulling strings again?), Corporal Lewis A. Riley of the Second Army found himself transferred overseas. This jarred Davis mightily, for not only had the corporal been a fantastic lover, but his boyish adoration had refreshed and renewed the healthier aspects of her self-image. Before he left, Riley asked her to wait for him. Davis decided she wanted to marry him immediately but he surprised her by hesitating. Then he told her he would rather wait until the war was over.

Later she said, "I grew tired of living my life in a mailbox." Soon she was back to work, and the distant Corporal Riley seemed a dream indeed.

Back in Hollywood, Davis went to a party at Laguna Beach. Her mother had a house there—one that Davis reluctantly paid for—and her uncle Paul Favor and his family lived nearby.

At the party a lean, craggy, muscular man handed her a drink. He didn't leave her side for the rest of the evening. He was William Grant Sherry. An ex-marine, he was just out of a service hospital for a condition about which he was reluctant to talk. He had been an unsuccessful boxer and was an avid painter whose enthusiasm far exceeded his talent.

Soon he was coming on strong and turned into the most persistent wooer Davis had yet encountered. Intense, but outwardly composed, he had a deep inner fierceness and bitterness which flashed out of his dark eyes more frequently than not. Miffed with the reluctant corporal, feeling uptight and lonely, carried away by Sherry's evident masculinity, she let herself be sucked into a relationship. Ruthie didn't approve of Sherry. She told Davis he was *déclassé*. His father had been a carpenter with the Theatre Guild; his mother worked an elevator in a San Diego hotel. Davis was tempted to tell Ruthie that Sherry's mother showed more self-respect than she did; at least she didn't sit back and let her children support her!

Ruthie was horrified further when Sherry took up physiotherapy to earn more money. His paintings weren't selling well. He was in awe of Davis, or pretended to be, but this was no boy-scout corporal worshipping at a goddess's shrine. Bobby, suspicious of him, had Sherry investigated. Pulling himself up by his bootstraps Horatio Alger—style was not for Sherry-boy. Bobby kept insisting that Sherry was not sincere. Then Ruthie hired a detective and came up with more dirt about Sherry. Davis refused to read the reports. She said later that the more Ruthie fought the Sherry involvement, the higher she got on him. He asked her to marry him. She agreed. Ruthie raised the roof. "You'll regret it," she said. "Why, Bette, why?" Davis replied succinctly, "He's damn good in bed—that's why!" Out she sailed from her mother's bedroom with the plaintive wail ringing in her ears, "But Bette, you don't have to marry him for *that!*"

They were married on November 29, 1945, at the Mission Inn in Riverside, California. Both families were represented. Ruthie took many pictures.

In August 1946, Davis became pregnant, though the doctors warned her that at her age, thirty-eight, the going might be rough. Nevertheless, she was anxious to be a mother and willing to take her chances.

Another of Davis's famous feminine rivals and would-be lovers surfaced at this time. Joan Crawford had signed a contract with Warner Brothers in 1943 after her five-year deal with Metro-Goldwyn-Mayer had ended. She had known she was washed up at the Lion Studio. "They laughed when I told them I wanted to do pictures like *Madame Curie* and *Random Harvest*," she later said of her final days at MGM. "They still saw me as the superficial clotheshorse and the ragged shopgirl on the make for riches." Joan had made a few quality pictures—*The Women, Susan and God, A Woman's Face*—and then found herself relegated to inferior stories while the big buildup went to Mayer's new favorite, Greer Garson. Greta Garbo had made her last film in 1941. Norma Shearer terminated her six-picture agreement in 1942. The last of MGM's original Big Three women stars to go, Crawford left the studio with a heavy heart. "Mr. Mayer didn't want me to go, but he saw how unhappy I was," she recalled. "I wasn't being taken seriously, I felt neglected and old-hat, something exploited as a certain commodity, then discarded."

By 1944, forty years old on March 23, Crawford was definitely running scared. That year she made a brief appearance in the all-star *Holly-wood Canteen*, then ruminated and agonized over the choice of vehicle that would get her off to a smash start at Warners. "What does the woman *want?*" Jack Warner asked his aides. "Good roles in good pictures!" she relayed back.

Finally producer Jerry Wald found *Mildred Pierce* for her. It was another rags-to-riches story but with a difference. Obsessed with nurturing and protecting her spoiled daughter, Mildred leaves her also-ran husband to start a restaurant, fights her way to wealth and success, her only objective being to give her girl a better life. But the girl (Ann Blyth) is rotten clean through and murders Mildred's playboy second husband (Zachary Scott) when he rejects her advances. For a time, Mildred takes the blame. And so forth and so on. Based on a lurid James M. Cain novel, the doings were wildly melodramatic, and yet director Michael Curtiz made something strong and realistic out of it that elicited heavy audience identification. "He took off my MGM shoulder pads and rubbed me down to some hardpan character," Crawford said of Curtiz. She seems to have gotten along far better with the feisty little director than Davis ever did, probably because she flattered him by going along with his ideas and because the hard-bitten Curtiz somehow sympathized with Joan's onward-and-upward struggle for success.

Mildred Pierce won Crawford an Academy Award for Best Actress of 1945, and this immediately launched her into top stardom at Warners, where within two years she had two other prestige smashes, *Humoresque* (she was the dissolute, filthy-rich mistress-patroness of violinist John Garfield) and *Possessed* (in which she gave Davis a run for her money in the unrequited-love tournaments as an unstable woman driven literally mad and murderous by the scornful and contemptuous Van Heflin's rejection).

She had by this time, of course, become Bette Davis's chief rival at the Burbank studio. If Davis were the Fourth Warner Brother, the triumphant and ever-more-ambitious Crawford had become Warner Brother Number Five—or even Bette the Second. There were rumors that Jack Warner had brought in Crawford deliberately to humble Davis and make her less cocky. Davis, though her dressing room was near Crawford's, went out of her way to avoid her. Not so the persistent Joan, who sent her flowers, perfume, notes—all of which were either ignored or politely but firmly returned.

At first, Davis was puzzled over Crawford's neurotically intense pursuit of her. Her first theory, as she later told a friend, was that Crawford was trying to assure her there were no hard feelings over Davis's brief affair with her *Dangerous* co-star Franchot Tone, Mr. Crawford Number Two, in 1935. Or Joan might be as embarrassed about the constant feud rumors as she, and wanted to be friendly. Her third theory, at first unthinkable, unimaginable, finally hit Davis like an electric shock, but everything pointed to its validity: Damn, the woman was attracted to her! Repelled because she had not the slightest interest in nor intention of reciprocating, yet fascinated because it built her overweening ego, Davis continued to be elusive, distant, cursorily polite when they passed each other in the hall or between sound stages. Crawford seethed at the implied rebuke. With an ego that was every bit as monstrous as Davis's, though filtered through a different personality and mystique, Crawford brooded—and proceeded to bide her time.

Joan Crawford's lesbian tendencies were, of course, no secret to Hollywood insiders. There had been rumors, back in the 1920s, of her crushes on such lovelies as Anita Page, Dorothy Sebastian, and Gwen Lee, her early MGM colleagues. She had been, by the standards of the time, reasonably secretive and discreet, and since her attraction to men equaled her passion for women, many in Hollywood, and the public at large, would have found fantastic such predilections in Joan (her standard ad copy, as in the 1947 *Daisy Kenyon*, ran along such lines as "Joan's Having Man Trouble Again!") And indeed she was—offscreen as well as on. She had had a flaming affair with Clark Gable while still married to her first husband, Douglas Fairbanks, Jr. Davis, who had made one picture with Doug, Jr., and sensed his unhappiness and humiliation over the Gable affair during the shooting, had heard plenty of scuttlebutt about that and considered Joan as of 1933 a pretty reckless trifler with the moral-turpitude contract clauses.

Joan, Bette, and Franchot Tone had formed, in 1935, that brief triangle during the making of *Dangerous*, and after that their paths had seldom crossed and then only superficially. Davis had known of Tone's infidelity, the beatings he had given Crawford, and their less than amicable 1938 divorce. After some years of finding consolation (discreetly) with a few women and (blatantly) with Hollywood's studs around town, Crawford had married handsome but dull Phillip Terry, a scholarly, homebody type (for an actor), whom she divorced in 1945 after a boring three-year marriage.

In addition to her straight and gay involvements, Joan had taken on additional emotional overload by adopting several children. Helen Hayes, who knew Joan well, later said, "Joan tried to be all things to all people—I just wish she hadn't tried to be a mother!" Truer words were never spoken, for Joan proceeded to abuse hapless daughter Christina and rebellious son Christopher so erratically and so sadistically, often when drunk, that many years later she was to reap a posthumous whirlwind of ridicule as Christina's *Mommie Dearest* blockbuster set loose bizarre stories involving wire coathangers and other weird forms of discipline.

This, then, was the woman who in 1945–1947 was rivaling Davis at Warners and lusting after her into the bargain. Adela Rogers St. Johns told me in 1960 (in a completely innocent context on Adela's part) that Joan had often rhapsodized to her about Bette's fire and excitement and "beautiful fierceness."

Confronted at last with the true nature of Crawford's neurotic and persistent overtures, Davis made herself as distant and unavailable to her overwrought Warner colleague as she could.

Crawford was deeply hurt when Davis refused her friendship. She talked of Bette often and compulsively. She seemed to want to take on some of Davis's feistiness and brazenness, her do-or-die, courageous, let-the-chips-fall-where-they-might approach to her objectives. For Joan, in her own way, was a tough cookie too. She could not have attained and held her major position in films for so long if she hadn't been. But in many ways she was more vulnerable than Bette, less self-confident, more emotional. She was bedeviled by her feeling that she had more personality than true talent. She envied Bette her unquestioned gifts.

Bette's basic attitude was that Joan was unstable, untrustworthy, insecure, and unreliable, in friendship and career. She made Davis ornery and nervous and tense. She told her associates that Crawford in her view was a phony and a hypocrite. "There's no way of telling in what direction that Crawford cat will jump!" she said.

Throughout 1947 Davis had fretted, during and after the pregnancy with her daughter B.D. that kept her inactive, over Crawford's rapid ascendancy at Warners. She asked for prints of *Humoresque* and *Possessed,* for which Crawford had won critical kudos, and studied them several times. "What an ambitious bitch!" she would scream to Sherry, who enjoyed watching her squirm as Crawford's face filled the screen. "But brother, she'll have to go some to put *me* out of business!" The Davis and Crawford paths were to cross again—and again—in the years to come, usually tensely, never pleasantly.

WHILE ENJOYING HERSELF at the canteen, Davis had gone into production with *The Corn Is Green* in the role of the selfless Welsh schoolteacher that Ethel Barrymore had made her own and which she played to great theatrical acclaim for several years on Broadway and on tour.

Ethel was more restrained than Tallulah Bankhead had been when Davis copped her stage roles as movie vehicles. She had not liked being passed over one bit, but realized she was hardly 1944 box-office fodder in a leading role in films, and accepted the inevitable with good grace. However, when asked what she thought of Davis playing her role, she snapped, "She's too young for it!"

Davis had caught Barrymore's performance in Chicago. She recalled that the audience gave her an ovation as she sat in the audience and that Barrymore looked out sourly at the proceedings from behind the curtain. It is true that she was only thirty-six when she played Miss Moffat, and the part had been written by Emlyn Williams to celebrate a teacher who was at least sixty. That was approximately Barrymore's age when she acted in the play. In future years Davis expressed the wish that she could have tackled the role at a more mature age. In fact, she was to do so, in a short-lived 1974 stage musical, *Miss Moffat*, which played out of town but never made it to Broadway. At that time Davis was sixty-six.

The story deals with the efforts of a heroic teacher in a Welsh mining village to inspire a gifted but recalcitrant young miner, played by the newcomer John Dall, to further his education. She inspires him to study hard and is instrumental in winning him an Oxford scholarship, which he almost throws away when a worthless, illiterate girl, Joan Lorring, snares him into fathering an illegitimate baby. Somewhat unrealistically, Davis assumes custody of the child and sends Dall to Oxford, after forcing him to realize that his duty to his genius outweighs every other consideration.

John Dall had played only so-so parts on the stage. His part was originally written for Richard Waring, who had been Davis's brother Trippy in *Mr. Skeffington*, but to the sorrow of all concerned, Waring was drafted into the service and Warners couldn't pull strings to release him for the part he was "born to play," as Davis regretfully put it.

Dall was handsome and talented, but he was not the most masculine figure in the world. Homosexual, he lived with his mother, whom he escorted to premieres. They were known unkindly as "The Dalls." Reportedly Dall had had no interest in what he called "butching it up" in the army, and had even told them about his sexual predilections when called up for service. "The way I like men, I'd have disrupted the morale anyway," he said. "They're better off without me."

After he was signed, Dall gave a number of gushy fan-magazine interviews about how "thrilled" he was to be acting with "a lady I have so long admired and sought to emulate [sic!]." He told them over and over how "kind" and "motherly" and "understanding" Davis was. Such was not the case with Irving Rapper and cameraman Sol Polito, who started getting nervous when Dall disappeared with some of the more attractive members of the professional Welsh Chorus, brought in to sing return-ing-from-the-mine songs—an inappropriate Hollywood touch. Mildred Dunnock, Rosalind Ivan, and Rhys Williams from the stage version were on hand, and while their styles did not blend easily at first with Davis's under Rapper's nervous direction, they all managed to accommodate eventually, and with consummate professionalism. In fact it was John Dall's style that worried Rapper—and Davis—more than the stage pro-fessionals'. As more than one account has it, Dall was absurdly uncon-vincing in scenes which called for macho marching in and out. Davis solved the problem by telling Rapper to tell the errant Dall to "think of soldiers marching in manly fashion on the parade field." This helped somewhat. Certainly Dall, a talented and sensitive actor, gave a good account of himself—that is, when his attention was not diverted to cruising the more attractive choir members. A large stage at Warners was drafted as the setting for the Welsh village, and Nigel Bruce, as the squire, counterpoised Davis's Miss Moffat very well in what constitute the liveliest scenes in the film.

Dall told many interviewers during 1944 and 1945 that he expected *The Corn Is Green* to "catapult" him into "great stardom." That it didn't do, given his reckless homosexual amours and his drinking and general unre-liability. He had some good chances after that, most notably in Hitch-cock's *Rope*, in which he was convincing enough playing a homosexual who murders for a lark. Farley Granger (on whom Dall developed a fierce crush during the shooting) was his co-star along with James Stew-art, top-billed. Jimmy, incidentally, emitted a shocked, *"Really?"* when I told him *Rope* had been one of his more compelling performances. Dall died, disappointed and largely forgotten, in 1971, at fifty-three. But still he had been luckier than the hapless Waring; at least he got his main chance.

Considering she was thirty-six in a sixty-year-old role, Davis shows much spirit and authority. She was greatly alarmed, however, in early August 1944, when an arc-light cover landed on her head; had she not been wearing a heavy wig, she might have been killed. "Not all crew members liked her; she could be a wear and tear," Hal Wallis later told me. *"Was* it an accident? Who knows?"

Some of the more interesting memories of *The Corn Is Green* came from Joan Lorring, who, in a 1988 interview for this book, said:

"The story of how I got to play Bessie Watty is a long and involved one, but the final link had to do with Rhys Williams, who played Mr. Jones in the film and, being Welsh, was also technical advisor. At this point I had been interviewed and rejected a couple of times for the role. One morning Mr. Williams's car broke down and he hitched a ride to Warners with an actor named Casey MacGregor. He mentioned to Casey that he was working on the film version of *The Corn Is Green* and that they were having great trouble casting the important role of the little strumpet, Bessie. Casey said, 'I just worked with a girl in a play about the Brontes you should see. She played Charlotte and her name is Joan Lorring.'

"Mr. Williams submitted my name, but Warners couldn't find me! Finally, the agent who had submitted me the other times did so again and they tested me. Jack Warner didn't want me at first; he favored Andrea King, a new contract actress he was hoping to build. But Bette Davis, who was going to star, saw my test and asked for me, as did Irving Rapper and producer Jack Chertok. I got it."

Joan Lorring recalled that Davis was rather private and aloof on the set, "but I was only in my teens then and was very retiring, too." Lorring remembered, "One day I came to the set not fully prepared. Oh, I'd studied my lines but when we started shooting I started going up [fluffing lines]. And Bette, in a no-nonsense, nonjudgmental way, said to this timorous girl who would have collapsed at outright disapproval, 'Do you know how much it costs to shoot for ten minutes?' The amount was staggering. She went on, 'Everyone has to come with his equipment. The electricians. The sound men. No one can come without the tools he needs. And we come with our tools: our words.' She wasn't angry. It was explanatory. It was illuminating for me! There was nothing I wouldn't have done for that woman. I have only had one or two teachers in my life about whom I felt as strongly and positively as I did about Bette Davis."

Lorring went on to recall that she had a real problem with the seduction scene with John Dall. "I'd never been kissed, didn't know where the noses went, didn't know where *anything* went! Now I had to seduce this young man. We did it, but later on we had to come back and shoot it again. By the time we got to the big final scene with Bette, where I tell her, 'I'm going to have a little stranger,' we were two or three weeks behind schedule—partly, I felt, because of me. Pink slips were coming down daily.

"Making matters worse, I had to tell Bette off in the scene. I had such respect for her—where was all the contempt and rage going to come from? First we did her close-ups for that scene. It was Friday and Bette was always given Saturdays off so she could go and rest at her Laguna home. To me, they said, 'We'll do your close-ups on Saturday.' When I got there the next morning, Saturday, there was Bette in gray wig, make-up, and costume so she could play her off-camera scene with me for my close-ups. She had a book in her hands—she was always reading; stacks of books were always being delivered to her dressing room."

According to Lorring, Bobby Vreeland, the first assistant director, informed her of Davis's special intercession that helped her get the part. Vreeland explained about the close-ups also. It seems that after she had done her own stint, Davis was told by Vreeland that he'd see her on Monday. Davis wanted to know when they were doing Lorring's close-ups, and when he informed her that they'd be done the following day, Saturday, she said, "I'll be there. I'll be a son of a bitch if I'll leave that girl all alone!" Joan Lorring was particularly grateful for this act of consideration because, as she recalled it, "Irving Rapper, the director, was prone to exploding on the set, and this was her chance to be protective of me so I'd not be affected by any of this temperament."

Lorring also recalled that Billy Roy, who played a young coal miner in the picture (and who later became a piano accompanist for Julie Wilson and other singers), did a devastating, highly accurate imitation of Bette that was in great demand at his friends' get-togethers. At the closing party, Billy worked up the courage to do the imitation for Bette for the first time. There were a lot of people around, and the collective breath was tensely held while everyone waited for the Great One's reaction. She sat there, all done up in her wig and costume, looking formidable and stern as all get out. Then, when the rash young Billy came to the hesitant stop, Davis's booming laugh came, and as Lorring remembered, "She literally laughed herself off the chair."

One day Lorring and Davis were looking at rushes. Lorring was sitting directly in front of the star. Suddenly a huge close-up of Lorring appeared on the screen. In those days Lorring held the firm opinion that her face would stop clocks, and she proceeded to slide so far down in her seat from sheer mortification that she landed on the floor, bottom first.

She looked up to see Davis standing over her, whispering, "When I was young and first came to this studio, there was a beautiful girl also under contract whose mother thought her the most gorgeous thing ever. Every time she'd see her on the screen she'd exclaim, 'Isn't she beautiful!' The girl's name was Anita Louise. She's forgotten. I'm still here!"

Lorring closed the interview with the proud recollection that for *The Corn Is Green* she won an Academy Award nomination for Best Supporting Actress.

Mildred Dunnock was another who held Davis's talents and character in high esteem. She told me, "I had had more stage experience than Bette, and knew that play well, but she gave her role the kind of disciplined dedication I associated with only the finest stage actresses. Oh, she could be imperious and definite about the effects she wanted, yes, but she was the star and the picture was riding on her box-office draw, and I couldn't blame her for that. She could be tough about what she wanted, but she was always fair, and could always be reasoned with, and could be resilient and flexible if someone gave her reasonable arguments and backed them up."

Rhys Williams remembered that, oddly, Davis wasn't too facile with the bicycle she had to ride in her opening scene. When it proved too awkward to bring off, she said to Irving Rapper, "Oh, the hell with it!" and entered with the bike beside her while she walked. Later she had to ride the bike across a bridge and, according to Rhys, "We were all wondering if she'd make it, but she did."

She said to Rhys one day, "God damn this goddamn bike! If Ethel Barrymore in the play hadn't used it for her trademark entrance, I wouldn't have bothered with it at all, but everyone who saw the play or heard about it expected it, and I didn't want to disappoint anybody!"

Rosalind Ivan remembered that Davis did have a disconcerting way of telling everyone what to do, including the grips, the cameraman, and director Rapper, who frequently lost patience and told her *he* was directing the picture, not she.

"Well, you're doing a damned lousy job of it," Davis yelled at him. "Why do I have to do everybody's work for them?"

"Maybe if you'd concentrate on your part and your lines you'd keep out of other people's hair," Rapper yelled back. After a parting shot— "I've had it with you, Bette. Go to hell!"—Rapper began to walk off the set.

"You go one step farther toward that door, you son of a bitch, and you're fired!" Davis screamed.

"Only Jack Warner can fire me, Bette; you know that. But he won't have to; I quit. I've had enough of your tantrums and your sadistic bullying!"

"Tantrums! Sadistic! Listen, you no-talent third-rater, you ought to go down on your knobby knees in gratitude that you're directing a Bette Davis picture!"

"I'm not directing; you are, Bette!" And so it went.

James Agee proved not only percipient but uncannily prophetic in his review of *The Corn Is Green* for *The Nation*.

Agee wrote in part: "I like and respect Miss Davis as a most unusually sincere and hardworking actress, and I have seen her play extremely well; but I did not find much in this performance to bring one beyond liking, respect, and, I am afraid, a kind of sympathy which no healthily functioning artist needs. It seems to me she is quite limited, which may be no sin but is a pity, and that she is limiting herself beyond her rights by becoming more and more set, official and first-ladyish in mannerism and spirit, which is perhaps a sin as well as a pity."

Agee continued: "In any case, very little about her performance seemed to me to come to life, in spite of a lot of experienced striving which often kept in touch with life as if through a thick sheet of glass. To be sure, the role [of Miss Moffat] is not a deeply perceived or well-written one, and the whole play seems stolid and weak. I have a feeling that Miss Davis must have a great deal of trouble finding films which seem appropriate, feasible, and worth doing, and I wish that I, or anyone else, could be of use to her in that. For very few people in her position in films mean, or could do, so well. But I doubt that anything could help much unless she were willing to discard much that goes with the position—unless, indeed, she realized the absolute necessity of doing so."

Other critics did not agree. E. Arnot Robertson in *Picture Post* rhapsodized about Davis's "impression of inexhaustible vitality under a prim exterior" and stated that only she "could have combatted so successfully the obvious intention of the adaptors to make frustrated sex the mainspring of the chief character's interest in the young miner." Otis Guernsey of *The New York Herald-Tribune* called her interpretation "sharp" and "vital."

18

The Quintessential
Bette Davis Movie

I N LATE 1944 Davis determined to produce her own films. As producer she would enjoy a tax break, but, more important, she would get to exert full control over every aspect of her films, and that appealed to her enormously. She contracted with Warners to do five films in which she would star. She wound up doing only one—*A Stolen Life*.

A remake of a 1939 Elisabeth Bergner film, *A Stolen Life* appealed to the sad, introspective, self-searching mood in which Davis found herself in late 1944. She had been a widow for a year, her romance with Corporal Lewis Riley had fizzled, and she was uncertain about her other involvements, including the one with Sherry. She admitted later that she was more lonely in that period than in any other in her life. Working closely with talented writer Catherine Turney, she put many personal touches and insights into the picture—her great love for New England, her continuing analyses of her inner nature—part dreamy romantic and part egoistic pragmatist—and her continuing enthrallment cum disillusionment with the many ways of love, in which by 1944 she had become one of the world's great authorities, on screen and off. Production on *A Stolen Life* began in the spring of 1945. Release was

delayed a year, when Warners used it to highlight the twentieth anniversary of sound.

The project also appealed to her vanity and offered her an exciting
challenge, for in *A Stolen Life* she would be giving her public what her
flacks styled "Double Davis"—she would play twins. One, the shy,
withdrawn Kate, would be counterpoised against the brazen, aggressive,
man-hungry Pat. She knew instinctively that she could do ample justice
to both.

Davis, a true New Englander, had long admired the works of such
fellow Massachusetts natives as Ralph Waldo Emerson, who wrote,
"Trust thyself: every heart vibrates to that iron string," and Henry David
Thoreau, who had written about the absolute necessity of each human
being stepping to the beat of his or her own drummer. One poem in
particular, by Emerson, guided her. It went: "Give all to Love;/Obey
thy heart; . . ./Nothing refuse. . . ./Let it have scope;/Follow it utterly,/Hope beyond hope;/High and more high/It dives into
noon,/With wing unspent,/Untold intent;/But it is a god,/Knows its
own path,/And the outlets of the sky./[Love] was never for the mean;/It
requireth courage stout./Souls above doubt,/Valor unbending."

A Stolen Life is one of Bette Davis's finest pictures (one of my three
personal favorites). It displays the then thirty-seven-year-old actress in
one of her most sensitive, introspective, and deeply felt performances. It
is also one of the most poetic and intense studies of the pangs of unrequited love ever put on the screen, its only peer being Joan Fontaine's
lovely, haunting romance of old Vienna, *Letter From an Unknown Woman*,
which followed it two years later.

In this, Davis, aided by Max Steiner's superior musical inspirations,
Curtis Bernhardt's understandingly cooperative direction, and Turney's
literate and probing script, explored the journey that the unrequited
lover must take, hopefully into the homeland of the beloved's heart.
Some reach that homeland; most do not, as Davis understood so well.
"Not being in love is such a relief," someone once said, "—like a long
journey one doesn't have to take."

As is the case with a few other Davis films, *A Stolen Life* bears detailed
recounting, for it represents a salient example of the all-pervasive effect
Bette Davis had on audiences of both sexes at the height of her career
and influence. It is a relatively simple story. Wealthy, blue-blooded,
identical twin sisters travel to an island off the coast of Massachusetts
one summer. (The locale, though shot in California, suggests both Nan-
tucket and Martha's Vineyard.) They both proceed to fall in love with a
shy, sensitive, yet manly and decent young idealist, an engineer work-

ing for a lighthouse offshore. But Glenn Ford's Bill Emerson (Davis, naturally, gave him the surname of her beloved Ralph Waldo), though intelligent and gentle-spirited, is also a young man of flesh and blood, and he comes to prefer the "frosting on the cake" of sexy, bold, aggressive Patricia to the far more spiritually worthy but outwardly drab Kate.

So heartbroken, helpless Kate loses her young man to the predatory, flashy Pat. But because Bill is more truly Kate's soul mate than Pat's, though he doesn't realize it, he is to find, in time, only misery with the sexy twin who cheats on him with other men, spends his money prodigally, and proves crassly insensitive to his deeper needs.

"Do you really *know* Bill?" the bereft Kate warns Pat before the imminent wedding. "Do you understand what kind of person he is, what he dreams of doing? When Bill's kind fall in love, they mean it!" But Pat scornfully brushes Kate off and merrily waltzes away with her bedazzled bridegroom—and soon enough has him boiling in a witches' brew of hurt and disgust.

For a time Bill continues to be deluded about his wife, and during that time the rejected Kate, cast into the darkness of loss and longing, endures all the horrors of being unwanted and occasionally patronized by Bill.

But all had begun well, Kate recalls, when she first stepped from a taxi onto the ferry landing to find she had missed the last boat to the island. At the beginning of the film, there is rich expectancy in the air, fed and fostered by the expressive Steiner score. One feels something important and meaningful is about to happen to this shy, drab, but gifted and prescient young woman—and it does, when Ford gives her a lift to the island in his launch.

Kate recognizes her soul mate in Bill at once, and later she maneuvers ingeniously to get out to lighthouse-keeper Eben Folger's (played by Walter Brennan) island where Bill works. An amateur painter, Kate convinces old Folger to pose for her daily. One night fog prevents her from returning home, so she wanders to the top of the lighthouse where Bill is working, and they stand outside in the swirling fog.

"It's like the end of the world," Kate whispers, looking out into the mist. "If it *were* the end of the world, then people could say all the things they wanted to say; then they would have the courage to say them." She has his attention now. "For instance?" he asks. "Honest things." "Such as?" She looks at him directly. "Such as telling you I didn't particularly want to paint Eben."

Alerted, suddenly gentle and compassionate, Bill asks quietly: "Then

why did you go to all that trouble?" "Because I wanted to see *you* again,"
she replies. And, with the foghorn punctuating every few sentences, she
adds: "Lonely people want friends, but they have to search terribly
hard—it's difficult to find—" "Other lonely people," he finishes for her
with a quiet intensity.

And so, because he is lonely, and because he likes and respects
Kate, Bill takes up with her for a time. Their favorite dating spot is a
cliff with a magnificent view of the Atlantic; there, he shares his quiet
thoughts with her.

"This is your proper place," Kate tells Bill. "Funny, you are the first
person to understand that," he tells her, and promises he will never
leave.

But one day on the dock, he encounters the vixenish Pat. He thinks
she is Kate, of course, and she proceeds to make him her own with all
the self-confident brazenness and aplomb that Kate lacks. Soon enough,
Bill is confessing to the amused Pat that "you've changed—before, there
seemed to be something lacking—it's as though you were a cake—without the frosting." "*They* say I'm well frosted," Pat snaps back. "I'll say!" is
Bill's boyish rejoinder.

Later Bill discovers the deception, but by then Pat has hooked him.
And so playgirl Pat gets the boy and drab painter Kate must suffer as
bridesmaid through an elaborate wedding ceremony in New York. As
Kate, Davis conveys wordlessly, in the high pantomimic style that is
purely hers, the agony of a soul incomplete and unfulfilled. Her expressive face and eyes convey the consternation and fright of a nonswimmer
who, emotionally speaking, has ventured beyond her depth—a bereft
spirit deprived of the feel of solid beach-sand beneath her feet. She is
drowning in an endless ocean of unrequited love.

Meanwhile she takes up with an indigent artist, Karnak (Dane
Clark), who is as rough, tough, and direct as Bill was shy and tentative.
A talented individualist, given to no-nonsense realism—"Man needs
woman; woman needs man—it all starts with that—art, music, the
works!"—Karnak tries to loosen Kate up by seducing her, and when she
resists he snarls, "Always running away—no wonder you lost that guy!"
On another occasion he barks, "Women like you want the grand passion! You want a guy to smother himself for you!" "Yes we do!" a finally
feisty Kate lashes back, and then, when one of Karnak's fierce kisses
obviously leaves her cold, she exits with the line, "I'm sorry, Karnak; I
guess it's the grand passion or nothing!"

Karnak, a Davis inspiration both in the writing and casting, has
distinct similarities to the masculine and direct painter William Grant

Sherry, who was then courting Davis. Oddly enough, in real life, the crass painter attracted her more than the passive idealist—possibly because he represented more of a challenge. Sherry reportedly did not like "his" persona as acted and spoken by Clark.

Bette Davis as unrequited lover proceeds to give herself a salient and definitive thespian workout in a subsequent scene that her fans and admirers have long delighted in. Bill, oblivious to what he has done to her, calls from Boston and asks if she will help him do some shopping in New York. With a fresh glow in her cheeks and a sprightly gait, Kate rushes to meet him at a department store. But it turns out he only wants to use her to model a birthday-present negligée for Pat. Kate holds up the negligée. "It will look wonderful on Pat," Bill enthuses. Later he is happily writing the check for the negligée and rattling on, ignorant of Kate's feelings, about how much he loves Pat and how they look forward to his new job in Chile. Earlier she had tried to reach out to him, saying, "Bill, I can't think of you away from the island, somehow." "I had to do something to make more dough," he replies offhandedly. She realizes then that he is totally oblivious to her and is longing only for his reunion with his wife. Grasping the pathetic futility of her presence there, she pleads an upcoming engagement and leaves. Steiner, with his usual inventiveness, concocted for this sad little scene a bittersweet, lilting theme, slight but compelling, that complemented Davis's emotions aptly.

Then, suddenly, she and Pat are in a sailboat (Pat has shown up on the island to join her after what appears to have been a spat with Bill) when bad weather overtakes them (a wonderfully graphic scene shot completely in a tank at the Warner studio) and Pat drowns. Kate allows herself to be mistaken for Pat and gets a chance to "steal" her sister's life. It is then that she learns how Pat had hurt Bill with her blatant infidelities and insensitivity to his feelings, and that they were on the verge of a divorce. Kate sees the misery in his handsome face, and when she asks him for another chance to restore his ideals, she mourns instinctively for the heartbreaking difficulties that lie ahead. Kate/Pat and Bill make a try of it, but more revelations of Pat's sordid two-timing life keep emerging, including an enraged lover (Bruce Bennett), who had arranged to divorce his wife for Pat.

And so, feeling that Bill will never again trust or love her while he thinks she is Pat, Kate runs away to the island. Bill, realizing at last who she is, follows her there, and high on the cliff where they had first communed, with the fog encircling them yet again and the sea pounding on the rocks beneath them, Bill tells Kate that he wants her to come home to him, that he realizes Pat was all wrong for him, that Kate had known all along what he didn't, that she had suffered so much for both of them. And then Bill enfolds Kate in his arms and says the long-delayed words that this weary, heart-sore wanderer had waited to hear: "Oh Katie, I love you so much!" Fadeout to one of Steiner's lushest musical alarums. The closing shot is one of the most famous in the Davis still-photo pantheon. Eloquent in its romantic lushness, it showcases both Davis and Ford to maximum advantage.

Bette Davis knew that *A Stolen Life* would appeal to those weary pilgrims of the soul who have far to go, and long, before their private homelands of the heart appear in the distance. And she sought to convey that, for those denied the ultimate reward, beauty and valor can still be found in the search, and in the courage to continue that quest, despite all discouragements.

She defended the picture vigorously, and she has had her allies, myself among them. Even the hard-boiled Walter Winchell, who would not be taken in by man, beast, nor movie, called *A Stolen Life* "short on logic but long on heart appeal." "The public liked it," Davis once said, "and the popular heart is more true a judge of a picture than an army of critics." In recent years filmic commentators have begun to understand what Davis was trying to convey and revisionism is upgrading it.

In a 1988 interview, Dane Clark told Doug McClelland: "Yes, I was in it, but I never saw *A Stolen Life*. I play an artist Bette Davis puts up in her home, but in the original script there was a scene where the two of us finally get to go out of the house together. She was the producer and for some reason she cut the scene out—maybe she wanted to concentrate on the romantic stuff with Glenn Ford. Anyway, I remember thinking it important to the story, and certainly to my part, and refused to see the picture.

"I'll never forget one scene that did get in. As a starving artist, I would read the papers to learn where there was an art show and go there and eat. This is how I meet Bette in the story. I'm this grubby street guy and I go to an art show, gorge myself on the food, meet Bette there and wind up in her house. I began the shooting of the scene like a ravenous animal, stuffing myself with everything in sight. I didn't realize that I would have to duplicate all the eating for everyone else's shots. By the second day on this scene I was deathly sick, by the third and final day I was out of my mind, throwing up and green in the face. They were three of the worst days of my life."

Dane Clark added, "Right after the picture was over and I was home recovering, a delivery truck pulled up in front of my house. The driver brought a huge, beautifully wrapped box up to my door. Inside was all the remaining food from the eating scene, with a note from Bette saying how lovely it had been to work with me. Since Bette Davis was not known for her sense of humor, I was flabbergasted.

"Then there was a very long scene in the picture between Bette and me at her house, where I was giving her painting lessons. We're talking about techniques. We did a master shot of the two of us, followed by her close-up, which went beautifully. Then it was time for my close-up. Suddenly I heard a little gay guy squeaking out the lines Bette was supposed to be saying. She had gotten bored, I guess, and gone to her dressing room. Now, I'd worked with many big stars, but they all read their lines off camera for me. I got angry and shouted, 'What is the bullshit? Where's Bette? I read for her, now she can read for me!' Curtis Bernhardt, the director, almost had a hemorrhage. I didn't realize that you didn't challenge a star who also happened to be the producer. Bernhardt kept saying, 'Shh! She'll hear you. She'll hear you.' I said, 'Let her hear me!' Suddenly, Bette tapped me on the shoulder and said, 'Dane, forgive me. I've been in this business too long. I've forgotten my theatrical manners. Of course I'll read the lines for you.'"

Walter Brennan, who played the lighthouse keeper, was distantly related to me. He told me of his feelings about her during my 1964 Hollywood visit, where I spent some time with him on a set. "I felt that trying to double as both producer and star was a bit too much for her," he said. "I noted that it made her tired and irritable at times, and after probably losing sleep all night worrying about stuff apart from her acting, she came to the set looking tired; she was in her mid-thirties then and the camera picks up on lines, bulges—and tiredness."

Walter laughed. "I was no spring chicken at the time [he was fifty-two] and since I was playing a crotchety old lighthouse keeper anyway, nobody gave a damn how I looked! The older, fuzzier, messier the better! But Bette was playing a highly romantic part and had to project youthfulness, and I remember thinking that she ought to get her sleep and look after number one and maybe ought to leave the nonacting chores to others. I really did feel she was taking on too much, and it showed in her work."

He added, "She was supposed to be in love with Glenn Ford in the picture, and he was playing a gentle idealist. But when I saw the film later, I thought she sparked up more with Dane Clark, who played a roughie-toughie big-mouthed bohemian painter. She seemed to like take-charge guys who talked up to her, both on and off screen. And I, for one, was not at all surprised when she married, later in the year, a real-life roughie-toughie painter. Now mind you, I wasn't given to gossip; I left that to Louella and Hedda, but when I heard stories about how Sherry kicked her around and threw things at her, I got the feeling she sort of enjoyed it all, deep down. Something in Bette craved excitement and danger, and I think she got bored in her marriages unless the man gave her some challenge. I'm afraid she often got more than she bargained for, but I've never been really surprised that her marriages never lasted. She was too much woman, hellcat-variety, for any man to keep up with. I think she just wore them out. They either took to drink or other women, or beat her up, or all three. And I have always suspected that something deep inside her enjoyed all the chaos, and that she went out of her way to generate it!"

Walter said of working with her as an actress: "Remember, in the scenes in *A Stolen Life* that I played with her, almost all of them early in the picture, she was supposed to be the shy, sensitive sister mooning over Ford. I was never in a scene where Bette let loose in her famous feisty manner. So I can't relate anything about playing off sparks of the kind for which she was famous. But I found her, in the characterizational mood she was in with me, a wonderfully sensitive and expressive artist. And she had more humor and self-deprecatory impishness than she was credited with. In one scene she had to run down a street after me. She had put on a few more pounds than she should have, and when she caught up with me, she was puffing so hard they had to reshoot. I think she liked my directness. I told her, 'Twenty pounds off would make you more fleet-footed,' and she laughed and said, 'Thirty pounds would be more like it, but I have to shovel it in to keep up my strength for all the work I'm doing on this picture! But thanks for taking ten pounds off what you could have estimated!'"

Catherine Turney, *A Stolen Life*'s screenwriter, shared interesting memories of the film in a 1977 interview. "Bette had liked my work on *My Reputation* with Barbara Stanwyck, which was a big hit and quite adult in treatment and concept, considering the Production Code strictures of the time. She asked for me to do *A Stolen Life*. She also thought my writing and Curt Bernhardt's direction worked well together." Turney found Curtis Bernhardt difficult to work with, however. "He was very Germanic and difficult at times. He was a product of the Berlin school of filmmaking, and they were quite sophisticated, those early German film directors." She remembered that Curt thought Americans of 1945–1946 were hopelessly, indeed laughably, naïve.

Turney also recalled that Curt and producer Henry Blanke taught her a valuable lesson: "Never attack a scene head on, always do it obliquely, if possible. Never have anything on the nose. It makes the audience more curious if you approach your points sideways." She remembered that Bernhardt insisted she avoid undue sentimentality. "Always there is that thin line between sentimentality and honest sentiment; it is easy to cross it. I'm afraid I did at times."

Turney recalled how new special effects were tried for *A Stolen Life*— original ones. "They went way out on a limb. It was difficult. They had to be very precise in the staging of scenes with both sisters. Bette would play one sister, and they would have another actress about her size and height playing opposite her. Then, on Stage Five, where they had the special effects, they would remove the head of the actress and substitute Bette's head." Bette, she recalled, got very upset when her head came off. "Now why do they have to do *that?*" she'd expostulate, nervously lighting a cigarette.

When Davis did such things as light and pass a cigarette to her "twin," it produced a startlingly novel effect. Bernhardt had warned Turney to write the sequence without regard to the projected effects. "Write it as two characters. Forget that Bette is playing both. Don't get involved in that or it will inhibit you."

Turney always claimed that she liked Davis personally and enjoyed working with her. "She was creative herself, always receptive, always fair, and if you overruled one of her ideas, she'd turn it over in her mind, and if she thought you were right, she'd go along with it." Turney had also worked with Joan Crawford on *Mildred Pierce* and Joan passed muster with her, too, though, it was obvious, Turney preferred Davis. She did not like Barbara Stanwyck very well, which secretly pleased Davis, who had had her own run-ins with Stanwyck on the set of *So Big* many years before. "I admired [Stanwyck] a great deal as an actress," Turney said, "but I never could get close to her." Turney felt that Stanwyck didn't really like women, adding, "I don't think there is a lot of warmth in her. If you think back on her performances, there isn't much warmth there."

Turney's analysis of Davis's producer status on *A Stolen Life* was: "At that time the studio was making deals with some of the big stars so they wouldn't have to give them raises in salary. They would make them producers in name only, and it allowed them to get capital gains, something taken off their income tax."

Errol Flynn, among others, served as "producer" on another Turney script, *Cry Wolf*, but he never functioned in that way, ever, was entirely indifferent to the functions of the job. But Davis took her duties very seriously, to the studio's considerable annoyance, and was always calling meetings. One meeting went on forever; it related to the dog she was to use in a particular scene. One subject was discussed: What breed of dog should be used, which would be most appropriate for the atmosphere of the scene? Numerous dogs of all breeds were paraded about while the producer-star cogitated furiously. Finally, after much soul-searching, a wire-haired fox terrier was selected. The dog got quite a directorial workout and ended up one of the best actors in the picture!

Davis gave her all to the scene, shot in the tank, where the twins' boat overturns in a storm. Tremendous waves were simulated mechanically. Tons of water came coursing down through a chute, accompanied by gargantuan splashes and tidal waves. At one point she almost drowned when the crew failed to pull her out in time after she went overboard as the bad twin. She insisted, nonetheless, on doing all the shots herself, and again and again she got knocked out of the boat. A double was on hand for this and other shots, but Davis didn't use her, even though memos from the front office warned her that she was endangering her health and life by going to such extremes.

During the shooting, writer Elliot Paul was sent by *Photoplay* to catch up with Bette. She was very excited about a current Russian discovery [since discredited]—a serum that would permit people to live several hundred years. One of its features was that it could arrest the aging process at any age the patient chose. At thirty-seven Davis felt the ideal age for a woman was thirty-five to forty. "By that time," she told Paul, "she knows enough so that her face is interesting, not like a magazine cover." She added, "Think what a wonderful inspiration [it would] be to an actress to know that after she has studied and worked fifty years to learn her trade, instead of being discarded, her looks and energy will be preserved and can be used to the best advantage another century or more."

Obviously carried away, Mr. Paul rhapsodized for *Photoplay* readers that the Davis face of 1945 was "a mirror reflecting changing emotions. To say that it is supremely beautiful is as true as to say that it is sometimes harsh and strained. It all depends on the moment."

Davis never produced again. Warners felt she was dissipating her energies and should concentrate on acting. She agreed.

Only thirty-six at the time, she played a middle-aged schoolteacher who inspires a miner to literary greatness in *The Corn Is Green*, 1945. *(Collection of Douglas Whitney)*

—◇—

Her favorite co-star Claude Rains, as a temperamental composer, stole the picture from her in *Deception*, 1946. *(Collection of Douglas Whitney)*

—◇—

ABOVE: William Grant Sherry, husband number three, and Davis with daughter B.D. at her christening, 1948. *(Collection of Lawrence J. Quirk)*

BELOW: Robert Montgomery was better at comedy than she was in *June Bride*, 1948, and she hated him for it—and for his political beliefs. *(Collection of Douglas Whitney)*

ABOVE: *Beyond the Forest*, 1949, with Joe Cotten, was ridiculed on its release, but is now an admired cult film. *(Collection of Douglas Whitney)*

BELOW: Marilyn Monroe was scared stiff of Davis in *All About Eve*, 1950, but Anne Baxter and George Sanders hold their own here. *(Collection of Douglas Whitney)*

LEFT: Davis with her mother, Ruthie, at the Hollywood premiere of *All About Eve* (*Collection of Douglas Whitney*)

BELOW: Davis and Mr. Bette Davis number four, Gary Merrill, celebrate her forty-third birthday in 1951 in England on the set of their ill-advised flop, *Another Man's Poison*. (*Collection of Douglas Whitney*)

Davis returned to Broadway in *Two's Company*, 1952, but succeeded only in proving that she was no musical-comedy star. Here she attempts a Sadie Thompson takeoff. (*Collection of Douglas Whitney*)

After two years of illness, she reprised Queen Elizabeth I in *The Virgin Queen*, 1955. *(Collection of Douglas Whitney)*

—◇—

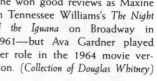

She won good reviews as Maxine in Tennessee Williams's *The Night of the Iguana* on Broadway in 1961—but Ava Gardner played her role in the 1964 movie version. *(Collection of Douglas Whitney)*

—◇—

Inappropriately cast as an apple seller, Apple Annie, in *Pocketful of Miracles*, 1961, here she clowns for co-star Glenn Ford on the set. *(Collection of Doug McClelland)*

—◇—

ABOVE: Davis and Joan Crawford (with Jack Warner here) paired for *What Ever Happened to Baby Jane?*, 1962—one more round in their famous feud. (*Collection of Douglas Whitney*)

BELOW: Director Robert Aldrich referees the contenders during a break in the shooting of *What Ever Happened to Baby Jane?* (*Collection of Doug McClelland*)

—◇—

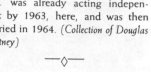
B.D. was already acting independent by 1963, here, and was then married in 1964. (*Collection of Douglas Whitney*)

—◇—

Davis plays twins in the murderous melodrama *Dead Ringer*, 1964. She played twins eighteen years before in the romance *A Stolen Life*. (*Collection of Doug McClelland*)

—◇—

Joe Cotten, Davis, director Bob Aldrich, and Crawford discuss the script of *Hush . . . Hush, Sweet Charlotte*, 1965. Later Crawford backed out, to be replaced by Davis's choice, Olivia De Havilland. (*Collection of Douglas Whitney*)

—◇—

Davis and De Havilland square off as feuding sisters in *Hush . . . Hush, Sweet Charlotte*. (*Collection of Doug McClelland*)

—◇—

ABOVE: Christian Roberts, as her son, watches as Davis manipulates a statue of a peeing boy in *The Anniversary*, 1968. The picture was a dud. *(Collection of Lawrence J. Quirk)*

RIGHT: Davis and Michael Redgrave did not fare well with *Connecting Rooms*, 1969. *(Collection of Douglas Whitney)*

LEFT: *Madame Sin*, 1972, was one of Davis's more colorful roles. Robert Wagner co-starred in this TV movie. *(Collection of Doug McClelland)*

BELOW: In the poorly received *Bunny O'Hare*, 1971, with Ernest Borgnine *(Collection of Doug McClelland)*

—◇—

Davis at sixty-eight in *Burnt Offerings*, 1976. She had a supporting role. (*Collection of Douglas Whitney*)

—◇—

Matching wits in *The Scientific Cardplayer*, 1972, with Silvana Mangano, Joseph Cotten, and Alberto Sordi *(Collection of Douglas Whitney)*

She grande-damed it with the best of them in *Death on the Nile*, 1978, here with Maggie Smith and Angela Lansbury in the rear. *(Collection of Douglas Whitney)*

Skyward, 1980, was one of her many television dramas. Here she is with co-star Suzy Gilstrap. (*Collection of Doug Clelland*)

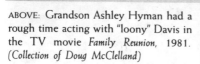

ABOVE: Grandson Ashley Hyman had a rough time acting with "loony" Davis in the TV movie *Family Reunion*, 1981. (*Collection of Doug McClelland*)

RIGHT: She did the first segment of the hit television series *Hotel*, 1983, with James Brolin and Connie Sellecca, but had to withdraw because of illness. (*Collection of Doug McClelland*)

Davis, seventy-four in 1982, enjoyed the role of matriarch Mrs. Vanderbilt in the television movie *Little Gloria, Happy at Last*. (*Collection of Douglas Whitney*)

———◇———

Lillian Gish found Davis a trial to work with in *The Whales of August*, 1987. *(Collection of Douglas Whitney)*

—◇—

19

Sliding Downward with Sherry

"I's LIKE GRAND OPERA—only the people are thinner!" That is how one critic summed up the lurid, highly melodramatic, and distinctly overblown *Deception*, which Davis shot in the spring and summer of 1946. Later the picture was dubbed *Conception* by some careless Davis chroniclers who claimed B.D. was conceived during the shooting. Since the picture was finished by August 1946 and released in October, the nine-month count between August 1946 and B.D.'s birth in May 1947 doesn't check out. B.D. was conceived in the weeks after *Deception's* completion.

Deception was a lurid bit of business about a concert pianist (Davis) who tries to conceal from her cellist lover (Paul Henreid), who was separated from her by the war, that she has been the mistress (kept in high style, too, with a penthouse and lavish clothes and gifts) of famous composer Claude Rains. Rains, angered by her marriage to Henreid, threatens to reveal all to her husband after he (Rains) has led an orchestra highlighting one of his own works with Henreid as the guest cellist. In a panic, Davis shoots Rains to silence him, then confesses the whole shoddy business to Henreid. They agree they must go to the police; it is just after Henreid's triumph playing Rains's cello concerto, and as they leave his dressing room for the exit, one of the onlookers gushes to Davis, "You must be the happiest woman in the world tonight!" The look Davis gives her has gone down in cinematic history as the most pregnantly campy she has ever bestowed and is often imitated by Davis fanatics and impressionists.

The film is indeed operatic, and Claude Rains as the tormented, egomaniacal composer Hollenius almost steals the picture from his co-stars. (In an unusual tribute to his performance, he was honored with his name above the title in the credits as the third star—"an honor he was long overdue," said good friend and fervent admirer Davis later.)

Cynical, jaded, despairing, yet haughtily brittle, Rains overplays in the best sense of that overused term, limning his viciously egocentric character with masterly dispatch. When Davis, who has come to beg him to remain silent about their affair, says, "Hollenius, what are you?" after he makes a pass at her, Rains ripostes, "What you've made me!" He is the most genuine character in the film. Henreid spends most of the picture looking troubled, perturbed, and increasingly suspicious, while Davis does frequent rechargings on her hysterical, agonized, pop-eyed "he must NOT learn the truth" shtick.

Even so, Davis has her moments. When she comes, gorgeously gowned and accoutred, with a gun in her purse to use on Rains if she cannot ensure his silence, and he tells her that he fears death and had a dream about it the night before, she hisses, "So you are afraid to die, Hollenius!" And later, when she shoots him with theatrical éclat at the top of a flight of stairs and he falls all the way down, her eyes pop, her chest heaves, and her breath comes in short gasps that would have done credit to any of the high tragediennes of the theater.

Erich Wolfgang Korngold went all out with a highly charged, lushly operatic score that highlighted all the melodramatic doings with expert selectivity. In fact, it is Korngold's own concerto that Henreid "plays."

The picture holds up well when seen today, but more than a few 1946 critics considered *Deception* overwrought, overstated, and over-colored in all departments.

Davis was extremely unwell through much of the shooting, which began in April, and due to delays because of her assorted accidents, health collapses, and temperamental demands, dragged on and on through the summer. She and Jack Warner exchanged a series of angry telephone calls, telegrams, and even on-set arguments, and she argued frequently with Irving Rapper.

Davis has always claimed that the picture was theatrically false from start to finish and that it should have followed the plotline of the original play more closely. To her, the only creditable thing about the proceedings was the performance of her idolized Claude Rains.

The screenplay, by John Collier and Joseph Than, was based on a play that had gone through several incarnations even during its theatrical existence. A two-character play called *Monsieur Lambertier*, designed for Parisian audiences, had been written in 1927. The title was later changed to *Satan*, then to *Jealousy*. Eugene Walter had then refurbished it to accommodate Fay Bainter and John Halliday. A Paramount film version, titled *Jealousy*, followed in 1929 with Jeanne Eagels and Fredric March. In the 1940s it was retitled *Obsession* and, under the refurbishment efforts of writer Jane Hinton, starred Eugenie Leontovich and Basil Rathbone.

The screenwriters revamped the stage piece completely and added a third character, writing in a number of juicy scenes tailored to the more flamboyant aspects of Rains's rich talents. Davis insisted later that she had wanted the piece kept a two-character affair; this seems inexplicable, as it was she who led the cheering for the scene-stealing Rains of the screen version.

Davis, who had studied piano as a child, even wanted to play Beethoven's "Appassionata Sonata" herself when it was required for a scene, but got talked out of it, wisely and tactfully, by Rapper who pointed out the public would think she was faking anyway, so why bother?

Irving Rapper, who always had a love-hate relationship with Davis, enjoyed telling one story about her in *The Celluloid Muse: Hollywood Directors Speak*. It seems that Davis, who had been ill, harried, and prone to accidents during the shooting, was particularly angry at Ernie Haller for not making her look more attractive. "Have you seen the rushes?" she asked. Rapper nodded and followed her into the projection room, where she and Haller were having a loud yelling session. Ernie had not been able to erase the ravages to her face caused by her misfortunes—to say nothing of her age in 1946—thirty-eight.

Davis reminded Haller at one point that he had photographed her very flatteringly in *Jezebel* in 1938. "Why can't you photograph me like that?" she demanded. Ernie, basically a civilized man who preferred stilettos to meat cleavers when delivering ripostes, topped her ace with his rejoinder: "Bette, I was eight years younger then!" Davis got his point immediately, flustered about a bit, and then gave out with one of her standard manic laughs. "Do what is humanly possible for a thirty-eight-year-old hag, then, Ernie," she snapped, and made a quick exit.

Haller was one of those who later made the point that if you gave her a sound argument and countered her protestations with a convincing answer, she was the first to concede.

When I interviewed Rapper on several occasions over the years, his love-hate attitude toward Davis continued to surface. "*Deception* was probably the toughest assignment I had with her," he said, "because her morale was shot, both at home and at the studio, and she was more than usually snappish and unreasonable. I tried to be understanding and flexible with her but boy, did she try my patience!"

Rapper recalled Jack Warner coming down to the set with producer Henry Blanke and telling him he didn't know how he got on with Bette without having a heart attack. "I'm a good listener," Irving replied, "and I keep detached, and I try to throw in a laugh now and then to relax her." "Well, that goddamned budget is going through the roof and we're weeks over schedule, and it isn't any goddamned laughing matter to me!" Jack Warner barked.

At this point, as Irving recalled, Jack sent Henry over to Davis's dressing room to report Jack's feelings on the matter and he could hear the famous voice all over the sound stage hollering, "Tell that son of a bitch to go straight to hell!"

Paul Henreid, one of Bette's good friends, preferred to talk about the clever hand work done for him during his "cello playing." According to Paul two cellists were on hand—one used his right hand for the bowing, the other the left to hold the instrument—then the scene was shot at three-quarter angles to heighten the illusion. "It was perfect!" he said. "I couldn't get over it." Once I had guided Paul, a kind and good-natured man, through his lavish praise of Rains, Haller, Korngold, and all other parties involved, I lured him into observing that "Bette was under great strain through that picture. I and my wife were close friends and we knew what she was going through. You will never get me to say anything unkind about a woman I and my family love dearly and cherish for her many acts of kindness toward us, but—well, her morale was not high, and the strain showed on the screen." Henreid, too, remembered her concern over the way the camera revealed her ravaged physical and mental state. "But on that I have no comment," he said.

Claude Rains, in the end, marched off with the good reviews. "If you want to call his flamboyant measures hammy," the *New York Post* chuckled, "you must add that they have quality, flavor and the so-called inner flame."

At home, Davis's domestic troubles with Mr. Bette Davis III matched her career worries.

Once Sherry was safely Mr. Bette Davis, as she was to recall, Dr. Jekyll promptly became Mr. Hyde. On their way to Mexico for their honeymoon (where she was also to receive an award from the Mexican government) he threw her out of the car during an argument. Later, on their honeymoon night, he threw a trunk at her. She began to wish that she had read Bobby's detective's report. The condition that had kept him in the marine hospital seemed to be something he was unreservedly acting out now that he was "home safe."

Back in California, they purchased a beautiful home on Wood's Cove, at Laguna Beach, high above the sea. The quarrels and the beatings were constant. She found herself saddled with someone who matched her in artistic temperament—but didn't have the talent to go with it. Frustrated in his Sunday painting, unsuccessful as a dilettante physiotherapist, annoyed because he was not seated up on the dais beside her at industry parties, Sherry turned ever more abusive.

After the outbursts he would be contrite, humble, gentle. Davis urged him to see a psychotherapist to learn to control his rages. Sherry agreed, but this did little good. When Ruthie saw some of the bruises on Bette's back and chest, she indulged in a round of I told you so's. Sherry's mother confessed that she had wanted to warn Davis about him before the wedding, but she was too afraid of Sherry; it seems he had hit *her*, too.

Meanwhile, love—of a sort—was in the air. Ruthie and Bobby decided it was time for them to get married, too. Ruthie chose a gentle, middle-aged specimen named Robert Palmer—yet another short-term marriage, as it turned out. Bobby, who was in one of her periods of relatively good mental health, married an innocuous man named David Berry. Davis laughed, "Now we're Mrs. Sherry and Mrs. Berry!"

For almost a year, Bette, Bobby, and Ruthie struggled on with their new marriages—each finding her own brand of disenchantment. Ruthie realized that she was too old, too set in her ways, too conditioned to being Bette Davis's chief parasite to acclimate herself to some nobody male's needs. Bobby's uncertain mental health took a turn for the worse yet again—and Mr. David Berry's term came, in time, to an end. But Palmer and Berry, as Ruthie later said, at least had their marbles, pussycats though they might have been, whereas Sherry was mad as a hatter.

A year later, pregnant by Sherry, Davis began entertaining hopes that a child would calm him down, make a man of him, give him something to live for, focus his energies. For a while—a short while—her hopes seemed confirmed.

Barbara Davis Sherry—named for Bobby at Bobby's frantic insistence, though Davis hated the name Barbara—was born by cesarean section in Santa Ana, California, on May 1, 1947. During the eighth month of Davis's pregnancy, the doctors had told her vaginal delivery was risky—something to do with one abortion too many in the Ham days—and that *she* could pick the date. May Day was her choice.

Sherry, his attention focused on the child and on his unaccustomed role as father, changed his tune for a while. He billed and cooed over her, insisted on changing her diapers and warming her bottle. Davis felt uneasy; something about this readiness to take on domestic duties reminded her uncomfortably of Ham. Soon Sherry also began whining à la Ham. He complained to the press that when Davis came home from a hard day at the studio he had her slippers ready, drew her bath, and then cooked her a nourishing meal. Again shades of Ham. All these protestations—public ones, too—smacked of weakness. It seemed he *wanted* to be Mr. Bette Davis. One night, during a fierce quarrel, he threw a heavy object at her while she was holding B.D. (as she called the child, because she hated the name Barbara). She told him that once the child's welfare was threatened she had had enough. She moved to the studio and hired bodyguards. He sent her threatening letters. Jack Warner offered to have him beaten up. Davis said no, she'd handle it.

He begged her for a reconciliation. Ruthie dug up a psychiatrist. Sherry promised he'd go and learn to control his "awful temper," become a true husband and father. This was in 1949, and Davis gave him one more chance. It didn't work. Sherry was on the loose again shortly, smashing windows and furniture and frightening the child into hysterical tears. Then Davis learned from her housekeeper that Sherry had fallen in love with B.D.'s nurse and planned to elope with her. Back to court they all went. Davis rehired the bodyguards, secured more restraining orders. Sherry threatened to sue for B.D.'s custody. Davis offered him alimony if he would desist. He promptly accepted and the divorce went through in early 1950—but not before he had appeared on a movie set and threatened to beat up Barry Sullivan, whom he suspected of romancing her. When the divorce was finalized, Sherry married the nurse and eventually wound up with a flock of children and grandchildren. As Ruthie observed, marriage to a nonentity like himself suited him far more comfortably than playing the role of Mr. Bette Davis.

But Sherry would be heard from again. In order to get the divorce, Davis had guaranteed alimony for three years. ("A wife paying her husband alimony—that was a new one on me!" she later said. "I guess I have to plead guilty to originating that trend!") Her next husband wanted to adopt B.D., so he asked Sherry's permission. Sherry put a

$50,000 price tag on his daughter, and when Davis refused, he sued for custody. Davis finally got rid of the bloodsucker once and for all when the judge, hearing that Sherry received alimony, threw the case out of court. Her lawyer, having advised her to withhold Sherry's latest alimony check, then managed to force his agreement to adoption by husband number four.

Davis had B.D. at age thirty-nine. She was told she could never have another child, either vaginally or by cesarean. Jack Warner sent her a priceless pearl each year on B.D.'s birthday.

In the 1947–1948 period, Davis was anxious to get two projects off the ground. She wanted to do a film version of the Edith Wharton novel, *Ethan Frome*, which had been dramatized successfully and had had a *succès d'estime* on Broadway. The story dealt with a farmer in nineteenth-century New England who is saddled with a cold, unattractive wife. He falls in love with the gentle hired girl, a relative of the wife's. When they run away, they are injured in a sledding accident, and the ironic conclusion has the wife carrying the maimed pair through many years and emerging the most sympathetic of the lot. Davis felt she would be perfect for Mattie, the hired girl, and she wanted either Gregory Peck or Gary Cooper for Ethan, and Mildred Natwick (who had made a perfect test) for Zenobia, the wife. Jack Warner was hesitant about the project—not only was it a period drama and he hated "costume stuff," but the theme seemed too drab and downbeat to be good box office. To Davis's frustration, he refused to go ahead. For years after she dreamt of doing *Ethan Frome*, even when she got too old for Mattie; then, she said, she'd do Zenobia. There were no takers.

The other project was *Mrs. Lincoln*, which was to be a film version of the often dramatized story of Abraham Lincoln's wife, who was emotionally unstable, accused of being a Confederate sympathizer because she had relatives in the southern army, and who lost several children to premature deaths. Years after Lincoln's death, her eldest son committed her to an Illinois mental institution.

Davis felt this was her kind of material, and she told Jack Warner that this role would win her a third Academy Award and that he must let her do it. She flooded his office with memos, letters, suggestions, injunctions, all-out demands—to no avail. All through 1947, 1948, and 1949 she kept up the pressure for Frome and Lincoln, but Warner remained adamant.

Jack's attitude seems puzzling when viewed from the hindsight of forty years. Her 1946 release, *A Stolen Life*, had done well at the box office, and so, for that matter, had her other 1946 picture, *Deception*. He knew she could carry a picture. It was true that he disliked "costume stuff," but some of her most successful pictures, including her all-time box-office hit, 1939's *The Old Maid,* had been period, costume material. So had *Juarez.* And *All This and Heaven Too.* And *Elizabeth and Essex.* Why the change in Jack's attitude circa 1947–1948?

Two factors might have influenced him. Times had changed, and the government in 1948 had forced separation of the exhibition and production aspects of the film industry as violations of antitrust statues. This, in turn, had affected the box office. From a high in 1946, the year after the war, the box office had dived by 1948, and television was coming up. Jack and his stockholders were more cautious; the halcyon days of the early to mid-1940s were over. The profits from the war period, when any movie made a neat killing in an entertainment-starved, escapist era, were things of the past.

Davis's instincts were true: *Ethan Frome* and *Mrs. Lincoln,* properly mounted, directed, and cast, would have advanced her already considerable prestige. But forced to play it safe, she settled, the September after B.D.'s birth, for two unworthy vehicles in a row.

The discerning critic Walter Kerr once defined the censors' and Legion of Decency's effect on the movies as "the tyranny of the well-meaning second rate."

Certainly Davis blamed these people specifically for her inability to convert her next picture, *Winter Meeting* (formerly *Strange Meeting*), into an honest, convincing motion picture. It was not to be the first—nor the last—time she castigated these "stupid, narrow, esthetically myopic people" for interfering with artistic truth and with the mirroring of life as it is lived and experienced.

Oddly enough, it was Sherry who had first read the Ethel Vance novel and enthusiastically recommended it to Davis for her first postbaby venture. When she read it, she was equally optimistic about its possibilities, and soon had her friend Catherine Turney preparing a screenplay. Nonetheless there was much about the project that worried her. The Ethel Vance novel had been trenchant, literate, and critically well regarded, but it had elements that Davis knew would not get by the 1948 censors. Complaining at the time to a *New York Times* interviewer, she lamented the lack of "vitality and honesty" in films because of the censorship stranglehold, adding: "Anyone who attempts to do something that hasn't been previously tested and approved soon finds that you can't do this because Mr. Binford [Lloyd Binford, the Memphis panjandrum of censorship] or somebody else won't approve."

In her screenplay, Turney had to deal with the honest discussion of

Catholicism versus Protestantism that had distinguished Miss Vance's work by watering it down to almost nothing. It would have offended the Catholics. Then she had to keep the hero and heroine from going to bed together, another crucial story thread. That, for obvious reasons, also had to go. All in all, Turney had to blur, blunt, or eliminate altogether about seven ideas.

The result, on screen, was a gutless, tepid, anemic tale of a repressed poetess and a naval hero who is struggling to become a priest. Davis's character, the daughter of a deceased minister, is a sexually starved sublimator who writes socially conscious poetry and volunteers at a local Manhattan hospital. The hero, handsome, muscular, and intelligent, has a psyche riddled with the horrors he has witnessed in action. He feels undeserving of the medals he has won and guilt-ridden and cowardly because he came back and his comrades didn't. He feels he is unworthy of the priesthood and is making an attempt to adjust to the realities of the postwar world. Invited to a nightclub dinner session by dilettante sophisticate John Hoyt (in the novel an obvious homosexual, in the screenplay a foppish neuter), the hero (Jim Davis, no relation) rejects the sexy Janis Paige for wrenlike, drab Davis and follows her home to her handsome apartment, where they exchange views on their respective life philosophies (in the novel, he seduces her). She tells him that her adulterous mother caused her minister-father's suicide. He teaches her compassion, and she phones her hospitalized mother. His vocation revitalized by his power to do good, Jim Davis waves good-bye to Bette Davis and goes off to his own world. Presumably, he gets the priesthood and she gets—her mother?

The absurdities, incongruities, and unlikelihoods implicit in Turney's bowdlerized version of the far more honest and incisive Vance original (*Winter Meeting*, the novel's title, became *Strange Meeting* and then *Winter Meeting* again—symptomatic of the studio's censorship concerns) doomed the picture with critics and public alike, and started a distinct downward trend in Davis's career.

Sadly enough, there was much that was admirable about the picture. Ernest Haller caught the ambience of the poetess's apartment and Connecticut farm very well (though Davis, possibly in an effort to look suitably drab and repressed, eschewed the mascara and eyeliner and smooth makeup, making her look very much her forty years—a mistake in boxoffice terms, given the romantic theme). She did manage to get off some shrewd and telling observations about loneliness and frustration (not wildly popular movie themes at the time).

Bretaigne Windust, a director from the New York theater who had never worked with Davis before (he had directed such stage hits as *Life With Father* and *Arsenic and Old Lace*) proposed to make a "new Bette Davis" out of his star, toning down her mannerisms (but not creatively and selectively, as had Wyler) and draining much of her surface emotion. This turned out to be a mistake, as Davis later complained, for her "scenery-chewing," as Bosley Crowther termed it, would have helped to make the finished result far more entertaining and exciting. Her explanation for letting Windust get away with it? "B.D. had made a drastic change in my life. I had no desire to give up my career, but somehow it didn't matter as much. My life seemed full without it. I had won my battle. I had reached my peak—inside. . . . I had had my Matterhorn. Now I was satisfied to be nestled in my little chalet. From Matterhorn to Jungfrau. . . . I had turned my back to warm some milk and my defenses were down. My claws had been manicured for the nursery."

Of Windust she said scornfully: "He wanted to bring a new Bette Davis to the screen. He would have been smarter to leave the old one alone." As it turned out, she was putty in Windust's hands and followed his every suggestion with an accommodating flexibility that was new to her. She even let Windust ruin the performance of her handsome new leading man, Jim Davis, who had been languishing in second-rate films over at MGM and who considered *Winter Meeting* his big chance. Davis later recalled in exasperation that the color and vitality that Davis had revealed in his test never showed up in any of the Windust-directed scenes. Windy, as she nicknamed him, adopted an overanalytical, nit-picking approach that dampened and defused both the Davis performances.

Windy, a cultivated Princeton man who had been one of the founders of the famed University Players in Falmouth, Massachusetts, loved to reminisce on the set about working in those early days on the Cape with the likes of Henry Fonda, Josh Logan, and Jimmy Stewart. His unfamiliarity with screen technique also exasperated producer Henry Blanke and photographer Ernie Haller, with the result that the shooting dragged through the fall of 1947 as he arranged fresh setups and retakes and other nonsense that Davis, anxious to get home to her baby, overlooked with a forbearance she never would have shown pre-B.D.

Windust never won distinction as a film director, and his only decent effort, *The Enforcer*, had to be fixed up by the far more cinema-wise Raoul Walsh, who did not get the credit. He did few films and died forgotten in 1960 at fifty-four—his chief distinction today being that he sidetracked the Davis career at a crucial point and nipped Jim Davis's romantic-lead prospects in the bud. Jim Davis went on to do many actioners and other low-budgeters, but he did not attain any measure of stardom until he played Jock Ewing on TV's *Dallas*. Within a few years, he died in 1981 at sixty-six.

In a double magazine interview, "Davis by Davis—Bette by Jim—Jim by Bette," in the March 1948 issue of the fan magazine *Motion Picture*, the Davises made the Warner publicity department happy by sparing the errant and meddling Windust his just chastisement and talking, honestly but affirmatively about working together.

Said Jim about Bette: "Bette and I have gotten along fine. If we've disagreed about anything, about a scene, for instance, I've found that she was usually right and I wrong, simply because she knows more about acting than I do." Significantly, considering the dismal result, he added, "She has the professional sense [!?] to leave the correction up to Mr. Windust. . . . If I ask for an opinion she gives it, but not until I ask. If she ever suggests anything, it's done in an off-hand manner, as one trouper to another, not as star to underling." Jim Davis recalled pleasant days off in Laguna, with Bette relaxing on a chaise longue while Jim and Sherry played pool.

Said Bette about Jim: "He's a fighter. He works hard, and has the sense to realize this picture is not the end but merely the beginning of his career. Basically he is a businessman. He was in the oil industry before going into pictures . . . and he's sold catsup, put up tents for circuses, done a dozen other things . . . he is deeply aware of his present inadequacy. I have never seen anyone try so thoroughly." In the interview Davis threw one consolatory sop to Windust, citing his thorough rehearsal period before shooting began. ("A lot of fuss for a lousy result," was her contemptuous summation many years later.)

When I interviewed Jim Davis on the *Dallas* set decades later, he denied any romantic interest in Bette but did recall that Sherry, who had been one of those boosting him for the part, was jealous of him, "though I did nothing to provoke it—nothing. Oh, those watchful, crazy eyes of his, though!" Bosley Crowther's verdict on *Winter Meeting*: "Interminable." Jesse Zunser of *Cue*: "To Catherine Turney goes a wreath, probably cactus, for writing a script that is the talkiest piece of 1948!"

The steady downward course of Davis's career continued with her next film.

June Bride, in its way, turned out to be as great a mistake as *Winter Meeting*. Tired of battles with the censors and unable to get the Frome and Lincoln projects into high gear, Davis wearily settled for yet another picture with Windust, who proved as unsuited for film comedy as he was for film drama, and again at Davis's expense, as she desperately needed a good picture to counteract the bad effect of *Winter Meeting. June Bride* was released in November 1948, the month Truman pulled his surprise victory over Dewey in the presidential election. One amusing sidelight of this was that Warners, which in *June Bride* had a line citing a stylistic shift from McKinley to Dewey, had to rush in a fresh reel to theaters with Truman substituted.

In her first comedy since 1941's *The Man Who Came to Dinner,* Davis once again exhibited her poor technical and temperamental equipment for comedy. Her timing was nonexistent, she was oppressively arch and heavy-handed when she should have been light and gossamer-humored, and her careful makeup and the handsome costumes of her new designer, Edith Head (whom she highly prized and whose clothes she bought for offscreen wear), did not disguise her obvious forty years.

The story, even by the standards of 1948, is silly and insubstantial, and halfhearted in its labyrinthine maneuverings. Davis is an editor of a woman's magazine who wants to shoot a layout of a June wedding in a "typical" Indiana home, and to meet her months-ahead deadline she shoots it in the dead of winter, turning the bride's home into a shambles via redecorating ideas that don't turn out and rearranging everyone's lives to a fare-thee-well, all of which arouses eventual resentment and confusion. Robert Montgomery co-stars as a roving war correspondent assigned as her reluctant assistant in these doings; at one time the two had been romantically involved until Montgomery reneged on it. They keep up a running battle during the Indiana assignment and when Montgomery discovers that the future "happy couple" are not even in love, and in fact have their hearts pointed elsewhere, he encourages them to break things up and rearrange the romances satisfactorily. Davis, enraged at first, finally sees he is right and plans her layouts to match the new pairings.

These lame and forced doings were written by Ranald MacDougall, a talented writer who was not at his best here. Ted McCord's photography did not disguise Davis's years, as one of her favorite lensmen would have done, and she later regretted using him. On the plus side she was delighted to be reunited with the fine actors Fay Bainter of *Jezebel* fame (who played her other assistant and had nothing worth her talents to show for it) and Jerome Cowan (of *The Old Maid* and *Mr. Skeffington*), who played her publisher, also thanklessly. The on-set conviviality between the old friends did not show up on the screen.

As Jerome Cowan recalled *June Bride* in 1964: "I was very sorry Bette had elected to do it, but she told me she was desperate at the time and felt a comedy (which was never her strong suit, in my opinion) would represent a 'change of pace.' Also I knew she was having troubles at home, and felt, as others did, that since having her baby, her attention was distracted and she was not using her best judgment as to vehicles. Windust had no talent for light comedy (it cried out for a McCarey or La Cava) and the depressing, spiritless atmosphere on the set carried over, regrettably, into the final result on screen."

Another negative factor that drastically affected the onscreen effect was Davis's opinion of co-star Robert Montgomery. She knew he had her cards and spades when it came to comedy timing and the light, fey touches for which he had become famous. He made her seem awkward and heavy in her efforts to keep up with his style and attack, and she hated him for it. Her quarrels with Windust, whom she resented for making her look "wrong, unlike myself" (as she put it) in *Winter Meeting*, also dissipated her energies. Only young Betty Lynn, who played the bride who runs off eventually with another man, brought out her kinder, gentler, nurturing side. Betty sang her praises constantly; they would do another picture together, and became lifetime friends.

Montgomery had another count against him: He was a strong conservative Republican and the year before, 1947, he had headed the Hollywood Republican Committee to elect Thomas E. Dewey. He had also testified that year as a "friendly witness" for the House Un-American Activities Committee. Later he became a special consultant to President Eisenhower on television and public relations, honing Ike's speaking style with admirable results. A no-nonsense, strongly opinionated character, Montgomery had served four terms, beginning in the 1930s, as president of the Screen Actors Guild, and had exposed labor racketeering in the movie industry. As Davis had with Warner, Montgomery had conducted a running vendetta with his boss, Louis B. Mayer of MGM, which resulted in his being assigned unsuitable roles later in a career that had begun sparklingly in the early thirties with leads opposite Shearer, Crawford, Garbo, and other feminine luminaries of Leo the Lion.

By 1948, Montgomery had served creditably in World War II and won the Bronze Star, among other decorations, as a navy PT boat commander. He had also won some fame as a director.

Davis's battles with Warner, however, had been over creative issues; Montgomery won Mayer's ire for political reasons, beginning with his SAG presidency. So the two could find no common ground there. And his vastly superior comic expertise frustrated and angered her. But worst of all, Davis, a dedicated Democrat and Roosevelt-Truman admirer, hated Montgomery's support of the Republican Dewey. Later, after the picture was released, she had the satisfaction of seeing Truman beat

Dewey. Reportedly she sent Montgomery a sarcastic telegram expressing her unmitigated glee—an act to which he did not take kindly.

So given all this, the relationship between the two stars was either red-hot combative or arctic frigid, depending on whose dander was up or down on a given day. Windust, among his other faults, exhibited a complete inability to mediate between his warring co-stars. As Jerome Cowan remembered it:

"Montgomery got Bette's pressure up more than Miriam Hopkins had ever done in the two films they did together, one of which I was in. Bob had a kind of feline, feminine talent for getting under a lady co-star's skin. I heard Joan Crawford had cordially hated him during their films together at MGM and I could see why. He knew he was better at comedy than Davis and it was like an antelope fighting a grizzly bear— on the antelope's ground, of course."

Years later, in 1961, I asked Henry Blanke, the film's producer, why Montgomery had ever been cast in *June Bride* when Davis disliked him on so many counts. "Oh, it seemed like a good idea at the time," he replied, "and we knew Bob was a fine comedian and felt he might lighten up Bette's style. Also Bretaigne Windust wanted him, and he and I talked Bette into it. She wanted to know why we didn't pick some Warner player under contract—she even mentioned Dennis Morgan, and, I believe, Jack Carson, but we made her see that they didn't have the co-star clout of Montgomery." Blanke then chuckled. "There was another reason, though we didn't underline it to Bette. Since she had her baby, she looked much older—fortyish, in fact—and Bob Montgomery was in his mid-forties then and we felt he might make *her* look younger, somehow. As it turned out, *she* made *him* look younger. I think he knew that when he saw the rushes, and it delighted him. He had a mean wit, and he was always trying to deflate Bette."

Blanke remembered also that when Davis lapsed, during what were supposed to be light comedy scenes, into some of her more stately, overembroidered posturings, Bob would chirp wickedly, "Bette, my dear, this is not the court of Queen Elizabeth, and certainly not the castle of Lady Macbeth!" According to Blanke, "She hated the guy's guts after that."

Many years later I met Montgomery at a party; he was then living in New York and winning distinction counseling the Rockefellers on their communications arm and fund-raising for Lincoln Center. When I brought up Davis and *June Bride*, he raised his arm, gave out with a cocked-eyebrow mock scowl, and replied, "Please, friend, spare me!"

But after I had informed him that I made a point of questioning every former Davis associate for the book I hoped one day to write on her, he sighed, and said, "Bette Davis is a great tragedienne but a terrible comedienne. She never should have tried comedy; it was poison for her. I have seen her perform most creditably in drama, but in the lighter things, she's simply—" He searched for the word, and finally came out with it, grinning, "elephantine!" I asked how he felt about her personally in retrospect. "On that, I pass!" was his reply. I wondered if he knew that Davis, on her end, had referred to him as "that superconservative Republican son of a bitch, always with his nose in the air!"

JACK WARNER, whose tastes and instincts had often been derided and downgraded by Davis, showed considerable wisdom and discernment in suggesting Stuart Engstrand's *Beyond the Forest* as a new picture for Bette in 1949.

"Hell, she has spent years screaming at me that she had to go on loan to RKO to get a really mean, bitchy part she could get her teeth into," he told Henry Blanke, who produced *Forest*. "She was a slut and a she-devil in *Of Human Bondage*, and it made her career, didn't it? And then she'd rant and rave about how we never found her a gutsy role like that here at Warners, and here we have one! Rosa Moline as Lenore Coffee has written her is every bit as strong and venomous as Mildred in *Bondage*. She's a manhater supreme, she does the guy dirt, she's scheming and climbing and ambitious in the same cheap, sluttish way Mildred is. So why doesn't she see, for Christ's sake, that in Rosa she has another Mildred! And it's how the public wants to see her. In Podunk they see her as a man-hating slut, ready to cut every guy's balls off—here's her chance to strut her stuff in her own inimitable style. *They'll eat it up!*"

Blanke and Lenore Coffee tried to get across Warner's thoughts on *Forest* to Davis, but she was having none of it. "I'm too old for Rosa! Brother, I was fifteen years younger when I did Mildred! I was twenty-six then; I'm forty-one now. How'll I look young enough? Give it to Virginia Mayo—she'll be great in it!" Mayo, a Warners contract player on the sluttish side, was then twenty-eight years old.

Still seething over missing out on *Ethan Frome* and *Mrs. Lincoln*, Davis was determined to give everyone concerned as hard a time as possible on *Beyond the Forest*. "She was just impossible at times," King Vidor said. "Here I was trying to help her give a performance worthy of her best efforts in a role that, in my opinion, was admirably suited to her, and she was fighting the whole idea of it, all the way, damn it!"

When I discussed *Beyond the Forest* with King Vidor, he was ambivalent about both the picture and Davis. "She did some really wonderful things in that," he told me. "I particularly admired a scene played entirely in pantomime, wordless from start to finish, in which Bette surreptitiously tried on a mink coat that the Ruth Roman character had left on a chair. The way she luxuriated in the feel of that mink, as she stood on a chair and preened in it in front of a mirror—she made it so vivid, so lifelike!

"Of course she overplayed at times," Vidor recalled, "but I think it was an excess of zeal more than anything else. She wanted to transform the material, get a good picture out of it by hook or by crook. And remember that we were fighting the Legion of Decency and the Production Code all the way—Bette was in absolute despair because that damned Code wouldn't allow her [Rosa] to go to an abortionist, for instance. When she did sneak over to one, the Code people insisted that the name on the office door carry the title of attorney rather than doctor—foolish stuff like that."

I told Vidor that I felt *Beyond the Forest* had a lot of vitality and bite— the kind he had given to pictures like *Ruby Gentry* some years later—and that it contained one of Davis's more vivid performances.

"But it didn't turn out as well as I had hoped," he added, "first because of those damned Code restrictions, which were forever interfering with the believability of the goings-on, and because of the hyped-up desperation of all participants."

Max Steiner gave *Beyond the Forest* one of his darker, more sinister scores, and his variations on the song "Chicago" were one of his happier inspirations.

Vidor found it amusing that the film had become something of a cult classic. Cult classic status, he felt, was always a wryly amusing mixture of admiration and contempt.

I asked Vidor what he thought of Davis's argument that she was too old for the role, that twentyish Mayo was more suited to it. "In the first place," Vidor rejoined, "Mayo, at any age, wasn't a powerful enough actress to carry the part. And in the second place, I know for a fact that in every state of this damned Union there are still attractive women in their early forties who want to chuck hubby and take off for more excitement in a bigger town. There's a desperation many women know in their early forties, when they're afraid life is passing them by, and Davis, I knew, could convey this desperation superbly—in fact, in many scenes in *Forest*, she did just that! But I could never make her understand the obvious logic in this; she was a stubborn one! When I joined Henry Blanke one day in her dressing room and made the points we thought salient—that it was a fine variation on Mildred and that women of forty-one were desperate for new experiences, she just dismissed it all. 'Don't give me that shit,' she screamed. 'Warner just thinks *Forest* would be less expensive than *Frome* and *Lincoln*; he wants something trashy and cheap that he thinks will sell to the lowbrows. I didn't work all these years for better pictures to be relegated, at this stage, to horseshit like this!'"

The irony regarding the financing of the picture, of course, consists in the fact that *Forest* wound up costing every bit as much as *Frome* or *Lincoln* would have. It was just one of the many ways in which Davis got a revenge of sorts on Warner.

Ruth Roman recalls being frightened to death of Davis. "I was twenty-four at the time, and the way she looked at me in our first scene—like she wanted to kill me! Her eyes narrowed into slits and she looked at me as if to say, 'What the hell right have you to look so young and pretty when *I'm* the star of this damned film!'

"In the scene, I had just showed up in town and was standing on the railroad station platform. Davis was supposed to look me over jealously and curiously. I must say, when I saw the sequence later on the screen, she certainly made it real. Too real. It all gave me the creeps."

I asked if Ruth would have wanted to work with Davis again. "I'll pass on that," she said.

In 1965 Joseph Cotten, one of Davis's good friends, expressed his admiration for her and said she had been a cooperative, concerned, delightful co-worker in *Beyond the Forest*. "I know she was having problems with the script, with King Vidor, with Jack Warner, with practically everyone, but there must have been something in our mutual chemistry that kept us calm and cordial with each other from the first scene to last." Cotten felt she had done some excellent work in the picture and blamed the censorship for the unrealities that cropped up.

"Bette is a really great artist," he said, "and I and my wife hold her in the greatest affection. I was on loan, and not a regular member of the Warner family, but she made me feel thoroughly at home at all times. I know others have found her temperamental and difficult, but maybe she had her reasons for acting as she did. I do know that she was always intolerant with mediocrity and false or slipshod work. She was a perfectionist, yes, but to me she was always fair and kind."

Lenore Coffee told me that fear of censorship was the main roadblock to her screenwriting efforts on *Beyond the Forest*. "The remarkable thing is that Bette, by sheer personality force and sensual innuendo, got across so much that we couldn't express in words. And I felt that some of her all-time best acting could be found in scenes in that picture. She even made a lot of 'What a dump!'" She threw the line away but high-lighted it in reverse. (Edward Albee featured the line in his 1962 play, *Who's Afraid of Virginia Woolf?*, citing its source and winning immediate response from an appreciative audience.)

Produced by Henry Blanke, and based on the novel by Stuart Eng-strand, the story deals with the bored and miserable Rosa Moline, wife of the town doctor in a stultifying Wisconsin community, who longs to escape "beyond the forest" to the Big Town, Chicago, personified by a millionaire who has a hunting lodge nearby and with whom she is hav-ing an adulterous affair. Later she goes to Chicago to find him, and when she is rejected, she returns in defeat to her patient husband (Cot-ten), by whom she later becomes pregnant. Then back comes mil-lionaire David Brian, and again she plans to lasso him. He is more amenable this time, having been disillusioned by a society girl who de-spised his humble origins. When her husband's friend (Minor Watson) threatens to expose her plan, Davis kills him during a hunting party. An expert shot, she aims with lethal efficiency, later claims it was an acci-dent, and is cleared. After trying to get an abortion, she throws herself down an embankment so she will miscarry, and later dies of peritonitis as she attempts to catch a train back to Chicago. Such is the basic plot, and Davis dresses up the proceedings with impassioned bravura. Made up garishly, her mouth smeared and her eyes rheumy, she is a horrible figure indeed as she staggers out of the house and toward the tracks to her doom. In a graphically realistic scene in Chicago after the mil-lionaire's rejection, she staggers through the rain while prostitutes jeer at her from windows and bar attendants refuse to seat her. She slithers and squirms in the best Davis style as she intones, "If I don't get out of this town, I hope I die!" and cites the undertaker as the best thing around: "He carries them out!" When one charitable housewife tells another at the post office that the town is tough on Rosa, her friend snaps, "She's tough on the town!"

Film critic William Schoell, in the film newsletter *Quirk's Reviews*, expertly nailed down the revisionist upgrading of *Beyond the Forest* (a crit-ical failure in 1949) in the 1980s. His August 1986 retrospective review read in part:

"It has been said that it was in this film (in which she utters the classic line, 'What a dump!') that Davis began to get set into her famous mannerisms and speech patterns and perhaps this is true. But she also gives, in her own larger-than-life way, one of the most impressive and strongest performances of her career. The scenes in the middle of the film, when she does run off to Chicago only to be rebuffed by Brian (and to discover that she wasn't really the urban sophisticate who could take the town by storm that she supposed she was), illustrate how good she can be at getting across loneliness, fear, and frustration. Her facial expressions mirror the conflicting, tormented emotions of her character perfectly. Davis is equally good in the final scenes, as her fever gets worse and she becomes delirious, literally dragging herself to the track in a futile attempt to catch another train to Chicago. This is an actress who, at her best, has the mesmerizing quality of a volcano."

According to Schoell: "The main problem with the story line is that Rosa Moline must be turned into a villainess because she refuses to conform to the values of Middle America. She wants a more exciting life, husband and environment, instead of the utterly drab ones she has been offered. She isn't interested in having children, in being maternal. She, in fact, tries at one point to get an abortion (horrors!) and even gives herself a miscarriage that doesn't work out by jumping out of a car and diving down an embankment (thereby getting the infection that eventually kills her). Naturally audiences of that day (1949) had to believe that anyone so lacking in wifely, womanly virtues would find it an easy step from abortion to murder. [The murder] is the only really 'evil' thing she does, and insures that whatever audience sympathy she may have garnered will be lost. This old-fashioned attempt to turn what could have been a tragic heroine (of sorts) into a murdering witch served to assure the 1949 audiences that any woman not content to stay home in dreary domestic bliss and raise babies was a most unnatural and evil creature who deserved only death and disdain. . . . it's a shame that its dated, conservative 1949-ish ambience prevents this film from finally getting the attention it deserves."

To add insult to injury, the Production Code bluenoses insisted that Warners insert a long, lugubriously puritanical foreword after the main titles to the effect that it was good for the collective public's souls to observe monstrous evil acted out, so that in recognizing its hideous face, they would be inspired to turn away and follow righteous paths!

Davis asked for a release from her Warners contract, conditional on her finishing *Beyond the Forest*. Her request was granted.

PAYMENT ON DEMAND had originally been titled *The Story of a Divorce*, appropriately enough, since shortly after its completion Davis finalized her own divorce from Sherry. Her old associate, Curtis Bernhardt, watched her Warners flounderings and the termination of her contract after *Beyond the Forest* and came up with an idea for a story he knew instinctively would be exactly right for Davis's talents and temperament. He and Bruce Manning turned it into a screenplay, and it was produced by Manning and Jack E. Skirball for an RKO release with Bernhardt directing.

Davis undertook it with high hopes in early 1950—hopes that were justified. It turned out to be one of her better pictures, a study of the twenty-year course of a marriage, with Davis playing an ambitious, driving, unscrupulous woman who forces her more easygoing husband, Barry Sullivan, into an upwardly mobile career that culminates in wealth and success as a corporation lawyer and steel executive. Disgusted throughout with his wife's corner-cutting expediencies, social climbing, and general ruthlessness, Sullivan suddenly asks her for a divorce.

When she discovers that he has been seeing a gentle, womanly schoolteacher (Frances Dee) who proffers the love and tenderness that his domineering, success-crazy wife has forgotten about, Davis takes him for all he has in a bitter divorce that leaves her with their two daughters (Betty Lynn and Peggie Castle), the property, and the money. Chastened by loneliness, however, Davis takes a trip and discovers the rootless, heartbreaking pattern of life for middle-aged divorcees after dallying with a married womanizer (John Sutton) and watching a friend (Jane Cowl) pitifully supporting a parasitical poet on a tropical island. She returns ready to resume with her husband, whom she sees again at their daughter's wedding.

Davis was later fit to be tied when Howard Hughes, the boss at RKO, insisted that she, Sullivan, and director Bernhardt return for a day to reshoot a new ending. In the earlier dénouement, which she thought was realistic and true, she was her old domineering, demanding self at a breakfast table scene; the leopardess had not changed her spots. Instead, Hughes forced a more muted ending on her, in which she told her husband, who had suggested reconciling, that she would take him back when he had a chance to think matters over. Hughes added insult to injury shortly thereafter by changing the title to *Payment on Demand*— which, Davis snickered, sounded like a quickie flick about blackmailers and underworld types. She pointed this out to him, but he refused to budge. "That was his stubborn, feminine side," Davis said later. "He stuck to his guns not because he didn't see the logic of my argument but because his ego demanded that he have the last word. I was so mad at that moment that if I had had a gun handy, I might have ended matters on my terms—it would have been worth getting the electric chair for!"

But regardless of the name change and the phony ending, *Payment on*

Demand won considerable praise from the critics and more than made back its $1,800,000 budget. In fact, it turned quite a nice profit. Shot from January to April 1950, *Payment* wasn't released until February 1951. Using his head, for once, Hughes decided to cash in on what was bound to be a smash, *All About Eve*—begun only ten days after *Payment* finished—by following close upon *Eve's* heels.

The Hollywood Reporter felt that "if *Payment on Demand* has been withheld from release until the Bette Davis hit in *All About Eve* had been cemented, it wasn't necessary. The picture, completed before the 20th-Fox comedy drama, stands on its own firm feet and Miss Davis on the powerful range of her acting talent. It's a superb part and the actress plays superbly, reading nuances of the modern woman into it that her fans will recognize and understand." The *Los Angeles Times* even rated it higher than the picture that preceded it by four months, declaring: "This is no such flashy performance as she gave in *All About Eve*. It is much finer grained."

B.D., almost three, played Davis's small daughter in an early sequence. She appeared in another of her mother's pictures years later, but as Davis declared, almost in relief, "It didn't seem to push her toward acting, and that was a mercy, too, all things considered, as I did not want her to go through all I had!"

Bernhardt and the cameraman, the great Leo Tover, devised a brilliant flashback sequence (when I talked to Tover in 1960, he generously credited the idea to Bernhardt) to show Davis and Sullivan as teenagers. In order to disguise their mature bulges and lines (Davis was then forty-two, Sullivan thirty-eight) he placed them middle ground in an impressionistic mélange of light and shadow. Then Tover darkened the foreground, lit up the background, and used specially made transparent walls for illumination. The careful arrangement of shadows gave Davis and Sullivan marvelously youthful appearances by shedding brilliant light on their faces and disguising their necks and chins with dark shadows. Bernhardt wondered years later why that technique wasn't used again. When I asked Tover if he or Bernhardt or both had patented it, he said he couldn't recall.

"That woman [Davis] understood lighting better than most lighting professionals," Tover told me. "Of course she had worked with the best, colleagues I greatly admired, like Ernie Haller and Sol Polito and Gaudio, and she must have picked up a hell of a lot from them because she knew all the lingo and all the terms. I would have been annoyed with her after she called, 'Watch that lighting, get the boom back there,

Leo!' just once too often, but she was usually right. *I learned from her during that picture!"*

When I talked with Barry Sullivan in the Polo Lounge of the Beverly Hills Hotel one afternoon in 1964, his memories of his one film appearance with Davis were vivid. "She was really the most talented individual I have ever acted with," he said, "and wonderful to you if she liked you. If she didn't like someone, she had ways of showing it—and believe me, they were mean ways. Diabolically inventive, in fact! Luckily for me I was one of those she liked. I remember being worried because my character was rather gentle, passive, and easygoing by nature and I was afraid I'd look wishy-washy up against her characterization that was so driving and vicious by comparison, but she showed me ways to subtly suggest the inner fierceness and resentment and manly sense of outrage my character was actually feeling, and miraculously it registered later on screen. I always felt Bette would have made a great director. She was full of suggestions, and Curt Bernhardt, who had worked with her before, had a knack of letting her have her head on things he agreed with, and pulling her up short when their ideas diverged. She was always reasonable if she realized someone else's idea was better than hers."

I asked him if he had been romantically attracted to her. "They said I was!" he laughed, "but much as I admired her, she wasn't my cup of tea that way. Her husband, whom she was in the process of divorcing, thought I was fooling with her, though, and he came on the set and knocked me down. He [Sherry] had a terrific inferiority complex—the 'Mr. Davis' stuff and all that—and *no* sense of humor." He recalled Davis came to his dressing room later to apologize for Sherry's behavior. "Bette had a humble, gracious side to her that not many people saw," he said.

Davis was delighted to work with the great stage star Jane Cowl, (who curiously had originated the role of Kit Marlowe in the 1940 stage version of *Old Acquaintance*, the role Davis played in the 1943 film). Davis had seen Cowl often on the stage and did everything she could to make her comfortable. They talked of doing another film, but Cowl, then sixty-three, was in the first stages of the cancer that killed her shortly after the film was completed. Manning and Bernhardt had written some excellent dialogue for Cowl in the telling scene in which, old and drifting, she is living on a remote island and keeping a man young enough to be her grandson. Warning Davis that she faces a similar fate, Cowl moans eloquently, "When a woman grows old, loneliness is an island and time is an avalanche!"

Not that the writers stinted on Davis's dialogue, one famous example being: "When you love a man and lose him, you may think it makes you an individual again—but it doesn't! It makes you a nothing!"

Davis continued her sister-daughter friendship with Betty Lynn (from *June Bride*), who played her daughter in *Payment*. Betty worshipped her, and was protective of her during the shooting. As Leo Tover chucklingly told me, "Davis, to cop from the old saw, when she was good with people she was very, very good—and when she was bad, she was horrid!"

Victor Young whipped up a perfect Bette Davis score for *Payment on Demand*. "I studied her carefully," he later said, "as I know Max [Steiner] did, and I tried to express the highs and lows of her personality in musical terms. I think I largely succeeded, as she was nice enough to tell me several times."

Except for the name change and the butchered ending, which she howled about for many years thereafter, Davis, on balance, held *Payment in Demand* in high regard. "The situations were adult and believable—and how I needed those at the time!" she recalled.

20

Renaissance—
and Gary Merrill

THE YEAR 1950 brought Davis a great new film role—and a fourth husband.

Davis was five days away from finishing *Payment on Demand* when she got a call from Darryl F. Zanuck. It seems he was in a serious bind. Claudette Colbert had been scheduled to star in *All About Eve*, but had hurt her back skiing in Switzerland and had to cancel out. Zanuck asked her if she could take over the role of Margo Channing. Davis asked to see the script, and Zanuck sent it over immediately. She read it at once and called to tell him she was born to play that part. He told her she would have to start in only ten days—five days after her last scene in *Payment* was shot, because they had rented the Curran Theatre in San Francisco for important interior shots. She told him she'd be on hand.

Years later Bette Davis had this to say about *All About Eve:* "I can think of no project that from the outset was as rewarding from the first day to the last. It is easy to understand why. It was a great script, had a great director, and was a cast of professionals all with parts they liked. It was a charmed production from the word go. After the picture was released, I told Joe [Mankiewicz, the screenwriter-director of *Eve*], he had resurrected me from the dead. He had, in more ways than one. He handed me the beginning of a new life professionally. I also say a thank you to Claudette Colbert for hurting her back. Claudette's loss was my gain. On what changed circumstances are whole lives changed. No broken back—no Gary Merrill."

In 1981 Claudette Colbert told me that she had cried for days when she realized the golden opportunity she had missed. With her usual honesty and candor, Colbert told me: "Bette said *Eve* rescued her from the doldrums. I was in some doldrums of my own at that time where my career was concerned, and I would have loved to be rescued. But it was not to be. I will always remember the year 1950 not only for the months-long pain I went through with my bad back—it took forever to mend—but for the emotional upsetment, indeed despair, I felt over losing such a plum role." Colbert, with characteristic generosity, added, "Bette was wonderful as Margo, though. I know how much it meant to her at the time, because she was having her full share of personal and professional woes. It was good to watch the law of compensation work for her."

Joe Mankiewicz was on a high in 1950; the year before, he had won critical plaudits (including Oscar honors) for his *Letter to Three Wives*, and he had just concocted a screenplay based on a story, "The Wisdom of Eve" by Mary Orr, that had won the enthusiasm of Darryl Zanuck. Mankiewicz had done duty as a producer at MGM earlier. His screenplays tended to smack more of theater than film; they were wordy and prolix and there was talk-talk-talk through many scenes that should have been cinematized, but even his flaws worked for him with *Eve*. With expert photography by Milton Krasner, a sharp, rousing musical score by Alfred Newman, and inspired costumes by Edith Head and Charles LeMaire that suited each of the main characters according to their personalities, *All About Eve* was a class production from the word go, and there was much advance excitement over it.

In the film, Davis plays Margo Channing, just turned forty and insecure despite her eminence as a Broadway star. She is in love with thirty-two-year-old director Gary Merrill and feels the age difference has her at a disadvantage. Her best friend Karen (played wisely and warmly by the sparkling Celeste Holm) introduces her to the stagestruck Eve Harrington (Anne Baxter), who insinuates her way into Margo's confidence with flattery and an overstated, wide-eyed obsequiousness that has Margo's dresser and confidante (Thelma Ritter) suspicious. First as Margo's secretary and then as her understudy, Eve furthers her own purposes, and when the innocently supportive Karen, who feels Margo has treated Eve with imperious insensitivity, maneuvers Eve into a one-time appearance in Margo's role by delaying the star in a faked auto mishap (she empties the gas tank), Eve proceeds to climb higher and higher, blackmailing Karen by threatening to tell Margo what she has done, winning the lead in Karen's husband's play and seducing him in the bargain. The only one besides the Thelma Ritter character who sees through Eve's machinations is Addison DeWitt (George Sanders) and he alone gets the last word—of a sort—with ambitious Eve. At the end Eve gets a dose of her own medicine. She is about to take on as assistant a young girl who is just as rapacious as Eve.

It was on the set of *All About Eve* that Davis met and fell in love with the man who was to become her fourth husband, Gary Merrill. Handsomely rugged, a fellow New Englander, and a newly acclaimed actor whom she had admired the year before in *Twelve O'Clock High*, Gary was just the tonic Davis needed after her debacle with Sherry.

Also, she liked the fact that Merrill had a mind of his own. Far from fawning, obsequious or "politely" considerate, he called the shots as he saw them. Once, she needed a light for her cigarette and stood waiting. He didn't take the signal, and she had to light up on her own. When she accused him of rudeness—hands on hips, the famous eyes flashing angrily—he told her that his character would never have lit Margo Channing's cigarette. She saw the logic of that, and liked and respected him all the more for it. Here, she felt, was a man of strength and purpose and true masculinity. She liked his directness and assertive ways. Soon it was apparent to Mankiewicz and his cast that Margo Channing and Bill Sampson were falling in love with each other off as well as on screen.

Davis brought to the role of Margo Channing all her seasoned discipline and charisma, as well as the wisdom she had accumulated about matters of the heart. Like Margo, Davis had had her full share of disillusionment, in love, in career, with people, and with life in general. And when she got down to making perhaps her most famous speech of the film in the stalled car with Celeste Holm, she spoke words that applied to her own life poignantly and pointedly. For at that point she was a forty-two-year-old woman alone again, with a three-year-old child, a threatened career, insecure and worried about the future. She conveyed all of this in that scene:

"Funny business, a woman's career. The things you drop on the way up the ladder—so you can move faster—you forget you'll need them again when you go back to being a woman. That's one career all females have in common whether we like it or not. Being a woman . . . and in the last analysis nothing is any good unless you can look up just before dinner—or turn around in bed—and there he is. Without that, you're not a woman. You're something with a French provincial office—or a book full of clippings. But you're not a woman. Slow curtain. The end."

Davis's continuing bitter feud with Tallulah Bankhead, more on Tallulah's side than hers—burst into flame again when Tallulah saw the film and claimed Davis was "taking revenge" on her, imitating her hairdo, her flamboyant life-style, and her voice. Davis and Mankiewicz protested that not Bankhead, but Elisabeth Bergner and her one-time protégée Irene Worth were the true models for Margo and Eve, but Bankhead refused to be pacified. She phoned both Zanuck and Mankiewicz and threatened a legal suit, which, in the long run she did not pursue. "That bitch stole my best stage roles for films, and now she is holding me up to public ridicule with her imitations of me!" Bankhead screamed at Zanuck in one of her hour-long coast-to-coast calls. Davis contacted Bankhead via letter, telegram, and telephone, all unanswered and unacknowledged, to explain that her voice had sounded the way it did because she had had laryngitis and throat trouble during much of the shooting, and *that* might have caused Tallulah to note a vocal similarity. But nothing mollified Tallulah, who continued to make capital of her complaints for years to come. Certainly Tallulah's then press agent, Richard Maney, got a lot of mileage out of it. It was well known that Tallulah's desire for a running publicity gimmick had more to do with the extended feud against Davis than any honest outrage or hurt feelings. "And it did wonders for Bette Davis's publicity, too," Maney later observed.

All About Eve is replete with brilliantly witty lines, courtesy of Mankiewicz: "Eve would ask Abbott to give her Costello." "She's like an agent with one client." "Not until the last drug store has sold the last pill" (Davis's retort to hypochondriacal producer Gregory Ratoff's claim to be a dying man). "When will the piano realize that it has not written the concerto?" (playwright Hugh Marlowe's crack at Davis, to which she replies that she has to rewrite and rephrase the dialogue to keep the audience from leaving the theater). And of course, "Fasten your seat belts—it's going to be a bumpy night!"

Davis always rhapsodized that she and the cast got along swimmingly and that everything was "a dream to do from start to finish." But there were tensions and hostilities that went unreported and, by her at any rate, publicly unacknowledged.

Some cast members, like George Sanders, later cued me in on the less glamorous doings behind the scenes of *All About Eve*.

When I discussed Davis with George Sanders in 1970, he was sixty-

four and nearing the end of a jaded, dissolute, totally cynical and disillusioned life. Two years after our talk, at sixty-six, he took an overdose of
sleeping pills in a Marbella, Spain, hotel, leaving behind a note that
expressed his boredom with life and his fundamental contempt for his
fellow human beings. One friend said of him at the time of his suicide,
"at least George went out with colors flying. To the end he maintained
his superior, condescending, contemptuous attitude toward life and people. Had George been a Catholic, which luckily for the Catholic
Church he wasn't, he would have been no 'deathbed' Catholic, begging
mercy for his sins after having done what he damn well pleased all his
life. He'd probably have left a lengthy letter for the pope and cardinals
telling them all that was wrong with their policies and their politics.
That was George. A lot of people didn't like his truths—but the funny
thing was, they were *true* truths, for all their malice and abrasiveness."
Sanders married four times. Two of his wives were the Gabor sisters Zsa
Zsa and Magda, another the actress Benita Hume, whom he inherited
from Ronald Colman after the latter's death. He published an autobiography in 1960, *Memoirs of a Professional Cad.* According to his close
friend Brian Aherne, who later wrote about Sanders in a book of his
own, he was as much a personal cad as a professional one. "He gossips,
he attacks people viciously, he has no respect for man nor beast—but
what an interesting man!" Aherne once said of him to me.

Sanders had pulled his punches on some people in his autobiography—by which I mean he was mildly disdainful when he could have
been all-out vituperative. And he could certainly be that, too.

Circa 1970, Sanders just didn't give a damn what he said about anybody, and what he had to say to me about Davis, especially during their
All About Eve encounter, was far from flattering. As Edward G. Robinson
had done before him, Sanders felt Davis was a sloppy actress who fell
back too often on mannerisms and standard tricks, and that she prima
donna-ed viciously to the detriment of her fellow players.

"She was lucky with *Eve* in that she had the benefit of a wonderful
script and an understanding director in Joe Mankiewicz—and she has
herself deigned to admit it," Sanders said, "but she was a very difficult
person to work with, and without that script and Joe's professionalism,
she would have taken all of us to the devil within a week of shooting.
She upstaged Anne Baxter at every turn, and drove Anne to distraction.
She was supposed to be playing a woman of forty who was jealous of a
much younger woman, Anne's character, and she played it as if it were
happening to her personally. Anne caught the underlying tensions and

the viciousness, and it is to her credit that it spurred her to act even better than she would have with a gracious co-star.

"And that poor Monroe child—Marilyn—Marilyn was terrified of her! She was very nervous in all her scenes with Davis, and understandably so. During one scene in a theater lobby involving Monroe, Davis, and me, Davis whispered to me after a shot—within poor Marilyn's hearing—'That little blonde slut can't act her way out of a paper bag! She thinks if she wiggles her ass and coos away, she can carry her scene—well, she can't!'"

Sanders found this all the more amusing because the pot was calling the kettle black—Davis, too, was wiggling her fanny and calling upon all *her* standard vocal tricks. "Her lack of fundamental graciousness toward her co-players disgusted me," Sanders sneered. "Hugh Marlowe was another player who was scared to death of her. In a scene where they are having a shouting match from stage to auditorium, Davis unleashed so much venom that the poor man forgot his lines completely!"

I asked Sanders how he himself had coped with her. "I think she got my message loud and clear—that I was not putting up with her nonsense. I matched her snarl for snarl and bite for bite. Of course it was great for the picture, as it made for some nice confrontational conflict, and I must confess I found it sort of an exhilaration. Later, when she lost the Best Actress Oscar for *Eve* and I won as Best Supporting Actor, I met her at a party and she turned her back on me without a word. I couldn't resist the temptation to purr over her shoulder, 'Sour Grapes, Bette?' and do you know what she did? She turned around and spit at me!"

It was not well known that George Sanders played both sides of the street sexually and that he was among the admirers of Tyrone Power, an actor notoriously generous with his favors to both sexes. Once when Henry Fonda asked Ty why he was known as "Mr. Round Heels," he replied, with a kind of backhanded wisdom, "Why frustrate people? If I'm feeling horny at the time, and I like them, I'll oblige them. Usually, once their curiosity is satisfied, they cool down and we resume as friends." "But doesn't it exhaust you to be such a *giver*," Fonda asked. "No, it exhilarates me, and it does wonders for my ego," the indefatigable Power replied.

Henry Fonda could be cruel and cynical at times, and when Power died in 1958 at forty-four after an intense dueling scene with Sanders while they were on location in Spain for *Solomon and Sheba*, Fonda joked around that Sanders had probably worn him out in the sack as well as on the set. The word got back to Sanders when Yul Brynner (who had taken over Powers's role) jokingly told him that Fonda had warned him to refuse tea in Sanders's dressing room if he wanted to finish the picture alive. "He refers to you as the man who killed Ty Power with love," Brynner told Sanders. For this he was rewarded with a nick on the arm in the first dueling scene—the one Power's heart attack had interrupted. Sanders never spoke to Fonda again, but he made nasty remarks about Fonda's own sexuality, citing his impotence with first wife Margaret Sullavan and a later wife's suicide, one of his milder observations being that Fonda was a "Don Juan homosexual who has to prove himself with one woman after another."

Davis had heard about Sanders from Fonda years before when they worked at Warners, and at the time *Eve* was shooting, she told Jerry Asher that Sanders was more bitchy to work with than Miriam Hopkins and that he had upstaged her at every opportunity. "He won that goddamned award at my expense!" Davis screamed to Asher. "I'd like to see him and Miriam go at it in a picture together—brother, would that be the Battle of the Bitches to watch!"

Reportedly Marilyn Monroe used to vomit after her scenes with Davis. But for all her fear, she gave a fetching performance. The role of Miss Carswell, the also-ran who, as Sanders's character puts it, belongs back in the Copacabana nightclub rather than on any stage, was, of course, ideally suited to Monroe's distinctly limited but nonetheless kinetic screen persona. Even so, she tended to be awkward in her scenes with Davis, as if afraid lightning was going to hit her any moment. At times it did. Gregory Ratoff told me in 1956 that Davis went out of her way to make cutting remarks to Marilyn about her entrances and exits; in one, as Ratoff recalled, Davis yipped at her, "I know and you know and everyone knows that kitten voice of yours is goddamned lousy— and it's lousy because you never trained it as a *real* actress does—a shame you never had stage training!" After such observations, Marilyn went away to cry as well as vomit, according to Ratoff. Ratoff, who had himself directed, felt that Mankiewicz let his delight in Davis's superb playing as Margo blind him to her objectionable ways off camera. "I would have tried to bring her to heel," he told me. "She always respected directors who drew the line with her, but Mank was a one-man Bette Davis Admiration Society and I think she secretly laughed at him for it!"

Celeste Holm has always been relatively reticent about working with Davis but it was common knowledge that she cordially disliked her. She told friends that Davis was always bristling to get the last word, on screen and off, and that she used all kinds of attention-getting tricks. In the famous automobile scene, in which Davis lets her hair down about love and men, it is true that Margo was supposed to dominate the action, but Holm felt she hogged it all unduly.

Anne Baxter later irritated Davis mightily by taking over the Margo Channing role from Lauren Bacall in the stage version, *Applause*. Davis deigned to visit Anne in her dressing room after a performance and infuriated the latter by purring, "I think you did rather well considering all the—er—limitations you had to work with." Baxter later told a friend, "I couldn't for the life of me figure out whether she meant *my* limitations or the *show's* or *what*? I don't think I wanted to know, either— I was angered enough as it was!"

One *All About Eve* co-worker who did seem to get along well with Davis was Thelma Ritter, who played her dresser. "I like Bette and she likes me," Thelma told me in 1963 between takes on a film called *Move Over, Darling*. "Maybe it's because I'm homely and she has always thought of herself as homely—how she hates to watch herself on the screen!— and when we worked in *Eve* there was so much humor between us, both in our lines and in our chemistry off screen, that she relaxed with me. I don't think she thought of me as competition; thought I complemented her, since we were such different types. There's no nonsense about her—none at all. She was so darned happy to be doing that role and knew it would help her a lot after something of a downslide she'd been through, and I was just the kind of no-nonsense good companion and boon buddy she needed. She was always nice in what she said of me to others, and I never had a single rough word with her. I think I amused and entertained her—at least, I hope I did!"

Sanders felt that Davis and Merrill were in love at first sight. "The chemistry was there—he looked solid and manly and take-chargeish, and they had their acting careers in common, and she didn't conceive of him as a leech or weakling as she did that painter she was in the process of divorcing. Later, his manly assertiveness, as I understand, got to be a pain in her behind, but it lasted ten years so there must have been something that kept them together besides the kids."

For *All About Eve* there was a total of fourteen Academy Award nominations, with Mankiewicz winning for Best Director and Best Screenplay and with George Sanders toting off the Best Supporting Actor award. Davis won the New York Film Critics Award and an Oscar nomination for *Eve*, but lost to Judy Holliday in *Born Yesterday*, there being speculation that Judy had sneaked in because Anne Baxter's nomination for Best Actress split up the vote. Also, Gloria Swanson had made a major comeback in *Sunset Boulevard*, and a number of votes went her way, confusing the issue still further. It was one of the great disappointments of Davis's career, as she said later; she had been positive she would get an Oscar for Margo.

Nonetheless she could take deep satisfaction in the glowing reviews she received for her performance. Alton Cook in *The New York World-Telegram & Sun* reported, "[Miss Davis] demonstrates what a vivid, overwhelming force she possesses. She plays a fading stage star with a sardonic humor so vicious it suggests that Miss Davis must have hated that character above all others on earth. Beneath that, there is also a wise understanding of the lady that leaves an audience finally idolatrous of both role and Bette."

In *The New York Morning Telegraph*, Leo Mishkin reported: "*All About Eve* is a movie in which Bette Davis gives the finest, most compelling performance she has ever played out on the screen."

In retrospect, Davis regarded *All About Eve* as one in a parade of what she called "my false new dawns." Within two years she found herself in yet another career rut—followed, in due time, by yet another renaissance.

Meanwhile there was a new man in her life, and there were big decisions to be made.

BETTE AND GARY MERRILL were married in Juarez, Mexico, on July 28, 1950. He divorced his first (and only previous) wife, Barbara Leeds, in the morning, and was married to Bette in the afternoon. Her divorce from Sherry had come through just in time for the nuptials.

It was as they drove across country to New England, where they planned to spend their honeymoon, that Gary and Bette first sensed their different attitudes toward life. He was laid back, easygoing, a make-do man. She was nervous, perfectionist. Davis fussed about poor accommodations along the way, whereas his attitude was, "If there's a bed in it, it'll do." He also lacked her competitiveness. He had had a so-so career on the stage, his chief hit, in 1946, being *Born Yesterday* with Paul Douglas and Judy Holliday, and he tended to fall into roles through luck or connections.

Gary had served in Army Special Services during the war, and had appeared in the films *This Is the Army* in 1943 and *Winged Victory* in 1944. After his discharge from the service in 1945, he did voice-overs, radio shows, and stage work, narrated the film *The Quiet One* in 1949 and acted in *Slattery's Hurricane* the same year. His first real break came in the Gregory Peck film *Twelve O'Clock High* as an Eighth Air Force squadron commander who has too much compassion for his men and is replaced by disciplinarian Peck.

Gary had not been all that much in love with his first wife, who was an actress, claiming he just needed someone to hang on to, and had ended the marriage without regret. He enjoyed the pleasures of life. He liked to drink, he liked to fish and drive around and take it easy in general. He often said he didn't have Bette's drive, was as good a sport when he lost as when he won. His attitude made Davis impatient. She had a high opinion of his acting gifts but said he wasted his opportunities because of his laziness. They did have in common their New England origins. Gary was born in Hartford, Connecticut, in 1915 and had been schooled at Loomis School in Connecticut and, briefly, at Bowdoin. After dropping out of college he had taken up acting in New York drama school productions and little theater plays, but right from the start he had schlepped along, often subsidized by his parents. By his own admission parts came to him because of his good looks, good voice, and easy charm. He had had his share of affairs, including a red-hot one in New York with Mercedes McCambridge.

He later explained his attraction to strong, driving women: "I don't like to be dominated; I give as good as I get, but I do like to see what makes these aggressive women tick. It's curiosity, I guess. Also their aggression translates well in the sack; they're never boring there!"

Gary and Bette honeymooned in Massachusetts and Maine. Ruthie was pleased because Gary's Yankee ancestry matched the Davises', his mother being one of the Andrewses who had come over on the May-flower.

Soon Gary was called away to do two films—*Decision Before Dawn* in Germany and *The Frogmen* in the Virgin Islands. He was continuously busy working over the next four years. Before they married Davis had told him there could be no children because of her abortions in the thirties and her cesarean in 1947. They agreed to adopt some. Gary wanted a boy first, then a girl. All was arranged by their lawyer, but Bette, in typical high-handed fashion, presented him with a little girl, named Margot (with a t) for her *Eve* character, when he returned from filming. A year later they adopted a boy, Michael. Gary and others felt that Davis's sudden desire to adopt was a belated expression of her long-standing guilt over the earlier abortions.

Douglas Fairbanks, Jr., was having a turn at movie producing in England, and he and his partner, Daniel Angel, offered Bette and Gary a chance to co-star again in a film to be called *Another Man's Poison*, based on the play *Deadlock* by Leslie Sands. Davis's old standby, Irving Rapper, was hired as director, and the screenplay was written by Val Guest. Robert Krasker was set as photographer.

Fairbanks's motivations for offering Davis the role seem confused in retrospect. He never really liked her. In his autobiography he refers to their one film together in 1933, *Parachute Jumper,* thus:

"I didn't . . . appreciate my new young leading lady . . . she was not particularly pretty; in fact, I thought her rather plain, but one didn't easily forget her unique personality. She was Bette Davis. We got on well enough, although she thought director Al Green's sense of humor as infantile as the story we were obliged to act out."

Fairbanks remembered her in that early film as "always conscientious, serious . . . devoid of humor of any kind."

Later in his book, Fairbanks erroneously claims that in 1938 Davis was box-office poison along with Dietrich, Hepburn, and other stars. The truth is in that period she was approaching her box-office zenith. He also refers to her as "fresh from the stage" in *Parachute Jumper* when in actuality she had been acting in films for a couple of years.

The most likely reason for his hiring her for *Another Man's Poison* eighteen years later was that she was on a box-office and critical high after the success of two pictures in a row—*All About Eve* and *Payment on Demand.*

If Fairbanks had held any kind of grudge against Davis over the years, he couldn't have taken a better revenge than he did in luring her into a film widely regarded as one of her all-time turkeys. It not only garnered bad reviews, but did only moderately at the box-office due to unfortunate distribution practices.

Fairbanks, it is obvious, realized his own mistake in commissioning *Another Man's Poison* under his production aegis, as his reference to it in his autobiography is: "Our only interest was to get the damned thing over with!"

Davis and Merrill were, however, heartened when Emlyn Williams, the author of *The Corn Is Green,* one of her great successes six years before, was cast in the film. Davis's respect for him was unreserved, and she even convinced him to work with her and Merrill on a script they regarded as eminently unsatisfactory. The talented Williams's input did strengthen the story somewhat, but the basic incredibilities implicit in it doomed the efforts of all—even the talented Irving Rapper, who had directed *The Corn Is Green* in 1945, and who enjoyed comparing notes with Williams on it during production. Williams also provided Davis with a pleasant bonus: He introduced her to the original of Miss Moffat.

Meeting this legendary woman, Davis later claimed, was one of her few consolations during shooting.

The story of *Another Man's Poison* is wildly melodramatic. Davis is a famous mystery writer who loves both her horse, Fury, and a handsome young engineer (Anthony Steel), whom she has stolen away from her wimpy secretary, Barbara Murray. "Do you love Larry?" Murray asks timidly. "I *want* him!" Davis snaps back.

Complications ensue when Davis's ex-convict husband reappears to blackmail her. Davis promptly kills him, fearful that she will lose the engineer. Then another convict, Gary Merrill, a pal of the deceased, shows up. After confessing to the murder, Davis convinces Merrill to hide the body in the lake. Merrill decides to stick around, and then kills her horse. "I loved that horse!" she yowls in her second major speech of the film. A veterinarian who has been treating her horse and who is given to philosophical, urbane comments (Williams has this thankless role) suspects there is monkey business going on. Davis tries to kill Merrill by sending him out in a jeep with faulty brakes. When this maneuver fails, she poisons him. Upon learning that the police are dragging the lake for the convict she and Merrill have hidden, Davis faints. Williams tries to revive her with a glass of the same poison she used to kill Merrill, and in the last shot—the best thing in the picture—Davis, realizing she herself will die, begins laughing with manic hysteria as the camera closes in, lingering on her face and wild eyes as she *laughs*—and *laughs*—and *laughs* . . .

The film was released at the very end of 1951 and was handicapped by a saturation booking in New York that ran through early 1952. The run unfortunately coincided with the popular *A Streetcar Named Desire*, and exhibitors chose this film over *Poison*—which also cut into the profits.

Davis and Merrill returned to America disgusted with the entire project—and at this point Fairbanks's evident dislike for her personally was heartily reciprocated. They never worked together again. "The only thing decent that came out of that mess," Davis later said, "was the wonderful friendship that evolved with Emlyn Williams. If only he and I could have worked on something decent!"

The reviews, from critics either stupefied or disgusted, ran along such lines as (*Hollywood Reporter*): "Bette Davis, queen of the vixens, combs her hair, lights cartons of cigarettes, snaps her fingers and bites her consonants, and it all adds up to a performance that you'd expect to find from a nightclub impersonation of the actress," and (*New Statesman and Nation*): "She does, in the cant phrase, The Lot . . . no one has ever accused Bette Davis of failing to rise to a good script; what this film shows is how far she can go to meet a bad one."

A number of critics questioned Davis's judgment in appearing in a small role in *Phone Call From a Stranger*, which starred Gary Merrill. Produced by Nunnally Johnson for Twentieth Century–Fox and directed by Jean Negulesco, with a screenplay by Johnson based on a play by I. A. R. Wylie, the story is an episodic affair in which Merrill, the sole survivor of a plane crash, goes about consoling, Good Samaritan style, the relatives of those who have perished in the crash. Having had occasion to hear their stories while the plane was en route from New York to Los Angeles, he restores a son's faith in his father (Michael Rennie), a drunk driver, by telling him he was on his way to confess to having killed some people in an accident; he builds up pathetic showgirl Shelley Winters to her husband and shrewish mother-in-law by leading them to think she was about to star in a big Broadway musical.

Merrill's last visit is to Marie Hoke (Davis), who had been described by loud, vulgar salesman Keenan Wynn as a bathing beauty. He finds her a helpless invalid, and she tells him she had an accident while running away with another man and that Wynn had forgiven her and then lovingly taken care of her for years, his raffish appearance belying his sterling inner nature. After this revelation, Merrill, with Davis's encouragement, phones his own wife, from whom he has separated because he suspects her of adultery, to tell her he forgives her and will return.

Nunnally Johnson drowned everyone in soapsuds in this film, including Davis, who, confined to bed with a pulley to raise herself, looks frumpy and unattractive, plump and matronly (at forty-three) and overacts considerably.

Some years later, while interviewing director Jean Negulesco, I found myself arguing with him about Davis's overdone, overcooked, and overstated performance. "She and Joan Crawford were in that period at the time," he protested. "Both were overacting all over the place and there was nothing you could do with them. I tried to get Bette to tone down, said she was overembroidering lines that were very simple and direct, but she wouldn't listen. She prided herself, for heaven's sake, on wearing a shapeless nightgown and bathrobe in the scene, and in knitting away, Granny-style, but it was all so actressy, so overdone! But you couldn't tell her what to do—no, sir!"

Negulesco felt Davis took the brief role just so she could be with Merrill. "That was still the early phase of their marriage, and she was still ga-ga about him. In fact, that was the third film they did together in a year and a half, and they were Bette's idea, not his. I think he wanted to establish his professional independence apart from her, and with other leading ladies. I don't think she realized that. Not then, anyway."

Davis has always maintained that she played Marie Hoke because she was more interested in the part than in its length. She thought Hoke was solid and true as a character. "And I wasn't just stuck in a bed, remember," she told Katherine Albert. "I had a swimming scene, where I injure myself; then I'm in an iron lung in the hospital. There was range and depth."

The critics were condescending, with "flashy play-acting" the term used by *Time* to describe Davis's performance. *Screen Slants* noted that Davis had overdone her scenes, with the critic remarking, "We know Miss Davis wants to give her fans steak rather than hamburger, but must she do the steak up to a blackened crisp?"

DAVIS'S NEXT VENTURE, *The Star*, represented yet another occasion on which Joan Crawford and Bette Davis's paths crossed—after a fashion. Katherine Albert, the fan-mag maven turned screenwriter with her husband, Dale Eunson, also a magazine veteran, had her friend turned enemy Joan Crawford in mind when she wrote the screenplay, a harsh, unflattering portrait of an aging movie star—not a stage refugee or dedicated artist but a *movie* star—whose whole world revolves around the unrealities of Hollywood. Obsessed with her appearance, her fan impact, her position in the Hollywood firmament, she is the personification of self-centeredness, replete with a childish ruthlessness that refuses to accept the reality that she is over forty, has lost that "fresh, dewy quality" her agent extols, and is washed up as a box-office draw.

Instead of trying the stage or radio or television or commercials, she continues to hammer at studio gates, believing that all it will take is one good role to put her back on top.

This is how Katherine Albert saw Joan Crawford in 1952. It was also her revenge on Joan, because a year or so before, Katherine had asked her daughter, budding star Joan Evans, to forgo marrying a young man named Kirby Weatherly because she was too young and should wait. Crawford, Evans's godmother, arbitrarily sided with the daughter, planned the marriage for her, and even held the reception in her own home.

Katherine Albert never spoke to Joan Crawford again.

Davis, of course, was in on all of this. She had never liked Joan, which was no secret to Katherine and Dale and everyone else in Hollywood, and she accepted the role with ill-concealed glee. The irony that Davis missed, of course, was that the role of Margaret Elliott had as many elements of Bette Davis in it as of Joan Crawford.

Henry Hart, the brilliant editor of *Films in Review* once said: "Bette Davis is an artist, and Joan Crawford is a trouper. There's a difference." By this Henry meant, of course, that Davis had a creative gift, while Joan took more essentially limited talent and enhanced it through sheer hard work and force of personality. Curtis Bernhardt, who had directed both actresses, once cited a salient difference between them. Davis's characters lived only while the cameras rolled, he said. Once "cut!" was shouted, she immediately reverted to her usual self, asking him if she had overdone or underdone anything, and so forth. Joan, on the other hand, went on weeping or raging or hystericizing or whatever for minutes, sometimes hours after the cameras stopped filming, so completely did she live and identify with her roles. Davis, with an artist's discipline, knew how to turn it on or off on command; Crawford simply *lived* it. "But both approaches could be equally effective," Curt added.

But in the role of the has-been Margaret Elliott there were many aspects of the real-life Bette Davis. Her scorn of producers, her ragings against the "tripe" they put her in, her determination to make a comeback through sheer will and determination against all odds, these were standard Bette Davis characteristics.

There is a wonderful scene early in the picture that only Davis could have played. She is broke and living in a small apartment court, her landlord is threatening to evict her, and then her parasitic sister and brother-in-law come for their monthly check. In this scene, Davis played out all the bitterness she had felt over supporting so many people, including her mentally ill sister, her spendthrift mother, and other relatives and hangers-on. The scene has a force and a reality almost frightening in its intensity as she reminds her munching, foolish-faced brother-in-law of the business she set him up in that failed, of the operations she has paid for, of her help to his twin boys, of the thousands she has loaned them that were not paid back. "It's too bad I forgot to give you a printing press!" she screams. "Then you could have printed your own money!"

And then she orders them out, slams the door behind them, and grabs her Oscar from the desktop and hisses, "Come on, Oscar, you and I are going to go and get drunk!" Her spree lands her in jail on a drunk-driving charge.

Bette Davis is written all over scenes like this. It is surprising, in retrospect, that she let Katherine get away with it. It is not possible that she saw *The Star* as a takeoff only on Crawford. Crawford herself saw what was intended ("That bitch is getting her revenge on me for interfering in her family affairs!" she screamed to Hedda Hopper), but she was perceptive enough to see that Katherine Albert and Dale Eunson had also trapped Davis into a rather blatant self-caricature. Oddly, when Hopper brought up the similarity between *The Star's* story situations and her own life, Davis merely snorted: "It's a damned strong part, the strongest I've had in some time, so why shouldn't I play it?"

Margaret Elliott does something neither Crawford nor Davis would ever have stooped to—she takes a job clerking in a department store. When two middle-aged ladies recognize her and talk about her recent jailbird stint and her faded appearance, she screams that she won't degrade herself a moment longer by waiting on "two old bags like you" and storms off the job screaming, "I'm Margaret Elliott and I'll *stay* Margaret Elliott!"

It is then that Margaret does something Crawford would have been more likely to do—pretends to accept the role of a drab older sister in a test for a picture in which she actually wants to do the lead—a young girl twenty years too young for her. She ruins her chances by dolling up, speaking her lines flirtatiously, and conducting herself so ridiculously that she loses the badly needed role to a more realistic middle-aged performer. The shots of Davis, in a projection room, registering the gradual horror at the spectacle of her forty-plus-year-old self trying to be young and sexy is in itself worth the price of admission to any revival theater. Her growing chagrin, her humiliation, her self-disgust in this scene are graphic and realistic.

A chastened Davis is offered another role at a party, that of a washed-up star living in pathetic illusions. Finally recognizing her true self, shocked and disgusted at her longtime flight from reality, she jumps into her car, grabs her daughter (Natalie Wood) from her father's home, and speeds to the docks and patient Sterling Hayden, a "wet-nurse for sick boats" who bailed her out of jail and has offered her his name and protection.

The ending was considered a copout by critics and audiences alike. The part Elliott ran away from might have put her back on top, but since the character was more Crawford than Davis she didn't see it as an artistic opportunity but rather as a fall from grace.

Ernest Laszlo's photography gave the picture a grayish, grainy, drab look (he doubtless thought he was achieving documentary realism but it didn't turn out that way, unfortunately). Certainly Davis, at the time forty-four, could have used more sympathetic lighting and camera angles, as in many shots, even the ones where she dolls up, she shows her true age rather brutally, complete with bags under the eyes, bulges (she was overweight), and harsh facial lines.

While it won a number of critical kudos at the time of its release, *The Star*, due to weak distribution, did poorly at the box office. It was shot in twenty-four days by producer Bert Friedlob and director Stuart Heisler and looks it, too. Twentieth Century–Fox released *The Star* in time for Academy Award consideration in December 1952, but it showed more widely in the early months of 1953. That January, Davis was feeling flushed with success in New York: *The Star* was playing at the Rialto Theatre on Broadway while around the corner she was starring in *Two's Company*, to full-house, appreciative audiences. My mother and I were among a group of well-wishers congratulating her on her double-header backstage in her dressing room after a performance. She chortled gleefully, "I'm on a roll—I'm on top of the world—couldn't feel better about things!" It might have been exhaustion from the demanding two hours she had put in onstage, or mere exuberance, or a reaction to the painkillers she was already taking for her bad teeth, but she seemed barely conscious of any of us—wrapped totally in a private euphoric universe, and looking for all the world like Margo in *All About Eve* in her dressing-room sessions.

She was happier still when her performance in *The Star* won her yet another Oscar nomination.

That same year, 1952, Joan Crawford got the last laugh when she made a smash comeback with her suspense thriller, *Sudden Fear*, and won an Academy Award nomination herself. But Shirley Booth beat both of them for the big prize with *Come Back, Little Sheba*.

Ironically, Shirley Booth's Oscar came for a role that Davis had refused—a refusal she later ranked with the most serious mistakes of her career. Two years before, Shirley had made a smash hit on Broadway in the role of a drab housewife whose marriage to an alcoholic, played in the theater by Sidney Blackmer, has disintegrated. The poignant title refers to the dog named Sheba that she lost years before. The sensitive playwright William Inge had concocted a heartrending study of the loss of illusion and hope in marriage—the sensitive husband losing himself in drink and the more earthbound but well-meaning wife finding escape in illusions of her own.

In a 1953 article, "Shirley Booth: Heifer in the Hollywood Crockery Shop," I commented on the unusual Booth mystique: a solid reality wed to a dreamy, vague, escapist projection that proved as irresistible on screen as onstage. She was not the type Hollywood usually took to its heart, as Davis had not been, either, twenty years before. She was not beautiful, svelte of figure, nor did she comport herself glamorously, on or off stage or screen. Davis was lost in admiration of Shirley Booth's performance and general mystique; she later said she refused the role because she did not feel she could capture the gorgeously defenseless dithering that was Booth's trademark nor did she feel she could come on quite that vulnerable and still hold on to her fans. It turned out to be a great mistake, as she later realized, but to her credit she also said that the part was Shirley Booth's and hers alone—on film as well as onstage.

TWO'S COMPANY, the revue with lyrics by Ogden Nash and words by Vernon Duke, was one of Davis's catastrophic career mistakes. In the summer of 1952, with *The Star* completed and no acceptable movie offers on the horizon (she had just rejected *Come Back Little Sheba*), it seemed like a lark. Gary agreed. Davis had been impressed by Judy Garland's one-woman-show success at the Palace in 1951, forgetting that Judy was a first-class singer. Davis did not want to do heavy drama, though it seems clear that would have been the logical move. Possibly she feared falling flat on her face and felt some singing and dancing in a light revue would be a way of easing back.

Even so, she was taking a risk. In my *Westchester Life* article in Fall 1952, "George Jean Nathan Versus Bette Davis," I pointed out that the great Nathan, a formidable and relentless theater critic of that day who had been originally instrumental in bringing Lillian Gish back to the stage in the early 1930s, would be among those she would have to face. She would have to measure up to the judgments of Brooks Atkinson and others, and was she *prepared?*

Had she elected to come back in a drama, Davis might have done well, but she feared the critical reaction, and *Two's Company* seemed a change of pace, what she thought was a stretching-of-wings. What Davis overlooked was that she lacked timing and singing-dancing expertise, to say nothing of physical stamina. She was inevitably an unprepossessing figure in that métier.

Gary, Bette, and the kids were living in a rather nondescript house on Camine Palmero in a not-too-fashionable section of Hollywood when an army friend, Ralph Alswang, called from New York to ask Gary to feel Bette out about the musical. When Davis heard the Duke music and the Nash lyrics she was enthusiastic, and agreed at once.

By September 1952, the Merrills were ensconced in a Beekman Place triplex with the kids, and sister Bobby on hand to protect B.D., Margot, and Michael from Bette's sudden fits of anger and frustration—as well as nerves, for she was beginning to realize what she had taken on. During the out-of-town tryouts there were several explosions over "creative differences." Davis fainted in her opening number, then, roused by a worried Gary, went out before the curtain and told the audience, "You can't say I didn't fall for you!"

There were rumors that the show was so bad it would close shortly after opening in New York, but in Boston her old drama school mentor, John Murray Anderson, was called in to do repairs. He and Jerome Robbins, ballerina Nora Kaye, and Jules Dassin, who directed the skits, worked so that a passable—but only passable—production opened in New York on December 15, 1952. Davis later recalled living on Dexadrine and emergency shots during the running. She was somewhat consoled by the frantic ovation on opening night and the continuously full houses. Indeed, the producers estimated that if her will and energy held out, the show could run until summer—or longer.

Davis alternated rather heavy-handed skits with musical turns such as "Roll Along, Sadie" (parodying Sadie Thompson) in which, as one critic wrote, she looked like a female impersonator done up in Sadie's garish costume, heavy jewelry, and elaborate feathered hat. She tried to torch a number called "Just Like a Man" and showed considerable strain trying to inject the requisite heartiness into her opening number, "Just Turn Me Loose on Broadway." All in all, she coasted on her personality, talk-singing the songs and dancing awkwardly, her flaws artfully covered by a watchful chorus. It was to her advantage that her audience, comprised of the curious, the die-hard Bette Davis film fans, and the gays came simply to see Bette Davis. In person. Do or die.

The New York World-Telegram & Sun critic nailed down her performance accurately: "Her dancing is likely to consist of hip rolls, marching, and none-too-steady lifts by a whole corps of male partners. Her singing is deep, husky, very articulate and rhythmic but not very musical." The reviewer for The New Yorker, after watching Davis attempt a hillbilly singer with pipe and minus front teeth followed by a parody of Tallulah Bankhead plus other misfires, wrote: "About half these items ought to be funny, but there is some quality in Miss Davis's technique that suggests she should confine her talents to Maugham's pale green and despicable Mildred and leave humor to the girls who just play for quick laughs."

Davis was puzzled by her fatigue during the run of Two's Company, which pills couldn't relieve. Then she discovered that she had an infected tooth that was draining poison into her system. Dr. Stanley Berman of New York Hospital's dental surgery unit removed the tooth and

discovered that she had osteomyelitis of the jaw, which, while noncan-
cerous, necessitated a serious operation, during which the jawbone
would be scraped to remove all diseased tissue. Upon hearing this, she
gave up her ill-advised effort at the Alvin Theatre in March 1953 and
went promptly into the hospital.

After only ninety performances, *Two's Company* had become theatrical history. The show's young producers, Jimmy Russo and Mike
Ellis, had nurtured hopes of a run of many months, possibly a year.
They were left to count their losses. The talented cast of actors, singers,
and dancers were left jobless.

Walter Winchell, the then-famous New York columnist, had been
one of the show's chief boosters. He often dropped in to catch parts of
it and ran plug items every other day in his column. Then Winchell
sprang a bombshell. He reported that Davis had cancer. Angered and
then horrified, Davis and Merrill insisted that Winchell publish a retraction. After checking with the hospital and her doctors, Winchell did so
gladly, assigning it a prominent place in his syndicated column. But as
Davis later noted, a retraction does little to lessen the initial impact of a
report, and during her lengthy convalescence many people were left
with the impression that cancer had figured in it.

Davis had been heavily insured for *Two's Company*. With the insurance money, she, Merrill and the kids repaired to Maine, where she was
absent for nearly two years from the screen or any other medium. During this time, as she recovered her health and strength, Davis devoted
herself to wifehood and motherhood. The Merrills bought a large,
handsome white-clapboard mansion that faced on the Atlantic Ocean at
Cape Elizabeth, near Portland. It was set back in woods and fields and
was difficult to find, so they named it Witchway. Davis later said they
had decided on the name given its location and because "a witch lived
there—guess who?"

They were hardly settled in when they were hit with a new disaster.
Three-year-old Margot had been acting strangely for some time. She
was enormously strong for her age and knocked heavy objects around.
She pulled out some of the year-old Michael's hair, to Davis's great
alarm, and then B.D., who was about six, announced she wouldn't sleep
in the same room as Margot because she was afraid of her.

Margot's temper tantrums grew worse, so Gary devised a little vest
to keep her confined to her chair and her bed. Finally Gary and Bette
decided to take her to a specialist in New York, who came up with the
horrifying diagnosis that Margot was permanently brain-damaged,

would never achieve an I.Q. above sixty or so, and should, for her and her family's sake, be institutionalized.

Ruthie, enraged at the agency that had sent Margot their way, declared that she should be returned forthwith, labeled "damaged goods." But Davis loved the beautiful child, whose appearance, at least in the early years, gave no indication of her affliction, and insisted on keeping her. Later, however, when the sleepless nights and the strain of coping with Margot became too much for her, Davis reluctantly agreed to send Margot off to a special school.

This was the Lochland School, outside Geneva, New York, run by a kindly, dedicated woman named Florence Stewart. Davis's heart was heavy when she left Margot there that first day, but later she came to feel that it was for the best, although the expense of maintaining her there was a terrible drain on the family finances, even with Gary's quick return to filmmaking. Under Miss Stewart's tutelage, Margot improved steadily, and eventually she came home to the family on holidays. There were rumors late in the 1950s that Margot had been lobotomized to keep her calm, cheerful, and tranquil. While vigorously denied by both Davis and Merrill, the rumors persist to this day. Certainly the mild, sweet, harmless Margot that Davis and B.D. Hyman describe in their respective books does not correspond to the earlier violent wildcat who had so disrupted their lives at Witchway.

Meanwhile, much of the mischief that eventually alienated Bette Davis from Gary and then in varying degrees from both B.D. and Michael was being played out from 1953 to 1955. Throwing herself into the role of housewife and mother, and having found—after much trial and error—a solid, dependable man-and-wife team to run the house for her, Davis so thoroughly domesticated herself that she began to turn Gary off. "He wanted Margo Channing—not a little wife and mother," Davis later said regretfully. Both have given their sides of the marital unhappiness that ensued. He painted her as temperamental, prone to fights over nothing, a maddening motormouth with an infuriating capacity for putdown. She painted him as refusing to accept the responsibility of his talent, lazy, irresponsible, drunken, and physically abusive. In her book B.D. wrote that Gary's and Bette's all-night fights and constant screaming frightened her and young Michael terribly. She recounted tales of Gary's obscene and abusive language to her mother, his accusations that she was a sexless bitch and a lousy lay and incapable of relating to a man in any context. She also recalled scenes of violence, Bette at Gary's feet while he threatened added physical abuse—and threatened B.D. into the bargain.

B.D. and Gary never liked one another. She felt he was cold to her because she was another man's child—and one who had cost them money. Michael was the one he adored. He considered Michael his true child. She remembered that after one of the more vicious domestic battles between Gary and her mother, Gary cried with Michael in his arms all night, crooning that he and Daddy might have to live elsewhere someday.

So unwanted and unloved by Gary did B.D. consider herself that when she came of age she insisted on resuming her original name, Barbara Davis Sherry, and setting aside any legal claim Gary might ever have on her.

Though Davis was a generous and indulgent mother to B.D., there was obviously always a coolness, a subtle alienation between them. B.D., as her own book reveals, was resentful about many things: the absent true father, Sherry; the constant domestic turmoil; Davis's cold, authoritarian ways; her frequent absences from home. She recounts the peace and quiet at Witchway when Merrill's brother Jerry and his wife stayed with the children while Gary and Davis were off on film assignments. Then she had known the atmosphere of a normal home. Then there had been an ambience of quiet domestic love.

Bette and Gary she came to associate with high-powered careerism, outrageous self-centeredness, and a love of turmoil and trouble.

Davis recalled the Merrill of those years at Witchway as rebellious, restless, drunken, often mean-spirited. She said that Gary saw life as some kind of jail he had to break out of, while she saw life as a coliseum where constant battle against a multitude of enemies had to be waged unrelentingly. It is obvious from her own words on the matter that B.D., for all the luxury, privilege, travel, gifts, the neurotic, ever-repeated protestations of love, felt essentially uneasy with her mother. She was, indeed, a bird of a different feather, as she was to prove.

AFTER A THREE-YEAR ABSENCE, the year 1955 brought Davis back to the screen.

Davis's portrayal of Queen Elizabeth I in *The Virgin Queen* is superior to her acting in *The Private Lives of Elizabeth and Essex* sixteen years before. She had been thirty-one when she made the earlier film; she was now forty-seven. Much had happened to her between 1939 and 1955 and it showed up on the screen. In the new picture, Elizabeth was nearly fifty;

in the earlier film she had been in her sixties. At forty-seven Davis could obviously empathize with and physically resemble her historical counterpart far more authentically than she had been able to do at thirty-one in the other film.

Robert Downing, in *Films in Review*, caught the improvement, stating: "Miss Davis' latest portrayal of Elizabeth I is better. . . . In *The Virgin Queen* Elizabeth is an elderly, watchful, suspicious, carping, greedy, lonely, proud, vicious and dangerous woman." Downing went on to observe: "Davis portrays all these human facets and royal ones as well. Her performance is a composition of shrewd intuitions about the complex sovereign who ruled an island kingdom that was being metamorphosed into an empire."

The plot this time around had Sir Walter Raleigh (Richard Todd) ingratiating himself with the queen while refusing her advances in order to win his dream of captaining three ships to the New World in search of riches. He adds insult to injury by falling in love with a court lady (Joan Collins), whom he marries. Davis first has him imprisoned, but later relents and sends him to the New World with his lady, taking comfort in the fact that her standard is waving from the mast.

Todd was extremely nervous in his first day of shooting and continually flubbed his lines in a court scene in which he approaches the formidable presence on the throne. Realizing his discomfiture was due to his fear of her, she later told him, "Under this getup, I'm on your side, Mr. Todd." He relaxed somewhat after that, but this was not to be one of Richard Todd's better screen performances. In my December 1955 *Films in Review* career study of Davis, I noted, "[Davis] played her role so effectively she took the picture away from Todd." Todd had little to say about *The Virgin Queen* in later years, other than to note that it had originally been meant to be "his" picture, with the original title *Sir Walter Raleigh*. Darryl Zanuck later changed it to *The Virgin Queen* in deference to Davis's feelings (some said her heavy hints that amounted to strong demands) after he had ordered screenwriters Harry Brown and Mindret Lord to build up her role.

Henry Koster, the talented German director who had guided Deanna Durbin to fame at Universal and who shot the first CinemaScope film, *The Robe*, in 1953, was assigned to this CinemaScope and DeLuxe color production because of his proven expertise in the new form. CinemaScope presented special problems, as it tended to be wavery around the edges and forced the actors to retain their characterizations and line readings longer, as on the stage, because the camera could not move in and out for close-ups and medium shots as fluidly. This Davis found disconcerting. She also engaged in a number of pitched battles with cameraman Charles G. Clarke, a testy old veteran of the D. W. Griffith days who had excellently photographed many creditable films of both the silent and sound periods.

Fifty-six years old in 1955 and every bit as autocratic and demanding and perfectionist in his chosen sphere as Davis was in hers, he showed little patience with her demands for special angles and lighting, feeling she was being self-centered and on her usual star trip. She told him what Tony Gaudio and Ernie Haller had done to favor her sensitivity to lighting, but an exasperated Clarke, in Henry Koster's words, "proved to be every bit as much a bitch as she was" and production was held up while the two argued at length, often at the top of their voices.

Meanwhile young Joan Collins, then twenty-one and being groomed for stardom at Twentieth Century–Fox (she would play Evelyn Nesbitt in *The Girl in the Red Velvet Swing* at Fox that same year), was having her own problems with Davis. Some thirty years later, Collins laughed that she got her earliest lessons in how to play the bitchy, demanding, vixenish Alexis in her long-running *Dynasty* TV series from testing her mettle against Davis in *The Virgin Queen.*

According to Koster, Herbert Marshall, and others in the cast, Joan aroused the same jealousies and insecurities in Davis that Eve Harrington and Barbara Lawrence, her pretty young rival in *The Star*, had. At that time she was fresh and dewy and her offscreen romances were already the talk of the town. Davis had yelled at "agent" Warner Anderson in *The Star*, "Just how *do* you keep that fresh, dewy quality in this town?" and here right in front of her was an archexemplar of just that.

Collins said she tried two approaches with the icy, ominous Davis. "I realized it was silly of her to envy me my youth and freshness in actuality when she was made up old and withered and bewigged anyway, and it fit her character perfectly to resent my taking handsome young Raleigh away from her. So I tried to be understanding and flexible—and keep out of the way of her icy glares and sharp tongue as much as possible—offscreen that is. She would finish a scene in which she was telling me off, and I always felt she wanted to keep right on going after Mr. Koster called 'cut!' So I would turn and walk away quickly as soon as my stint was completed. I'd go to a corner of the set and recharge my batteries, so to speak, for the next onscreen-offscreen encounter."

Her second technique for countering Davis? "Olivia De Havilland had had a role in the earlier picture similar to mine, but the script allowed her to be sassy and mean and humiliate Elizabeth, poking fun at her appearance and so forth, but I had to be servile, begging her for

Raleigh's life and protesting my love for him and so forth, so my only recourse was to smilingly, indifferently ignore her attitudes and snipings—I let it roll off me, I never reacted to her digs and carpings—I think that infuriated her more than anything else I could have done!"

Henry Koster recalled that he must have been lucky; his European sophistication plus a certain modicum of tact, got him through the project without a major blowout with Davis. "Clarke and the CinemaScope process were drawing most of her fire—I guess she didn't have much energy left over to take me on, too!" He didn't escape completely, however. When, in Davis's opinion, he failed to direct a court scene with the majesty and solemnity she thought it required, she shot at him: "Mr. Koster, this is not one of your Deanna Durbin musicals or whatever they were. This we should re-do!" Instead of arguing, Koster re-did the scene at a "slower, more majestic" pace, with the fussy Clarke grumbling, "Prima donnas, all of them!" behind the cameras.

Producer Charles Brackett later told Zanuck: "I didn't think matters would go as easily as they did, actually. I think she yelled at me only three times!"

Anxious to get the picture properly launched, Davis asked Zanuck and Brackett to give the film a world premiere in Portland, Maine. They acceded, reluctantly. It was to be her first premiere in her New England stamping grounds since *The Great Lie* in 1941. Portland's Strand Theatre was drafted for the occasion on July 22, 1955. Newspaper publisher Jean Gannett led off with a clambake in the afternoon, and over a hundred personalities and press people flew in from New York and other communities. This was followed by a cocktail party at Witchway, with the Merrills, children, and entourage on their very best behavior, although Conrad Nagel, one of the guests, later recalled that Merrill's face looked puffy as if he had a fierce hangover, and Davis looked tense "and more shockingly overweight than I had ever seen her." He wondered if Davis was eating more than she should at the time because of her marital problems. The children, however, with their ready, bouncy charm, made up for the slightly Macbeth-ish aura of their elders.

After the party was dinner at the Eastland Hotel. Then came the theater, the lights, the crowds, estimated at 15,000 by the Portland police. A contented Davis quipped: "Hollywood Boulevard was never like this!"

Soon, however, Davis was firing telegrams and letters and phone calls to Hollywood, complaining that a picture of her as Margo Channing was being used for ad illustrations. "It's *The Corn Is Green* all over again!" she hollered to (or rather, at) Merrill. "They'll sex it up and bitch it up, as usual—they're incorrigible!" Chastened Twentieth ad officials removed the Channing picture, but the ad copy still implied all manner of sexual delights, both aspired to and fulfilled. This elicited more protests from Maine, but this time the studio held firm.

"They threw the film away with bad promotion," she later said, "first those silly, sexy, inappropriate ads, and then the complete failure to book it and sell it as they should have!"

While *The Virgin Queen* was in production, the Academy of Motion Picture Arts and Sciences asked Davis to present the Best Actor award at the ceremonies of 1955.

Delighted with the honor, Davis still hesitated because her hair had been shaved back two inches to simulate Elizabeth's baldness and she had cut it so short for the totally bald scenes (she wore a bald piece also) that no matter how she arranged it, she would look eccentrically coiffed. After experimenting with several wigs, all of which looked artificial, ill-fitting, and inappropriate, she appealed to Mary Willis, who had designed her costumes for *The Virgin Queen*.

"I thought it over very seriously from all angles," Mary Willis later related, "and finally I came up with an idea that met Miss Davis's hearty approval. First I whipped up a dignified black gown that had a sixteenth-century look to it with its flounces and sweeps; then I devised an Elizabethan cap that had a peak, and jewels placed strategically. I figured that would do it!"

Nonetheless, her overweight figure, the hastily designed dress and the odd-looking cap drew negative, if muted, comments from the audience, until Davis explained her hair problem for her newest role. At the time Davis also wondered how the Hollywood audience would react to her after her three years away. She needn't have worried. The wave of applause that greeted her warmed her heart—and it went on at length.

Marlon Brando turned out to be the actor in her envelope, for his role in *On the Waterfront*. These two performers from different eras and sporting radically different styles did not seem completely at ease together on the great stage. Whatever she may have thought about "method" acting (and she had plenty to say about it at a later point), Davis was gracious to Brando on that occasion: "I . . . was thrilled that Marlon Brando was the winner. He and I had much in common. He too had made many enemies. He too is a perfectionist."

Her next film, *Storm Center*, proved to be an apt name for what was happening to Davis in real life.

After resting in Maine that summer of 1955, Davis proceeded to make a career mistake. Producer Julian Blaustein offered her a screenplay by Daniel Taradash and Elick Moll called *The Library*. It had been written some years before by the liberal Taradash, who had reacted strongly against the Red-baiting of Senator Joe McCarthy's committee and the Communist witch hunt.

Circa 1952, Mary Pickford had almost signed to do the picture, as she had been assured it would be a great comeback for her, but when columnist Hedda Hopper, a fervent anti-Communist, and other conservatives asked why she had considered something so un-American, the great silent and early-talkie star, an Oscar winner for the 1929 *Coquette*, got cold feet and backed out. Attempts were then made to enlist the likes of Barbara Stanwyck and Loretta Young for the part, but both actresses shied off from the theme. Result: The project remained for some years in limbo.

And what was this theme? Well, it seems that a loyal, dedicated, hard-working head librarian in a small New England town, Alicia Hull, who is the widow of a World War I soldier killed in action, is pressured by the library overseers and the city council to remove a controversial book from her shelves: *The Communist Dream*. They feel it is subversive because it tries to put a positive light on Communist aims and ideals. Hull thinks the book is preposterous, its ideas unsound and unrealistic, but she decides to keep it on her shelves in the interests of American principles of free speech. For her pains she is labeled a Communist sympathizer and removed from her position. Later, when an impressionable child who had worshipped Hull for her learning and inspiration to him is swept up in the anti-Red hysteria and burns the library, the town realizes what they've been doing, asks Hull back, and together they pledge to rebuild the library.

Davis, a Democrat with pronounced liberal leanings, felt that the picture had much to say about true Americanism and the necessity for society to be free and open to all opinions and points of view. The times, however, were not conducive to liberal thought in this regard. She won the ill-will of Hedda Hopper and others of the super-right in Hollywood, and there were numerous mutterings among the politically conservative that she had recklessly endangered her career with such an ill-timed message. It is significant that she did not work in a feature film for three years after making what eventually was retitled *Storm Center*.

When the furor over the picture began Davis said, "I am one of the *loyal* opposition. The principle of free speech is being extolled in this film—not pro-communism—the book in question is downgraded and

discredited by my character in the book—but the right in a free country
to air one's opinions without fear of the consequences."

Harry Cohn was approached to do the film for Columbia and he
blew hot and cold on it, but finally agreed. Taradash, Davis, and others
took small salaries, gambling on the picture's eventual success. The picture was shot quickly in the early fall of 1955, but the studio ner-
vousness over its theme became apparent when it was shelved upon
completion and not released until July 1956, almost a year later. Even
that release was limited, and the film did not even open in New York
until October.

Martin Quigley, the publisher of *Motion Picture Herald*, the most conservative of Roman Catholics (he had helped draft the Production Code
and had figured prominently in the formulation of the Legion of Decency), was most concerned about *Storm Center* in the summer of 1956.
He was anxious that its message be correctly understood as anti-Communist, and behind the scenes urged Blaustein and Taradash to make
changes. They acceded, somewhat nervously and uncertainly, and this
accounts for the erratic release schedule, with an early showing in Philadelphia in July but the New York opening delayed.

I was assigned to review *Storm Center* (I was then film critic for Mr.
Quigley's *Motion Picture Herald* and *Motion Picture Daily*), and Mr. Quigley
discussed the film at length with me in his office. He had never interfered with me before, and would not again, but this film plainly had him
worried. He asked me what I thought of it. I stressed that while its point
was well taken—there must be free speech in a free America—the
theme was fuzzily presented, and the picture itself was not very good. I
later stated these opinions in my review. Even Bette Davis, in her autobiography, wrote that she didn't think it turned out to be a very good
picture, not because of the theme, but because of the way it was handled.

Obviously Davis regretted having done the film for the reasons she
gave. But that three-year period in which she was not offered decent
feature roles has ominous implications. It was widely rumored that
Hedda Hopper and her friends did not forgive Davis for doing the picture and applied pressure to keep her from getting decent offers after her
next picture, *The Catered Affair* (which was released before *Storm Center*).
Davis continued to suffer the aftereffects of this unfortunate venture
clear up to 1961, when she finally made a decent comeback in *Pocketful of
Miracles*, and an even bigger one in 1962 with *What Ever Happened to Baby
Jane?*

In 1957, a year after the release of *Storm Center*, I wrote a magazine piece called "Hollywood's Neglected Genius," in which I stated that the film studios' failure to find decent roles for Davis was a waste of her great talents. This elicited a letter from a congressman asking if, in my opinion, Bette Davis was a Communist! I replied that I most certainly did not believe so, that she might be a liberal Democrat, a member of the loyal opposition, but as loyal an American as anyone could be.

During filming in California, Davis mistakenly believed that producer Blaustein and director Taradash were snubbing her when they did not accept her invitations for dinner after the day's shooting, and some hollering on the set resulted. Later she realized that they were spending the nights nervously rewriting the script to make the characterizations more believable and the dramatic elements more compelling. Davis did not get along well with the little boy, Kevin Coughlin, who burns the library. There was some trouble getting him to cry on cue, and when she saw his mother pinching and hitting the boy to get him to react properly on camera, she was horrified.

Henry Hart's *Films in Review* had some serious reservations about *Storm Center* when it opened that summer of 1956.

"[The] script is replete with irrelevancies, changed intentions, and implausible melodrama," the magazine stated, "and is altogether synthetic. Bette Davis' performance as the middle-aged librarian is adequate, but does not elicit the sympathy it should. Miss Davis' failure to win the audience is due more to the gauche things the script obliges her to do and say than to the asperity which recently has increasingly infected her performances."

Time magazine put its finger on the problem as well as any publication, stating:

"*Storm Center* is paved and repaved with good intentions; its heart is insistently in the right place; its leading characters are motivated by the noblest of sentiments. All that writer-director Taradash forgot was to provide a believable story. . . . *Storm Center* makes reading seem nearly as risky a habit as *dope.*"

Davis was to be troubled over *Storm Center* for some years to come. One of her co-actors who appeared with her in the film, later told me:

"It could have been a fine picture; if the points had been made more clearly in the writing and direction, every thoughtful member of the audience would have seen it for what it was—a thoroughly pro-American discussion of the necessity of free speech. But it was all too murky, too confused. I know Bette was worried about it. I don't think Danny Taradash was following his own convictions and writing from his heart, all the way. He was too afraid he would be misunderstood, politically.

The irony," the actor stressed, "was that if he had written straight ahead out of deep conviction, as I am sure he really wanted to, he would have given us all real roles to act, realistically, and he would have made his points, among them being that political censorship, be it Communist or Democratic, of films, plays, books, whatever, is dangerous to our individual liberties. That is what attracted that loyal American, Bette Davis, to it, and it is a shame that she wasn't supported by better writing and surer direction, and she'd have made her point just fine!"

Davis's fundamental problem in her next picture, *The Catered Affair*, was her miscasting as Aggie Hurley, an Irish-American Bronx housewife who wants to give daughter Debbie Reynolds the elaborate formal wedding that *she* had missed when she married cabdriver Ernest Borgnine.

Not only was Davis not Irish (and her assumed Irish-Bronx accent was wobbly at times), she also, unfortunately, overacted her role and overstated her character, with the result that this is not one of her more notable performances.

When the film was released, critics on both coasts picked up on the miscasting and the overacting. The *Los Angeles Times* reported: "Miss Davis, required to be realistic in a role that is alien to her—from the dumpy figure to the dropped 'g's' of her speech—summoned all her admirable resources to meet the challenge. But the more she succeeded in meeting it, the more she became a triumphant Bette Davis first and a beaten Mom Hurley second."

The *New Yorker* critic felt that *The Catered Affair* was "a confused and wearying account of a family squabble in the Bronx," adding, "In the role of the mother, Bette Davis is done up to resemble a fat and slovenly housewife, but even so she conveys the impression that she's really a dowager doing a spot of slumming in the Bronx."

With the lack of objective self-criticism that was to pop up often during her career, Davis always opined, and doubtless felt, that *The Catered Affair* contained one of her best performances. She was blind to the "set, official, first-ladyish" mannerisms James Agee had noted and the querulous crabbiness and humorlessness throughout that kept her performance from winning the audience sympathy that the role should have elicited. At forty-seven she was right for the part age-wise, but her fussy, domineering, inflexible approach to the simple tale of Aggie Hurley's frustration had more of the elements of the Queen Elizabeth she had recently played than those of a frustrated Bronx housewife who is denied her last pathetic dream.

Many wondered why the forceful, no-nonsense Richard Brooks, who directed, did not pull a William Wyler and give Davis a solid Dutch-uncle talk about her approach to the role. Brooks, forty-three at the time he did *Catered Affair*, and later the husband of actress Jean Simmons, had a reputation as a man's man with a catnippish appeal to women. Starting as a sports reporter and radio writer, he did screenplays before marine service in World War II. His 1945 novel, *The Brick Foxhole*, about antihomosexual bigotry (a startlingly advanced theme for its time), was later made into a tough-minded, no-nonsense movie called *Crossfire*, with anti-Semitism substituted for the gay theme Hollywood was not yet up to handling. After writing several more novels, Brooks debuted as a director with a political thriller, *Crisis*, in 1950. By 1955 his *Blackboard Jungle*, about crime in city schools, added to his cachet as a powerful realist of the cinema.

With Davis in *The Catered Affair*, however, Brooks turned, oddly enough, soft and sentimental. He spent many hours on the set reminiscing with her about her great films with Wyler and Goulding. Davis, always a pushover for handsome, sexy, and strong men, fell in love with Brooks. She told friends she felt she had found another Wyler. She was wrong in both instances. Brooks, much as he admired her, did not return her erotic interest.

For one thing, she was overweight and forty-seven, and Brooks's preference went to young, slim women. For another, he was not temperamentally suited to cater to her demanding nature and her neurotic needs, as he conceived them. Nor was he equipped at the time to be a Wyler and take a firm hand with her. Far from attempting to tone down her mannerisms and grossly overstated line readings, he gave her, in general, a free rein. The result was a ruinous performance on most counts.

In 1957 producer Sam Zimbalist said of the Brooks-Davis rapport—or lack of it:

"Richard was much too soft with her, catered to her illusions about herself. I personally had reservations about casting Davis in this, and so did Paddy Chayefsky. Paddy's original teleplay called for an actress who could be simple, sincere, somewhat beaten down but inarticulately valiant, but in a drab, understated way. Davis gave the role grand opera, Queen Elizabeth, everything that was wrong for it. I asked Richard why he let Davis get away with it. He said, 'I felt sorry for her; she had been ill for years, she needed praise, help.' 'Bull!' I replied, 'you should have been cruel only to be kind; she might have given a great performance if you had given her a double dose of the Wyler treatment—toned her down, got her to understate. You couldn't have made her Irish, no, but you could have made her real!'"

When I talked with Paddy Chayefsky on the set of *The Goddess* in 1958, he felt that Davis's overplaying had thrown *The Catered Affair* hopelessly off balance and changed its tone for the worse. "Ernie Borgnine was as real in it as he was in my *Marty*," Paddy said. "Everyone else fit in just fine—it was Davis who was all wrong! She was all signed and into the picture when I saw some of the rushes and realized how wrong she was—but I just wasn't up to a battle, knowing how nasty she could be. And I sure as hell felt Brooks would handle her in such a way that she would be an asset to the film. Instead, given her head the way she was, she turned out to be its major liability!"

There was some amusement over the choice of perennial bachelor and international sophisticate Gore Vidal to do the screenplay for such a simple, homely story. "Gore knew about as much about the Bronx way of life as I knew about Florentine vases," Zimbalist said. "I didn't really want him, felt he was all wrong, that he put in precious, effete, bitchy touches that didn't belong there. This further hampered Davis's performance. A prima-donna bitch writing for a prima-donna bitch, that was Gore and Bette, and he should have been writing some goddamned spinoff of *All About Eve* or *The Star* for her, not Irish Bronx stuff. Chayefsky agreed with me, but felt Gore was a name, and swallowed it."

Chayefsky's version of this was: "In retrospect I should have fought to do the screenplay myself. Gore and I mixed like oil and water—he spoke a different language from me; we lived in separate worlds in more ways than one. But the studio wanted him, and he had some inside pull, and that's how the cookie crumbled. Crumbled is the word for it."

Davis had a few good moments in spite of Brooks's pussycat direction, Vidal's sly digs at the very life-style Chayefsky was trying to portray with human realism, and her own self-destructive overacting and hopeless miscasting.

For instance, toward the end of the picture, when Aggie Hurley realizes that there will be no big wedding, that her daughter and son will be leaving, that relative Barry Fitzgerald will be marrying the woman he has long dallied with and will also leave, and that she and Borgnine will be alone together, stuck with each other till death, she goes into her bedroom and has an epic crying spell. Davis insisted that she work up the crying spell according to her own instincts; she told Brooks that she could do it only once. After meditating and preparing herself psychologically for hours, she did it in one take, perfectly. It is the most convincing, authentic moment in the film.

Barry Fitzgerald, the brilliant Abbey Theatre veteran who had won an Oscar for his role as a priest in *Going My Way* in 1944 (his star, Bing

Crosby, won Best Actor honors for the same film), is one of the major assets of *The Catered Affair* because he has the right look, the right tone, and the right attitude. And Dorothy Stickney, who plays the widow who finally wins his hand, plays her role the way Davis should have played hers—simply, sincerely, honestly, and with wise understatement. The Fitzgerald-Stickney scenes and the romantic scenes between Debbie Reynolds and fiancé Rod Taylor are in the correct mood as, for that matter, is Ernie Borgnine when he is not encumbered by Davis's presence. And Madge Kennedy and Robert Simon are also absolutely right as Taylor's parents.

One of Davis's greatest admirers was the actor Ray Stricklyn, who appeared with her in *The Catered Affair*. As Ray recalls it:

"Upon arriving in Hollywood in late 1955, I recall the first movie set I was taken on (by my agent) was at Columbia. Miss Davis was shooting *Storm Center*. I was in awe seeing the Great One working. I didn't meet her, however. Little did I know, a short time later, that I would be cast to play her son in MGM's *The Catered Affair*. My agent arranged an interview for me with director Richard Brooks at the studio. I don't remember having to read for the role of Eddie but I do remember Brooks chatting with me and, finally, saying: 'Yes, you'll be fine—except that you're prettier than Debbie Reynolds.' Laughs were exchanged and that's how I was cast.

"Though I had done a small role in *The Proud and the Profane* (Paramount) and a featured role in *Crime in the Streets* (Allied Artists), this was to be my third movie and my best break so far—certainly in terms of prestige. Just working with Davis, Ernest Borgnine, Debbie, and Barry Fitzgerald was a thrill for a novice movie actor. Plus Richard Brooks directing! If I recall correctly, we had a few days of rehearsal—a rarity—before we started shooting the film. I'd already heard rumors that Brooks usually had a whipping boy on each film—usually the youngest one in a film—and I was afraid that just might be me. As it turned out, that wasn't the case. Debbie Reynolds, surprisingly, seemed to attract most of his attention and ire.

"This was at the height of Debbie's publicity buildup and, more important, her upcoming marriage to Eddie Fisher. And, of course, Fisher was tremendously popular and the trade papers were constantly filled with the fabulous deals he was making with the networks, record companies, etc. I remember Debbie coming onto the set sporting a [reportedly] $10,000 engagement ring—which she forgot to remove when we were shooting a scene. Since we were portraying a poor Bronx family, the sparkler didn't set too well with Brooks. 'Cut!' he screamed, and

Brooks, in colorful language (to say the least) berated Ms. Reynolds for her lack of concentration. He seemed to be constantly needling her—about her relationship with Fisher, 'all the money' she'd have [once she married him], etc."

Ray Stricklyn felt that Brooks was doing this to get the performance he wanted out of her, and according to him, Brooks succeeded, because he thought it her best screen performance. Reynolds later recalled the rough treatment she got from Brooks in her autobiography. She felt he had not wanted her for the role, and held her abilities in low esteem—an attitude he did not trouble to hide from her or others. Davis, she recalled, was concerned, encouraging, and protective.

Stricklyn added: "I don't remember having any particular problems myself—the role certainly wasn't demanding." (Stricklyn had next to no scenes, in fact, and was given no opportunity to establish his character in the ones he *did* have.) He remembers Davis as "the complete pro." He recalls coming to the set the morning after the Academy Awards that year—Anna Magnani had won for *The Rose Tattoo* and Ernest Borgnine for *Marty*—to find that Davis had attached a large sign reading ITALIANS GO HOME! to Borgnine's dressing room door. This was a rather typical example of Davis's sometimes outré sense of humor, and she ran the risk of giving ethnic offense. But as Stricklyn recalled, "She seemed quite fond of Borgnine and she was a great admirer of Magnani's."

Stricklyn said that at the wrap party for the picture, "Debbie proved the main attraction by doling out outlandish gag gifts to the cast and crew." She gave Davis a ratty old fox stole, Stricklyn a draft card, and Brooks a pair of ear muffs so that, in her words, "He wouldn't have to listen to himself talk," as well as a bank ledger book so he could keep better track of his money. "So she got her little digs in after the film was completed," Stricklyn summed up.

Stricklyn had not seen the last of the Great One. Some years later she did a Schlitz Playhouse television segment called *For Better, For Worse*. "Apparently my name was one of the juveniles submitted for her approval, and she, I was told, said, 'Get Stricklyn.' So again I played her son—adopted, I believe—in this half-hour segment. It was a much larger role than I had in *The Catered Affair* and the wonderful character actor John Williams played my father. I had several scenes with Davis, in which she tries to take the blame for a driving accident in which I'd killed someone.

"The final night of shooting at the old Revue Studios, only Davis and I were working, doing a shot in a Thunderbird convertible on the process stage. This time we had a lot of time together on the set, and our relationship grew more intimate. We worked late—till around nine P.M.—and when we finally finished she asked me into her dressing room for a drink. While her sister, Barbara, packed up Davis's belongings we sipped several scotches. Davis said she'd rented a beach house (she was married to Gary Merrill at the time). We must've talked for over an hour and finally we heard someone shout, 'Miss Davis, we're closing up!' So we said our farewells—certainly reluctantly on my part."

Stricklyn continued, "It was raining when I left the sound stage to go to my car. As I was driving down the deserted studio streets, another car, headlights flashing, stopped me. It was Bette and Barbara. She rolled down her window, as I did, and she suddenly said, 'What are you doing this weekend?' It was a Friday night. I said nothing in particular. 'How would you like to spend the weekend at our house in Newport Beach? I'm having a small dinner party and you can be Barbara's daughter's date.' I quickly hopped out of my car, got her address and phone number, and said I'd be down the next day. I was elated, to be sure.

"She'd also said that Gary wouldn't be there, as he was rehearsing a *Playhouse 90* with Claire Trevor" (a role, incidentally, Davis had accepted and then reneged on).

Young Ray Stricklyn said the weekend was "enchanted. We lolled on the beautiful white beach, with her daughter B.D. and young son Michael. Later that night [Saturday] we dined at a Mexican restaurant with about five other people—her doctor, his wife, Barbara, etc. On Sunday evening she was cooking in . . . the children were there and Barbara and her daughter and myself. It seemed a wonderful, relaxed evening and the drinks were flowing."

Ray particularly remembered what happened after the dinner party. "We went back to the house. It was maybe eleven P.M. and the two of us had a nightcap and turned on television. For me it was a scene out of a Joan Crawford movie—the pounding of the ocean outside—a fire roaring in the fireplace—Davis in her robe, stretched out on the couch, and me sitting at her feet on the floor. To me, a scene right out of *Candida*."

A Warner movie came on TV. It was *Dust Be My Destiny* with John Garfield and Priscilla Lane. When the credits rolled, Davis suddenly said, "'There goes my whole life,' referring to the listings of the Warners people who'd made the movie, the crew, the wardrobe people, the makeup people, etc. There seemed a tinge of sadness in the remark. Then she asked me what I thought of Garfield. I quickly said I'd liked him as an actor very much [Garfield had died in 1952]. 'Overrated,' she commented. She said Claude Rains was her favorite actor—'such a *wonderful* actor!'"

Ray Stricklyn didn't discuss what happened next in this "Joan Craw-fordish" late-night tête-à-tête with Davis. Instead he cut to the next evening—Sunday. "We were about to sit down for dinner when suddenly headlights glared into the house. 'Oh Christ,' Davis commented. '*He's* home!' That could only mean Gary. And indeed it was. They'd finished rehearsal earlier than he'd expected and he decided to make the drive to Newport Beach instead of staying in town."

Ray got the distinct impression that Gary wasn't pleased to see him. "I was introduced, and I'm sure he wondered who I was, but possibly he really thought I was Barbara's daughter's date. Which I was—though, in my mind, I was really Davis's date!

"Following dinner, more drinks were served. Now, both Davis and Merrill liked to drink—but she seemed to hold hers better than he. I remember him saying something about 'Claire Trevor is going to be terrific' in the *Playhouse 90*,' adding, 'She'll probably win an Emmy.' Davis didn't seem to like that remark, particularly since she'd turned the role down. The bickering started.

"Finally she recommended the children go to the other room and watch TV. I was relegated to 'one of the children.' I didn't like that too well but dutifully followed her order. But I must admit, my ear was more tuned to the conversation they were having than what was on television. Suddenly I heard Merrill say, 'I wish I were Gregory Peck, so I'd only have to do one good movie a year and make some decent money.' To which Davis growled, 'If you're going to pick an actor to be, at least pick a good one.' And they were off."

Ray Stricklyn also recalled that the following morning Gary Merrill asked him to go sailing with him and Michael, but "I declined, much preferring to spend the little time left with Miss Davis. She heard me decline and later said, 'I'm glad you didn't go with them.' We wandered down to the beach, though she was fully clothed, and sat on the sand for a while. I got the distinct impression she was quite sad. I bid my adieus and drove back to Hollywood."

A few weeks later, while Davis was shooting another television movie, Ray read in the morning paper that she and Merrill had separated and went to visit her on the set.

"She greeted me warmly and we went into her dressing room. Then she suddenly burst into tears and wept about the end of her marriage. How difficult it was, at her age, to start all over. I felt very close to her, that she would share this unhappy moment with me."

It appears Stricklyn was on hand at other Davis low points in the 1956–1958 period. He spent time with her at her Brentwood home when she was confined to her bed after falling down a flight of cellar steps and severely injuring her back. Ray remembered how disappointed she was at the time because the injury prevented her from doing the Broadway version of Thomas Wolfe's novel, *Look Homeward, Angel*. The role went to Jo Van Fleet, who was a success in it.

Stricklyn sometimes gets his dates mixed up—she and Merrill did not divorce until 1960 and her cellar-stairs accident was in 1957, not after the divorce, as he states. But emotionally his memories ring true.

After that, Stricklyn and Davis didn't see each other until years later, when Davis won the American Film Institute Award for Life Achievement. Stricklyn, who had become a publicist, found himself representing her and was warned that because he had acted with her in the past, given her quixotic nature, that could be an advantage or a disadvantage.

As he recalled it, "It turned out, thank God, to be a great advantage. She always (if she liked you) preferred working with people she knew and trusted. She also knew the great value of this award and she was on very good behavior. She was the belle of the ball again, and she relished that position. She did dozens and dozens of interviews, did many shots with her favorite photographer, George Hurrell, and was always the consummate pro. 'I like you, Ray. You're a survivor like me,' I remember her saying."

At that point, Ray remembered Davis as "firm, definite in her likes and dislikes, what she would do and wouldn't do—but you always knew where you stood with her. And she knew the value of publicity. The old studio training had taught her that. The event was a smashing success and she relished the attention and eminent position she was in once again.

"That and handling the Henry Fonda AFI tribute the next year were the highlights in my twelve years as a publicist. Davis appeared, of course, on the Fonda tribute—and I remember her seeking me out at the affair and we went into a secluded room off the main ballroom and chatted for a good half-hour. Then she wanted me to get her 'out of there' once it was over—so, of course, I graciously escorted her to her limo."

Ray remembered that as they made their way through the crowded room, Davis stopped suddenly and tapped Cloris Leachman on the shoulder. Leachman almost collapsed when she saw who it was. Davis said, "I'm doing a television movie—a great script—you might be very right to play my daughter." As Ray recalled it, "Leachman was loud in her praise and said, 'Oh, I think my agent's mentioned it.' There was a pause and then Davis said, 'I understand you don't allow smoking on your sets.' Leachman was very flustered (she was a very vocal non-smoker advocate) and lamely replied, 'Ohhh, I'm sure there can be an adjustment.' Davis said tartly, 'Hmmmm,' and we walked off. . . . Gena Rowlands played her daughter."

Ray said that he rarely saw her after that. He thinks the last time was when she autographed her album, *Miss Bette Davis Sings*, at a small record shop in West Hollywood—"and the lines were blocks long." Ray added, "She's a tough, difficult lady. But she's also one of the greatest . . . one of a handful of truly great movie stars." He said, "I've heard a lot of disparaging stories about her in recent times, but certainly my relationships with her were, for the most part, ones I will always cherish."

I had heard, of course, of Ray Stricklyn's on-again/off-again relationship with Davis for years. Jerry Asher, the publicist who knew Davis well, felt that Davis had been in love with Ray for a while—which may or may not be news to Ray circa 1990. When they met, she was pushing fifty and he was in his early twenties. He seems to have been the first of a line of young men half her age—later even a third her age—with whom, as she admits in her second autobiography, she was destined to fall in love, never happily.

"Ray was a gentleman with her, compared to the way some of the other pups treated her," Jerry told me. "She had a side of her that was consummate vulnerable-romantic. I think she was trying to recapture some of her own lost youth by osmosis with these young men. Remember that she was a virgin until she married that first man, Nelson, at the overripe age of twenty-four. With these kids she could imagine herself sixteen or eighteen again, going all the way, totally, without her mother standing guard over her, without her puritanical ideas [at that long-gone time] about passion unleashing itself only in the sanctity of holy matrimony."

Circa 1967, Jerry Asher opined, "Romantic ideas like that will get Bette into a lot of emotional hot water yet—in that respect she doesn't learn from her mistakes." In the years after that, Davis would prove him right more often than she cared to remember.

21

Back in the Doldrums

I N MAY 1958, Davis set out for Europe on the S.S. *Independence* with
eleven-year-old B.D. and Bobby. They were bound for Spain and
France, where she would shoot her cameo role (as Catherine the Great
of Russia) in *John Paul Jones*, produced by Samuel Bronston. It pleased her
that the film would be distributed by Warner Brothers. Bronston had
offered $50,000, which she was in no position to refuse, 1958 being one
of her leanest years ever.

Robert Stack was the star of this somewhat episodic historical
drama, which eventually ran 126 minutes. The founder of the U.S.
Navy, John Paul Jones was an advocate of sea power for the newly
independent United States. Temporarily frustrated in his aims, he tours
Europe seeking alliances and winds up in Russia, where Catherine the
Great claims she wishes to employ him as commander of her Black Sea
fleet. She also has romantic designs on him, which become apparent to
the serious, dedicated Jones, so he leaves Russia and goes on to France
and other adventures.

As soon as Davis arrived in Spain, she was dispatched to the Palace
of Versailles outside Paris, where many of her scenes were shot. She did

not get along well with John Farrow, once a talented director who was
nearing the end of his life and was crotchety, fidgety, and every bit as
temperamental as she was. Humiliated over her cameo part, Davis tried
bits of business that Farrow hated. He informed her he wanted Catherine the Great played as an all-out bitch in heat and that she was to
underline the sexiness in the part, pursuing the handsome Stack with
mad abandon. "You are to be the Queen of All the Rushes," he laughed,
and found that his attempt at sardonic humor went right by her. She
told him his concept of Catherine was vulgar and shallow, that she,
with her predecessor Peter the Great, had guided Russia into the modern era, and while she was willing to be flirtatious and vain, she wanted
to stress Catherine's more statesmanlike aspects. All this went over and
around Farrow. Ill and disgruntled at fifty-four (he was to die a scant five
years later), the macho and posturing Farrow was in no mood to indulge
Davis's whims, and her attempts to cultivate his friendship off the set
met with chilling silence.

As a director he was a martinet, demanding that things be done his
way all the time, but Davis, sensing he was no Willie Wyler on whom
she could depend implicitly, resisted and fought him, which led to
many screaming matches. Then word came that Bronston had run into
money troubles and corners would have to be cut, which meant that the
script Farrow and Jesse Lasky, Jr., had concocted on a day-by-day basis
would have to be tightened.

In actuality, Davis filmed many more scenes than appeared in the
final print, and she later resented the cuts that made her performance
seem perfunctory, abrupt, and off balance.

The picture had a large cast. In addition to Stack, Marisa Pavan,
Charles Coburn (as Benjamin Franklin), and Bruce Cabot, there were
such cameo stars as Macdonald Carey, Jean Pierre Aumont, David Far-
rar, and Peter Cushing.

Max Steiner composed one of his later, less felicitous scores for the
film, which was photographed by Michel Kelber in Technicolor and
Technirama. The Technicolor did not favor the fifty-year-old Davis,
making her look lined and tired. Even the magnificent gown of velvet
trimmed with sable that designer Phyllis Dalton concocted ran afoul
with an off-the-shoulder effect that overemphasized the cruel bulges and
lines in Davis's neck. When she saw the rushes, she was so infuriated at
the way she looked that she threw an ashtray at Kelber in the screening
room. The ashtray contained a match that was still smoldering, so, for
his pains in photographing her—or rather lack of pains—Kelber

sported an ash-spattered face and a small red spot on his chin from the smoking match.

Robert Stack, always mellow and relaxed in an interview, was in high spirits at the time he made *John Paul Jones;* he had just gotten an Oscar nomination for the 1956 *Written on the Wind.* But mention of Davis in *John Paul Jones* brought on one of his rare low moods when I asked him about it in 1964. "Her role was small to begin with—I always thought cameo a cruelly sarcastic term," he told me. "And after Bronston went on a cost-cutting jag, what scenes she had were cruelly cut—and I don't blame her for screaming loud and long about it," Stack said, "but working with her was not easy. She and Johnny Farrow did not get along, she overplayed her scenes and she seemed very tense and nervous and went right off to her dressing room to rest when we were through. Farrow used to wink and tell me Davis had romantic designs on me, but I think she played her scenes *très intime* because Johnny insisted on it, not because she was after me. Certainly I got no invites to the dressing room, so we can't plead her guilty on that. But she knew the project was doomed, I think, and it kept her in a sour mood. I can't really blame her, either."

John Paul Jones turned out to be a monumental, elephantine bore when it was released in 1959, and the few critics who mentioned Davis patronized her. *Current Screen* observed, "Bette-Davis-is-Bette-Davis-is-Bette-Davis, to crib from Gertrude Stein. Say that, and you've said it all. . . ."

After the picture's completion, Davis took B.D. on a vacation in Italy. They did all the sights, photographed the pope, and Davis later recalled the interlude as one of the most relaxing of her life.

Davis left Italy for England feeling sanguine about her new project, *The Scapegoat,* playing opposite Alec Guinness. Guinness was forty-five then, and at the height of his acclaim. That same year, 1958, he had been knighted for his many distinguished performances on stage and screen, and the year before, he had won an Academy Award for his role in *The Bridge on the River Kwai.*

Co-workers felt Davis resented the fact that her co-star was attaining his peak of fame and success while she was on the downslide. She was doubtless irritated, too, because Sir Alec was doing the *A Stolen Life–Dead Ringer* twin bit. Daughter B.D. later quoted Davis as saying of Guinness: "He's overbearing, egotistical, haughty, snotty, insensitive to play opposite and a dreadful actor!" Guinness was more temperate in his comments, but his dislike for Davis was obvious. He remembered that she refused his dinner invitations, kept aloof, and warded off all his friendly overtures. Certainly there is no question that Davis felt Guinness was getting all the attention, and soon she was accusing cameraman Paul Beeson of favoring Sir Alec and quarreling bitterly with director Robert Hamer, a confirmed alcoholic who died of his affliction a scant four years later. Beeson didn't like the chalky white makeup she insisted on, and told her so. Daughter B.D., a frequent visitor to the set, recalled the constant tension and hostility.

When word reached Davis that Daphne DuMaurier, the author of the novel on which the film was based, didn't approve of her in her role and felt she was not injecting enough life and vitality into her scenes, Davis refused to have dinner with her. Eventually, Guinness, DuMaurier, the unfortunate tippling Hamer, and photographer Beeson reacted to Davis by withdrawing. "At times I felt I was acting in an absolute vacuum," Davis later complained, and her co-workers let it be known that the vacuum was of her own making.

The story deals, somewhat murkily, with an Englishman and a Frenchman who are identical in appearance. The Frenchman, upon meeting his lookalike, conceives a scheme whereby he will murder his wife and take up officially with his mistress by pinning it all on the Englishman. Plot ramifications abound, and at the end the mistress is not completely sure if the man who claims her is the Frenchman or his counterpart.

Davis played the role of the Frenchman's dowager-countess mother, who is addicted to drugs and cigars. Most of her scenes were shot in bed. Overdressed, overmade-up, frowsy and fussy and furbeloved, Davis acted up a storm, throwing the film off stride. In the finished picture, Guinness dominated the action, and Davis was reduced to an also-ran supporting player, a fact that enraged her.

The truth, according to producer Michael Balcon, was that the film had to be severely edited, especially the Davis scenes, because her grotesque attitudinizing and overplaying hopelessly unbalanced the flow. Characteristically, Davis put the blame on Sir Alec, saying he had demanded that her scenes be cut so that he could appear in a more commanding light. In turn, the cuts injured the film's continuity and deprived the picture of all sense. Alec Guinness later conceded that it was one of his poorer efforts.

In later years, Davis refused to speak of the film, treated it as if it didn't exist, as well she should have, as it was one of her more humiliating ventures. She and Guinness not only never acted together again, but they also never spoke to one another.

—◇—

HOPING TO GIVE HERSELF a new start in the theater, Davis toured the country in 1959–1960 in *The World of Carl Sandburg*. It consisted of readings from the works of the noted American writer and biographer and had Sandburg's hearty approval. Simple, homespun Americanisms abounded in the text, which was directed by Norman Corwin. Davis and Gary Merrill won plaudits in their seventy-two-city tour.

Worthy as the Sandburg project was, it did not provide Davis's talents with an appropriate showcase, however, and she quarreled with Merrill constantly during the production, which resulted in his being replaced by Barry Sullivan and then by Leif Erickson right before the New York run.

Davis later admitted that firing Merrill, then divorcing him, just as the readings were picking up speed had been a serious mistake. Merrill, who physically resembled Sandburg and captured something of the author's flavor, would have been ideal for the New York opening in the fall of 1960, as Davis later admitted.

She has said of *The World of Carl Sandburg*, "A reading is a total departure from an acting performance. You become the servant of the author. The audience, which you play to in a reading, is one of the characters of the play. Norman Corwin, our director, gave us practically every gesture, every reading. So it was not a matter of time mellowing or quelling my 'famed mannerisms.' It was a question of a new, to me, form of theater—a form I grew to love."

The public in New York did not agree with her. The project had a short run, drew small audiences, and closed within weeks. "It wasn't the Bette Davis they came to see," one commentator noted succinctly.

After Davis divorced Merrill in May 1960, she began a series of unseemly and undignified public custody battles over eight-year-old Michael. She resented the fact that he preferred to be with Merrill; the child had had enough turmoil in the Cape Elizabeth house to last him for the rest of his life, and he wanted only peace, a permanent school, and his friends.

Michael resented being the pawn in a custody suit that had his schoolfellows talking, and was more annoyed by Davis's public castigation of the father he adored as a drunken, irresponsible, unreliable parent.

After the divorce, Gary took up with Rita Hayworth, who was between men. Once when Gary and Rita brought Michael home after an excursion, Bette stuck her head out of a second-floor window and called

Rita a whore. Fed up with scenes like this, tired of Davis's overbearing insistence that she was his only real parent, Michael gradually pulled away from Davis, while his devotion to Gary remained unswerving. Gary assuaged Michael's insecurities about being adopted by telling him his actual lineage was probably better than the Merrill and Davis lines combined, and he did all he could to make Michael feel that he was his child, that he loved and cared about him.

It is a tribute to Gary Merrill's fatherly nurturing that Michael Merrill turned out as well as he did—he is now a lawyer in Boston, with a wife and two sons. Since Michael is totally uninterested in "bookwriting histrionics," as he has reportedly called them, it is unlikely that we will ever see a Michael Merrill tale of family woe. Davis eventually realized that Michael preferred to steer his own course, so she kept on good, if somewhat distant, terms with him until she died.

With the divorce (and its accompanying costs) implemented and the rent due on an expensive townhouse on East Seventy-eighth Street in New York City, Davis found herself desperate for money in the fall of 1960. When a publisher offered her a solid advance for the first of two autobiographies she started to work on it immediately with the help of author Sandford Dody, who in a book he wrote later recalled the daily horrors of trying to wheedle, cajole, and finally force Davis into facing the facts of her life honestly. She went over every sentence, every word, with a fine-tooth comb, as he recalled, cutting out large segments that Dody felt would have improved the work. Gary Merrill would drop in occasionally during the bookwriting sessions, but never interfered. "I trust Bette," he'd smile.

Disspirited by her mother's death in July 1961, bickering with her publisher over the autobiography, concerned over the reception of her just-completed film, *Pocketful of Miracles,* Davis needed something new to think about, so she decided to go along with Tennessee Williams's insistence that she appear in his new play, *The Night of the Iguana.*

The trouble began as soon as *The Night of the Iguana* went into rehearsal in the fall of 1961. Davis was not at ease around Margaret Leighton and Patrick O'Neal, her co-stars. She also knew that Leighton deeply resented having to alternate top billing with her on the marquee. Both performers considered her a personality first and an actress second and did not feel she had developed the stage discipline necessary for *Iguana.*

Tennessee Williams, who looked in on the rehearsals, had second thoughts about Davis's suitability for Maxine, the sexy, pot-smoking, freewheeling landlady of the Mexican resort hotel where the action takes place. He thought O'Neal and Leighton perfect, though—O'Neal was admirable as the alcoholic former clergyman and Leighton affecting as the sad woman with the aged father. Short on plot and strong on Williams atmosphere, *The Night of the Iguana* had a fair success on Broadway and in 1964 was made into a movie with Richard Burton, Deborah Kerr, and Ava Gardner in the Davis role.

Davis felt resentful when she was not asked to repeat her role on film, but in fact she was much too old for it, and had been in the play as well. Her carryings-on seemed inappropriate, given her haggard face and matronly figure.

During the run, whenever Davis appeared on stage the outbursts of applause disconcerted her fellow actors and interfered with the flow of the play. Later she said unkind things about her co-stars' efforts to reason her into a disciplined, ensemble-type performance. By April she walked out on the production. The critics tried to be kind, calling her "marvelously brash and beguiling" and referring to the "tattered and forlorn splendor" of her aura as Maxine. But Davis knew that *Iguana* had been an ill-advised theatrical excursion for her.

In HER FIRST MOVIE in two years, Davis was flagrantly miscast.

May Robson had made a solid hit with the 1933 film *Lady for a Day*, in which she played Apple Annie, a pathetic alcoholic who sells apples on the New York streets during Prohibition. Frank Capra directed. The story has Annie rehabilitated and gussied up to masquerade as society lady Mrs. E. Worthington Manville in order to receive her daughter, whom she has not seen for years. The young lady is engaged to marry a Spanish aristocrat who is coming with his family to New York for a visit.

Robson, a fine old character actress with a solid stage background, made a career playing grumpy, grouchy, baggy-eyed, dumpy characters. She won the hearts of film fans who sensed the warmth beneath the crusty exterior. *Lady for a Day* was a one-of-a-kind film and May Robson a one-of-a-kind actress perfectly suited to the role. (Capra's mistake, circa 1961, was his attempt to remake it.)

Based on Damon Runyon's story "Madame La Gimp," from which Robert Riskin had written a sprightly screenplay back in 1933, it was beyond the talents of the two new writers assigned, Hal Kanter and Harry Tugend. In addition, Capra and company failed to realize that the subject matter and sentimental theme were extremely dated for 1961 audiences. Capra was desperate for a hit, however, as his career had languished over the previous years.

Glenn Ford joined Capra as co-producer and took over the lead, a gangster who helps Annie create the proper atmosphere in which to receive her long-absent daughter (Ann-Margret in her debut film). His quiet, introverted, hesitant on-screen persona turned out to be totally unsuited for the dapper, witty underworld character that Runyon had conceived for the original. Nor was Hope Lange, Ford's girlfriend at the time, right for the role of his showbusiness moll who also takes a personal interest in Annie's transformation.

Capra later admitted that he had made a mistake with this pathetic retread, and said it had been "shaped in the fires of discord and filmed in an atmosphere of pain, strain, and loathing."

Two other actresses rejected the role of Apple Annie before Davis took it. After viewing the original film, Shirley Booth said no actress could possibly duplicate Robson's perfect characterization. Capra then approached Helen Hayes, who hemmed and hawed, reportedly because she agreed with Booth, but who eventually begged out because of a State Department tour.

Glenn Ford claims he then suggested Davis to Capra. Davis was hesitant to accept the role until daughter B.D. told her (in a notorious example of fourteen-year-old bad judgment), "You'd be the best Apple Annie in the world!"

Production began inauspiciously in the spring of 1961 when Glenn Ford let it be known that he wanted current love Lange to have the dressing room next to his. Davis went off on a wild tirade and made everyone miserable until the dressing room was declared hers, firmly and finally.

Next Davis read in a newspaper interview that Ford had gotten her the Apple Annie part as a token of his appreciation for the boost she gave him sixteen years before in *A Stolen Life*. Davis screamed a stream of outraged, ego-affronted obscenities of which the mildest example was: "Who is that son of a bitch that he should say he helped me have a comeback! That shitheel wouldn't have helped me out of a sewer!"

Word of this got back to Glenn, who remained distant toward Davis for the remainder of the shooting. And Hope Lange had gotten off on the wrong foot with the dressing-room incident. Davis let it be known that Lange was an inadequate actress who was inauthentic in manner, style, and looks for her role. That resulted in *two* people not speaking to Davis on the set of *Pocketful of Miracles*.

Frank Capra was not well at the time and began to get migraine headaches trying to cope with Davis's tantrums and demands. Later he tried to excuse her egomaniacal ravings on the grounds of her "inner insecurity and delicate-spirited fears, especially after having been off the screen for so long." To which Lange—in one of her milder rejoinders—snickered, "Bette Davis is about as delicate-spirited as a tank!"

Certainly this was not one of Davis's more felicitous assignments. She was hopelessly miscast as Apple Annie and played her with a heaviness and awkward overstatement that fell far short of the heart and vulnerability with which the great May Robson had invested the part. As the rehabilitated Mrs. E. Worthington Manville, Davis was one-dimensional, lending the transformed "society lady" grande-dame airs without the subtle hesitancies and insecurities Robson had gotten across so well. Because Ford, Lange, and Peter Falk were also lamentably miscast, their performances were wan, tepid, and lackluster. Only Thomas Mitchell and Edward Everett Horton managed to summon the proper panache.

Playboy tried to be charitable, saying that Davis "slices the *jambon*" and that Glenn Ford seemed "like a very nice fellow from the studio accounting department who stumbled onto the set by accident."

22

The Horrors

THE YEAR 1962 was the start of Bette Davis's six-year horror film period.

What Ever Happened to Baby Jane?, based on a novel by Henry Farrell, is not a good picture by any standards, and it is apparent now that it was cynically designed by director Robert Aldrich and producers Eliot and Kenneth Hyman to lure film audiences in and then shock them. The film certainly fulfilled its perpetrators' dreams: In time its bonanza box-office performance totaled a cool nine million dollars.

Davis had her doubts when Aldrich offered her the script. She realized the role of demented Jane Hudson, a former child star, would call for messy makeup, outlandish clothes and hairdo, and a loony acting style that could either be ridiculed or applauded by her fans. But no one around was offering her anything better at the moment, so she even agreed to take a low salary in return for a percentage of the picture after Aldrich and the Hymans told her the quick shooting schedule (twenty-one days) and the low budget necessitated all manner of cost-cutting. The picture is B-movie cheapjack and grotesque, but what puts it over is the spectacle of Bette Davis and Joan Crawford, both symbols of old glamorous Hollywood, looking worn and totally out of character, but acting up a storm.

Davis is a former kiddie star now gone to seed, and Crawford the once beautiful sister who was a famous romantic film star who has been crippled since a mysterious accident. Bitter and half crazy, Davis torments her sister and then goes downstairs to conspire with overweight mama's-boy Victor Buono about revitalizing her career—a pathetic travesty of her kiddie act in vaudeville in which she will reprise her maudlin, dated song, "I've Written a Letter to Daddy." When she learns that Crawford is going to sell the house they live in and put her away, she locks her up.

Crawford crawls downstairs in a pathetic attempt to escape, and Davis hits her and then ties her up in her room. Later, a drunken Buono finds the near-dead Crawford and rushes to notify the police, but Davis bundles her sister into a car and takes her to the beach at Malibu to bury her. There, Crawford confesses that she perpetrated the accident which Davis had always thought her fault. It is too late to save Baby Jane's sanity however; the police find her cavorting and singing while her dying sister lies on the sand.

Such is the plot. It was ridiculous enough when Henry Farrell made it into a novel; it is outlandish when acted out on the screen. The dead rat (and later dead parrot) for lunch is grotesque, and Davis's Mary Pickford hairdo, pasty face, and kohl-lined eyes, plus a mouth that, as one critic put it, looks like "a messy black bow tie shunted up to her lower face," are pathetic.

And yet the public ate it up. It had a saturation booking in the major cities in November 1962 where it ran up huge grosses. The movie made back its modest cost in eleven days and went on to reap a huge profit, which enriched Davis's and Crawford's coffers as well as the producers'. In July, Jack Warner gave a big luncheon on his movie lot for returned prodigal Davis (away thirteen years) and long-departed Crawford (out of Warners ten years) to celebrate the Warner release of the Hymans' Seven Arts Production.

Davis's daughter, B.D., played the daughter of a neighbor, and her memories of the film were vivid—and nasty. On the first day of shooting Crawford insulted her by telling her to stay away from her twins, Cathy and Cindy, who were also on the set part time. Crawford said that because B.D. had been exposed by her mother to far more sophisticated surroundings and situations than her sweet, protected, innocent girls, she might prove a contaminating influence. After a "Bless you"— her insincere, condescending benediction to friend or foe—Crawford

left Davis and her daughter open-mouthed and seething at her effron-
tery.

Next, Crawford, a Pepsi-Cola executive, began carrying a Pepsi bottle everywhere, which infuriated and disgusted Davis, because she knew
it was half Pepsi-Cola, half vodka. In the privacy of her dressing room,
after reining in her fury and frustration all day, Davis would scream,
"That bitch is loaded half the time! How dare she pull this crap on a
picture with me? I'll kill her!"

The next bone of contention, which arose when Davis was obliged
to lean over Crawford for long periods of time, was the size of Joan's
legendary and often ridiculed falsies. They were so sharply-pointed that
they threatened to tear through Joan's blouses. They stabbed Davis's
chest like miniature stilettos until she hollered, "I keep turning into them
like the Hollywood Hills!"

But worse was to come. Joan Crawford began sending Davis gifts—
just as she had fifteen years before. Grumbling and swearing, Davis
opened perfumed boxes containing lingerie, candy—and even flowers,
all accompanied by sugary "Bette dear"-style notes. Davis gathered all
the items into a bundle and sent them straight back to Joan, with a terse
note stating she appreciated the thought but was much too busy to go
out and select suitable reciprocal gifts. Crawford was deeply hurt by this
and even looked teary-eyed on the set. After a few days of heavy silence, however, the gifts and notes started arriving again.

"What *is* this crap?" Davis hollered. "Christ, I'm fifty-four years old
and my figure is shot to hell. *She's* fifty-eight if she's a day, and she's still
coming on like a dikey schoolgirl with a crush on the boobs and twat at
the next schoolroom desk!"

Davis seethed for a while, then sent the next batch of presents back
with a note that said, "Other than ripping my toilet seat off and wrap-
ping it up to send you, I can't think of any other way to answer. Except
to tell you: *get off the crap!*"

After that, Davis-Crawford relations were icy. But since both knew
that on the limited budget they would have to be ultraprofessional and
finish on time or before, they did not flare up at each other on set. The
tension, however, as Robert Aldrich and cameraman Ernie Haller recalled, was thick and mean. Crawford began planning a subtle revenge,
which, when it came off, was, to her credit, a dilly!

Meanwhile there was the picture to get through. Davis's insistence
on having Ernie Haller photograph her seems strange in retrospect, as
Haller, one of the greats in his field, had specialized in making her look
beautiful in the old Warner days. Now, to his bewilderment, he was

forced to follow her strident commands to make her look as horrible as possible. This he succeeded in doing. So well, in fact, that when she finally got to see the picture straight through the following year at the Cannes Festival, she turned to Aldrich and wailed, "Did I look *that* bad? Did I really?" He replied, "You wanted to look your worst, Bette; you insisted on it, raised hell about it, and Ernie gave you your wish!" After that she grumbled and grumped through the rest of the showing, then left abruptly when the closing credits rolled. Aldrich recalled, "She drew herself up and marched out of that auditorium so quickly and briskly— like someone in the military would have—that I couldn't catch up with her, and when I got out to the limousine she slammed the door on me and told the driver, 'Drive on, for Christ's sake!'"

Joan Crawford had her own ax to grind. She realized that Davis had the showier role, and that she—as in real life—was consigned to playing beseeching masochist to Davis's rejecting sadist. Crawford's role is admittedly passive. She sits sweetly in her wheelchair in the upstairs bedroom, widening her eyes and covering her mouth in horror when she lifts up silver plate covers to find dead rats for lunch. Later Davis said to Aldrich, "The scenes I most enjoyed playing were the ones where I had to beat the shit out of her! They were nothing she'd simper 'bless you' about later!"

Inexplicably, considering the grotesque nature of her role, Davis won another Academy Award nomination—her first in ten years. Crawford, enraged over being ignored, set her special revenge plan in motion. On Oscar night, while Davis, who had been presenting other awards, stood waiting tensely backstage, primping and clearing her throat for her big acceptance speech, she saw Crawford standing serene and composed nearby. Then the winner was announced—Anne Bancroft for *The Miracle Worker!* "Shit!" Davis muttered, but before she had decided whether to stalk angrily off or stay and smile grimly in good-sport fashion, Crawford sidled by her with a smirking, "Excuse me!" and went out to accept the award for Anne Bancroft, who was in New York. As surrogate, she graciously acknowledged the waves of applause. Unbeknownst to Davis, Crawford had made deals with all the other nominees to accept in their place if they could not be on hand!

Prior to this catastrophe, Davis made extensive personal appearance tours for *Baby Jane* that reached as far as London. She bowed and preened in city after city. "What a glorious comeback! Oh how wonderful it is!" she glowed to fan writer Ruth Waterbury, who told me later, "The comeback she thought was so glorious was for a trashy little cheapjack film that was neither fish, fowl, nor good red herring!" Ruth said that she never could figure out if *Baby Jane* was horror, pure and simple, or suspense or Grand Guignol. "You'd think she had scaled the heights in something classic, something prestigious like in the old days; she thought she'd given a great performance. What she had actually tendered her audiences was just a grotesque stunt, overembroidered and overacted at that!"

What was the secret of *Baby Jane's* success? Certainly Seven Arts' cynical but effective promotion approach helped. One advertisement presented the stars' names at the top of the layout in type so faint one didn't even notice them. The body of the ad showed both ugly, lined faces jammed together with the legend, *Sister sister, oh so fair, why is there blood all over your hair?*

Also, in 1962 the bulk of the audience had a fairly fresh memory of the prestigious stardom both actresses had once enjoyed. Fickle, jaded film audiences enjoy seeing the mighty fall. *What Ever Happened to Baby Jane?* presented both actresses as sad caricatures of themselves. The 1962–1963 audiences came for two things—and sometimes stayed for a second viewing: the cheap horror effects and the comical and outlandish parody of two cinema grande dames making fools of themselves.

The critic of *The New York Herald-Tribune* was rather tactful but his message is very clear:

"If Miss Davis's portrait of an outrageous slattern with the mind of an infant has something of the force of a hurricane, Miss Crawford's performance as the crippled sister could be described as the eye of that hurricane. Both women are seen in the isolated decay of two spirits left to dry on the desert by the receding flood of fame. 'I didn't bring you your breakfast because you didn't eat your din-din,' Miss Davis tells Miss Crawford. She then howls a witch's laugh that would frizzle the mane of a wild beast. It is the mingling of baby-talk and baby-mindedness with the behavior of an ingenious *gauleiter* that raises the hackles."

Bosley Crowther in *The New York Times*, however, told it as he saw it, writing, "Joan Crawford and Bette Davis make a couple of formidable freaks . . . but we're afraid this unique conjunction of two one-time top-ranking stars in a story about two aging sisters who were once theatrical celebrities themselves does not afford either the opportunity to do more than wear grotesque costumes, make up to look like witches, and chew the scenery to shreds."

When I interviewed Victor Buono in 1964, his memory of *Jane* was still as fresh as if he had shot it the week before. "It was a real break for me, appearing with Bette and Joan," the actor recalled. "I had always dreamed of being the Charles Laughton of the 1960s, especially when he died the year the film came out, and *that* got me off to a flying start! I was a mother-ridden, pixillated, neurotic mess in that, helping Bette with her terrible song and discovering Joan nearly dead upstairs, and it was a stimulating, indeed galvanizing experience." But with a candor that was refreshing, Buono admitted: "Bette was a real bitch to work with. One time we were doing a little rehearsing before a scene, and I wanted to show her the courtesy of leading off, and she turned and prodded me and said, 'You're being paid to act and react, you fat slob, so react! Don't stand there like a damned idiot!' When Bob Aldrich, who was guiding us, attempted to make Bette understand that I was only deferring to her courteously, she just grumbled, and continuing to stand her ground, didn't even offer a grunt of apology."

Robert Aldrich later told me that he felt Davis and Crawford both imagined he was in love with them. "Hell, I just wanted to charm and seduce them through the picture! Personally—forget it!" he huffed.

IN SEPTEMBER 1962, with *Baby Jane* only weeks in the can, Davis did a strange, unpredictable, and self-destructive thing. And it indicates that with the release of the film only two months away, she had little faith in its restoring her to the top, though it *would*—for a while. All during 1960 and 1961 she had been railing away at the journalists who, usually sympathetically, pointed out that her career was in decline. She would rant and rave and threaten to sue, while giving interviews such as the one with Bob Thomas (*Newark Evening News*, March 15, 1960) in which she was quoted thus: "Let's face it! I'm simply not on the green list. There's a list, you know, of a few top stars who are supposed to be the only box office draws . . . stars of my era don't have a chance. If there is a good role for one of us they change it and give it to some cutie." She told *Variety* on April 4, 1960: "I sat around Hollywood last fall and didn't get a call from the studios. Oh, yes, I had a chance to play Burt Lancaster's mother in *The Unforgiven*, but I'll be damned if I'll play Burt Lancaster's mother after thirty years in this business." Some time before that, she told Vernon Scott in *The Morning Telegraph*, "The tragedy is we can't sit around and wait for good things. We have to take whatever comes along. I've done many TV shows I didn't want to do, just to keep busy . . . but we all have to make a living doing whatever we can."

In 1961, her depression was exacerbated by her mother's death in July and her unhappiness playing second fiddle to Glenn Ford and Hope Lange in *Pocketful of Miracles*. By 1962, despite the publication of her *Lonely Life* autobiography (many wondered when Bette Davis had ever had a chance to be lonely) and her part in *The Night of the Iguana*, she still considered herself over the hill and discriminated against. Which leads to what she did in September 1962.

Obviously uncertain as to the fate of *Baby Jane*, she put an ad in the Hollywood trade papers on September 21. It read:

> Mother of Three—10, 11, and 15—divorcee, American. Thirty years' experience as an actress in motion pictures. Mobile still and more affable than rumor would have it. Wants steady employment in Hollywood. (Has had Broadway.)
> Bette Davis. References on request.

The late Dorothy Kilgallen, a superbitch who nonetheless leveled truthfully, let Davis have it in her column of September 26, 1962, writing:

"Will the real advisor of Bette Davis please step forward? That Hollywood trade paper ad saying she was available and needed work certainly caused talk, but not the right kind for an actress of Miss Davis' stature. Needless to say it made the producers of her latest picture furious, because it made her seem like a broken-down 'has-been,' and they were doing all they could to promote her for an Academy Award. Martin Baum . . . who gets credit for being her agent (not much of a compliment, when she's indicating she's desperate for work) ought to go into a corner and blush quietly for not talking her out of the ad."

When she realized that she had made a major blunder in not consulting with her agent, Davis tried to say that she had been "facetious" and "sardonic," but it was generally agreed that she had made a stupid mistake.

But with *Baby Jane*, Bette Davis was on top again.

Shocked into the awareness that Davis was still a hot box-office property after he saw *Baby Jane*'s receipts, Jack Warner decided to find a vehicle for her that would combine the high-gloss, "prestige" look of the films of her Warners heyday with the grotesque elements that her fans—in his view—would certainly expect after *Baby Jane*. The story he selected was *Dead Pigeon*, filmed in 1946 in Mexico with Dolores Del Rio. William H. Wright would produce and Albert Beich and Oscar Millard would write the screenplay from the story by Rian James. Jack Warner decided to retitle the picture *Dead Ringer*.

Production was due to start in the spring of 1963, but there were delays due to Davis's European tours with *Baby Jane*, her radio appearances, and the necessity of getting her out of a commitment she had made with Robert Aldrich to guest-star in a western, *4 for Texas*, which starred Frank Sinatra and Dean Martin. Since she had taken the role because it was all that was available, she was glad to get the release from Aldrich. "The role in the Sinatra picture was not that long, and I'm afraid 'guest star' didn't apply in truth to it, as it was a small supporting role, and going the cameo route or whatever they call it would have been a strategic blunder at that point," she said later. "The only real consolation would have been to have worked yet again with that delightful character actor Victor Buono, who had been cast in it."

Dead Ringer was a sort of retread of *A Stolen Life* in that Davis again played twin sisters, both murderous. Davis has an acting field day. Again the clever use of process shots and the added boon of a double, Connie Cezon (who was indeed a dead ringer for Davis herself, and who had imitated her successfully in revues on the stage), promised a felicitous result.

The plot is reasonably complicated, at least for a melodrama. Davis is a poor sister, down on her luck, who hates and resents her twin, whom she hasn't seen for years, because she stole the rich man she loved by pretending she was pregnant. After the rich man dies, Davis lures the widow to her apartment, murders her, puts her own clothes on her, leaves a "suicide note"—and walks out in her sister's clothes to the limousine and into her sister's life.

There she finds matters more complicated than she imagined, what with a lover (Peter Lawford) who helped her sister murder her husband for his money. When she has to sign important papers, she burns her hand deliberately with a hot poker (a wonderful Davis scene, expertly played) to avoid giving herself away. The lover tries to blackmail her, so she sets her fierce dog on him. The detective (Karl Malden), who loved the poor sister and planned to marry her, comes around asking questions and eventually has Davis arrested for her "husband's" murder. At the end, she is off to jail—not for the murder she actually committed, but for the one she didn't.

All this wild melodrama and theatrical posturing is reasonably entertaining, in no small measure due to the sympathetic and understanding direction of Davis's old co-star, Paul Henreid. He and Davis got along famously, as he told me in 1964. "We always had simpatico," he said. "I understood her temperament and her peculiar gifts—I had acted opposite her in two pictures and I knew what she thought was effective for her. There was never a romance between us, but there was always a warm mutual regard, and my wife and I counted her among our greatest friends. She also kindly and thoughtfully suggested that my daughter

Monika play her maid in several sequences. It was a big thrill for Monika, believe me."

Asked if he underwent the usual *sturm und drang* Davis was notorious for inflicting on her directors, Henreid replied, "Not at all. Perhaps because we had acted together, Bette felt instinctively I was, in spirit, on her side of the camera with her at all times, and I did feel like I was doing double duty—keeping things going smoothly from in front and empathizing with her back there. In any event, it turned out very well indeed."

The process shots from *Dead Ringer* were created with the same technique used in *A Stolen Life*. Ernest Haller was again the photographer (it was his last assignment; he died later in an automobile accident at seventy-four), and he and others from the process and research departments availed themselves of the lessons they learned during the filming of the earlier picture. One innovation was nailing down all the furniture on the set where the one twin murders the other, so that re-shooting would be a breeze. Connie Cezon's resemblance to Davis was so uncanny that she even appeared in the final print in some minor throwaway shots. Haller did his best to make Davis up as effectively as her fifty-five years on earth would permit. In this endeavor he was aided by the clever Gene Hibbs, a protégé of Perc Westmore who had developed a clever technique for making older actresses look younger via "painting." As Davis later put it, "Gene paints a face as if he were painting a portrait."

It must be admitted, however, that despite the valiant and highly skilled efforts of Haller and Hibbs, Davis still looks middle-aged in even her best shots.

Peter Lawford, who played her lover, was someone she was prepared to like, as he was the brother-in-law of President John Kennedy. But Peter, then forty and already declining, was not at his best, and she and Henreid both felt he was not giving the role his full attention and seemed distracted by outside problems. Davis was not surprised when Pat Kennedy later divorced him—his deterioration during shooting was all too evident. But even at a dissipated forty Peter could still call on a certain rakish charm, and some of his scenes with Davis come off effectively. Reportedly, concerned and sympathetic Henreid gave him some Dutch-uncle lectures when he failed to show up on the set, and managed to instill enough self-respect into him to ensure some solid scenes.

A few years later, Peter told me: "Bette had always had a reputation as a holy terror on the set, and I didn't know what to expect, but she was understanding, kindly, patient—even maternal, if that is the word.

I suspect she felt sorry for me." Jerry Asher told me that she said of Peter, "I'm sad about him. He's unfortunate, and it's too bad."

Time magazine had fun with Davis in its review of *Dead Ringer.* "Exuberantly uncorseted," the review ran in part, "her torso looks like a gunnysack full of galoshes. Coarsely cosmeticked, her face looks like a U-2 photograph of Utah. And her acting, as always, isn't really acting; it's shameless showing-off. But just try to look away."

Next, Davis allowed herself to be talked into an Italian-made movie. It turned out to be one of her most unfortunate ventures. Joseph E. Levine and Carlo Ponti persuaded her that *The Empty Canvas,* based on Alberto Moravia's novel *Boredom* (a prophetic title, as it turned out), would be just the thing to raise her spirits after another project, *Faster, Faster,* produced by Jack Dietz and written by William Marchant, failed to get off the ground in England. Accordingly it was on to Rome and director Damiano Damiani, with whom she had little rapport and who, she said later, "spoke a different language, verbally and creatively"; the pretty Belgian actress Catherine Spaak, a sassy eighteen-year-old whom Davis dismissed with, "She thinks trading on her looks is acting—well, it isn't!"; and the popular young German star Horst Buchholz, whom she disliked on sight.

She claimed later that Buchholz frustrated her at every turn, and was "the male equivalent of a self-centered prima donna." Since Buchholz didn't have a strong command of the English language, he fell back on what he did know and called her, in turn, "a meddling bitch." Born in Berlin in 1932, he had survived the Allied bombings of Germany as a child and had had to scrounge during Germany's postwar chaos and bitter poverty. After dubbing foreign pictures into German, he had attracted the attention of director Julien Duvivier, who was bowled over by his performances at Berlin's Schiller Theatre. In 1955 he debuted on film in the French/German co-production *Marianne of My Youth,* in which Duvivier showcased his dark good looks and lithe body.

From there he achieved international fame in the film version of Thomas Mann's *The Confessions of Felix Krull,* in which his character seduces an old man. Critics raved about the "realism" and "sophisticated sensibility" of this film, and wrote that he "played it to the life."

By the time he crossed swords with Davis in 1963, he had won added acclaim in films like *The Magnificent Seven* and *Fanny,* and was a "ravishingly sexy" thirty, as one Italian reviewer called him, and ready to do battle with Davis or any other formidable dragon.

Damiani irritated Davis mightily by siding with Buchholz in all arguments concerning the film. When she was overruled by the two men, who were every bit her match in opinionated arrogance, she retaliated by bitching up the project to "enliven" it and "give it some direction and form."

Soon Davis was largely directing herself. Since the script was terrible (she felt), and since Carlo Ponti had not kept his promise (she maintained) to improve on it, she compensated in typical Davis style by adopting a garish blond pageboy bob and sporting a broad Texas-Louisiana accent. The wig did not always fit, and the accent was not always consistent, especially when Damiani's direction and Buchholz's upstaging got her rattled—which was often.

The screenplay, an uneasy tripartite concoction by Damiani, Tonino Guerra, and Ugo Liberatore, featured Buchholz, the son of rich American Davis and a deceased Italian nobleman, as a typical specimen of New Wave anomie and directionlessness, dabbling away at painting. Thinking he has found the image for his "empty canvas," Buchholz takes up with man-mad nymphet Spaak, who refuses to marry him—even after he covers her nude body with 10,000-lire banknotes. She does agree to become his mistress—until a more interesting man comes along. The dénouement of all this weary existentialism comes when Buchholz has a breakdown and is guided back to health by Davis. He tells her at the fadeout that now he has suffered, and he thinks he might be able to fill that empty canvas.

One of the film's intentional comic highlights comes when Davis walks in on her son and the nude Spaak, who is covered with the banknotes, and deadpans, "Put the money you don't want back in the safe—I don't want the maid to find the room in this curious state." "This," one critic laughed, "was the apogee of permissive, mom-istic existentialism."

Davis later said, "All this talk of the anomie and the *weltschmerz* and the existentialist what-of-it aspects is a lot of poppycock. What that damned picture needed was a clear, linear, progressive beginning-middle-and-end plot and a part I could make credible to audiences—it had neither—and I refuse to accept any of the blame." One commentator offered the wistful hope that "Miss Davis at least got well paid for it."

Brendan Gill in *The New Yorker* thought the result, seen on American screens in the spring of 1964, "shockingly miscast" and "one of the worst pictures of this or any year." *Time* threw Davis a consolatory dandelion by commenting that the picture was "chiefly notable for the fun of watching Davis breast the New Wave plot with bitchy authority." Davis's final comment on the film was: "It alerted me to choose my pictures with greater care henceforth."

About this time Davis had some drastic personal changes in store for her.

In 1964, at the age of sixteen, B.D. married. Her husband, Jeremy Hyman, almost twice her age, was the nephew of the Eliot Hyman of Seven Arts Productions. They met in London and fell in love with each other almost on sight. B.D. liked Jeremy's low-key, quietly assertive manliness; it was obvious that he was the father/older-brother figure she had sought all her life. As of January 1990 they have been married twenty-six years and have two boys, Ashley and Justin.

At first Davis opposed the marriage, citing B.D.'s youth. But in matters of the heart, the sixteen-year-old showed she had a will as strong as her mother's. Davis eventually gave in, feeling that worse might follow if she didn't accept Jeremy Hyman as her son-in-law. She also realized that, unlike herself, B.D. was a one-man woman. Davis had set her up with many a glamour boy, such as George Hamilton, and B.D.'s virtue *and* virginity remained intact. It was obvious that B.D. had set out to be everything her mother was not.

Davis was humiliated to realize that B.D. held her in contempt for her four marital failures and for her restless peregrinations among men young enough to be her sons. And B.D. would be particularly angry when Davis tried to alienate her from patient, forbearing Jeremy. When Davis visited them, there was always tension, and several times B.D. had to cut the visits short.

B.D. was particularly disgusted in the mid-1960s, when Davis, approaching sixty, got involved with many unsuitable young men. In her later autobiography, Davis admitted having been a "fool for love" right up to the gates of old age. She recounted one instance in England when she and her swain went into a gift shop and the woman asked if she could wait on her "and your son." And to B.D.'s exasperation, Davis took up with another handsome pup who lived at Malibu Beach and who was gay. When she tried to warn her mother about him, Davis laughed that he wasn't gay anymore, "now that he had a real woman!" Davis took to parading around the beach in tight bikinis that outlined every bulge and line in her aging body. Finally, after trying to force the kid into one sexual position too many, they split up rather noisily—and when B.D. called, Davis admitted that she had been right all along.

Davis herself recalled, in *This 'n' That*, her second book, another instance of a young man, circa 1967, who courted her in England. She wanted very much to marry him, though he was some thirty-five years her junior. Her lawyer told her she would have to have him sign a prenuptial agreement stating that what was hers was hers, even after they became husband and wife. The kid disappeared the next morning from the hotel where they were both staying, and she never saw him again.

During the 1960s Davis took up with a series of gay men whose wit and campiness amused her. She even brought them along with her to B.D.'s and Jeremy's. None of them lasted, however. Invariably they did or said something to annoy her and were promptly banished. Then there was a succession of lawyers, such as Tom Hammond and later Harold Schiff, who were saddled with a number of assignments, not the least being to keep B.D. in dutiful contact—until B.D. lost patience with the ploy. When they told her that she should be more daughterly and understanding toward her busy mother, B.D. told them that her mother was an unbearable egotist who thought of no one but herself.

On her end, Davis was a very generous mother and on occasion lent Jeremy money when his businesses failed. B.D. insisted that her mother used the loans to establish a hold over her and her family, but the fact is that the help was forthcoming.

Davis never tired of reminding her daughter that she had given her a very expensive Hollywood wedding in 1964, with all the trimmings— thanks to the $125,000 she had been paid for a picture (*Where Love Has Gone*) she hadn't particularly wanted to do.

Jeremy found Davis a chore and a bore—and worse, a threat to the peace of his marriage. Gifted with uncommon patience, he tried to understand his wife's deep ties to her mother, but Davis's unreasonable conduct (she once sneaked him a sleeping pill when he asked for an aspirin, to embarrass him at a public restaurant) and her constant cracks at his expense were more than he was willing to take. He and his formidable mother-in-law thereafter lived in a state of armed truce.

Michael, a sturdy, sensible boy, was essentially disillusioned by the domestic fights at Witchway, then by the nasty custody battles in which he was a helpless pawn. He, too, asserted his own individuality and independence in time.

DAVIS WAS SOON engaged in another of her famous on-set feuds.

She had a low opinion of *Where Love Has Gone* from the moment she read John Michael Hayes's pedestrian screenplay. But she needed the money offered so she reluctantly signed on.

In this instance, she was not on particularly good terms with anyone connected with the proceedings. She thought the Harold Robbins novel on which Hayes based his screenplay trashy, vulgar, and exploitative— its inspiration being the notorious murder of Lana Turner's lover,

Johnny Stompanato, by her daughter Cheryl in 1958. Robbins and Hayes had skirted the libel laws by changing the profession of the lead, played by Susan Hayward, from actress to sculptor, and the father's (Mike Connors) from restaurateur (like Stephen Crane, Cheryl's father) to architect, and giving Hayward a monster-mother (Davis) written along the lines of Gladys Cooper's monster-mother in *Now, Voyager*. The ending, too, was changed, with the lover getting killed protecting Hayward from her murderous daughter, who, in the book and film, ends up in an institution.

Edward Dmytryk had been assigned as director by producer Joe Levine, who thought he was making up to Davis for the *Empty Canvas* fiasco. Davis didn't particularly respect Dmytryk, as she felt he had sold out on his early promise as a director of such arresting films as *Crossfire* (about anti-Semitism in the armed forces) to make glossy, commercial potboilers. She also didn't care for his politics; he had been one of the "Hollywood Ten" and later tattled on his confederates to get back into Hollywood's good graces. The atmosphere between director and star was therefore on the frosty side, and a timid, tentative Dmytryk let Davis direct herself for the most part. When he ventured a suggestion now and then, Davis tongue-lashed him viciously in front of the whole crew. "That woman has the temper of a *fiend!*" he said later.

Joe Levine avoided visiting the set, as Davis thought as little of him as she did of Dmytryk. "True, she was taking all that nice money from Joe, but she thought him a purveyor of pap and let him know it," Susan Hayward later said.

Susan herself found Davis a holy terror and avoided her as much as possible. Nervous and uncertain about how to interpret her part, Susan was in no mood to fuss with her co-star, and beat a hasty retreat after their scenes together. Davis, feeling more than usually paranoid, interpreted this as disdain and returned Susan's attitude in kind. Eddie Dmytryk later remembered, "When Susan ventured to suggest a change in the blocking in one scene, Davis angrily tore off her gray wig and threw it in Susan's face. Susan turned white—yes, you could see the paleness even under her makeup—and wheeled around and stomped toward her dressing room hissing, 'Bitch! Bitch!' under her breath. 'What did you say, Miss Hayward?' Davis shouted imperiously, unable, as usual to relinquish the last word. Angered beyond control, Susan Hayward wheeled around and yelled, 'Bitch! That's what you are. An old bitch!'"

Startled, Davis was for a moment speechless. Later she sent a note to Susan suggesting they talk over the problems of what she called "a stinking, lousy script." Susan gave her the silent treatment. Later, when Susan learned that Davis was shouting that she was going to "rewrite this crock of shit," she went to Levine to protest. Levine, himself rattled with Davis, sent down word that every word in the script would be retained.

After that, except for onscreen interchanges, Susan Hayward and Bette Davis never spoke to each other again.

"They were both on the defensive," their co-star, Mike Connors, later recalled. "Bette felt insecure up against a ten-years-younger woman, Susan, who was better-looking, and, moreover the real star of the film, the person the proceedings revolved around. And Susan, who was sullen and defensive anyway, found that hers and Davis's temperaments were too much alike for pleasant socializing off-camera. I remember it, and so did Eddie Dmytryk, as an atmosphere of armed truce—and a mean, icy truce it was, too!"

The critics greeted *Where Love Has Gone,* when it opened in November 1964, with frosty disdain, which occasionally took a jocular turn. One critic made sport of one of Davis's terribly overwritten speeches in which she rattles on, Gladys Cooper—fashion, about the decline of standards—and this in a picture that was a perfect example of what she was gassing off about.

Davis proceeded to complement the mixed reviews with an endlessly repeated story she gave out during interviews of how they had wanted her to go insane at the end and slash her own portrait, a majestic, grande-dame affair that closely resembled the over-the-fireplace portrait of Cooper in *Now, Voyager.* When she refused to do this, claiming it was out of character for such a strong-minded matriarch to go bonkers, the producers threatened to sue her. But she—and her battery of lawyers—held firm, and the original ending was retained.

Newsweek, on Bette's side in its review, called her "splendid, with her eyes rolling and her mouth working and her incredible lines to say." *The Saturday Review,* also in her corner, said she lent "all her old verve and intensity to the role of the domineering dowager."

DAVIS'S NEXT FILM, *Hush . . . Hush, Sweet Charlotte,* was shot in the summer of 1964, released briefly in California in December to qualify for Oscars, and then opened in New York in March 1965. She has always insisted that it was *not* a horror film, but rather a drama in which she gave a strong, fully realized characterization. Unfortunately, this is just not true.

Based on yet another Henry Farrell story (he of *Baby Jane*) with a script by Farrell and *Baby Jane* writer Lukas Heller and produced and directed by *Baby Jane* director Robert Aldrich for Twentieth Century–Fox release, the film's original titles shamelessly tried to trade on the *Baby Jane* phenomenon. *What Ever Happened to Cousin Charlotte?* was one. When Davis vociferously objected, the title became finally *Hush . . . Hush, Sweet Charlotte* (which Davis liked very much, curiously enough). Many critics though *Hush* a ripoff of the film *Diabolique.*

In this ghoulish fiasco, Davis is a half-demented aging chatelaine of an old Louisiana plantation house, whose married lover had been savagely beheaded by unknown persons many years before. Suspecting that her late father (Victor Buono) killed him, Davis's Charlotte Hollis is fearful that his memory will be incriminated if evidence is discovered during the razing of Hollis House, which is being forced by the Louisiana Highway Commission. Her cousin from abroad comes, ostensibly to help and comfort Davis, but it turns out her mission is to drive Davis even crazier with disembodied heads and hands rattling around downstairs. The cousin conspires with a confederate to pretend Davis has murdered him so that he can appear at the top of the stars muddy and bloody, and so forth and so on. When Davis hears them plotting, she topples a piece of statuary from the balcony of the mansion, killing them. Then, after her lover's widow dies, she is handed a letter in which the widow admits to the murder and also to having paid the cousin to remain silent. Davis is purged and liberated.

Aldrich pulled out all the stops on this one, so it is impossible to believe that Davis ever considered *Hush . . . Hush* a legitimate drama of any kind.

Films in Review, Henry Hart's feisty and honest magazine, declared, "Bette Davis and producer-director Robert Aldrich here attempt to duplicate their success with *What Ever Happened to Baby Jane?* Though not so effective as their earlier effort, this film will please all who like the macabre. *Baby Jane*, despite its contrivances, had a better story and was more believable than *Charlotte*, but the supporting cast and production values of the latter are grander."

This was followed by a condescending pat on the back to Davis, to wit: "No matter. Miss Davis, as Charlotte, gives another of her bravura performances and one which will disappoint none of her admirers."

Time magazine minced no words, stating, "[The picture] is a gruesome slice of shock therapy that, pointedly, is not a sequel to *What Ever Happened to Baby Jane?* The two films are blood relatives, as [Aldrich] well knows, but *Charlotte* has a worse play, more gore, and enough bitchery to fill several outrageous freak shows . . . choicest holdover from *Jane* is

Bette Davis, unabashedly securing her clawhold as Hollywood's grande-dame ghoul."

As photographed by an obviously indifferent Joseph Biroc with frumpily fustian costumes by Norma Koch, Davis looks every year, month, day, hour, and minute of her fifty-six years—meaning like hell.

And her "acting" is anything but that. Robert Aldrich showed himself the most craven pussycat of her many pussycat directors by letting her run wild and throw in anything that occurred to her, resulting in a performance that is as excessive as anything she ever essayed.

As if manically determined to top the ace of his *Baby Jane* screenplay, Lukas Heller rang all the gongs. It is hard to imagine how Davis thought she was giving a strong dramatic performance when the script insisted on keeping her hysterical, deranged, and wild-eyed all the way through. Still, she had her critical defenders for this film, including reviewer William Schoell, who felt that her delineations of fear and incipient madness were convincing, and at times, even touching and true.

Davis's hysterical cavortings and wild-eyed gesticulations might possibly have been due to all the trouble she was having with—who else?—Joan Crawford, who had been persuaded to join this rehash of *Baby Jane* horrifics. Joan was not keen on the idea; she had had enough of Davis the first time around, but Aldrich persuaded her that a Joan Crawford–Bette Davis repeat was good business and good box-office, and besides, the money was excellent. Satisfied with her fee and determined to brave Bette on her own terms and her own ground, Joan showed up for work—and immediately there was trouble.

She became convinced that Bette and Agnes Moorehead, who was very effective as Bette's protective servant, were conspiring to trip her up, embarrass her in her line readings, and make her life on set as miserable as possible. So nervous was Joan that she fluffed her lines once too often, and Davis icily declared to Aldrich in front of the whole crew that she could do nicely by herself, thank you, reading her lines straight into the camera, and that "Miss Crawford can withdraw and compose herself."

As Bob Aldrich remembered it, "There were no gifts from Joan to Bette *this* time! It was all business, and they didn't even bother to conceal their deep dislike of each other. Soon Bette was sneaking around to me asking for rewrites and new camera setups, all of which, I couldn't help but notice, favored her over Joan."

Then Davis began calling Aldrich on the phone every night complaining about Joan—how she was overdressed, how her jewelry jan-
gled, how she read her lines "amateurishly," adding, with a sardonic
laugh, "and when she's been around for centuries, too!"

Joan tried to mask her anger under her usual sweety-sweet "bless
yous" but began to develop psychosomatic symptoms and shortly
was complaining of a respiratory ailment. "She's just bluffing, grand-
standing, trying to cadge sympathy!" Davis told Aldrich con-
temptuously. Then Joan came down with a real fever and went into the
hospital. Determined to finish the movie, she recovered in short order,
returned to the set, then collapsed again. This was three weeks into the
filming.

Back again in Cedars of Lebanon hospital, Joan fretted and steamed
and finally began to scream at the hospital help. I was in Hollywood
that summer, and I visited Joan at the hospital. She pulled a series of X
rays out of a drawer, got out of bed, and began stalking back and forth.
A nurse came in to tell her to get back into bed, and Joan told the
frightened woman to get out, pronto—or else. She began holding the X
rays up to the light. "I can't figure them out," she said over and over. "I
know there's something wrong and they won't tell me and I have to do it
all myself!"

She grew more and more agitated. "Have you been to the set, Larry?
What is Bette up to? How are they handling my absence? Are
they shooting around me?" The nurse came in again, accompanied by a
handsome young doctor who proceeded to tell Joan that he had been
an admirer of her screen performances for years. Joan calmed down,
began to primp and purr, and when the dreamboat medico gently suggested it would be nice if she were a good girl and took her sedative,
she climbed back into bed, opened her mouth dutifully, and swallowed.
It must have been a knockout sedative for she was already yawning
when I left.

Over on the set, Aldrich was arguing with Davis, who at one point
screamed that she would walk off the set and off the Twentieth-Fox lot,
never to return, "unless you do something, anything about that malingering bitch!" Joan began calling Aldrich from the hospital. Caught
between the irresistible force and the immovable object that were Joan
and Bette, Aldrich took the coward's way out.

The insurance company had assured him that huge fees could be
collected to compensate for Crawford's illness. They sent their own doctors over to the hospital, and they confirmed (or so Aldrich always
claimed) that "the malingering bitch" was actually quite sick and would

not recover in time to finish the film. One day, while listening quietly to the radio and looking forward to having her pulse checked by the white-coated dreamboat, Joan heard that she had been removed from the film and replaced by Olivia De Havilland.

On my next visit to Cedars of Lebanon, Joan was cursing Aldrich's perfidy. "He didn't even have the manhood to come and tell me to my face or even over the phone! I had to hear it from the radio!" Joan screamed over and over. And yet I sensed a kind of backhanded relief that she was out of the picture and free of Bette. In typical Crawford schizoid style, she changed her manner and tune in a matter of seconds when the handsome young doctor reappeared, a trembling nurse behind him, to take her pulse and speak soothing words. I suspect she had taken a slow-acting tranquilizer before I arrived, because she began to nod, smile sleepily, and ask for a good-bye kiss. Her last words before wafting off to dreamland were: "Don't you think Doctor Charles is handsome as all get out? Don't you think he ought to be in the movies?"

Aldrich had great difficulty getting De Havilland to sub for Crawford. She and Davis were on excellent terms, had always been good friends since the Warner days when they had co-starred several times. But De Havilland felt the role of Miriam was too murderous, too sinister for her. In spite of the fact she had been a naughty girl in films like *The Dark Mirror* and *My Cousin Rachel*, now, at age forty-eight, she wanted to be beneficent, kindly, and feminine. No, she repeated, the role of Miriam wouldn't do at all. Before clinching it with De Havilland, thanks to a special long-distance phone plea from Davis, Aldrich had braved the likes of Vivien Leigh and Loretta Young. Loretta dismissed the role as totally wrong for her; Vivien was more tart about it:

"I could just about look at Joan Crawford's face on a southern plantation at seven o'clock in the morning," she purred venomously from London, "but I couldn't possibly look at Bette Davis!" When Leigh's words were relayed to Davis, all her repressed anger and frustration over Leigh's copping her Scarlett role and beating her out for the 1939 Oscar burst forth, and she smashed several mirrors and overturned a number of expensive props from the drawing room set of Hollis House. Katharine Hepburn, yet another headliner who had been asked to replace Crawford, declined with more verbal economy. She said but one word, "No," and informed Aldrich she was going to Connecticut, and her car couldn't wait.

When things finally got going, Olivia did well in her role, and she and Joe Cotten, as the family doctor who is in league with her to declare Davis insane, worked well together. When I asked Cotten in 1965 how things had gone on the set and location of *Hush . . . Hush, Sweet Charlotte,* he said, with his usual tact and kindly obliqueness, that he felt Olivia had done well considering she had been brought in at the last minute and that "Bette, as always, was a pleasure to play with. She went out of her way to be considerate to me."

Another cast member who spoke well of Bette during *Hush . . . Hush* shooting was Mary Astor, who in the second of her autobiographies commented that Davis made it a point to visit her before her few scenes (Astor was the murderous wife who is not exposed until the dénouement) and compliment her on her appearance. Davis reportedly told Aldrich, "Pay attention to this woman—you may learn something."

Agnes Moorehead walked away with critical kudos for her role as the protective servant. She later said, "Working with Bette was a real pleasure. I don't think the role made the most of her talents, but she gave it everything she had, and then some. It's a shame they can't find roles that would do justice to Bette's gifts."

Aldrich later admitted he was relieved when shooting ended. "I can't think of a picture that took more out of me," he said. "There was so much unpredictability throughout—Joan's illness (I was terribly disappointed she couldn't complete her role; it would have helped her at that stage) and Bette's tensions. The last time I called 'cut' on closing day I felt profound relief."

Davis next took off for England, where she did *The Nanny,* from a screenplay by Hammer Films' Jimmy Sangster, based on an Evelyn Piper novel. Assigned as director was Seth Holt, a creative but erratic forty-two-year-old who was troubled with weight problems, a "nervous" heart, and chronic alcoholism that would kill him six years later while he was directing a strenuously horrific film called *Blood From the Mummy's Tomb.* (Michael Carreras completed it and shared co-directing credit.)

A kindly, bluff, outwardly placid individual, Holt was a churning mess of tensions and neuroses on the inside, and Davis, as he told me later, got on his nerves exceedingly. Several times he almost told Jimmy Sangster that he found her impossible to work with and wanted to be taken off the film. Holt told me:

"She got the flu during shooting, and sometimes she'd stay away altogether, holding up shooting while she sent in day-to-day reports on her condition—'It's worse!'—'It's better!'—'Oh God, I've relapsed!'—and so forth, and when she was on set, still sniffling and coughing, she was drinking out of everyone's glasses and wheezing in her co-actors' faces in the best show-must-go-on manner—oh it was hell! Then she was always telling me how to direct. When I did it her way, she was scornful; when I stood up to her, she was hysterical. I managed some kind of middle course and got through the film and stayed calm, smiled sweetly, and got my way when I could. But I'd never have wanted to work with her again."

Holt felt she overacted, but when he tried to tell her this, "She'd say, 'I act larger than life; that's what my audience paid me for all these years. If they wanted ordinary reality they'd go out and talk with their grocer!' I knew she hated rushes, hated to look at herself. I'd ask her what did it matter since she was made up and dressed to be a frumpish, unattractive, middle-aged nanny anyway—and she was fifty-seven or so and how did she expect to look, even if Dior were dressing her and her old pal Perc Westmore making her up—but I couldn't get her to look at those rushes. If I had, I might have made her realize that she was pouring it on too much!"

Co-star Jill Bennett was afraid of Davis. She said Davis was always ready with advice and suggestions, including one to the effect that "making love to the furniture" helped enliven a scene. She told Jill that one should always dress up like a star on public occasions and then ridiculed archrival Joan Crawford the next day for doing the same thing! Jill also recalled that when she and Bette went to an event together and Bette felt she was dressed better than Jill, she would make her walk behind her like a servant.

The plot deals with a neurotic nanny who is responsible for a child's death through neglect. She railroads the young son of the house into a home for disturbed children claiming he is the culprit—her attitude being that nannies have to keep up appearances. Naturally the little boy hates her. When he's released, she almost drowns him in the bathtub, but finally comes to her senses and revives him—then exits the family's life.

The story holds up in the telling, but Davis overacts. Seth Holt's reservations about her style and approach to the material show up clearly on the screen. When the picture opened in America in November 1965, *Time* magazine gleefully reported, "*The Nanny* is her definitive essay on the servant problem, and may be taken as antidote by those who found Mary Poppins too sweet to stomach."

It was becoming increasingly apparent with her next film, *The Anniversary*, made in England for Hammer Productions in mid-1967 and released in early 1968, that Davis was not only increasingly devoid of judgment where appropriate scripts were concerned, but could not recognize the faults in her performance which were apparent to everyone else. She was also falling into the cantankerous, abrasive, on-set habits for which she had castigated Miriam Hopkins.

The Anniversary had opened as a hit black comedy on the London stage in the spring of 1966, with Mona Washbourne scoring a signal success as the domineering one-eyed mother. Once again, Davis would be repeating the monster-mother *shtick*. Moreover, she did not get along with the director, Alvin Rakoff, and had him replaced by Roy Ward Baker, with whom, she informed producer Jimmy Sangster, she was sure she would "enjoy the requisite simpatico." Rakoff later told associates that she was demanding and impossible, had ridiculed what she called his "trash-TV methods" (Rakoff hailed from television), and kept insisting that all the good films she had done had been shot in an atmosphere of tension and the bad ones in hale-and-hearty felicity. Over and over she said to the baffled crew, "Tension breeds creativity! Relaxation and conviviality breed mediocrity!"

Sheila Hancock and others from the original London production found her impossible to work with. Hancock recalled that Davis wanted to be treated deferentially, as a sort of queen. When she made her first entrance, coming down a flight of stairs, she received loud applause and was so gratified by this that she went upstairs and did the whole thing over again!

The story, which was an excellent black comedy on the London stage, turned into what Davis insisted would be, after she dictated rewrites and directorial changes by Baker, a comedy-drama acceptable to American as well as British audiences. "This star-turn changeover, plus the script changes designed to favor her front and center, and overacting to beat the band," Rakoff later charged, "ruined the balance of the original stage concept of MacIlwraith and Washbourne and Co. and resulted in a mess of a film built around Davis's foolish, overbaked posturings and camera-hoggings."

Unfortunately the picture is as bad as Rakoff said it was. Davis hams it up as never before, complete with glass eye (one of her sons had accidentally shot out her real one years before). She gathers her grown children together yearly to celebrate her wedding anniversary. And quite a collection they are, too: One is a transvestite, the second is a hen-pecked husband, and the third is a satyriacal womanizer with a new "fiancée" every few months. She proceeds to insult the latest fiancée by telling her she has body odor, pokes fun at the transvestite, raises every kind of vicious hell she can, and is finally brought up short by the spirited fiancée, who tells her she might well shoot out her other eye. This results in a sort of truce, with Davis planning future anniversaries.

Davis gave pathetically obtuse and short-sighted interviews at the time, saying that the film was meant to be a high-powered attack on monster-momism, to which too many American women were given. The truth was that she had so confused the intent of the play's author and star and had so weighted the total effect with her confused, unbalanced performance that the film ended up neither fish, fowl, nor good red herring fare. "So exaggerated that it shatters the credibility needed to be effective satire," sniffed the *New York Post*.

23

Bette Davis: Survivor

AFTER "MAKING DO" with more television shows to keep the income flowing, Davis at last found a script that she felt might kill her horror-film cycle conclusively.

Connecting Rooms has gone down in the Bette Davis pantheon as the Mystery Film. It was never distributed in America, had only a limited release in England, and hasn't even made it onto American television, let alone the videocassettes or cable showings. I was one of the few to see this film in England in 1971, courtesy of a friend who pulled strings to get me a screening-room look.

Connecting Rooms was shot at Pinewood in the spring of 1969. British release was held up until 1972, for reasons that are still obscure. While it is a far cry from being one of Davis's best films, it doesn't deserve to be situated toward the bottom of her deck either. It should have art house exposure now, some twenty years later, and certainly would register better on television and videocassettes than other widely shown Davis films that are inferior to it.

It is easy to see, in retrospect, why Davis decided to do *Connecting Rooms*. After the grotesqueries of *The Anniversary*, she felt it represented a definite change of pace for her—and she was right. Based on a play of the same name by Marion Hart, with screenplay and direction by Franklin Gollings, it was produced by two Englishmen, Harry Field and Arthur Cooper.

The producers clinched it with Davis, who had been considering the script for two years, by getting Sir Michael Redgrave, the distinguished star of stage and screen, to co-star with her. Each admired the other and had wanted to work together for some time. Once roped into it, Davis and Redgrave found themselves in mutual agreement as to the script's deficiencies. It tended to be maudlin, sentimental, and unconvincing. A downbeat story of the inhabitants of a seedy London boarding house, it displays Davis as a middle-aged cellist, on the mousy and drab side, who supports herself by playing in front of theaters. Sir Michael plays a former schoolteacher, sacked because he was suspected of a homosexual affair with a handsome student protégé. In the third lead was the young, handsome Alexis Kanner as a pop artist, song writer, and would-be gigolo. Davis becomes emotionally involved with Kanner and befriends her next-door neighbor, Redgrave. Kanner is a cynical, opportunistic type, however, for all his charisma, and Davis predictably winds up with Redgrave after Kanner unkindly exposes his past.

Davis—whose cello work was faked by Ian Fleming's sister, Amerlis—is subdued and kindly and well-meaning in this. Obviously she felt that after playing horror-film grotesques and one-eyed harridans, a sympathetic, warm role—in the tradition of *The Sisters* and *All This and Heaven Too*—was called for. But in this instance she did not have the talented Anatole Litvak to guide her—only the insecure Franklin Gollings, who spent most of the picture acting frightened to death of her. As usual, this "scaredy-cat" approach irritated her mightily and soon she was bullying the hapless Gollings mercilessly. "I was trying to rouse him to tell me what to *do*, for God's sake!" she later reported. "I can't stand a director who doesn't direct!" If Gollings had stood up to her even once, things might have gone more smoothly—but this he didn't do. Once, out of sheer panic and the worse for wear after an unaccustomed drink or two, he even fainted dead away on the set. This aroused her contempt further.

Davis and Redgrave spent a lot of time in her dressing room bluepenciling and rewriting the script, and Gollings hemmed and hawed indecisively when presented with the results.

Then there was the problem of young Alexis Kanner. Sassy, tactless Kanner had an unshakable belief in the power of his own charm and his photogenic capacities, and it was obvious he was not impressed with the

Great Bette Davis. Soon the two were arguing loudly, and after pushing him at Gollings and demanding that he be thoroughly rehearsed, Davis began looking for a replacement. "That was her idea, not ours!" Harry Field later said. "She just took things into her own hands without consulting us, even directed a scene when Gollings passed out one time. She wanted Keith Baxter to take over for Kanner, but we had to tell her he wasn't young enough (the kid was supposed to be a late teenager) and she grumblingly backed down." Again Davis and Kanner rehearsed, and some compromise was obviously reached, because they function well enough together in the final result.

Much of *Connecting Rooms* is touching and real. In low-keyed fashion Davis and Redgrave make the weak script look better than it is, via sincere, honest acting. Davis seemed to curb her usual tendency to overplay, inspired perhaps by her co-star Redgrave's subtle, more muted technique. Redgrave is touching as a man who feels himself unjustly buffeted by fate, and Kanner is so masculinely charismatic as the gigololike young heel that it is surprising little was heard from him thereafter. Reportedly Kanner told an interviewer, "If working with Bette Davis is an example of what movies are all about, then I want no more of them!"

As a study of loneliness and emotional distress, the film has its fine moments. At times it is overly sentimental, the pace lags, and there is an undue drabness, but despite these faults, it certainly deserved an American release and wider distribution.

THE YEAR 1971, when Davis turned sixty-three, brought her yet another failure in *Bunny O'Hare* (formerly known as *Bunny and Billy*). Davis had been intrigued by the script and felt the role would be good for her, but it was yet another instance of her poor judgment during this period.

Producer-director Gerd Oswald, who had directed her for television, and the American-International entrepreneurs James H. Nicholson and Samuel Z. Arkoff had sold her some months before on a story by Stanley Cherry, which Cherry and Coslough Johnson had worked into a screenplay. They had also enlisted the help of Davis's ex-co-star of *The Catered Affair*, Ernest Borgnine. Davis said she liked Borgnine and would be glad to reteam with him.

The story deals with a widow (Davis) who, after her home is foreclosed on by a bank, takes up robbing similar institutions with the help of a former bankrobber (Borgnine). In this manner the widow intends to continue supporting her hapless, foolish, dependent children (Reva Rose and John Astin). The bank robber and she proceed to career around in harsh New Mexico locations on a motorcycle, wreaking assorted mayhem and sporting wild hippie clothing (the ad copy for the film implied they were the geriatric answer to Warren Beatty's and Faye Dunaway's *Bonnie and Clyde* of four years before).

Borgnine and Davis are trailed by cop Jack Cassidy and criminologist Joan Delaney. Cassidy hates hippies, especially old ones, and pursues them assiduously, but later, through a fluke, the pair get off the hook. The picture ends in a burst of vulgarity, Davis shucking off her children with the words "Fuck 'em!" and Borgnine being revealed as a purveyor of toilets to disadvantaged Chicanos. Many of Davis's fans wondered why she, who said she was so concerned about good taste and high standards, ever stooped to four-letter words and vulgar situations, and she herself felt guilty for doing the film because she had permitted the bad language and vulgar dénouement.

Davis and Borgnine began the film agreeably enough, but, according to Gerd Oswald, soon they began coming to him separately, asking to have the scenes built up to their respective advantages. It was also noted that when Borgnine and Davis were forced to career along New Mexico roads on the motorcycle, he didn't take particular care for her safety as she clung to him frantically. Davis objected loudly to everything—the harsh sun, which bothered her skin; the strange New Mexico weather, which was alternately icy cold and unbearably hot; and the ludicrous, unbelievable situations which a frantic Oswald tried to hype up from the foolish, poorly motivated screenplay in which he, the stars, and everyone else had lost faith.

Back in Hollywood Arkoff and Nicholson were getting frantic phone messages and telegrams from the director, the stars, the cameraman (who was trying to lens all the chaos in widescreen *and* Movielab Color), and even some prop people, who threatened to complain to their union about the impossible conditions on location.

When Davis saw the first rough cut, she screamed and threatened to sue the company, claiming that they had edited all sense out of the story. After some changes and more recutting, Davis dropped her much-publicized suit threats, claiming that *Bunny O'Hare* was a lost cause and she wanted to forget it and move on. The critics hated it, with *Variety* saying it needed "a swift kick in the movieola." The *New York Post* felt the picture was "weak" and "let her down" and added, "I don't know how they sold her on it in advance."

Next Dino DeLaurentiis talked Davis into flying from California to

Italy to make *The Scientific Cardplayer* (*Lo Scopone Scientifico*), also known as *The Game*. Alberto Sordi, the beloved Italian comedian, would appear opposite her.

The project was in for trouble from the start. Davis did not get on well with Sordi because, though he spoke good English, he insisted on yelling at her in staccato Italian. She suspected it was a ploy to disconcert her and show her who was boss, so she gave as good as she got, screaming some of her best obscenities at him. She never apologized for her behavior, acidly observing, "What good would it have done, for Christ's sake? Except for Sordi, who was bluffing, they would no more have understood English civilities than they did my curses!"

The plot deals with an egomaniacal American millionairess who enjoys playing regular card games with impoverished Italians who hope to win a fortune from her. Of course she rigs it so that she is always the winner, but hope beats eternal in the breasts of her Italian suckers, and the game goes on and on. The *Variety* reviewer threw her a critical posy with: "Bette Davis dominates with a neat display of egomania and cruelty beneath a stance of gracious dignity." Silvana Mangano is one of her opponents at the perennial card game—known as Scopa—and almost beats her at it several times. Then at the end, one of the outraged Italian youngsters presents her with a poison–filled cake. It is obvious she won't be coming back for her usual sport.

Joseph Cotten made yet another appearance with Davis as a faithful friend who plays with her and offers ruefully tactful comments. Sordi is effective in his usual style and Silvana Mangano offers a vivid performance as the card-game opponent without illusions.

I caught the film at the Museum of Modern Art in 1986, where it played to an appreciative audience. The picture reportedly made money in Italy (primarily on the strength of Sordi's name), but got scant distribution in both England and America, which is surprising, as the Eastman color is handsome, the production values fair enough, and the direction by Luigi Comencini extracts all that is good from the Rodolfo Sonego script.

Davis never liked the film, however, citing not only Sordi's rudenesses and prima-donna posturings, but the fact that she didn't know the dialogue would be shot in Italian, with dubbing.

Joseph Cotten, who later admitted he did the film only because he admired Bette and needed the money, felt that she was not shown due respect and that Sordi was regarded by the Italian cast and crew as the star while Davis was treated as a cameo player. Her role is actually large, and she manages to project a kinetic energy and sense of move-

Fasten Your Seat Belts

ment while being confined to a wheelchair. It is an odd blend of the fantastic and the realistic, not always successful, but the Italianate ambience lends flavor and spice, so *Scientific Cardplayer* is not a film that Davis need apologize for.

Sordi told several interviewers that he had no wish to work with Davis again, as she had been consistently rude to him and accused him of selfishly hogging the camera. He tried, he said, to pass off her tactlessness with humor, but this only succeeded in enraging Davis further. "Then I gave up," he said.

DAVIS'S CLOSE FRIENDSHIP with the actor Robert Wagner dated from the early 1970s. He had used his influence to cast her in a segment of his television series, *To Catch a Thief*. In "A Touch of Magic," Davis played a safecracker who assumed different personas. First she was a frail convalescent, then she dressed up as a grand lady, and then got into nun's "drag" and did a comic *shtick*. She gave Wagner credit for influencing the writer to enlarge her role in order to display her range.

Davis watched with regret when Wagner's marriage to Natalie Wood broke up and was delighted when they remarried some years later. Natalie, as she often said, was "another daughter" to her. (Davis had appeared with her in *The Star* years before.)

Then in 1972 Robert Wagner came to her rescue again. She starred with him in *Madame Sin*, originally shown as a TV pilot but later released in European theaters.

In this she is a sinister-looking, totally evil, half-Chinese woman who indulges in endless machinations. Ensconced in a Scottish castle that, as one reviewer put it, "is loaded with typical spy-movie gadgetry," she runs afoul of the Wagner character, who is out to counter her plots. As one critic said, "Evil genius (Davis) uses former C.I.A. agent (Wagner) as pawn for control of Polaris submarine. Elaborate production has Bad beating out Good at end; with Bette in charge, it's well worth seeing."

Davis is sinister and serpentine indeed, and garishly made up, with black wig, snappy black gown, and jangling jewelry. Her poisonously powerful performance won good reviews here and abroad.

DAVIS HAD BEEN doing television shows since the early 1950s. She never took them very seriously, but now and then landed good parts on *Wagon Train*, *Perry Mason*, and others. Many were done as pilots that never caught on as a series.

Two of her television movies in the 1972–1973 period illustrate the quality of her work in that medium. In *The Judge and Jake Wyler*, Davis contributed an ironic, humorous portrayal of an eccentric jurist who decides to open a detective agency and takes on an ex-con as her partner. Together they solve the murder of a businessman. The story has ingenious twists and Davis plays with a light, throwaway style that is unusual for her, though the familiar overcooked, sometimes hammy Davis mannerisms did show up at times when director David Lowell Rich obviously wasn't looking. Doug McClure and Joan Van Ark supported her ably. Davis told an interviewer later that McClure was "all man and very cute."

The Judge and Jake Wyler, like so many of her other television appearances, had originally been designed as a pilot for a series, but footage was added to bring it to feature length, and it debuted as a TV Movie of the Week for NBC in December 1972. Kent Smith, who had a supporting role in it, told me: "Bette was always a good sport in the television shows she was forced to make because she needed money or had nothing else on tap. I was on hand to watch her make something out of nothing with *Judge*. She always went all out, even in drek. That was part and parcel of her professionalism."

Scream, Pretty Peggy, a 78-minute 1973 television movie, got the treatment from William Schoell, author of the book on horror films, *Stay Out of the Shower*: "[The picture] is a ridiculous rip-off of *Psycho* that has yet another crazed cross-dresser as the killer. You have to see Ted Bessell running around in drag to believe it. The plot deals with a college girl who becomes a housekeeper at a place with a dark secret. Jimmy Sangster's screenplay is ludicrous, Gordon Hessler's direction never rises above the routine, and Bette Davis as Bessell's mother doesn't put herself out too much, to put it charitably."

IN 1973 BETTE DAVIS began appearing in a one-woman show, a sort of retrospective of her life and career. Her first appearance at Town Hall in New York was a smash success, so she took it all around the country and even to Australia and Europe.

The program for the evening never varied. The first half was a series of film clips, cleverly chosen by film historians like Don Koll. The second half had Davis fielding any and all sallies and queries, personal as well as professional.

These sessions drew a large contingent of gay men, who delighted in her reminiscences and witty, tart remarks about former co-workers and, of course, her complex relationships with Miriam Hopkins and Joan

Crawford. Michael Ritzer, then a reporter for *Quirk's Reviews*, stupefied Bette and the audience at the 1973 Town Hall event when he stood up and told her that *Beyond the Forest* had always been his favorite picture. Davis gave him one of her steely-eyed looks and snorted, "Oh really . . ." Whereupon the audience roared with laughter. Oddly, Ritzer proved a pioneer in his evaluation of *Beyond the Forest*, for today it is an ever-more-acclaimed cult film.

On the tour, Davis was endlessly accommodating. She answered as many questions (written and sorted-out in advance) as time and energy permitted. Over and over she reviewed the two-cigarette scene in *Now, Voyager;* told what a bitch Miriam had been during *The Old Maid* shooting; refused again and again to admit that William Wyler had been the only man she truly loved but refused to surrender to. She recited the get-set-for-a-bumpy-night speech from *All About Eve* until it was running out of her ears, praised Eddie Goulding and Willie Wyler as her favorite directors, discussed her feuds with Jack Warner, her marriages, fellow actors such as Charles Boyer, Leslie Howard, Paul Henreid, and her favorite-of-favorites, Claude Rains.

Before Davis began this tour, she had appeared with three other luminaries in a Town Hall series called "Legendary Ladies"—the others being Sylvia Sidney, Myrna Loy, and Joan Crawford, with each assigned her own evening. Since Joan was involved in the same project under the same auspices, Bette kept a civil tongue regarding her, and Crawford returned the favor, although many felt the series would have been even more lively had the ladies really let loose on each other. Later, off on her own, Davis was more frank, but still restrained for her. She recalled that when she told the press in 1962 that before *What Ever Happened to Baby Jane?* no bank had wanted to take a chance on a picture starring "two old broads" like her and Crawford, Crawford had sent her a sharp note telling her not to refer to her in that way again.

Like many observers, I am curious about what seems to be a Bette Davis and Joan Crawford obsession on the part of many gay men. Despite the fact that the mannered and incisive Davis persona is very easily imitated, Crawford, too, has attracted a cult, as has Judy Garland. But it was the Crawford-Davis gay cult phenomenon I was concerned with, and in 1973, I wrote an analytical article about it for *Quirk's Reviews*.

After reading "The Cult of Bette and Joan," as I titled it, Joan Crawford said she was not quite certain what the gays saw in her, though she had an easier time comprehending the gay fixation on Davis. Up in her apartment over dinner one evening, we covered the topic comprehensively.

Joan led off by saying that she and her friends had found "The Cult of Bette and Joan" most amusing and incisive, and recalled that Leonard Frey, as Harold in the 1970 movie version of *The Boys in the Band*, had held up my 1968 book, *The Films of Joan Crawford*, in plain view of the camera. Joan added that gays were wonderful people, that she had many gay friends, and was happy to join such as Garland and Davis in their pantheon of goddesses, but remained a little puzzled as to whether she deserved the honor of being included.

I explained that many gay men identified with Joan's and Bette's *struggle*—for careers, for men, for self-respect, for social acceptance, for all the good things in life, as exemplified in their 1930s–1950s movies. I pointed out the ads on their movies, for instance: "Bette Davis as a Twelve O'Clock Girl in a Nine O'Clock Town" (*Beyond the Forest*). "No One Can Hold a Candle to Joan Crawford When Joan Is Carrying the Torch" (*Good-bye, My Fancy*). "It Happens in the Best of Families but Who Would Have Thought It Could Happen to Her?" (*Now, Voyager*). "Joan's Having Man-Trouble Again!" (*Daisy Kenyon*). "Disillusioned, Sick with Men, Does Joan Dare Love Once More?" (*Humoresque*). "She's Meanest When She's Lovin' Most!" (*Jezebel*). "Deep in Her Heart, She Knew She Could Never Hold Him!" (*The Corn Is Green*). "He *Strayed* and He *Paid*—*She* Saw to *That*!" (*Payment on Demand*).

Then I described the standard Bette and Joan plots with which many gay men identified: Joan climbing, on a ladder of rich and powerful men, from rags to riches (*Sadie McKee*); Bette determined to break out of the stultifying small town to glamour and men in Chicago (*Beyond the Forest*); Joan, unrequitedly and obsessively in love with a guy, goes bonkers and shoots him to death when he takes up with someone else (*Possessed*); Bette and Miriam fighting over men with *both* of them losing out (*Old Acquaintance*); Joan suffering unrequited love for a loser, winding up in a house of ill fame, then going for a smash finish as the wife of the richest guy in town (*Flamingo Road*); Bette defying the conventional monster-mother to go out and fight for happiness and love (*Now, Voyager*); good Bette and bad Bette in a dual role as twins fighting over a guy, who—for a while—prefers the frosted naughty girl to the unfrosted goody-goody (*A Stolen Life*); Joan on the rags to riches *shtick* again, loving a no-good son of a bitch and winding up with a squeaky-clean boy scout (*Mannequin*).

At the end of this recital, Joan said she understood her and Davis's appeal to gay men. Davis, for her part, said often that gays were among the most appreciative, tasteful, and artistically aware members of her audience. She appreciated their loyalty and love for her, which, at times, it is true, was a bit excessive. A popular Greenwich Village joke has it that two gay guys are drinking in a bar and one says to the other, "You must be in love with Bette Davis the way you go on about her at such length!" The other replies, *"In love* with Bette Davis! I AM Bette Davis!"

On her tour, Davis said she always enjoyed seeing nightclub comedians, drag queens, and others parody her, but claimed she could do it better herself. She would proceed to demonstrate with cigarette, twitching pelvis, bugging eyes, and elbow wavings. She maintained that she never said "Petah—the Lettah!" in any picture. It was actually a synthesis from two of her films—*The Letter,* and *In This Our Life,* in which a man named Peter (Dennis Morgan) is driven to suicide by her.

THE YEAR 1974 brought Bette Davis, at age sixty-six, a big opportunity, one she truly cherished—but it ended as an all-out disaster. There is still a running debate in show business circles as to whether Davis was victim or perpetrator of what came to be known as "the *Miss Moffat* mess."

For thirty years Davis had longed to repeat her role of the valiant Welsh schoolteacher in *The Corn Is Green.* Though the film (shot in 1944) was a hit, she felt that, at thirty-six, she had been too young for the role, recalling that Ethel Barrymore, its originator, had been sixty-one when she did it on Broadway. It was the talented director and writer Joshua Logan, a longtime admirer, who approached her with the idea of a musical version to be toured and taken to Broadway. Mary Martin had been the original choice for the lead, but she had declined at the last moment. Emlyn Williams wrote the lyrics, Albert Hague the music.

Davis told Logan that her *Two's Company* musical attempt of 1952–1953 had "left a bad taste" in her mouth; she didn't think she was up to it. She brightened up when Logan told her that he was relocating the story from Wales to the Deep South and that the racial question would be addressed four-square by making Morgan Evans a black boy of singular brilliance whom Miss Moffat's tutelage inspires to future greatness.

Delighted with the updating of the theme, assured that the musical score and lyrics would be adapted to her limited abilities, and that dancing would be sparse and discreet, Davis took the bait.

Trouble began at once. She had difficulty remembering lines. The young black actor-singer Dorian Harewood, whose big chance this would have been, was nervous trying to cope with her erratic, unpredictable style, and they did not work well together. In Philadelphia she collapsed from nerves, finding little consolation in the knowledge that advance ticket sales in New York guaranteed that the show might run for a year at least.

Josh Logan and Davis emerged from the ill-starred venture as all-out enemies. "She was tactless, overbearing, did not blend in with the cast," he claimed, and, in his view, faked a succession of illnesses in order to get out of her commitment. She disconcerted her cast by stopping the action dead to complain about a scene. She threw young Harewood off stride by failing to pick up his cues. Then the sore throats and neuralgic pains and hysterics began, and Davis took to her bed in a Philadelphia hotel. Then she claimed that the back injury from the 1957 fall had flared up. Logan visited her room and surrounded her with two doctors, a lawyer, and an insurance representative. He all but accused her of malingering and then asked her to show some professionalism, some consideration for the cast of young hopefuls, especially the despairing Harewood, whose future she was "mangling beyond the point of return."

Angered, Davis called in her own set of doctors, who, upon examining her, informed the distraught Logan he was dealing with a woman at the gates of old age who had no business in such a stressful endeavor, and that if she continued, she might die on his hands. Logan, a director of many Broadway hits, had a history of mental breakdowns, and he told his wife Nedda Harrigan that "the Wicked Witch of the West," as he called Davis, might well bring on "the grand extravaganza nervous breakdown of my life." He insisted angrily that Davis was exaggerating her assorted afflictions to cop out." She's always calling other people cowards, but she's the biggest coward of all!" he said. Davis ignored all pleas, and at a cost of hundreds of thousands of dollars, withdrew. Logan closed down the show—and never forgave her.

Davis went into temporary retirement. For most of the year 1975 she rested, amidst recurring rumors about her health, and soon she was game for more activity. But, she stressed to the press, never again, ever, in the theater!

24

A Legend—But Alone

IN 1976 DAVIS appeared in a gory film called *Burnt Offerings*—at least it was supposed to be gory. Trouble was, the gore was at a minimum and the boredom preeminent—at least for the audience. She played the aunt of a married couple (Karen Black and Oliver Reed) who take over a strange old house for the summer and gradually fall under its evil spell (the house grows newer and sprucer while the inmates grow older and more decrepit). Reed turns murderous and tries to drown his son, Davis tries to combat the evil influence and is killed, and Black winds up a zombie taken over by Satan who serves meals to a mysterious person in the attic, and so forth and so on.

Davis didn't get along with anyone during the shooting of *Burnt Offerings*. She yelled so often at producer-director Dan Curtis that he walked off the set and disappeared for days. She was nervous about how the DeLuxe Color would make her look and argued endlessly with cinematographers Stevan Larner and Jacques Marquette, frightening them into dropping and smashing valuable camera lenses. She walked in and out of other people's dressing rooms hollering that the original novel by

Robert Marasco "stank," that the screenplay was lousy, and that she might have to rewrite the whole thing herself.

Then she started giving out interviews saying, "There's practically no rehearsal, and the sloppy attitude on the set is unbelievable. These people that have been bred on television production have no sense of pacing or style . . . it's all 'just get it into the can!'"

When Producer Curtis sent a mild-mannered publicity man to point out to her the disadvantages inherent in the unfortunate publicity such negative interviews would attract, which might affect bookings and future reviews, she yelled at him so furiously that the poor man retreated in tears and later vomited in the men's room. When told of this later, she said, "Good—it got all the damned puke out of him. Let's hope he took a good crap, too—he was full of it when I talked to him!"

Soon she was giving Karen Black acting lessons, telling her she was too "improvisational" and "lacked discipline" and "needed the seasoning of more stage training." Davis would stage-whisper, "You missed your marks, girl" and Black would sweat profusely. Oliver Reed's behavior also annoyed Davis no end. "That man seems to be perpetually on a hangover," she told producer Curtis. Reed hated her so much, he would say his lines and retreat immediately to his dressing room. "Get him to use a mouthwash," he overheard Davis tell Curtis. "His breath stinks to high heaven!"

There was general relief that Davis's character was to get killed off early, as this meant Davis would no longer be on the set. She surprised them, however, by hanging around anyway, even after her few scenes were shot. "They can use a veteran's experience; they might want to ask me something!" No one did, to her exasperation.

Variety gave her a coup de grace with: "As for Davis, she doesn't have much to do. Her role is that of a weak and pathetic old woman, hardly the kind of thing she does best. Unkind lighting and costuming make her resemble Baby Jane Hudson."

Meanwhile Oliver Reed and Karen Black were letting it be known that they would never act with her again.

During the 1970s Davis alternated between film and television.

She did not like working with Faye Dunaway in *The Disappearance of Aimée*, a *Hallmark Hall of Fame* television drama that debuted in November 1976. Chief among Davis's complaints was Faye's alleged failure to get to the set on time, her "prima-donna habit," as Davis put it, of sulking in her dressing room while costs mounted, and her frequent disappearances in her limousine while all production activity came to a halt.

As late as 1987 Davis was telling Johnny Carson that during the long periods Dunaway kept everyone waiting she'd have to entertain the cast and crew by singing "I've Written a Letter to Daddy" and other songs associated with her. She called Dunaway blatantly unprofessional and inconsiderate and said she'd never work with her again. Dunaway, for the most part, ignored the criticism and, patronizing Davis's by-then sixty-eight years, told an interviewer, "She's been around for ages and is getting on, and I cannot believe that she would speak of anyone the way she has spoken of me!" Driving the knife home, Faye added, "Of course she hasn't been well for a long time."

Dunaway could have mentioned that for many years Davis had wanted to play Aimée Semple McPherson herself—and now here she was in a secondary role as her mother! McPherson had been a famous radio evangelist and mesmerist who galvanized audiences of the 1920s from coast to coast. Although suspected by many of being a fake and a charlatan, the magnetic Aimée won millions of fans who would rise en masse to clobber any dissenters in the hall. Directed by Anthony Harvey, who had triumphed with such movies as the Katharine Hepburn–Peter O'Toole *The Lion in Winter* in 1968, the television film dealt with the strange disappearance of Aimée in 1926. She claimed she had been kidnapped, but rumors persisted that she had shacked up with a man with whom she had temporarily fallen "into lust." Davis, as her mother, joins with Faye to hoodwink the public into accepting the kidnapping theory. Davis didn't have as many scenes as she would have liked, but she got in her innings in a flamboyant scene in which she drives the audience to hysteria with the wild declaration that she believes her daughter has been murdered.

Whatever her problems with Faye, Davis garnered some good reviews for her performance in *Aimée*, with the *Los Angeles Times* television critic noting, "[She] summons her familiar crisp authority as a dominating mother who, believing her daughter has met foul play, is full of skepticism and demands for the truth." Other reviewers cross-country called her "forceful" and "attention-getting," with a few commenting on her familiar tendency to overact and overembroider. Indeed, frustrated by the fact someone else was playing a character she had long wanted to do, and fueled by her personal dislike for Dunaway, Davis did cut loose with some fancy scenery-chewing on occasion. She enjoyed the 1920s costumes, wearing them with flair.

In 1977, Davis was on hand to accept the American Film Institute's

Life Achievement Award, which was presented to her on March 1. The first woman to receive it—a fact she made sure the press duly noted—she appeared with hostess Jane Fonda, whose imminent birth had speeded up the *Jezebel* shooting nearly forty years before. On hand were old lover and mentor William Wyler ("Sometimes she wanted more takes than I did!"), Olivia De Havilland ("She got the roles I always wanted!"), and Robert Wagner, Henry Fonda, Geraldine Fitzgerald, and other stars she had worked with.

Davis got a roar of laughter hissing, "I'd love to kiss ya but I just washed ma hair" and saluted Ruthie, by then sixteen years dead, as someone who "worked and slaved for many years to help make my dreams come true."

After *Aimée*, Davis was not seen on television for over a year. Nursing her uncertain health, disdainful of much she was asked to do, she finally accepted the two-part television dramatization of Tom Tryon's *The Dark Secret of Harvest Home*. She got off on the wrong foot at her first meeting with the producers by telling them that Tom Tryon had been a lousy actor but was obviously a better writer or she wouldn't be gracing them with her presence.

In this Davis is a mover and shaker in a small New England village that visitors find strangely old-fashioned. There is an obsession with the town's corn crop, and it turns out that the townsfolk practice some arcanely sinister fertility rites to assure that it grows properly. Included in the rituals are unabashed human sacrifices.

A young couple moves into the town. Soon enough they are drawn into the horrific proceedings, wishing fervently that they were back among the jangling unpredictabilities of bold, bad New York, from whence they came.

The television offering ran five hours (with commercials), several of them monumentally slow and tedious. As the ringleader of the morbid and bloody doings, Davis wears granny glasses, a strangely angled pilgrimlike cap, and a severe high-necked dress, and the camera does nothing to hide all the lines and bulges of her seventy years. To her annoyance the producers decided to go on location in Ohio rather than her beloved native New England, where the story was laid. Later she wrote critics who had demurred at her rather overwrought and unbalanced performance that if she had been allowed to cut loose "in the proper locations" instead of "drab, flat Ohio" she might have summoned the proper creative inspiration. Among her problems in Ohio was a local witch's coven that harassed her for "misrepresenting" their calling and threatened to burn down her trailer. One paper called the film's garishly ominous proceedings "terrifically earnest."

Again giving the press her standard excuse, "I needed the money and gambled it would turn out well," Davis appeared in *Return from Witch Mountain* in early 1978. A sequel to *Escape to Witch Mountain*, a popular release of three years before, the film featured young Ike Eisenmann and Kim Richards as two aliens villain Christopher Lee and his accomplice, Davis, try to manipulate—he to gain world power, she for riches. After much rushing about, the kids foil the bad guys. The original picture reportedly grossed over nine million dollars in rentals, chiefly because children liked it; the sequel did nowhere near as well.

The movie was Davis's first feature appearance for Disney (she did one other, two years later). The *Variety* critic put his finger on what was wrong, writing: "Davis doesn't quite click as [Lee's] partner in crime," adding, "It's interesting to note that Disney villainesses are triumphantly cruel in animation, a quality difficult to duplicate in live action. For the men, it's the opposite way around, which should give sociologists something to ponder."

Janet Maslin in *The New York Times* wrote: "John Hough's direction, ungainly at its best, is occasionally downright cruel, [such as] shooting Miss Davis in close-up when her heavy makeup seems designed for long shots. She's supposed to look frightening much of the time, but there's such a thing as gallantry, too."

The witty Harry Haun summed up the problem succinctly in the *New York Daily News*, writing: "Good roles for 70-year-old grandmothers are in such short supply these days that Bette Davis sometimes has to settle for pictures every bit as slim as her pickings . . . it would have been nice if the elves in charge had been ready for her [and] had come up with something in the way of a character to play—but apparently even Disney witchcraft has its limits. . . . however, the real trick in *Return from Witch Mountain* is a dubious one: making a formidable force like Bette Davis seem invisible. A working grandmother deserves more."

That year, in a series of press interviews, Davis held forth on the "execrable, monstrously bad" pictures that had been forced on her in that period. "Money," she then screamed to one and all, "it's the bane of my existence. People expect a star to live high no matter how old she gets, or whatever the state of her finances may be. And when they learn who you are, they deliberately charge you more—more—more!" Her voice rose: "Some people can never get it into their stupid, stupid heads that a star can work for fifty years and still not have any decent money put away. Certainly *I* don't! So I slave and slave and grub and grub and take a lot of perfectly terrible stuff for the money—and yes, the continued exposure."

One reporter asked her if she'd forego trash like *Return from Witch Mountain* if she had a private fortune. "Would you hold out only for quality fare, then?" he ventured. "And would you go back on the stage, do Albee, Williams, Chekhov perhaps?"

To this she thundered, puffing furiously away at her cigarette: "I would hold out for parts that showcased my particular talents, yes. But I don't know about the classics—they're for another type of artist" [she did not elaborate on this statement]. As for the stage, "I've had enough of theater. It's too hard on me at my age. Everyone depends on you because you're the star. An understudy will never do in an emergency. And the repetition and the touring and the physical strain—no, the stage is now firmly in my past." And more pictures like *Witch Mountain*? "Regrettably, in my future. The money, remember?"

AT FIRST it looked like Bette Davis would go against type, so to speak, by behaving like an absolute angel on the set of *Death on the Nile,* an Agatha Christie mystery following in the wake of the highly successful *Murder on the Orient Express* of four years before. Ingrid Bergman had won a supporting Oscar for her brief but telling role in that, and Davis told friends that she might get one herself this time around. "I'm not proud—a supporting Oscar would be fine," she said. "Ingrid won two best actress Oscars and then that one, and a two and a half would be gratefully received in my case, too."

But soon it became obvious to her that her role, a haughty dowager who bullies secretary-companion Maggie Smith, was not the stuff of which Oscar nominations are made. Before long she was overacting in her usual style, frantically trying to make her few scenes "pay off big," as she put it. Then she and director John Guillermin began having what she called "constructive sessions" in far corners. She insulted color photographer Jack Cardiff when she told him that he didn't understand her "special problems" and was not photographing her "with the professionalism" to which she was accustomed.

The small size of her role ate at her continually, and she was forever coming up with "bits of business that will help the picture as a whole," as she put it, but that were actually designed to further her advance toward that ever-more-elusive third Oscar.

Thinking to enlist the other actors to her cause, she went out of her way, as George Kennedy later recalled, to be nice to them—at least in the beginning. "But keeping herself reined in was taking its toll on her," he felt. Certainly even *she* was somewhat put off by the major-league talent that surrounded her; the cast included Peter Ustinov, Angela Lansbury, David Niven, Maggie Smith, and Harry Andrews.

The plot concerns the murder of spoiled heiress Lois Chiles during a cruise down the Nile. Detective Hercule Poirot (Ustinov), who happens to be aboard the houseboat, determines to find the killer, and is confronted with her fortune-hunting, weakling husband (Simon McCorkindale); the crooked lawyer who has been preempting her money (Kennedy); jilted fiancée Mia Farrow; socialite Davis and her companion, Smith; radical politician John Finch; a doctor, Jack Warden; and Lansbury, who is delightful as a writer of elegantly sexy novels. Poirot bags the murderer, of course, but not before two more people are killed.

The film was shot on location in Egypt, and Davis was thrilled at first by the geographical novelty. Soon, however, she was reacting adversely to the hot weather and dusty terrain. The weather got her so down that instead of giving a visiting English journalist the nice interview she had rehearsed—just in case Oscar beckoned—she reverted to her usual brittle carping, telling him that back in the Great Warner Days they'd have put the whole shebang on a nice, convenient back lot, but that "nowadays, films have become travelogues, and actors stuntmen!"

She became particularly angry when the handsome costumes prepared for her began to wilt in the brutally hot weather. One hat, large and impressive and shaped like Napoleon's famous headgear, began to wilt at both ends, and wound up framing her haggard, lined face comically. Maggie Smith, who as the drab secretary wore simple dresses, coats, and hats, ventured to commiserate with Davis one day over the condition of her wardrobe, and Davis snapped back; "Well, at least they'll look at me in my costumes, but they'll overlook you!"

Davis took a shine to handsome young Simon McCorkindale and began giving him tips on his acting—some he found workable, others he quietly discarded. "She was such a nice old lady," he said later. "They told me she was just turning seventy. I wanted to be nice to her. I know the weather got her down." Had Davis overheard these sentiments, she doubtless would have exiled McCorkindale, resenting his condescension.

"Angela Lansbury seemed to get along well with her," Peter Ustinov later observed, "but then Angela gets along well with everybody." Asked how he himself had weathered the Davis presence, he hesitated, then observed: "Well, the poor lady is getting on in years, and the weather is hard on people that age, and, well, I let things roll off me—no sense getting my blood pressure up!" A statement that hinted at far more than it revealed.

David Denby in *New York Magazine* did not hold *Death on the Nile* in high esteem, calling it "a great lummox of a movie," adding, "What is the point of this dreadnought approach to a basically frivolous genre?" He continued: "Apart from a satirical duet between dragon-eyed rich-bitch Bette Davis (wearing a cloche—or is it a toque?)—and her cranky-tweedy companion, Maggie Smith, the performances are demoralized and stale. This is one formula whose charm has run out."

Davis closed out the uncertain and unsatisfying 1970s, at age seventy-one, with her television appearance in *Strangers: The Story of a Mother and Daughter*, which aired in May 1979. Gena Rowlands, whom she found pleasantly rewarding to work with, played opposite her.

In this television drama directed by Milton Katselas and written by Michael deGuzman, Davis is an aging widow confronted with the knowledge that her daughter, from whom she has been separated for twenty years, has come home to die. Together the two women work through and resolve, after a fashion, their lifelong differences, with Davis learning to accept her daughter's imminent demise.

Gena Rowlands told the press how "happy and proud" she was to be playing "with such a distinguished legend" while Davis said how gratifying it was "to note that younger performers have among them people who understand the disciplines and dedication of my day!"

The critics noted, however, that Davis offered practically a self-parody in most of her scenes, and that she was forbidding and dour throughout, leaving little room for sincere emotion.

John O'Connor in *The New York Times* described the trouble well when he stated, "Miss Davis is an institution, very much a national treasure. But her thoroughly familiar mannerisms can be a handicap, and they are precisely that in the opening scenes. She is overwhelming in her passionate withdrawals."

A pleasant, easygoing woman in private life, Gena Rowlands, wed for years to the late actor-director John Cassavetes, has said of Davis in *Strangers*: "I felt that life had left her worn and tired, and that her work, while it was the important thing in her life, was not yielding the consolations that she had hoped for. We had many talks, and I found her more objective about herself than her publicity would lead one to believe."

The 1980 Emmy that Davis received for *Strangers* was widely regarded as a sympathy vote.

Skyward, another TV movie, was aired in November 1980. In this, Davis is a veteran airplane pilot who helps a paraplegic confined to a wheelchair, Suzy Gilstrap, actually a paraplegic, fulfill her dearest ambition—to fly. It was Ron Howard's first directorial assignment, and he was nervous around Bette, who couldn't help but see him as the boy from *Happy Days*. Addressing him icily as Mr. Howard and "Richie," she recalled, she didn't begin calling him what he had requested, Ron, until she was sure he "had what it took." Howard later told an interviewer that a combination of tact and good cheer carried him through his debut as a "Bette Davis director," and that she "wasn't *that* tough—if she knew she was in good hands and was sure I knew what I was doing."

While Davis kept a stiff upper lip with her co-workers, she screamed bloody murder to B.D., who recalled that she had said scornfully of Howard and his producer, Anson Williams, "They're going to tell *me* what to do? Jesus! Someone has to be kidding!"

Davis also complained that the two didn't have any idea what they were doing, and improvised atrociously. She sarcastically observed, "All those kids care about is that dear, darling little crippled girl. She gets to sit in the shade in her wheelchair while I'm out on the burning-hot pavement with blisters on my feet and my sneakers stuck to the tar. Shit!"

Skyward got a sympathetic reception from the press, but the kudos had a rather dutiful tone. After all, it would not do to put down a picture that attempted to deal affirmatively with the aspirations of the disabled to live normally. Amidst all the hollow praise, one Baltimore critic dared to assert that Davis made "rather forbidding and cold" company for the aspiring paraplegic, and that the proceedings were "soap."

In 1980, age seventy-two, Davis was telling the press that she was returning to live in Hollywood permanently. She spoke a lot about the elaborate pink mausoleum she had erected at Forest Lawn Cemetery, emphasizing that it was so situated so that it looked down directly on her old stamping grounds, the Warner lot in Burbank. She buried Ruthie there in 1961, and now her sister Bobby, dead from cancer, was duly installed in the monument. She told Mike Wallace on *60 Minutes* that it comforted her to think about the crypt reserved for her beside Ruthie and Bobby, and that one of her reasons for "staying put" in Los Angeles was to be near it, thus saving people the trouble of making "that long trip across the country with me."

To reporters who interviewed her that year, she seemed to show as practical and realistic an attitude toward death as she always had toward life, saying it had become a familiar phenomenon, with so many rela-

tives and friends dead, and that one had to make ready for it sensibly.
"But one doesn't have to sit around waiting for it, either," she added, "I
intend to go right on working. Work is my morale source. And work
keeps me from thinking too much."

As of that year, Davis seemed realistic regarding her family. Though
she claimed that she had never tried to interfere with B.D.'s affairs, she
seemed wistful because their paths had diverged and said often that she
loved B.D. more than anyone in the world. Her attitude toward Michael
and Charlene, ensconced in the Boston area, was equally resigned. She
had long since accepted the fact that he felt closer to Gary than to her,
and Gary's proximity in Maine, his political activities, his continuing
work as an actor and as a voice-over for commercials kept him busy and
happy and ready and able to visit the Michael Merrills whenever the
spirit moved him.

As Gary revealed later, he had been supporting Margot at her
school for a number of years. Davis tried to put her in a series of what
can only be called "boarding homes" in order to cut down on expenses
as her income became more uncertain. When he heard of it, Gary
tracked Margot down and put her back in the school where she had
been most happy and where she had felt most secure. By 1980 Margot
was almost thirty, and Gary recalled that when he had told Davis he
was taking her back to her old school, she yelled, "Okay, then *you* pay
for her!"

At seventy-two Davis could hardly be called a model of balance and
mellowness. There was still much she was bitter about. Michael and
Charlene dutifully visited with her, but she sensed their quiet determination to live lives of their own. B.D. and Jeremy, with their two boys
Ashley and Justin, had also drifted apart from her, though, as she noted,
whenever they needed financial help they didn't hesitate to ask. She
realized that she and Jeremy would never get along, and she had also
come to accept that B.D. had a successful marriage, had no beefs with
her husband, enjoyed motherhood and domesticity, and showed no hint
of her mother's restlessness and unease with the male sex.

In her book, *My Mother's Keeper* (1985), B.D. later recalled her
mother's mischievous attempts to set her up for adulterous involvements
when she visited her and her impatience with Jeremy's "English macho"
attitude toward his wife and family, which, B.D. declared, suited *her* just
fine. But B.D. finally lost patience when Davis tried to insinuate—without a shred of evidence—that Jeremy was cheating on her. B.D. wasn't
buying the "men are shits" line—then or ever.

Davis doubtless thought she was being revolutionary when she did

White Mama in 1980. In this CBS-TV movie, Davis co-stars with a young black actor, Ernest Harden, Jr., in a story about a down-and-out widow who is too proud for welfare and too young for social security, and who tries to augment her income by taking in a vagrant black youth in order to get a state stipend for his room and board.

Of course the two start off disliking each other intensely, and "White Mama" is the derisive epithet he throws at her. She wants him to get an education and make something of himself. He wants to win purses in boxing matches so he can take off and get away from her. Harden gets stabbed in a street fight and disappears, and Davis, penniless, becomes a bag lady wandering the streets of New York. Then they get back together, and Harden fights a match to win enough money to pay Davis's rent for a year, after which he goes in the army.

Some of Davis's friends felt she was trying to make up for having let down Dorian Harewood, the promising young black actor-singer, when she defected from the aborted *Miss Moffat* six years before by giving Ernest Harden, Jr., the benefit of her experience. But it didn't work out that way, and young Harden found that *White Mama* was not the breakthrough he had hoped for.

Part of the problem lay in the impersonal, icy script, which threw together a series of events without offering any enlightening insights into the strange juxtaposition of aged white widow and rebellious black youth.

The critic at *TV Guide* sensed the underlying trouble with the movie and noted that Davis "doesn't sentimentalize the role, but, in going so far to the opposite, hard-bitten extreme, she closes out sympathy."

IN THE LESS SOPHISTICATED 1930s, a woman as masculinely aggressive, feisty, and "ballsy" as Davis was bound to excite gossip along certain lines. Rumors about her alleged lesbianism were rife from the beginning of her career. As early as 1932, she was extravagant in her praise of Katharine Hepburn, who had just made a sensational debut in *A Bill of Divorcement* with John Barrymore. She often commented on Hepburn's high-cheeked "beauty" and expressed much curiosity about the actress's myraid friendships with women such as Laura Harding. Of course, Hepburn, too, was the subject of rumors, as she had deserted her first and only husband, socialite Ludlow Ogden Smith. She contented herself with her family and a series of women friends. Even her famous liaison with Spencer Tracy smacked of the intimacy of two male buddies rather than lovers. Circa 1936 Davis had been most anxious to

get the role of Queen Elizabeth in Hepburn's *Mary of Scotland*, but director John Ford laughed her off, and Jack Warner refused to lend her to
RKO, because he felt the role, a one-scener, was too small for her.

Davis was, it is true, more likely the object of lesbian addresses than
the instigator, as in the cases of Miriam Hopkins and Joan Crawford,
both of whom she spurned, but rumors about her and Mary Astor, dating from their appearance together in 1941's *The Great Lie*, continued to
proliferate. Decades later, while primping together in a powder room,
Liz Taylor asked Davis about Astor and Davis vigorously denied any
involvement, insisting she liked men.

Then there were Davis's friendships with such younger women as
Jane Bryan and Betty Lynn, with whom she had appeared in films, and
with whom she remained permanently friendly. She seemed to have
been more a sister or motherly figure to them, but still the rumors continued.

As late as 1979, when Davis was seventy-one, there were unfounded
rumors about her and twenty-two-year-old Kathryn Sermak, a beautiful
young woman, and by all accounts heterosexual, whom she hired as a
secretary-companion for her trip to England during *Watcher in the Woods*.
Sermak remained with Davis for ten years. Patient, understanding, and,
according to Davis, devoted as B.D. had not been, her presence and her
supportiveness seemed literally to have prolonged Davis's life.

DAVIS'S SECOND DISNEY FILM, *Watcher in the Woods*, was a confused
affair, a blend of gothic horror and science fiction, that wound up with
three endings—one original, the other two reworkings, and none of
them offering a clear resolution to the mystery.

The story is murky horror nonsense about an American composer
and his wife who come to England and rent an old estate whose owner,
the reclusive, eccentric Mrs. Aylwood (Davis), lives in the caretaker's
cottage. The couple's two children, a seventeen-year-old girl and her
ten-year-old sister, promptly become aware that something is wrong.
Strange things begin occurring—a ghostly image of a blindfolded girl in
a mirror, a light in the lake nearby, the older daughter's awareness that
someone or something is continually watching her from the woods. The
younger girl gets a puppy with the strange name Nerak—Karen spelled
backwards. Karen was Mrs. Aylwood's daughter, who disappeared in a
flash of lightning thirty years before. Davis gathers her daughter's grown
playmates together to reenact the secret society initiation in which her
daughter vanished, which results in the three aforementioned endings,

one abrupt, the second featuring a strange, shapeless creature, and the third a jumble of science-fiction special effects.

I was at the first preview of the picture in early 1980. I wrote: "Among other inanities, the final reel was not finished in time so the film ended with unseemly abruptness for preview audiences and critics— what kind of undisciplined, self-indulgent production sloppiness is this?"

Disney then sent out press releases to the effect that new endings and special effects were being tried. The picture was released with another ending late in 1980, and yet another in 1981. Audiences and critics proved equally indifferent to all three dénouements.

During 1980 and 1981, Davis gave out interviews casting her own bolts of lightning on the production, the camerawork, the writing, and her dialogue—all of which she branded as execrable. The director, John Hough, the screenwriters, Brian Clemens, Harry Spalding, and Rosemary Ann Sisson, were all excoriated, as was Technicolor photographer Alan Hume and composer Stanley Myers. Carroll Baker, David McCallum, and their onscreen girls, Lynn-Holly Johnson and Kyle Richards, the unfortunate actors involved, were somehow spared.

But Davis failed to realize that her own performance left much to be desired. I wrote in my review:

"I am second to none in my admiration for Miss Davis. But the Bette Davis of 1980 is not the Bette Davis of 1940, and it isn't age that has done it. Her work in recent years has been oddly off-kilter. Her latter-day directors have been afraid of her and she has been given too loose a rein, with the result that she has over-played, over-attitudinized and postured outlandishly. There is also something oddly unpleasant, stiff and withdrawn about her personality onscreen in recent years; it shows up in TV work of hers like *Strangers* and *White Mama*, too. Unlike Helen Hayes, who has matured benignly, Davis seems to look out at the world through baleful blue spectacles, at least in her performances."

I went on to make the point that if Davis would just relax before the camera and allow the humane, sensitive, and aware personality that graced so many of her films of the thirties and forties to shine through, she could flower in her old age, as grand old troupers like May Robson, Jessie Ralph, Alma Kruger, and others such as Helen Hayes and Lillian Gish have done. And I expressed my puzzlement that this onetime aspect of her wasn't waxing far stronger now that she was older; in fact it seemed somehow dimmed. I closed with the observation that her audiences needed the benefit of her mature insights and the accumulated wisdom of her seven decades, yet she wasn't giving them to viewers, and I wanted to know why.

After passing over Carroll Baker and David McCallum perfunctorily, Rex Reed, in his New York *Daily News* notice, continued with, "And that leaves Bette Davis, looking like Beulah Bondi with a hangover, one eye on the camera and the other eye on her paycheck."

Another *Daily News* writer, Kathleen Carroll, seemed equally baffled by Davis, and after noting that she played with "her usual flourish," went on to say that Davis was "delivering each of her lines with such biting force she tends to resemble an angry duchess who's been forced to mingle with the servants."

Carroll also observed, "[It is] a somewhat tantalizing, but ultimately ridiculous suspense movie; [it] not only completely ignores the fate of the little girl who appears in the opening sequence, it offers only a garbled explanation as to just who this creature is who likes to spy on young girls, particularly blonde teenagers."

Wherever Davis went during 1980 and 1981 she was forced to explain why she had bothered to appear in *Watcher in the Woods*. She gave many reasons: She was short of money; she thought the script was intriguing, at least on paper; she felt that with Technicolor and other production furbelows the picture might at least turn out to be "photographically handsome." And when reasonably tactful observations were offered concerning her overacting she gave out with her usual rationalization that she had to "play the damned thing larger than life to keep what audience there was from leaving the theater!"

But even she eventually conceded that the picture had been "unfortunate."

IN 1981 Davis's private and professional lives intersected briefly, when her eleven-year-old grandson, J. Ashley Hyman, made his first and only appearance with his grandmother in *Family Reunion*. NBC-TV telecast this four-hour drama over two nights in April 1981. At first it seemed a cute idea to put Ashley in his grandmother's telemovie—think of the press attention it would attract. But Bette and Ashley did not hit it off, and B.D. later said she thought his grandmother's handling of him was "old-fashioned," "cold," and "strict." While Ashley had some fun with his role, he told his parents upon his return, "Never again!" and declared his grandmother "real looney tunes" with her erratic, unpredictable behavior and sudden changes of mood. He was also disconcerted by her quarrels with fellow actors, and the prima donna attitudes he had never before encountered firsthand.

In this movie Davis is a retired schoolteacher who has never married and is something of an institution in her new England town. The usual villainous conglomerate wants to tear up sections of Winfield, as the town is named, to build a shopping mall. Davis gets an unlimited-fare bus ticket and goes around the country rallying members of the Winfield clan (her family founded the town) to show some family spirit and return en masse to defeat the forces of crass commerce. All ends well, of course.

Variety labeled it "not a family portrait. It's a cattle call" (whatever *that* meant). Other critics noted Davis's usual stiff posturings and cold demeanor, and young Ashley was patted on the back as "pleasing" and "self-assured." *Family Reunion* was one of those projects that Davis had been promised might develop as a weekly series, but, as in other cases, nothing came of it.

The whole experience dampened J. Ashley Hyman's acting ambitions permanently.

THE YEAR 1982 brought Bette Davis's finest performance of the 1980s, a television movie called *A Piano for Mrs. Cimino*. As Esther Cimino, a music teacher who has reached retirement age, Davis finds that her mental faculties are slipping somewhat. The picture is a trenchant, realistic study of the ravages and displacements, socially, physically, and mentally, that are visited upon a once-proud, sensitive, and still highly intelligent woman who is declared mentally incompetent by her children. She is subjected to a hearing, where her blurred responses prompt the judge to put her in a nursing home, and she begins to deteriorate. However, a granddaughter who loves her rouses her back to life and helps her learn how to live again. Not that she needs all that much rousing, for this is a proud, spunky, resilient woman who gradually wins back her life, her self-respect, and control over her circumstances. Keenan Wynn (who was sixty-six to Davis's seventy-four when he made *Cimino* but managed, through his own considerable art, to suggest a much older man) is affecting as the musician who meets her in the nursing home, and with whom she begins a galvanizing semi–love affair.

The part met the woman here. Davis put into *A Piano for Mrs. Cimino* all her own valor in the face of advancing age and physical attrition. She is in perfect control here, seems to feel the part, to actually live it.

The New York Times said of her in this: "Miss Davis plays Mrs. Cimino with reserve, intelligence, and suitable irascibility, and her initial senility is convincing, too."

Keenan Wynn later told me: "The pluck of that woman! I could see that her health was not the best but she never complained, was always cheering us on!"

CIRCA 1982, the television movies were coming thick and fast for Davis. In *Little Gloria, Happy At Last,* an NBC-TV two-part movie that aired in October 1982, Davis starred as Alice Gwynne Vanderbilt, Gloria Vanderbilt's formidable grandmother. The story, based on Barbara Goldsmith's best-seller, deals with Gloria's difficult coming-of-age when, at eleven, she was a pawn in a custody battle between her sybaritic mother and her aunt, played by Angela Lansbury. Maureen Stapleton, Christopher Plummer, and Glynis Johns also graced this fine cast.

Davis won a Supporting Actress Emmy nomination for this stint, even though her strong role was brief and her character died before the first of the two parts ended. She does her standard bit as the frosty, haughty, domineering matriarch of the Vanderbilt clan, putting across some strong, biting confrontational scenes. She looks majestic and every bit her seventy-four years here, with lined, haggard face, large veiled and sequined hats, beaded, laced dresses, and choker and pearls.

Reviews cross-country were uniform, calling her "strong," "forceful," "formidable," "keeps you thinking about her straight through Part II, even though her character has died," and so on. *Variety's* critic questioned the taste of the entire enterprise with, "Getting a look at all those pearls, fishknives and furs, and watching Bette Davis get a shot at being imperious again probably makes the venture amusing, but the telefilm, with its awkward exposition and sensationalism . . . pokes around in lots of areas that seem better left undusted."

Angela Lansbury, a tolerant and relaxed woman in private life, spoke well of Bette, with whom she had a number of scenes. "She knows what she wants to do," she said, "and she wants a professional atmosphere. I had no problems with her, and I parted from her at the end of shooting with a great respect for her discipline and willingness to work."

The years 1981 through 1983 were for Davis a pleasant mélange of honors for her acting, some TV work, and lively social events. Settled permanently in Hollywood in a pleasant apartment filled with mementos of her past, Davis was no recluse and went out often to dinners, screenings, and parties, accompanied by good friends like Roddy McDowall, whom she described as "a kind compassionate man who always makes me laugh and still shows his national origin, being an English gentleman through and through."

In 1981 Davis was delighted with the success of the song "Bette Davis Eyes," written by Donna Weiss and Jackie DeShannon, which is about a forceful blond actress who has led a glamorous and successful life. The lyrics are witty and charming, and Davis found the entire concept flattering and amusing. Singer Kim Carnes won considerable fame as a rock singer after she recorded this, and the song itself went on to win a Grammy as Best Song of 1981. Kim and Bette got together at a party where they toasted the song's success in champagne. Davis told interviewers, "My grandson has finally sat up and taken notice of me. He loves the song and goes around saying he now realizes how famous Grandma is!"

Davis admitted she missed New England at times but liked the swirl and excitement of Hollywood life, and even began to entertain old and new friends at the West Hollywood townhouse that she had recently taken. Her old friend Joan Blondell told Mike Wallace in 1980 that it was good for Davis to be back in her old stamping grounds, that the atmosphere gave her strength. And of course work offers poured in constantly, mostly from TV, and this kept her in good spirits. By 1982 she was feeling so well that she even ventured a few plane trips East to visit relatives and friends there, but continued to say that Los Angeles—and the loved ones in the mausoleum at Forest Lawn—was her "final stop."

Another old friend, Ginger Rogers, who bore her then-seventy-one years lightly, appeared with Davis at the historic, memory-filled Cocoanut Grove nightclub in 1982, where Davis received the American Movie Award in honor of her fifty-four years in show business. She and Ginger later had dinner together, full of good spirits and plans, and even began planning a benefit appearance together in Paris at the Olympia Theatre. But this never materialized because Davis did not feel she was up to a six-thousand-mile plane journey. Katharine Hepburn came up in the conversation and they recalled how they had both wanted to play the small but telling role of Queen Elizabeth in Hepburn's *Mary of Scotland* back in 1936. "Certainly we both look old enough to play her *now!*" Ginger laughed. "We wouldn't need any makeup either!" With a graciousness people found atypical of her, Davis replied, "I could play her—you still look too young, Ginger!"

Also in 1982, an amusing memento of Davis's past reappeared in the shape of a statue called "Spring" that Davis had posed for as a teenager in Massachusetts. People were startled when they found out she had posed for it *nude*. "Virginal, protected teenage Bette Davis posing for a nude statue? Why it sounds like something out of Marlene Dietrich's *The Song of Songs!*" one of Davis's Hollywood friends laughed. (In that 1933 film, Dietrich, with sexy abandon, had posed naked for sculptor Brian Aherne.) Word of the Davis statue set in motion a great "Bette Davis Statue Hunt" all around Massachusetts. It was discovered that it had stood in the midst of a fountain in a square near Boston, but there had been a crusade to remove its "shameless nakedness," and it had disappeared into a warehouse. It was finally traced to the Museum of Fine Arts. Retitled "Young Diana," it languished in a back room. Careful study of the statue by museum experts established its authenticity. Indeed it *was* teenage Bette Davis! Asked about it in far-off Hollywood, Davis laughed and said, "It represented me at an uncharacteristically rebellious moment. If I had known then what I know now, I'd have broken some other rules, too—lots of them!"

In April 1982 Mayor Tom Bradley of Los Angeles officially announced Bette Davis Day, April 3, two days before her seventy-fourth birthday. At that time one honor was following another—she said she didn't have room for all the plaques and citations she was receiving. B.D. remembered Davis saying she was sick of all those awards, they were a nuisance and a bother. She had to dress up and go down to some place and smile at people and express her thanks. With her customary directness B.D. suggested that she simply pack them away or throw them out if they were such a bother, and Davis drew herself up and declared that if people were kind enough to show her honor, she in turn should treat their citations with respect. End of subject!

In 1982 alone, Davis was honored with the Film Advisory Board's Lifetime Achievement Award, the first Golden Reel Trophy from the National Film Society, and the Valentino Award (Burt Reynolds was the male recipient), given in memory of Rudolph Valentino (1895–1926). In their tribute the donors stated that this award was a special salute to stars who had "persevered and endured."

In early 1983 Davis and perennial companion Roddy McDowall were among the more glittering guests at the banquet honoring Queen Elizabeth II during her American visit. It was held at Twentieth Century–Fox Studios, and Davis got almost as much attention, Roddy later recalled, as the queen.

Shortly after this, Davis was particularly happy to receive a Defense Department award for her work with the Hollywood Canteen during World War II. At the ceremony, her hard work on bond-selling tours was also acknowledged. On hand with her were such other honorees as

Bob Hope, who had made many tours overseas to entertain servicemen, and Martha Raye, who was honored for her work in Vietnam.

There was much celebration for Davis's seventy-fifth birthday on April 5, 1983, and she went to numerous parties and luncheons. She seemed to thrive on all the attention, all the reminiscing, and she talked freely and joyously to any reporters who wanted to interview her.

In the spring of 1983 during one of these sessions, she set forth her attitudes toward life and her career at age seventy-five. She acknowledged that young married people such as Michael and Charlene Merrill had adjustments to make and should be left in peace. She said she tried to steer a middle course between reminding her children of her existence with calls, gifts, and occasional visits, and leaving them to what she called "their reality" as against "my reality." Philosophically, she maintained that her life was drawing to a close and that she had learned the truth of the adage: "Accept wisely the counsel of the years, surrendering gracefully the things of youth." When asked if she had given up on romantic love, a shadow crossed her face, she sat pensively for a minute, then said, "I accept the realities of my years—yes. . . . All that is gone now, for good."

IN THE FALL of 1982 Davis appeared with James Stewart in their first movie together, *Right of Way*. It was shown during 1983 as an HBO cable television production.

George Schaefer directed the Richard Lee script, and Davis, not in the least put off by the fact the picture would not be a theatrical release, began referring to it as the answer to Henry Fonda and Katharine Hepburn's *On Golden Pond*, which had won them both the 1981 Oscar. There was, however, little relation between the plots of *On Golden Pond* and *Right of Way*. Stewart and Davis play an elderly couple who decide to commit suicide together after they learn that she is terminally ill.

Both Davis and Stewart were saddened by Henry Fonda's death that year (he had been one of Stewart's closest friends) and when they worked particularly hard on a scene and felt it went well, Jimmy whispered, "this was for you, Hank!"

In *Right of Way* Davis plays Miniature Dwyer, her unusual first name coming from her mother, who was making miniature doll houses when Minnie was born. Minnie, too, has built doll houses for years, and when she and Teddy Dwyer (Stewart) begin planning their joint suicide, she makes sure that her dolls are placed with people who will appreciate and cherish them. The couple refuse to allow their grief-stricken daughter

(Melinda Dillon) or the solicitous social worker or anyone else to fore-stall the death they are determined is right for them, so in the end they die together in the family car of carbon monoxide poisoning.

It is the precise, ordered, matter-of-fact objectivity displayed by the couple that vitiates this film's impact. It lacks the emotion and poignancy that, properly orchestrated, make for a moving and cathartic experience.

Davis's performance, especially, is much too detached and icy. She deprives her character of any sympathy. Stewart, on the other hand, makes his character human and understandable. Humble, down-to-earth, quietly determined to accompany the wife he loves into their last adventure, Stewart was the essence of kindly realism. But even he is hampered by the impersonal, methodical quality of Lee's script and Schaefer's direction. Obviously, everyone feared that the picture would sink into a morass of sentimental bathos and that the plight of these two old people might be limned as Hollywoodishly maudlin. Unfortunately, the net result goes to the other extreme and comes across as uninvolving and cold.

After receiving a Best Actress testimonial from the International Television Festival in early 1983 for her performance in *A Piano for Mrs. Cimino*, Davis took on a new television series, *Hotel*, which became a long-running success (four years) and made permanent television stars out of James Brolin and Connie Sellecca. Davis was set to play Laura Trent, the owner of a San Francisco hotel. Her part would run through the series, though she asked that her appearances be limited to nine episodes per season, feeling that, at seventy-five, she could not sustain a more intense workload.

Davis started work on *Hotel* in April. But after filming only two episodes, she visited her doctor, Vincent Carroll, complaining of a breast lump and a circulatory dysfunction. When her lawyer, Harold Schiff, learned that hospitalization would be necessary, he recommended that she go to Manhattan's New York Hospital—Cornell Medical Center, as it was near his office and apartment, and the hospitalization, in his view, could more easily be kept secret from the press.

The breast lump was found to be malignant, and a mastectomy was performed. Davis remained in the hospital for testing on the circulatory disorder. Shortly after, she suffered three strokes in a row. She had been in the hospital for weeks when she began to suffer severe attacks of chronic itching. B.D. learned from Dr. Vincent Carroll that Davis's drinking was causing the itching, but Davis prohibited any discussion of her smoking or drinking habits.

Ever more intractable, she heaped abuse and obscenities on the staff and the therapists who worked on her limb and circulatory disorders. And she began to recover, she grew more temperamental. Kathryn Sermak was exhausted by her demands, and B.D. began to dread visiting her. Soon therapists refused to work with her as she was so difficult. She would throw dinner trays on the floor, holler with high-decibel impatience at all comers, and make a thorough nuisance of herself. Later in the summer of 1983 Davis was pronounced fit for discharge but she insisted on remaining in the hospital for weeks longer, claiming she knew better than anyone else her true condition.

B.D. recalled one occasion when Davis had been screaming at her helpers. Her room was in a shambles, she flicked cigarette ash over her bed, shouted orders and commands with ever more frenetic restlessness. Then word came that a handsome young doctor, who had nothing to do with her case but was an admirer of hers and liked to drop in, was about to pay one of his periodic visits.

The transformation in the hospital room was dramatic. Davis had her hair brushed, she perfumed and dolled herself up, moved to a chair, rearranged her features into an expression of martyred composure, and was utterly charming with the handsome pup in the white coat. According to B.D. she was every inch the great star, the consummate survivor, talking with chin-up bravery about her condition and referring to her daughter's "beautiful farm" and how she hoped she'd see it again soon. The young doctor expressed his admiration and made a respectful withdrawal, at which time it was back to Madame Hyde time, and the screaming and ash-scattering and general disorder started up all over again.

Eventually Davis was persuaded to leave the hospital and the handsome young doctor and repair to the Lombardy Hotel, where she rested for some time before returning to her West Hollywood townhouse. A friend later said that Davis's behavior with the doctor convinced her that even at seventy-five, she still hadn't given up on romance, and that her actressy declaration to the press about "surrendering gracefully the things of youth" was her usual brand of public relations hogwash.

All was well as 1983 progressed, but back in West Hollywood Davis fell and broke a hip. A fresh period of disablement ensued, and her temper was worse than ever. But, as usual, when in the company of Robert Wagner or other friends from the show-business world, she was the soul of dignified behavior.

Though hundreds of thousands of dollars were involved—money she desperately needed—she abruptly informed Aaron Spelling that she would not be returning to *Hotel*, and that as far as she was concerned that episode in her life was over. There were reports that in exchange for release from her *Hotel* commitment, she would star at a later date in one of Spelling's television movies. Her reasons for walking out on her lucrative *Hotel* commitment were, as usual, complex and dichotomous. She claimed she hated the scripts, thought them "garbage." She felt, also, that Brolin and Sellecca were the real stars because they were "young and cute" and that she, with all her hard-won expertise, was being "cameo-ized" and "downgraded" and "pushed aside." Whatever the reasons, *Hotel* was definitely a thing of her past by early 1984.

In October 1984, after nearly two years without work, Davis flew to England with Kathryn Sermak to do a television movie, *Murder With Mirrors*, in which she would co-star with Helen Hayes. John Mills, Leo McKern, Liane Langland, and Dorothy Tutin were also in the cast.

Helen Hayes had the actual lead, playing the legendary Agatha Christie detective Miss Marple. In one of Christie's more popular mysteries, adapted by George Eckstein, Miss Marple visits the ancestral home of an old friend. Among the guests are several suspicious characters, one of whom commits a murder. The shocked and horrified hostess has more faith in Marple's ability to solve the murder than she has in the police's methods. Davis has a distinctly secondary role as an aged dowager who comments on the proceedings, which puzzle and annoy her mightily.

What with the mastectomy, stroke, and then a broken hip from which she had recently recovered, Davis was nervous about the long flight and the five weeks of shooting in the misty English climate. But she weathered it nicely, commuting from the Savoy Hotel to the set daily. She had long talks with Mills, McKern, and Tutin and felt comfortable and relaxed, except for some problems with makeup and costuming.

Davis claimed that she and Hayes did not work together until near the end of Davis's shooting schedule, and then had scenes for only a day or two. According to her, Hayes wrote a cordial letter expressing her pleasure in working with her for the first time, and she and Sermak selected a gift for her, an antique mirror on which she had "H.H. from B.D." engraved.

She seemed to respond well to Dick Lowry's direction, and she said later that he and the adapter, George Eckstein, went out of their way to be accommodating.

Murder With Mirrors, telecast in 1985, is standard Christie, with reasonable suspense elements, but nothing calculated to advance either Davis's or Hayes's careers.

In a 1988 interview, Helen Hayes gave her own version of what it was like to work with Bette Davis in *Murder With Mirrors*.

"Dear Bette Davis," she purred. "I love her, admire her and I certainly admire her work. But that time, she seemed determined to make life difficult for us all!"

Hayes continued, "She started by snapping at me the first day. I said, 'Good morning,' and she looked right through me. Later, when the cast gathered for introductions, our eyes met, and I waved. 'What's that mean?' she snapped. 'I was saying good morning,' I answered. 'You already did that!' she snapped back."

Coming to the defense of her longtime close friend Lillian Gish, Hayes added, "While Bette Davis has indeed always been one of my idols, she did make mincemeat out of poor Lillian when they made *The Whales of August*, a lovely picture. Lillian swears she'll never act again [whether with Davis or with anyone, ever, Hayes did not make clear]. So first she drove *me* from the screen, now she's driven Lillian. She's making a clean sweep of everyone our age!

"When the film was over, I asked John Mills, who was in it, if he'd enjoyed himself. 'I was never so scared in my life,' he said. 'And I was in the war!'"

Hayes's anger toward Davis is unusual coming from her, as she is balanced and sweet-natured in her dealings with most people. She has said that at eighty-eight she isn't going to get her blood pressure up unnecessarily fussing and feuding. Davis obviously goaded her into suspending her usual rules.

During 1986, while struggling off and on with a new autobiography, aided by writer Michael Herskowitz (it was rejected by one publisher as lacking bite and honesty and inside material of a lively nature), Davis ventured on an HBO movie for television called *As Summers Die*. In this she is an eccentric lady in a small town in the 1950s South, who helps lawyer Scott Glenn defend a poor, underprivileged, black woman. Jamie Lee Curtis is on hand as her niece.

The 90-minute film was shown in 1986, and garnered some respectful but restrained reviews, with one critic declaring:

"Bette Davis is always touching and honest when she is sincere about what she is trying to get across, and in *As Summers Die*, her liberal beliefs in civil rights and equality of opportunity and human respect for all are given a thorough, and wholesome showcase. And more power to her!"

During the making of *As Summers Die*, Davis found it necessary to pace herself, as this was only her second television movie after her serious illnesses, and at times she tended to overdo. Scott Glenn and

Jamie Lee Curtis both publicly commended her durability and courage in 1986 interviews, and she, in turn, pronounced them thorough professionals who were "delights" to work with.

WITH KATHRYN SERMAK'S help she had found a spacious eight-room apartment in West Hollywood, near Sunset Boulevard. There was nothing pretentious about the place or the neighborhood, which was nondescript. In a foyer, near her terrace, she kept her two Oscars and other trophies. Ashtrays and cigarette cases were all over the place. She had problems with help, going through cooks, butlers, secretaries at a fast clip. Taylor Pero, who, like the others, lasted an average of a week, found her testy, nervous, abrupt. "No," he said, was her favorite word, on the phone and in person, and No finally got to him.

BETTE DAVIS AND LILLIAN GISH made a strange pair indeed when they co-starred in *The Whales of August*, her first theatrical film in seven years. It was shot for eight weeks on location in Maine in the fall of 1986 and was released a full year later. At the time they made it Lillian Gish was ninety and Davis was seventy-eight, yet Gish played the *younger* sister. She looked younger, too, as Davis's assorted illnesses and the considerable weight loss she had sustained left her looking ravaged.

Playing with them were Vincent Price, Ann Sothern, Harry Carey, Jr., and Mary Steenburgen, with Tisha Sterling playing her mother, Ann Sothern, as a girl.

In his October 16, 1987, review, the *New York Times* critic called *The Whales of August* "a cinema event, though small in scale and commonplace in detail," adding, "It's as moving for all the history it recalls as for anything that happens on the screen." Earlier he had said of the Gish-Davis combine that they "together exemplify American films from 1914 to the present." Gish, who had spanned the silent and sound eras, becoming a star in Griffith's 1915 *Birth of a Nation*, went on to starring roles in the 1920s that made her, for a time, the screen's most prestigious star. Her later career in sound films brought her added fame as a character actress and won her, in 1970, a special Oscar.

In *Whales*, Davis and Gish are two elderly sisters who have vacationed in Maine for decades. Davis is crabby, withdrawn—and blind. Gish is sunny, outgoing, and solicitous. They interact with their own brands of sarcasm and putdown, though Davis's is the sharper and meaner. "Busy-busy-busy," she crabs at Gish, whose forbearance and humorous flexibility approach the saintly as she applies herself night and day to making her disabled but unappreciative sister comfortable. Price is on hand as a Russian émigré of aristocratic pretensions who is put down in short order by Davis. Ann Sothern is a friend and neighbor, sunny and ebullient, and Harry Carey, Jr., is present as a perennial handyman. There are flashbacks to their youth—old loves and old regrets are paraded—and Gish's memories are more enriching and consoling to her because she is a widow of philosophical bent. Her life is serene while Davis's is dark and withdrawn. Most of the action is centered on the installation of a window that will give a picture-frame view of the bay: Gish wants it; Davis doesn't. She prefers their closed-in life just as it is. So slight is the story line, that the dénouement involves Davis's assent to the installation of the window.

This lack of action makes the film a strangely uninvolving, tepid affair. Most of the critical huzzahs seemed to come as kudos to the film history the two stars represent and the legendary quality of their famous faces. The picture itself, its story, its direction, its photography were shunted into secondary coverage—where, frankly, it belonged.

Lindsay Anderson directed, from a David Berry screenplay based on his play.

Most of the publicity (the picture being so forgettable) centered around how Davis and Gish got along—and the reports were not good. Davis started the ball rolling by demanding first billing, which Gish agreed to without demur. Then, as one writer put it, "Bette flew into Maine on a four-jet broomstick." The setting might have been Casco Bay but the atmosphere became Witchway-dour. Davis was distant and cold with Gish from first to last. Often she wouldn't even look at her and played out their scenes as if in a vacuum.

Hurt at first, Gish resorted to sympathy and concern that to an enraged Davis emerged as lofty condescension. Gish's references to Davis did not help, either: "That face! Have you ever seen such a tragic face? Poor woman! How she must be suffering! I don't think it's right to judge a person like that. We must bear and forbear."

Irritated with the "bear and forbear" sweetness-and-light attitude Gish had adopted, Davis waited to get in her innings. When someone commented how wonderful Gish had been in a close-up, she snapped, "She ought to know about close-ups. Jesus, she was around when they invented them! The bitch has been around forever, you know!"

Even Gish had her breaking point, and soon she was jabbing back, only her technique was stiletto to Davis's meat-cleaver. "I just can't hear her," she commented helplessly to director Anderson, forcing Davis to speak louder. But onscreen their contrasting personalities somehow registered to good effect. One writer waxed flowery about the Davis-Gish juxtaposition: "Bette crawls across the screen like a testy old hornet on a windowpane, snarling, staggering, twitching—a symphony of misfiring synapses. Lillian's performance is as clear and simple as a drop of water filled with sunlight."

Of the two performances, Gish's is the better. She is open, honest, clear in her technique; she gets across much compassion, humanity— and resignation—in her performance. And in one scene in which she is recalling her lost husband, she offers a deeply moving rendition of aged loneliness evoking happier days.

Director Lindsay Anderson found Davis a trial to direct and didn't mind telling the world. He recalled testily that when he tried to help her portrayal by suggesting she read a line differently or employ a more emphatic gesture, she would snap, "That's nonsense!" Lindsay later opined: "I think [Davis] sees the world as the enemy, and you have to go through a process with her." He ascribed her intractable prickliness "part to temperament and part to the experience of having to fight all those years in Hollywood."

When I interviewed him concerning the film in the fall of 1987, Anderson did a variation of what Irving Rapper had said years before. Rapper had snapped "Tough!" when I asked him what it was like to direct Bette Davis. Thirty years later, Anderson said crisply, "Difficult. Very difficult."

Davis showed her disdain for Gish in other ways. When a preview of the film was held in New York on Gish's ninety-first birthday, Davis was absent. "Let *her* hog the attention!" she told a reporter in Los Angeles, three thousand miles from what she called "the Gish event." Both ladies were deeply disappointed at not getting Academy Award nominations. To their great surprise, a supporting nomination for the film went to Ann Sothern, whose role, while hearty and humorous and vital, was rather peripheral to the main action. Later, with a cattiness that for once had more subtle overtones, Davis said she thought Sothern had gotten the nomination because people in Hollywood felt sorry for her because she had been crippled by a bad fall.

Davis did not think well of *Whales of August*. She thought the title (which refers to the disappearance of the whales from the Maine coast) "awkward and obscure" and said the story as written was not strong enough to allow her a meaningful characterization.

Many feel that if, in the years 1986 through 1989, Bette Davis had spent just one tenth as much time on acting as she did on peregrinating between Europe, New York, and Hollywood, partying, accepting awards, and giving endless interviews to the press on anything and everything, she might have given at least four image-enhancing performances that would have made her a candidate for good parts.

After B. D. Hyman's *My Mother's Keeper* emerged in 1985, with a frank recounting by B.D. of her mother's darker side, Davis turned into a whirling dervish of largely profitless activity, backed up and supported as always by her faithful sidekick Kathryn Sermak, and cheered on by her contingent of loyal friends and admirers, including Robert Wagner, Roddy McDowall, and columnist Robert Osborne of *The Hollywood Reporter*, a helpful and compassionate man, who kept her comings and goings continually before his readership.

In 1987 Davis was out with her book, *This 'n' That*, a second autobiography of a sort following upon the 1962 *The Lonely Life.* Disjointed and superficial, the book conceals more than it reveals about her recent life, but she did respond to B.D.'s criticism, commenting on her generosity to her and her husband in tough times and calling B.D. a great purveyor of fiction.

Gary Merrill joined the Bette-book sweepstakes in 1988, and while castigating B.D. for her attacks on her mother, proceeded to make some of his own, reminding the world that he had paid for Margot's schooling since 1965 and commenting that Davis kept her distance from her and from her grandchildren by Michael and Charlene Merrill. One gossip columnist called Gary's book *Wifey Dearest*.

A cute commercial for Equal sweetener, a dietary sugar substitute, was made by Davis in November 1988, and aired in the first months of 1989. Lip-synching the distinctive Davis voice is a little girl of no more than ten, done up in a Margo Channing hairdo and gown and lipsticked and rouged à la the original. She is sitting in imperious command at a restaurant table and orders a waiter to bring her "the finest chianti." When he asks for her driver's license she tells him to bring her iced tea instead. When he asks how she likes it, she tells him, in true grande-dame style, "I'm letting it breathe!"

DURING 1988 AND 1989, *Wicked Stepmother*, known as "The Bette Davis Picture That Wasn't," created a great deal of fuss and feathers. References to it appeared in columns and magazine and newspaper articles at the rate of one every other day.

Davis started shooting it in May 1988, then quit after one week to go to New York for dental surgery. After that, she took off for Europe, sending word that her health would not permit her to resume for a while. She said that after the surgery she had sustained severe weight loss—from eighty-eight to seventy-five pounds. Soon Davis declared that she had decided to withdraw altogether from the film because director Larry Cohen was concentrating too much on the camera effects and not enough on her. She also said he made her look "terrible." "People will be horrified at the footage on me," she declared. "For the good of my future in films I had no choice but to withdraw."

Blind to the fact that even before the weight loss she had looked like a skeletal gargoyle ("*Of Human Bondage's* Mildred: Age 80," as one commentator put it unkindly but accurately), she blamed Cohen and his photographer, saying, "I'm not a vain person [really!] but at eighty years old I don't want to look the way I looked. It seriously could be the end of anybody ever hiring me again!"

Larry Cohen proved to be a patient man, his patience doubtless sweetened by the waves of publicity the project was receiving thanks to Davis's loud complaining.

After it became apparent that Davis would not under any circumstances be persuaded to fulfill her commitment for an additional two weeks of filming, Larry Cohen rewrote the script, utilizing the roughly twenty minutes of film Davis had shot to accord her a "cameo" role as a wicked witch who marries herself into a family of innocents and proceeds to wreak all kinds of mayhem. In the earlier version she metamorphosed a household cat into ravishing Barbara Carrera. Davis's loss turned out to be Carrera's gain, for in the updated script Davis *becomes* Carrera, who then goes on playing her part throughout.

Cohen's publicity cake was further sweetened when he revealed that the insurance company had paid him a handsome million dollars to compensate him for Davis's precipitate exit. Many in New York and Hollywood felt that Davis made a serious mistake in walking out. "She should have finished the film no matter how much she disliked her role or the way she was handled. Then she could have bitched about it to high heaven afterward without getting herself labeled a quitter," one commentator noted.

Davis complained that Cohen had ignored her suggestions on how she should play her role and said that when she saw the rushes she was horrified by her performance and her appearance. Columnists had a field day for months with the Cohen-Davis feud, with Cohen underplaying beautifully, calling her a wonderful woman and a fighter whom he greatly respected. He claimed that he had written the role especially for Davis, and that if she had seen the completed picture with her role amplified as he had planned, she would have been more sanguine about it. Cohen also got the last word: "Many people give Bette Davis dinners and awards but very few give her jobs. I gave her a job!" The film finally made videocassettes in November 1989.

25

The Lioness in Winter

As of 1989 Davis was a frequent print subject. Her appearance continued to arouse much concern, as her face looked ghoulishly skeletal under the garish makeup and flashy blond wig. The awards kept coming in—a Kennedy Center tribute in late 1987 which she felt had been withheld for years because of her liberal Democratic convictions. (Whenever they had sent her a questionnaire asking for her recommendation of a winner, she had always written in: "Me!") In between bouts with Larry Cohen over *Wicked Stepmother*, she managed, in summer 1988, to wing off to the Villa d'Este in northern Italy, where she picked up yet another award for her artistic achievements at Campione Casino, near Lake Como. In April 1989 she was at last honored by the Film Society of Lincoln Center with a lavish tribute followed by a VIP party at Tavern on the Green. Earlier in 1989 she was honored, with Clint Eastwood and Julio Iglesias, at the American Cinema Awards in Hollywood, which benefited the Motion Picture Country Home and Hospital. At this last function, she alarmed her friends and fans by fainting briefly. Liz Smith revealed that after all these decades she had finally added longtime friend Olivia De Havilland to her crowded enemies list because, Davis claimed, Olivia had "upstaged" her when she got a French government tribute in 1987.

A more ominous note was struck when a tabloid detailed her afflictions: a hip that had failed to heal properly and that kept her in constant pain; a sapping of her strength that had her wondering if she could ever work again; her disappointment over getting no solid job offers; her dashed hopes of playing the cosmetician Helena Rubinstein, a role she insisted she was "born" to create.

Davis's estrangement from her family (completely on the outs with B.D.; cordial but distant with Michael in far-off Boston) continued apace. Margot was essentially out of thought and out of mind by then, Gary's responsibility, with $15,000 per year paid by him to Lochland School for her care. Her apartment with its mementos and New England furnishings was still a West Hollywood rallying place for friends and fans—to a point—but as one friend reported, "She's not even tending to her patio garden anymore, something that used to give her so much pleasure . . . she's gotten to the point where she's almost unreachable. She doesn't want anyone in her life."

And then the friend added, "It's like she's holed up in her house just waiting to die."

Unmentioned in the public prints was the cancer that was steadily eating away at her.

She remained close to daughterly and faithful Kathryn Sermak, but realized that at thirty-three Kathryn had a life of her own. And so she kept the reins loose. She had learned, the hard way, the truth of Mrs. Aphra Behn's famous lines: "I hold my love but lightly, for things with wings held tightly, want to fly."

Those who watched and waited felt that Bette Davis's thoughts were often on the beautiful spot in Forest Lawn where Ruthie and Bobby lay. Two of the four husbands (Ham Nelson and Arthur Farnsworth) who had brought her so much grief had preceded her into the Beyond.

The handsome young men whose love she sought even into her sixties were now but dim memories. Though hurt by them, she continued to maintain, right to the end, that it was better to lead with one's heart and get wounded, than to close up and withdraw, for when one did that, one was no longer alive.

She still had fans, but their adoration, their persistence, their obsession with her and her legend had taken on the quality of a tale told once too often. The friends were there to the end, but they could not truly penetrate her ever-deepening solitude, that profound aloneness that she had predicted for herself decades before as her final chapter.

But there was to be one final hurrah. In September 1989 she left Hollywood for the 37th San Sebastian International Film Festival, where she was to receive an award. Later her attorney, Harold Schiff, told the world that the breast cancer she had been weathering since her 1983 mastectomy had recurred, was metastasizing, and was terminal. "The doctors said," he added, "let her go on going about her business."

Davis's good friend Robert Osborne, the *Hollywood Reporter* columnnist, went along with her desire to put up a brave front for press and public. In his September 1 column he quoted her as saying, "I hope this will prove to the world I'm not dying. The only thing that's making me sick are all those awful reports and rumors about how ill I'm supposed to be. Where do they start? And how do you get them to stop?"

V. A. Musetto, the *New York Post* film critic, was in San Sebastian on September 22 and described her thus: "She was a tiny, pencil-thin old woman who had trouble walking unassisted. But she still had the unmistakable look of a Hollywood queen. Bedecked in a sequined purple gown, she emerged from her car in front of the Victoria Eugenia Theater. In the background could be heard the sounds of police firing tear gas at protesters, who in turn were lobbing bottles and rocks at the cops. But the residents of San Sebastian paid little attention to the street fighting, which these days is a common occurrence in the hotbed of the Basque separatist movement.

"Besides," Musetto added, "Their minds were really on that fragile 81-year-old woman."

"Bette! Bette!" The Spaniards' shouting was—it was obvious to all present—music to her ears. Inside the theater, puffing away furiously on her cigarette, she spread out her arms and shouted back over and over again, despite the effort it evidently cost her, "Muchas gracias! Muchas gracias!"

The next night, when she presented a festival award to Andrei Konchalovsky for his film *Homer and Eddie,* the director made a gesture that delighted the audience. He went down on his knees before her to accept. Onlookers recalled later that this spontaneous token of his esteem seemed to touch her deeply.

At another point she held a press conference, at which "more than 400 of the world's journalists gave her a standing ovation," according to Musetto. She told the assembled reporters that she loved her work, wanted always, always to act. Her favorite roles were those in *Dark Victory, Jezebel, Now, Voyager, All About Eve,* and *What Ever Happened to Baby Jane?* She didn't think Ronald Reagan much of an actor but felt he had been "very good" as president and "made us all very patriotic." Of her

Right of Way co-star Jimmy Stewart she said, "If I had met him way, way back, he would never have escaped me, but it's too late now." Relatively gentle with Joan Crawford, she called another co-star, Miriam Hopkins "a bitch. Impossible to work with." She hated colorization of her old films, called it "heartbreaking." And she thought Hollywood's current movies "very sad."

Elated by her Spanish reception, she then set off for Paris, accompanied by faithful companion Kathy Sermak. During the journey, people who saw her felt she was still shaking up busily the dimming embers of what had been a fiery, furnacelike eighty-one years. Old age, as she had often declared, was not for sissies. But when she reached Paris, her strength compeltely failed her, and Kathy rushed her to the American Hospital.

For some time she lingered. Liz Smith and other columnists in the know kept her condition a secret. What she had to do she wanted to do alone, without reporters and other intruders.

"Accommodation to life's inescapable realities is not surrender," she had said, at twenty-eight, in London fifty-three years before, when she realized she would have to go back to fulfill her Warner contract after the hard-fought court battle that she had lost. And late on the night of Friday, October 6, 1989, in Paris—three thousand miles away from the city in Massachusetts where she was born eighty-one years before, six thousand miles away from the Hollywood of her triumphs—Bette Davis, feisty and realistic to the end, accommodated.

When the news broke the next day, the press accorded her a send-off that would have made her very proud. She was front-page news, and the encomiums were deservedly lavish.

Harold Schiff and Michael Merrill made arrangements to ship her body back to Hollywood, where her funeral was held on October 12 at Forest Lawn Memorial Park, with the Reverend Robert M. Bock of the First Christian Church in North Hollywood officiating. The private service was attended by no more than twenty-five family members and close friends. The marble sarcophagus, marked DAVIS and bearing a statue of a woman that B.D. claimed was modeled after her (B.D.'s) face and figure, had now seen three interments. Bette, Ruthie, and Bobby were at last reunited.

Kathryn Sermak, Robert Wagner, George Schaefer (who directed her in *Right of Way*), and others later organized a public memorial service at a sound stage on the Warner Brothers lot attended by all the people in Hollywood who knew and loved Davis. The devoted Robert Osborne commented, "It's no accident that [Bette] chose as her final resting place a plot of Forest Lawn that overlooks the Burbank Studios and all those soundstages where she churned out the good work for eighteen years."

A month after her death, Davis's will was published. Daughter B.D. was totally cut out of it, as was Margot. B.D.'s sons were also snubbed. The estate, valued at between $600,000 and a million, was divided equally between Kathryn Sermak and Michael Merrill. Some small bequests were made to her niece Faye Forbes, childhood friend Robin Brown, and Mrs. Michael Merrill. The general assumption regarding the unfortunate Margot was that Davis had arranged for Michael to assume her expenses. (Gary Merrill, Michael's father, by then in his seventies, had paid Margot's fees for years.)

Attempting to explain why Davis didn't include B.D.'s sons in her will, Harold Schiff said, "Unfortunately their mother chose to have them follow her rather than their hearts. Twenty years from now they'll say, 'That was our grandmother; why didn't we know her?'"

B.D., who was given until December 5 to contest the will, told reporters on November 7 that she had no intention of challenging it. Now living in Charlottesville, Virginia, where she trains Arabian horses, Davis's only natural child scornfully said, "I would be shocked if [the will] mentioned me." She added with a chuckle, still referring to her mother in the present tense, "That's the way she is with everyone. Either she owns them or they're the enemy." B.D. had often described her mother as "a totally destructive force in my children's life and my life." Told that Davis's maid would have prevented B.D. from attending the funeral, she laughingly declared she had had no intention of going anyway.

No shrinking violet, B.D. went on Connie Chung's TV talk show to say that as far as she was concerned her mother had died years earlier for her, that she was a great star, yes, but a star in private as well as in public, and that she, B.D., had done her thing and her mother had done hers.

One fan wrote in to say of all this, "Nobody expected a movie queen to be an exemplary wife and mother—that was not her destiny. Great artists live by their own rules. Bette Davis would have been far happier if she had never married and never had children. She belonged to the world. Her gifts were meant for the world, and to the world she gave with ultimate generosity."

"She will never really die," another admirer wrote in. And it is true. Bette Davis's vivid and individual mystique will keep her firmly ensconced among the eternally creative living thanks to the magic of film.

A Bette Davis Film Listing
(With Stage Roles and Some TV Films)

The year noted is the film's formal release date. Those films marked with an asterisk (*) were never formally released in the United States.

1. *Bad Sister* 1931
2. *Seed* 1931
3. *Waterloo Bridge* 1931
4. *Way Back Home* 1932
5. *The Menace* 1932
6. *Hell's House* 1932
7. *The Man Who Played God* 1932
8. *So Big* 1932
9. *The Rich Are Always With Us* 1932
10. *The Dark Horse* 1932
11. *Cabin in the Cotton* 1932
12. *Three on a Match* 1932
13. *20,000 Years in Sing Sing* 1933
14. *Parachute Jumper* 1933
15. *The Working Man* 1933
16. *Ex-Lady* 1933
17. *Bureau of Missing Persons* 1933
18. *Fashions of 1934* 1934
19. *The Big Shakedown* 1934
20. *Jimmy the Gent* 1934
21. *Fog Over Frisco* 1934
22. *Of Human Bondage* 1934

23. *Housewife* 1934

24. *Bordertown* 1935

25. *The Girl From Tenth Avenue* 1935

26. *Front Page Woman* 1935

27. *Special Agent* 1935

28. *Dangerous* 1935

29. *The Petrified Forest* 1936

30. *The Golden Arrow* 1936

31. *Satan Met a Lady* 1936

32. *Marked Woman* 1937

33. *Kid Galahad* 1937

34. *That Certain Woman* 1937

35. *It's Love I'm After* 1937

36. *Jezebel* 1938

37. *The Sisters* 1938

38. *Dark Victory* 1939

39. *Juarez* 1939

40. *The Old Maid* 1939

41. *The Private Lives of Elizabeth and Essex* 1939

42. *All This and Heaven Too* 1940

43. *The Letter* 1940

44. *The Great Lie* 1941

45. *The Bride Came C.O.D.* 1941

46. *The Little Foxes* 1941

47. *The Man Who Came to Dinner* 1941

48. *In This Our Life* 1942

49. *Now, Voyager* 1942

50. *Watch on the Rhine* 1943

51. *Thank Your Lucky Stars* 1943

52. *Old Acquaintance* 1943

53. *Mr. Skeffington* 1944

54. *Hollywood Canteen* 1944

55. *The Corn Is Green* 1945

56. *A Stolen Life* 1946

57. *Deception* 1946

58. *Winter Meeting* 1948

59. *June Bride* 1948

60. *Beyond the Forest* 1949

61. *All About Eve* 1950

62. *Payment on Demand* 1951

63. *Another Man's Poison* 1951

64. *Phone Call from a Stranger* 1952

65. *The Star* 1952

66. *The Virgin Queen* 1955

67. *Storm Center* 1956

68. *The Catered Affair* 1956

69. *John Paul Jones* 1959

70. *The Scapegoat* 1959

71. *Pocketful of Miracles* 1961

72. *What Ever Happened to Baby Jane?* 1962

73. *Dead Ringer* 1964

74. *The Empty Canvas* 1964

75. *Where Love Has Gone* 1964

76. *Hush . . . Hush, Sweet Charlotte* 1965

77. *The Nanny* 1965

78. *The Anniversary* 1968

79. *Connecting Rooms* 1969*

80. *Bunny O'Hare* 1971

81. *The Scientific Cardplayer* 1972*

82. *Burnt Offerings* 1976

83. *Return From Witch Mountain* 1978

84. *Death on the Nile* 1978

85. *Watcher in the Woods* 1980

86. *The Whales of August* 1987

87. *Wicked Stepmother* 1989

A Selective List of Bette Davis TV Films

1. *Madame Sin* 1972

2. *Scream, Pretty Peggy* 1973

3. *The Disappearance of Aimée* 1976

4. *The Dark Secret of Harvest Home* 1978

5. *Strangers* 1979

6. *White Mama* 1980

7. *Skyward* 1980

8. *Family Reunion* 1981

9. *A Piano for Mrs. Cimino* 1982

10. *Little Gloria, Happy at Last* 1982

11. *Right of Way* 1983

12. *Murder With Mirrors* 1985

13. *As Summers Die* 1986

Stage Appearances

1. *The Earth Between* 1929

2. *The Wild Duck* 1929

3. *The Lady From the Sea* 1929

4. *Broken Dishes* 1929

5. *The Solid South* 1930

6. *Two's Company* 1952

7. *The World of Carl Sandburg* 1959

8. *The Night of the Iguana* 1961

9. *Bette Davis on Film and in Person* 1973

10. *Miss Moffat* 1974

A Selective Bette Davis
Bibliography

Astor, Mary. *A Life on Film.* New York: Delacorte Press, 1971.

Davis, Bette. *The Lonely Life.* New York: G. P. Putnam's Sons, 1962.

Davis, Bette. *This 'n' That.* New York: G. P. Putnam's Sons, 1987.

Higham, Charles. *Bette: The Life of Bette Davis.* New York: Macmillan: 1981.

Higham, Charles, and Joel Greenberg. *The Celluloid Muse.* London: Angus and Robertson, 1969.

Hirschhorn, Clive. *The Warner Bros. Story.* New York: Crown Publishers, 1979.

Huston, John. *An Open Book.* New York: Alfred A. Knopf, 1980.

Hyman, B. D. *My Mother's Keeper.* New York: William Morrow & Co., 1985.

Kaminsky, Stuart. *John Huston, Maker of Magic.* Boston: Houghton-Mifflin, 1978.

McGilligan, Pat. *Backstory. Interviews with Screen Writers.* Berkeley: Univ. of California Press, 1986.

Merrill, Gary. *Bette, Rita, and the Rest of My Life.* Augusta, ME.: Lance Tapley, 1988.

Nickens, Christopher. *Bette Davis.* Garden City, N.Y.: Doubleday, 1985.

Quirk, Lawrence J. "Bette Davis." *Films in Review,* December 1955.

————. *Bette Davis: Her Films and Career.* Secaucus, N.J.: Citadel Press, 1985.

————. "Bette Davis: Hollywood's Neglected Genius." *Hollywood Stars,* 1957.

————. *Joan Crawford. Films in Review,* December 1956.

————. *The Films of Joan Crawford.* Secaucus, N.J.: Citadel Press, 1968.

————. *The Great Romantic Films.* Secaucus, N.J.: Citadel Press, 1974.

————. *Anthology of Photoplay.* New York: Dover Publications, 1971.

————. *Claudette Colbert.* New York: Crown Publishers, 1985.

————. *Margaret Sullavan: Child of Fate.* New York: St.Martin's Press, 1986.

————. *Lauren Bacall: Her Films and Career.* Secaucus, N.J.: Citadel Press, 1986.

————. *Norma: The Story of Norma Shearer.* New York: St.Martin's Press, 1988.

Stine, Whitney. *Mother Goddam.* New York: Hawthorn Books, 1974.

Swindell, Larry. *Charles Boyer.* Garden City, N.Y.: Doubleday, 1983.

Walker, Alexander. *Bette Davis.* New York: Weidenfeld & Nicholson, 1986.

Selected Periodicals

Quirk's Reviews, Films in Review, Photoplay, Motion Picture, Modern Screen, Time, Life, McCall's, The New York Times, Variety, People, Vanity Fair.

Index